D0223629

REAL WORLD
MICRO

NINETEENTH EDITION

EDITED BY SMRITI RAO, ALEJANDRO REUSS,

BRYAN SNYDER, CHRIS STURR,

AND THE *DOLLARS & SENSE* COLLECTIVE

REAL WORLD MICRO, NINETEENTH EDITION

Copyright © 2012 by Economic Affairs Bureau, Inc.

All rights reserved. No portions of this book may be reproduced, stored in a retrieval system, or transmitted in any form or by any means, electronic, mechanical, photocopying, recording, or otherwise, except for brief quotations in a review, without prior permission from Economic Affairs Bureau.

ISBN: 978-1-878585-92-9

Published by:
Economic Affairs Bureau, Inc. d/b/a *Dollars & Sense*
1 Milk Street, 5th floor, Boston, MA 02109
617-447-2177; dollars@dollarsandsense.org.
For order information, contact Economic Affairs Bureau or visit: www.dollarsandsense.org.

Real World Micro is edited by the *Dollars & Sense* Collective, which also publishes *Dollars & Sense* magazine and the classroom books *Real World Macro, The Economic Crisis Reader, Current Economic Issues, Real World Globalization, Real World Latin America, Real World Labor, Real World Banking and Finance, The Wealth Inequality Reader, The Environment in Crisis, Introduction to Political Economy, Unlevel Playing Fields: Understanding Wage Inequality and Discrimination, Striking a Balance: Work, Family, Life,* and *Grassroots Journalism.*

The 2012 *Dollars & Sense* Collective:
Ben Collins, Leibiana Feliz, Ben Greenberg, Vera Kelsey-Watts, Shirley Kressel, James McBride, John Miller, Linda Pinkow, Paul Piwko, Lauren Price, Smriti Rao, Bryan Snyder, Chris Sturr, and Jeanne Winner.

Co-editors of this volume: Smriti Rao, Alejandro Reuss, Bryan Snyder, and Chris Sturr
Editorial assistant: Zachary SantaMaria
Production assistants: Molly Cusano, Sandra Korn, Zachary SantaMaria, and William Whitham
Design and layout: Chris Sturr

Printed in U.S.A.

CONTENTS

INTRODUCTION

It sometimes seems that the United States has not one, but two economies. The first economy exists in economics textbooks and in the minds of many elected officials. It is a free-market economy, a system of promise and plenty, a cornucopia of consumer goods. In this economy, people are free and roughly equal, and each individual carefully looks after him- or herself, making uncoerced choices to advance his or her economic interests. Government is but an afterthought in this world, since almost everything that people need can be provided by the free market, itself guided by the reassuring "invisible hand."

The second economy is described in the writings of progressives, environmentalists, union supporters, and consumer advocates as well as honest business writers who recognize that real-world markets do not always conform to textbook models. This second economy features vast disparities of income, wealth, and power manifested in a system of class. It is an economy where employers have power over employees, where large firms have the power to shape markets, and where large corporate lobbies have the power to shape public policies. In this second economy, government sometimes adopts policies that ameliorate the abuses of capitalism and other times does just the opposite, but it is always an active and essential participant in economic life.

If you are reading this introduction, you are probably a student in an introductory college course in microeconomics. Your textbook will introduce you to the first economy, the harmonious world of free markets. *Real World Micro* will introduce you to the second.

Why "Real World" Micro?

A standard economics textbook is full of powerful concepts. It is also, by its nature, a limited window on the economy. What is taught in most introductory economics courses today is in fact just one strand of economic thought—neoclassical economics. Fifty years ago, many more strands were part of the introductory economics curriculum, and the contraction of the field has imposed limits on the study of economics that can confuse and frustrate students. This is particularly true in the study of microeconomics, which looks at markets for individual goods or services.

Real World Micro is designed as a supplement to a standard neoclassical textbook. Its articles provide vivid, real-world illustrations of economic concepts. But beyond that, our mission is to address two major sources of confusion in the study of economics at the introductory level.

The first source of confusion is the striking simplification of the world found in orthodox microeconomics. Standard textbooks describe stylized economic

1

interactions between idealized buyers and sellers that bear scant resemblance to the messy realities of the actual economic activity that we see around us. There is nothing wrong with simplifying. In fact, every social science must develop simplified models; precisely because reality is so complex, we must look at it a little bit at a time in order to understand it. Still, these simplifications mystify and misrepresent actual capitalist social relations and excise questions of race, gender, and class from the analysis.

Mainstream economic analysis calls to mind the story of the tipsy party-goer whose friend finds him on his hands and knees under a streetlight. "What are you doing?" asks the friend. "I dropped my car keys across the street, and I'm looking for them," the man replies. "But if you lost them across the street, how come you're looking over here?" "Well, the light's better here." In the interest of greater clarity, economics often imposes similar limits on its areas of inquiry.

As the title *Real World Micro* implies, one of our goals is to rub mainstream microeconomic theory up against reality to direct attention to the areas not illuminated by the streetlight, and particularly to examine how inequality, power, and environmental imbalance change the picture. The idea is not to prove the standard theory "wrong," but to challenge you to think about where the theory is more and less useful, and why markets may not act as expected.

This focus on real-world counterpoints to mainstream economic theory connects to the second issue we aim to clarify. Most economics texts uncritically present key assumptions and propositions that form the core of standard economic theory. They offer much less exploration of a set of related questions: What are alternative propositions about the economy? Under what circumstances will these alternatives more accurately describe the economy? What difference do such propositions make? Our approach is not to spell out an alternative theory in detail, but to raise questions and present real-life examples that bring these questions to life. For example, textbooks carefully lay out "consumer sovereignty," the notion that consumers' wishes ultimately determine what the economy will produce. But can we reconcile consumer sovereignty with an economy where one of the main products in industries such as soft drinks, autos, and music is consumer desire itself? We think it is valuable to see ideas like consumer sovereignty as debatable propositions and that requires hearing other views in the debate.

In short, our goal in this book is to use real-world examples from today's economy to raise questions, stimulate debate, and dare you to think critically about the models in your textbook.

What's in This Book

Real World Micro is organized to follow the outline of a standard economics text. Each chapter leads off with a brief introduction, including study questions for the entire chapter, and then provides several short articles from Dollars & Sense magazine and other sources that illustrate the chapter's key concepts—74 articles in all. In many cases, the articles have been updated or otherwise edited to heighten their relevance.

Here is a quick overview of the chapters:

Chapter 1, Markets: Ideology and Reality, starts off the volume by taking a hard look at the strengths and weaknesses of actual markets, with special attention to weaknesses that standard textbooks tend to underemphasize.

Chapter 2, Supply and Demand, presents real-world examples of supply and demand in action. Dollars & Sense authors question the conventional wisdom on topics such as the minimum wage, rent control, and rising gas prices.

Chapter 3, Consumers, raises provocative questions about utility theory and individual consumer choice. What happens when marketers shape buyers' tastes? What happens when important information is hidden from consumers? Does consumer society threaten environmental sustainability?

Chapter 4, Firms, Production, and Profit Maximization, illustrates how business strategies often squeeze workers to boost profits and challenges students to think about other ways of organizing work.

Chapter 5, Market Structure and Monopoly, explores market power and monopoly, just one example of the unequal power relationships that pervade our economic system. The chapter critiques market power in the pharmaceutical, oil, and financial services industries, but also questions whether small business dominance would be an improvement.

Chapter 6, Labor Markets, examines the ways in which labor markets can be affected by discrimination, unionization, globalization, and a host of other factors beyond supply and demand.

Chapter 7, The Distribution of Income, discusses the causes and consequences of inequality and counters the mainstream view that inequality is good for growth.

Chapter 8, Market Failure, Government Policy, and Corporate Governance, addresses when and how public policy should address both particular and systemic failures of markets, from environmental issues to health care.

Chapter 9, Taxation, explores issues of incomes, wealth, and taxation, including who actually pays taxes and at what rates. Changing relative prices of commodities and activities can lead to changes in behavior. This proposition is explored in the areas of health care and the environment.

Chapter 10, Trade and Development, covers key issues in trade policy and the world economy, questioning the value of free trade for development.

Chapter 11, Labor Movements and Unions, this year's policy spotlight explores microeconomic implications of organized labor.

What's New in This Edition?

This 19th edition of *Real World Micro* adds a chapter on taxation as well as a new policy spotlight on labor movements and unions. The book includes 25 new articles written over the past year.

Chapter 1

MARKETS: IDEOLOGY AND REALITY

Introduction

Economics is all about tradeoffs. The concept of opportunity cost reminds us that in order to make a purchase, or even to make use of a resource that you control (such as your time), you must give up other possible purchases or other possible uses. Markets broaden the range of possible tradeoffs by facilitating exchange between people who do not know each other, and in many cases never meet at all—think of buying a pair of athletic shoes in Atlanta from a company based in Los Angeles that manufactures shoes in Malaysia and has stockholders all over the world. As the idea of gains from trade suggests, markets allow many exchanges that make both parties better off.

But markets have severe limitations as well. The economic crisis that began in 2008 has made those limitations all too clear. Even lifelong free-marketeers such as Alan Greenspan have been forced to question their belief in the "invisible hand." Markets are vulnerable to excessive risk-taking that leads to speculative bubbles like the one that recently "popped" in the U.S. real-estate market.

Even if regulatory oversight prevented excessive risk-taking, markets have other problems. Markets ration goods to those most able to pay, as Ellen Frank points out (Article 1.1). More generally, if we rely on markets to distribute goods that we think of as basic needs or even rights—health care, housing, education, and so on—lower-income people will be "rationed out," receiving fewer or poorer-quality goods, if not any good at all.

Markets and price determination, in neoclassical economics, have been idealized into an elegant utility maximizing perfection. Chris Tilly, in "Shaking the Invisible Hand" (Article 1.2), uncovers the curious assumptions necessary to allow for the market mechanism to be the most efficient allocator of scarce resources. He provides us with eight "Tilly Assumptions" underlying perfectly functioning markets. If any of these assumptions are violated, then there is a possibility if not probability of market failure or less than optimal market results.

Alejandro Reuss provides us with a stellar example of this idealized neoclassical view of exchange in "Freedom, Equity, and Efficiency" (Article 1.3). Ideal neoclassical markets offer the promise of freedom of choice, equity (fairness), and efficiency, but fail to deliver on all three counts. Reuss walks us through these neoclassical standards and offers a not so ideal reality of labor-market competition and exchange.

Mainstream theories justify increased consumption by arguing that this must reflect decisions made by consumers to maximize their happiness (utility). Thad Williamson uses survey data for the United States to challenge that connection (Article 1.4). The data suggest that beyond a certain level of material comfort, which he argues has already been widely achieved in the West, more money does little to increase happiness. Instead, the pursuit of money makes it harder for individuals to seek out those things that do indeed make them happier, such as connections with family and friends and participation in religious and other community organizations. He points out that the structure of the political economy today makes economic stability, another factor that increases a sense of satisfaction with one's life, impossible to attain for most Americans. He argues that it is time to shift the focus from increases in material wealth towards broader moral concerns that would truly result in increased well-being.

With the "invisible hand of the market" efficiently allocating scarce resources, such as housing, what could possibly go wrong? In "Bubble Trouble" (Article 1.5), Dean Baker provides a prescient analysis from 2005 about a dangerously inflating housing bubble in the United States.

The reality of our present distribution of income and wealth has been revealed starkly by the Occupy Wall Street movement over this past year with the simple observation of the seriously polarized distribution of income and wealth in the United States. The issue of class and the ongoing class struggle are embodied in the graph provided by Alejandro Reuss in his brief primer, "The 99%, the 1%, and Class Struggle" (Article 1.6), which concludes this chapter.

Discussion Questions

1) (General) What things should not be for sale? Beyond everyday goods and services, think about human bodies, votes, small countries, and other things that might be bought and sold. How do you draw the line between what should be for sale and what should not be?

2) (General) Advocates of unregulated markets often argue that deregulating markets doesn't just promote mutually beneficial exchanges, but also fundamentally expands freedom. Explain the logic of their argument and the logic of the opposing view, and evaluate the two points of view.

3) (General) If not markets, then what? What are other ways to organize economic activity? Which ways are most likely to resolve the problems brought up in this chapter?

4) (Article 1.1) Ellen Frank claims that markets erode democracy. Explain her perspective. Do you agree? Do all markets undermine democracy?

5) (Article 1.2) Write out the eight "Tilly Assumptions" and corresponding realities using Tilly's exact terms for the assumptions. Are these assumptions reasonable? Why or why not?

6) (Article 1.2) For each of the eight "Tilly Assumptions," explain how the market mechanism would fail if the assumption were violated.

7) (Article 1.3) According to the neoclassical theory of exchange how do markets deliver "efficient" results if all "barriers" to exchange are removed? In what sense are these results "efficient?"

8) (Article 1.3) How is the word "freedom" defined by neoclassical economists?

9) (Article 1.3) Does the unfettered operation of the market mechanism deliver "equity" to society?

10) (Article 1.4) According to the survey data Williamson cites, what is the connection between income/consumption and happiness? How does this contradict the standard economic model of consumption?

11) (Article 1.4) Williamson argues that the moral task set out by Adam Smith of ensuring enough economic growth to allow everyone to live in material comfort has in fact been attained. Do you agree with him? What is your reaction to Williamson's argument that the focus from here on should not be on economic growth as currently defined, but rather on the fulfillment of other "real goods of human life"?

12) (Article 1.5) What is a "bubble?" Provide Dean Baker's suggested cause for such a phenomenon in the housing market. What happened to the bubble? Why didn't anybody (regulatory body and/or the Federal Reserve Bank) do anything about this bubble back in 2005?

13) (Article 1.6) Stare deeply into the graph that Alejandro Reuss has provided. Explain what is happening in the graph over time (in particular from 1962 to the present). Is this an example of class struggle? Who won?

14) (Article 1.7) What are the advantages of working at a worker-owned and democratically controlled business? What are the disadvantages? Evaluate the long-term viability of such forms of "popular production."

Article 1.1

THE IDEOLOGY OF THE FREE MARKET

BY ELLEN FRANK
February 1999

When the County Commissioner for Lake County, Florida, proposed in 1998 that the fire department be turned over to a private, for-profit company, he unleashed a torrent of opposition and the idea was dropped. Throughout the United States, similar proposals to "privatize" public schools, education, and health services face strong resistance from taxpayers and state workers. Yet the overall trend in U.S. public policy for at least 20 years has been toward greater reliance on market forces and the profit motive to provide what used to be considered public goods and services.

In liberal Massachusetts, substantial portions of the public bus system are now run by private businesses; in New York City, private security forces patrol sections of Manhattan. Nationwide, some 15% of hospital beds are now owned and operated by for-profit corporations. Privately run prisons, trash disposal companies, social service providers are growing in importance everywhere.

"The era of big government," President Clinton announced a few years ago, "is over." In its place we have the market. But can the market deliver?

Market Myths

Markets, boosters contend, foster individual freedom. Consumers in market economies are free to express their individuality, assert their unique identity, by buying the precise things they want. For Americans raised on 28 choices of breakfast cereal, one-size-fits-all, big-government fire departments and health-care programs just won't do. Competition, so the story goes, will lead to more and better choices. Why? Because firms can only make money by producing what consumers are willing to pay for.

Governments and non-profit institutions might be less greedy, more humane in their motives, but they are under no particular pressure to cater to consumer demand. The profit motive is the consumer's best friend, forcing firms, as the textbooks say, to allocate resources efficiently, producing only the goods consumers desire.

Market Realities

The problem with this rosy view of things is that all voices are not equal in the market place. Upper-income consumers, with cash to spare, can bid up prices and walk away with the lion's share of society's output. For poorer folks, the vaunted "rationing" function of prices often means being priced out of the market, unable to afford the goods they want and need.

There is no question that market economies deliver goods in abundance. Wherever capitalism has been given free reign, streets are choked with automobiles and shops overflow with goods. When the former Soviet countries embraced capitalist markets several years ago, for example, commentators noted the extraordinary increase in goods available for sale. Formerly barren store shelves suddenly burst with local and imported goods of every manner and description. Unfortunately, though, few people in Russia could afford to buy any of it. The markets operated mainly for the benefit of a small and wealthy elite.

Market Inequities

Evidence abounds that markets, unless tempered by active government interventions, open up vast chasms of social and economic inequality, generating unprecedented affluence but also astounding poverty. The United Nations in its most recent report on human development found that, as markets expanded throughout the world, the richest one fifth of the world's population consumed 86% of the world's output, while the poorest fifth received just over 1%. The richest 225 people in the world today have assets equal to the annual income of the poorest 2.5 billion people.

In the United States, where faith in markets amounts to a state religion, such issues are rarely broached. Staggering levels of inequality are everywhere to be seen, yet rarely discussed. In a country where exclusion on the basis of race or gender is widely regarded as intolerable, Americans routinely accept exclusion on the basis of income. Imagine if every upscale suburb were to post signs at their borders saying, "Minimum Annual Income of $1,000,000 Required for Residence." Americans might be shocked by the candor, but not by the sentiment.

In America, the wealthy are distrusted, but not despised, and Bill Gates, whose personal wealth (now some $40 billion) equals the total wealth of the poorest 106 million Americans, is feted in the press, a kind of cultural icon.

Markets and Freedom

Advocates of free markets don't apologize for these tremendous inequities. The freedom to choose, they contend, isn't only about breakfast cereals and fashion statements. Individuals in market economies must compete for the rewards the market doles out. People can choose to be rich, or not to be; to work hard or to take it easy; to succeed or to fail. In a market economy, people get what they deserve, or so the myth goes.

But this myth ignores the very serious inequities in power that flow, inevitably, from inequities in income. High incomes lead to wealth and wealth to the exercise of power, the ability to control others, to command their labor and constrain their freedom, including their freedom to buy and sell. This is why it is illegal, in most countries, to sell your organs for transplant, though there is no lack of willing buyers and sellers. It is legal to sell your blood for transfusion or (in some places) your body for sex, and studies of the markets for blood and for prostitutes come to the same finding: when human bodies are exchanged for money, the poor lose control of their bodies.

Markets and Democracy

The freedom promised by markets is, for this reason, incompatible with democratic ideals of free, self-governing citizens. In democratic countries, governments provide basic goods and services and restrict market transactions not because doing so is "efficient," but because the freedom from want and exploitation is a precondition for meaningful citizenship. For example, 43 million Americans currently lack even minimal health care coverage; as the health care system shifts into for-profit mode, these people are at risk of falling too ill to compete in the marketplace or even to participate freely in governance.

If education were to become a buy-and-sell proposition, as some conservatives advocate, large numbers of citizens (and prospective citizens) will go uneducated and unable, therefore, to exercise their rights or protect their freedoms.

Economic inequities are not the only injury markets cause to democratic practice. The insatiable quest for gain that propels behavior in the marketplace disrupts the ecology of the earth and uproots communities. All over the world, clear-cutting, deforestation, strip-mining, toxic-dumping, and other environmentally damaging excesses of unrestrained markets have torn apart stable, self-governing towns and villages, turning secure citizens out on the open road; the hobos and homeless of our modern era.

The competitiveness engendered by markets is also at odds with democratic ideals. Psychologist Alfie Kohn has shown, for example, that people in competitive situations are more likely to cheat and to express feelings of distrust. Yet a spirit of trust and cooperation is essential to successful governance.

In opposing the private takeover of their fire department, the citizens of Lake County, Florida, seem to have understood a basic truth about limitations of markets. It may well be that private, for-profit firms can fight fires or patrol the streets more cheaply than the government can, but a trusted government can fight fires and patrol streets more democratically. ❑

Article 1.2

SHAKING THE INVISIBLE HAND
The Uncertain Foundations of Free-Market Economics

BY CHRIS TILLY
November 1989; updated March 2011

"It is not from the benevolence of the butcher, the brewer or the baker that we expect our dinner, but from their regard to their own interest... [No individual] intends to promote the public interest... [rather, he is] led by an invisible hand to promote an end which was no part of his intention."

—*Adam Smith, The Wealth of Nations, 1776*

Seen the Invisible Hand lately? It's all around us these days, propping up conservative arguments in favor of free trade, deregulation, and tax-cutting.

Today's advocates for "free," competitive markets echo Adam Smith's claim that unfettered markets translate the selfish pursuit of individual gain into the greatest benefit for all. They trumpet the superiority of capitalist free enterprise over socialist efforts to supplant the market with a planned economy, and even decry liberal attempts to moderate the market. Anything short of competitive markets, they proclaim, yields economic inefficiency, making society worse off.

But the economic principle underlying this fanfare is shaky indeed. Since the late 19th century, mainstream economists have struggled to prove that Smith was right—that the chaos of free markets leads to a blissful economic order. In the 1950s, U.S. economists Kenneth Arrow and Gerard Debreu finally came up with a theoretical proof, which many orthodox economists view as the centerpiece of modern economic theory.

Although this proof is the product of the best minds of mainstream economics, it ends up saying surprisingly little in defense of free markets. The modern theory of the Invisible Hand shows that given certain assumptions, free markets reduce the wasteful use of economic resources—but perpetuate unequal income distribution.

To prove free markets cut waste, economists must make a number of far-fetched assumptions: there are no concentrations of economic power; buyers and sellers know every detail about the present and future economy; and all costs of production are borne by producers while all benefits from consumption are paid for by consumers (see box for a complete list). Take away any one of these assumptions and markets can lead to stagnation, recession, and other forms of waste—as in fact they do.

In short, the economic theory invoked by conservatives to justify free markets instead starkly reveals their limitations.

The Fruits of Free Markets

The basic idea behind the Invisible Hand can be illustrated with a story. Suppose that I grow apples and you grow oranges. We both grow tired of eating the same fruit all the time and decide to trade. Perhaps we start by trading one apple for one orange. This exchange satisfies both of us, because in fact I would gladly give up more than one apple to get an orange, and you would readily pay more than one orange for an apple. And as long as swapping one more apple for one more orange makes us both better off, we will continue to trade.

Eventually, the trading will come to a stop. I begin to notice that the novelty of oranges wears old as I accumulate a larger pile of them and the apples I once had a surplus of become more precious to me as they grow scarcer. At some point, I draw the line: in order to obtain one more apple from me, you must give me more than one orange. But your remaining oranges have also become more valuable to you. Up to now, each successive trade has made both of us better off. Now there is no further exchange that benefits us both, so we agree to stop trading until the next crop comes in.

Assumptions and Reality

The claim that free markets lead to efficiency and reduced waste rests on eight main assumptions. However, these assumptions differ sharply from economic reality. (Assumptions 1, 3, 4, and 5 are discussed in more detail in the article.)

ASSUMPTION ONE: *No market power.* No individual buyer or seller, nor any group of buyers or sellers, has the power to affect the market-wide level of prices, wages, or profits.

REALITY ONE: Our economy is dotted with centers of market power, from large corporations to unions. Furthermore, employers have an edge in bargaining with workers because of the threat of unemployment.

ASSUMPTION TWO: *No economies of scale.* Small plants can produce as cheaply as large ones.

REALITY TWO: In fields such as mass-production industry, transportation, communications, and agriculture, large producers enjoy a cost advantage, limiting competition.

ASSUMPTION THREE: *Perfect information about the present.* Buyers and sellers know everything there is to know about the goods being exchanged. Also, each is aware of the wishes of every other potential buyer and seller in the market.

REALITY THREE: The world is full of lemons—goods about which the buyer is inadequately informed. Also, people are not mind-readers, so sellers get stuck with surpluses and willing buyers are unable to find the products they want.

Note several features of this parable. Both you and I end up happier by trading freely. If the government stepped in and limited fruit trading, neither of us would be as well off. In fact, the government cannot do anything in the apple/orange market that will make both of us better off than does the free market.

Adding more economic actors, products, money, and costly production processes complicates the picture, but we reach the same conclusions. Most of us sell our labor time in the market rather than fruit; we sell it for money that we then use to buy apples, oranges, and whatever else we need. The theory of the Invisible Hand tells us a trip to the fruit stand improves the lot of both consumer and seller; likewise, the sale of labor time benefits both employer and employee. What's more, according to the theory, competition between apple farmers insures that consumers will get apples produced at the lowest possible cost. Government intervention still can only make things worse.

ASSUMPTION FOUR: *Perfect information about the future.* Contracts between buyers and sellers cover every possible future eventuality.

REALITY FOUR: Uncertainty clouds the future of any economy. Futures markets are limited.

ASSUMPTION FIVE: *You only get what you pay for.* Nobody can impose a cost on somebody else, nor obtain a benefit from them, without paying.

REALITY FIVE: Externalities, both positive and negative, are pervasive. In a free market, polluters can impose costs on the rest of us without paying. And when a public good like a park is built or roads are maintained, everyone benefits whether or not they helped to pay for it.

ASSUMPTION SIX: *Price is a proxy for pleasure.* The price of a given commodity will represent the quality and desirability and or utility derived from the consumption of the commodity.

REALITY SIX: "Conspicuous Consumption" (Veblen) and or "snob effects" will often distort prices from underlying utility.

ASSUMPTION SEVEN: *Self-interest only.* In economic matters, each person cares only about his or her own level of well-being.

REALITY SEVEN: Solidarity, jealousy, and even love for one's family violate this assumption.

ASSUMPTION EIGHT: *No joint production.* Each production process has only one product.

REALITY EIGHT: Even in an age of specialization, there are plenty of exceptions to this rule. For example, large service firms such as hospitals or universities produce a variety of different services using the same resources.

—Chris Tilly and Bryan Snyder

This fable provides a ready-made policy guide. Substitute "Japanese autos" and "U.S. agricultural products" for apples and oranges, and the fable tells you that import quotas or tariffs only make the people of both countries worse off. Change the industries to airlines or telephone services, and the fable calls for deregulation. Or re-tell the tale in the labor market: minimum wages and unions (which prevent workers from individually bargaining over their wages) hurt employers and workers.

Fruit Salad

Unfortunately for free-market boosters, two major short-comings make a fruit salad out of this story. First, even if free markets perform as advertised, they deliver only one benefit—the prevention of certain economically wasteful practices—while preserving inequality. According to the theory, competitive markets wipe out two kinds of waste: unrealized trades and inefficient production. Given the right assumptions, markets ensure that when two parties both stand to gain from a trade, they make that trade, as in the apples-and-oranges story. Competition compels producers to search for the most efficient, lowest-cost production methods—again, given the right preconditions.

Though eliminating waste is a worthy goal, it leaves economic inequality untouched. Returning once more to the orchard, if I start out with all of the apples and oranges and you start out with none, that situation is free of waste: no swap can make us both better off since you have nothing to trade! Orthodox economists acknowledge that even in the ideal competitive market, those who start out rich stay rich, while the poor remain poor. Many of them argue that attempts at redistributing income will most certainly create economic inefficiencies, justifying the preservation of current inequities.

But in real-life economics, competition does lead to waste. Companies wastefully duplicate each other's research and build excess productive capacity. Cost-cutting often leads to shoddy products, worker speedup, and unsafe working conditions. People and factories stand idle while houses go unbuilt and people go unfed. That's because of the second major problem: real economies don't match the assumptions of the Invisible Hand theory.

Of course, all economic theories build their arguments on a set of simplifying assumptions about the world. These assumptions often sacrifice some less important aspects of reality in order to focus on the economic mechanisms of interest. But in the case of the Invisible Hand, the theoretical preconditions contradict several central features of the economy.

For one thing, markets are only guaranteed to prevent waste if the economy runs on "perfect competition": individual sellers compete by cutting prices, individual buyers compete by raising price offers, and nobody holds concentrated economic power. But today's giant corporations hardly match this description. Coke and Pepsi compete with advertising rather than price cuts. The oil companies keep prices high enough to register massive profits every year. Employers coordinate the pay and benefits they offer to avoid bidding up compensation. Workers, in turn, marshal their own forces via unionization—another departure from perfect competition.

Indeed, the jargon of "perfect competition" overlooks the fact that property ownership itself confers disproportionate economic power. "In the competitive model," orthodox economist Paul Samuelson commented, "it makes no difference whether capital hires labor or the other way around." He argued that given perfect competition among workers and among capitalists, wages and profits would remain the same regardless of who does the hiring. But unemployment—a persistent feature of market-driven economies—makes job loss very costly to workers. The sting my boss feels when I "fire" him by quitting my job hardly equals the setback I experience when he fires me.

Perfect Information?

In addition, the grip of the Invisible Hand is only sure if all buyers and sellers have "perfect information" about the present and future state of markets. In the present, this implies consumers know exactly what they are buying—an assumption hard to swallow in these days of leaky breast implants and chicken à la Salmonella. Employers must know exactly what skills workers have and how hard they will work—suppositions any real-life manager would laugh at.

Perfect information also means sellers can always sniff out unsatisfied demands, and buyers can detect any excess supplies of goods. Orthodox economists rely on the metaphor of an omnipresent "auctioneer" who is always calling out prices so all buyers and sellers can find mutually agreeable prices and consummate every possible sale. But in the actual economy, the auctioneer is nowhere to be found, and markets are plagued by surpluses and shortages.

Perfect information about the future is even harder to come by. For example, a company decides whether or not to build a new plant based on whether it expects sales to rise. But predicting future demand is a tricky matter. One reason is that people may save money today in order to buy (demand) goods and services in the future. The problem comes in predicting when. As economist John Maynard Keynes observed in 1934, "An act of individual saving means—so to speak—a decision not to have dinner today. But it does not necessitate a decision to have dinner or to buy a pair of boots a week hence...or to consume any specified thing at any specified date. Thus it depresses the business of preparing today's dinner without stimulating the business of making ready for some future act of consumption." Keynes concluded that far from curtailing waste, free markets gave rise to the colossal waste of human and economic resources that was the Great Depression—in part because of this type of uncertainty about the future.

Free Lunch

The dexterity of the Invisible Hand also depends on the principle that "You only get what you pay for." This "no free lunch" principle seems at first glance a reasonable description of the economy. But major exceptions arise. One is what economists call "externalities"—economic transactions that take place outside the market. Consider a hospital that dumps syringes at sea. In effect, the hospital gets a free lunch by passing the costs of waste disposal on to the rest of us. Because no market exists where the right to dump is bought and sold, free markets do nothing to compel the hospital to bear the costs of dumping—which is why the government must step in.

Public goods such as sewer systems also violate the "no free lunch" rule. Once the sewer system is in place, everyone shares in the benefits of the waste disposal, regardless of whether or not they helped pay for it. Suppose sewer systems were sold in a free market, in which each person had the opportunity to buy an individual share. Then any sensible, self-interested consumer would hold back from buying his or her fair share—and wait for others to provide the service. This irrational situation would persist unless consumers could somehow collectively agree on how extensive a sewer system to produce—once more bringing government into the picture.

Most orthodox economists claim that the list of externalities and public goods in the economy is short and easily addressed. Liberals and radicals, on the other hand, offer a long list: for example, public goods include education, health care, and decent public transportation—all in short supply in our society.

Because real markets deviate from the ideal markets envisioned in the theory of the Invisible Hand, they give us both inequality and waste. But if the theory is so far off the mark, why do mainstream economists and policymakers place so much stock in it? They fundamentally believe the profit motive is the best guide for the economy. If you believe that "What's good for General Motors is good for the country," the Invisible Hand theory can seem quite reasonable. Business interests, government, and the media constantly reinforce this belief, and reward those who can dress it up in theoretical terms. As long as capital remains the dominant force in society, the Invisible Hand will maintain its grip on the hearts and minds of us all. ❑

Article 1.3

FREEDOM, EQUITY, AND EFFICIENCY
Contrasting Views of Markets, Competition, and Labor

BY ALEJANDRO REUSS
April 2012

The basic world-view of neoclassical economists is that, in markets, people engage voluntarily in exchanges with each other, and that this means market exchanges leave both parties better off. If someone cannot be forced to make a trade, they will only do so if it leaves them at least a little better off than they would have been otherwise. Any exchange between rational and self-interested people will, therefore, leave *both* of them better off, since either one would therefore have turned down an offer that left them worse off than they would have been otherwise. If a trade between two parties does not affect anyone else—if the two parties are better off, and no one else is worse off, as a result—then it adds at least a little to the sum total of well-being in society. Left to their own devices, people will find and exhaust all the possibilities for trades that boost the overall social well-being. Policies that interfere with people's ability to make voluntary trades, then, can only subtract from the well-being of society as a whole. This kind of story is sometimes referred to as a "master narrative"— the basic idea underlying the views of a particular school of thought on almost all issues. As we will see, neoclassicals tell this same basic story about all kinds of markets. However, we will focus here on the implications for "labor markets"—that is, the bargains made between wage workers (those who work for other people for pay) and employers.

The neoclassical narrative depends on many (often unspoken) *assumptions*. The assumptions of a theory are statements that have to be true for the theory to be true, but which are not proved to be true by the theory itself. For the basic neoclassical narrative to be true, individuals must be rational and self-interested. The assumption of "rationality" means they must act in ways that further their objectives, whatever these objectives may be. The assumption of "self-interest" means that, in making decisions, they must only take into account benefits and costs to themselves. They must have perfect information about all factors (past, present, and future) that could affect their decisions. Their actions must not affect any "third parties" (anyone other than those directly involved in the exchange and agreeing to its terms). There must be many buyers and sellers, so that no single buyer or seller (and no group of buyers or sellers colluding together) can impose the prices they want. Several other assumptions may also be important. If any of these assumptions is not true, then the neoclassical story at least partly breaks down.

The neoclassical master narrative also depends on several key *normative* concepts. Normative concepts are ideas about what is desirable or what "should" be. People often make normative statements using words like "good," "right," or "fair." (Contrast to *positive* statements, which are statements of fact, or statements about what "is," rather than about what should be.) Implicitly, the neoclassical story appeals to ideas about freedom, equity, and efficiency. Almost nobody would say they are against "freedom." But different people have very different views about what people should have the freedom to do, and what "freedoms" would impinge on the freedoms, rights, or well-being of others. So really the issue is, when neoclassical economists say that unregulated market competition is desirable as a matter of "freedom," what view of freedom are they basing this on? "Equity" is another word for fairness. Almost nobody would say they were against "equity"—which would be the same as saying they were against "fairness." People often disagree about political or economic issues, however, because they have different views of fairness. Finally, most people think of themselves as being in favor of "efficiency." Hardly anyone would openly celebrate "inefficiency." Again, however, neoclassicals have a very specific definition of efficiency. Other views of efficiency might lead to different conclusions about what kinds of social arrangements are desirable.

Freedom

By "freedom," neoclassical economists mean freedom from force or threat of force. They would recognize that someone making an exchange when threatened with violence—when confronted with "an offer they can't refuse," in the *Godfather* sense of that phrase—is not really engaging in a voluntary transaction. That person could very well make an exchange leaving them worse off than they would have been otherwise (except that they may have saved their own neck). On the other hand, suppose a person is faced only with very undesirable alternatives to engaging in a trade. Suppose they have "no choice" but to accept a job, because the alternative is to starve. Neoclassical economists would point out that these circumstances are not of the potential employer's making. It is quite unlike, in their view, conditions that are directly imposed by the other party (like having a gun held to one's head). If the impoverished worker accepts a job offer, even at a very low wage or under very bad working conditions, the neoclassical economist would argue that this is evidence that he or she really is made better off by the exchange. Restricting his or her freedom to engage in this exchange, in the neoclassical view, only makes him or her worse off.

Markets, neoclassical economists argue, basically force people to compete by *offering a better deal* to potential trading partners (since the trading partners are free to choose the best of all competing offers). They can do this in two ways, by offering more or by demanding less. For example, one company can increase its sales by offering more or better goods for the same price as its competitors (offering more). It can also increase its sales by offering the same goods for a lower price than its competitors (demanding less). Barriers to market competition, in the neoclassical view, restrict market participants' freedom to do one or another of these two things. Imagine, for example, a law that sets a minimum price that one can charge for a certain good (called a price floor). This prevents a producer from offering that good at a lower price, even if they are willing to do so, and prevents a consumer from buying that good at a lower price.

How do these ideas apply to labor markets? Neoclassical economists' story about price floors applies directly to labor markets, only we have a special name for a price floor in the labor market—the "minimum wage." In the neoclassical view, minimum-wage laws deprive workers of the freedom to accept a wage *lower* than this minimum. If workers were not willing to accept a wage lower than the legal minimum, neoclassical economists note, the minimum wage would have no effect. If it has any effect, then it must be by preventing workers from making agreements—to work for less than this minimum—that they would freely accept. They make similar arguments about labor unions. To the extent that unions impose on employers a higher wage than the employer would otherwise have had to pay, it can only be by preventing workers—for example, those who are not members of the union—from entering into a voluntary and mutually beneficial agreement with the employers.

Equity

Neoclassical economists argue that restrictions on market competition can unfairly benefit some market participants (buyers or sellers) or potential market participants at the expense of others. This kind of equity concern enters into neoclassical theory in several ways:

First, restrictions on competition may affect the ability of different people (or firms) to participate in a market—to offer what they have for sale or to bid on what other offer for sale. Suppose that the government issues special licenses to some people or firms that permit them to engage in a certain trade, while denying such licenses to others. (Such policies create "barriers to entry," in the language of neoclassical economics.) Such restrictions are, in the neoclassical view, unfair to the unlucky (or less-influential) individuals or firms who did not receive licenses and so are locked out of the market. Neoclassical economists argue that some special licenses required to engage in a certain occupation (like taxi medallions, legal licenses, and so on) are basically unfair barriers to entry. They favor people in that particular occupation, driving up their pay by restricting competition from other people who would like to be able to practice that trade as well. On a larger scale, restrictions on immigration act as "barriers to entry" into the labor market of an entire country.

Second, restrictions may affect the ability of different people to use whatever advantage they may have, to compete in a market. A price floor, for example, prevents lower-cost sellers from using their cost advantage (their willingness to accept a lower price) to compete in the market. In the neoclassical view, this favors higher-cost sellers at the expense of their lower-cost competitors. Minimum-wage laws, in this view, favor higher-skill workers over lower-skill workers, since it prevents the latter for competing by offering to work for less. The same is true of labor unions which, if they are to win higher wages from their members, must keep employers from hiring lower-wage workers.

Third, restrictions may affect the ability of sellers to fetch the highest price they can, constrained only by competition from other sellers, and of buyers to pay the lowest price they can, constrained only by bidding from other buyers. A price floor, by restricting producers from competing on price (preventing any from offering prices below the floor), may favor producers in general at the expense of consumers. By the same token, a price ceiling (a maximum legal price) may favor consumers at the expense of producers. When it comes to minimum-wage laws and labor unions, neoclassicals tend not to focus so much on the effects on buyers in the labor market (employers) as on the indirect effects on buyers in goods markets. Higher wages, imposed by government or union power, they argue, eventually drive up prices for the end consumer.

Efficiency

In the neoclassical view, a resource is used "efficiently" as long as the benefit from using that resource (to society as a whole) is greater than the cost (to society as a whole). Let's think about a company—say, an auto company—that has to decide how many machines to rent or how many workers to hire for its operations. It will consider how many extra cars it can produce if it rents one additional machine, or hires one additional worker. (We'll assume, as neoclassicals do, that it does not change the amounts of any other resources it uses.) The company will figure out how much income it will get from the sale of those additional cars. That is, it will multiply the number of additional cars by the price it will get per car. Ultimately, it will compare this extra income against the rental cost paid for the machine, or the wage paid to the worker. The company will rent a machine, or hire a worker, as long as the extra income it gets is more than the additional cost it has to pay.

In the neoclassical view, this is "efficient" not only from the standpoint of the company, but from the standpoint of society as a whole. As long as there are no effects on third parties (known as "externalities" or "spillovers"), the *benefit* to society of the use of one extra machine is the value of the extra cars produced. How much society values these cars is reflected in the price of the cars. The *cost* to society, on the other hand, is the cost of using the machine for the period of time that it is rented, during which it cannot be used for another purpose and probably undergoes some wear-and-tear. How much society values the use of the machine, in turn, is reflected in its price. If the value of the extra cars produced is greater than the cost of using the machine, then, the use of the machine is also "efficient" from the standpoint of society as a whole.

There's just one more problem. In the neoclassical view, for private actors to make decisions that are also "efficient" form the standpoint of society as a whole, the prices they base their decisions on have to be the *right* prices. That is, each price has to reflect the true cost of a good to society as a whole. The "price of labor," in the language of neoclassical economics, is the wage. So how do we know, in this view, what is the "right wage"?

The "Right" Wage

Suppose that the going wage in a certain place (for a certain kind of labor) is $20 per hour. According to neoclassical economists, a company will hire a worker as long as the extra benefit it gets from each extra hour of labor (the extra units produced times the price the company gets per unit) is at least as much as the additional cost it pays for that extra hour of labor ($20 per hour in this example). Suppose, however, that the wage was only this high because there were barriers to competition in the labor market (such as unions, minimum-wage laws, barriers to migration, etc.). If the wage without barriers would have only been, say, $10, then a company would hire an extra worker as long as the extra benefit it got from each extra hour of labor was at least $10 per hour. The company would hire more total labor hourse at a wage of $10 than at a wage of $20.

How do we know whether the "right" wage is $20 or $10, or something else, for that matter? In the view of neoclassical economists, the right wage—like any other right price—reflects the true cost to society of the good involved (here, an hour of labor). The cost of labor is whatever pains the worker endures as a result of that hour of work. This includes having to show up for work, when one might prefer to be someone else, having to follow the employer's orders, when one would rather be "doing one's own thing," putting up with the conditions at work, which could be dangerous, unhealthy, or unpleasant, and so on. If the worker is not *forced* to accept the offer of any particular employer, neoclassical economists argue, then all these costs are reflected in the wage. Remember, the wage must be enough to compensate the worker for all the pains they endure, or they would not accept the offer.

All workers would presumably rather have a higher wage than a lower one, all other factors being equal. It is competition in the labor market that makes workers reveal what they really require to compensate them for the burdens of labor. They may *say* they require a higher wage, but competition from other workers makes them lower their wage demands, down to an amount that is just enough to balance the costs to them of the last (or "marginal") hour they choose to work. This, in the neoclassical view, is the "right" price of labor: In the labor market, *as in all other markets*, unrestrained competition among all market participants results in the right price.

If the price of labor, due to barriers to labor-market competition, is "too high," then employers will use "too little" labor. If the wage is $20, due to barriers, then employers will not hire an extra hour of labor unless it results in the production of at least $20 of additional goods. That means that they will not hire an extra hour even if it results in the production of somewhere between $10 and $20 of additional goods. But the real cost of the labor, to society, is only $10. As a result of the inflated price of labor, society will have turned its back on who-knows-how-many opportunities to get between $10 and $20 of goods at a cost of $10 of labor. In other words, wages that are inflated by barriers to competition result in an "inefficient" use of resources.

Critiques of the Neoclassical View

Economists associated with different schools of thought may use normative concepts like "freedom," "equity," or "efficiency," but mean something very different by these ideas than what neoclassical economists mean. (Some may choose not to use these terms, and instead invoke other normative concepts, like "justice," "equality," "the good life," and so on.) Here, however, we will focus on contrasts with the neoclassical views of freedom, equity, and efficiency described above.

Equity

What is the "right" wage? According to neoclassical economists, the "right" wage is just barely enough to compensate a worker for the pains and burdens of work. Unrestrained competition is good because it forces workers to reveal the *lowest* wage that they will still accept. Is this a "fair" wage?

In the neoclassical view, only barriers to competition can result in a higher wage. These barriers, neoclassical economists argue, favor some workers at the expense of others and workers at the expense of consumers. An alternative view is that restraints on labor-market competition allow workers to get a better deal from employers. Such restraints may, indeed, benefit some people at the expense of others. Restraints such as unions, minimum-wage laws, regulations on hours and conditions, and so on may benefit workers while cutting into employers' profits. The absence of these restraints, on the other hand, may result in higher profits for employers while relegating workers to lower pay and worse conditions. Which outcome one prefers depends on how one values benefits to one group of people (workers) compared to benefits to another (employers).

There are several reasons that someone might favor the interests of workers over those of employers, and therefore approve of changes that benefit workers even if these benefits come at the expense of employers:

1. Ideas of "fairness" based on social "custom" or "convention." In most societies where people work for wages, there are evolving ideas about what is a "fair" wage or "decent" living. Partly, such ideas may be based on what people have become accustomed to in the past. Partly, they may reflect expectations that conditions of life will improve over time, and especially from one generation to the next. If wages and conditions fall below past levels, or fail to improve as fast as expected, some people may see improvements in workers' wages and working conditions (even at the expense of employers) as tilting the distribution of well-being in society back toward a "fair" balance between workers and employers.

2. Commitment to greater economic and social equality. People who get most of their income from property (ownership of businesses, land or buildings, or financial wealth) are likely to be at the top of the income ladder. Most of the people at the bottom or in the middle, on the other hand, get most of their income from work. Therefore, changes that benefit workers as a group (at the expense of employers) tend to bring about a more equal distribution of income in society. A more equal distribution of income may, in turn, create greater equality of opportunity from one generation to the next. The children of the well-off may no longer start with as great a head start, in terms of opportunities for education, resources for starting a business, and so on, over the children of the less-privileged. Moreover, greater economic equality may create greater political equality, to the extent that high incomes and wealth are a source of political power.

3. Ideas about who creates and deserves to keep society's wealth. Some "radical" economists argue that labor is the source of all new wealth produced in society. Owners of property take a piece of this wealth by controlling things (like farms, mines, factories, etc.) that everyone else needs in order to work and live. In this view, there is no such thing as a "fair" distribution of income between workers and employers, since the employing class exists only by virtue of taking part of what workers produce. Radical economists would like to see a different form of economic organization, in which workers no longer have to work under the authority of employers and no longer have to give up part of the value they have produced to the employer as profit. In the meantime, however, most radicals look favorably on changes that favor workers at the expense of employers, and allow them to keep more of what they have produced in the first place.

Much of the history of labor movements around the world centers on attempts to *restrain* competition between workers, to keep workers for undercutting each other on the wages or conditions they will accept, and therefore to benefit workers as a group. When workers all make their own separate deals with employers, each worker is put into competition with the rest. Each can be tempted to offer the employer more (longer hours, harder work), or to offer to work for less (lower wages, worse conditions), in order to out-compete fellow workers for a job. If some workers reduce their wage and conditions demands, however, other workers will be tempted to do the same. They will undercut each other until they get to the minimum they are willing to accept.

Labor unions and other restraints on labor-market competition may keep workers from undercutting each other by accepting lower wages, longer hours, or worse working conditions. Unions, for example, are compacts by which each member agrees *not* to accept a lower wage or worse conditions than the other members. Unions also set conditions on hours, benefits, and conditions of work. No individual can bargain a lower wage or worse conditions, in order to get a job, and thereby force other workers to do the same. Labor legislation like the minimum-wage laws, maximum hours (or overtime) laws, and laws regulating labor conditions are, likewise, all restrain competition between workers.

Labor Market Segmentation

Restraints on labor competition may benefit workers at the expense of employers. However, they may also benefit one group of workers at the expense of another. Some restraints may protect one group of workers by excluding other workers from certain kinds of jobs. (Racial and gender discrimination in the United States, for example, have historically excluded African Americans and women from many jobs—including professional, civil service, skilled trades, and industrial jobs.) In effect, these jobs are reserved for members of the included group. Protected from competition for jobs (from members of the excluded group), they can demand higher wages or better conditions than they would otherwise enjoy.

The exclusion of certain workers from certain jobs creates what economists call "segmented labor markets." In effect, different groups of workers are divided into different labor markets. There is no reason to expect the wages and conditions for workers in two different labor markets to equalize—even if workers in the two groups have, on average, the same skills. Racial and gender discrimination, then, have helped maintain higher wages for white workers than for African Americans and higher wages for men than for women. (Some economists argue that, by creating divisions and undermining solidarity between workers, discrimination may have harmed workers of all groups.)

Barriers to international migration also create segmented labor markets. Critics of such barriers argue that, just like racial or gender discrimination, they create different opportunity levels for different people based on something over which they have no control (in this case, place of birth). Barriers benefit native-born workers at the expense of workers born elsewhere (and may also benefit workers born elsewhere who "win the lottery" to enter and work). They create inequalities between the two groups of workers, and create a temptation for employers to use workers in the excluded group to undermine the wages and conditions of workers in the included group. They also drive a wedge between different groups, encouraging workers in the included group to view workers in the excluded group as a threat.

Many radical economists recognize the problems of unrestrained labor-market competition. They argue, however, against restraints that specifically protect a high-wage group at the expense of a low-wage group. Instead, they argue for policies that will benefit both groups of workers—raising the wages and conditions for workers in lower-income groups toward the level of those in higher-income groups.

Freedom

Neoclassical economists emphasize workers' freedom of choice to accept low wages, long hours, bad working conditions, and so on. Workers would not accept those conditions, they argue, unless doing so would leave them better off than they would be otherwise. For example, workers may accept "poverty wages," but only because the alternative (not having a job at all) would be worse. They may, for the same reason, agree to work under unpleasant, unhealthy, or unsafe conditions. In this view, institutions like unions or policies like minimum-wage laws interfere with workers' freedom to make a deal that would leave them better off.

Many liberal and almost all radical economists, on the other hand, emphasize how the conditions that an individual will "freely" accept depend on the alternatives available to them. If people have no alternatives, or only very bad alternatives, they are likely to accept very bad conditions. While they may be entering formally voluntary agreements—where they are not coerced directly (as by threat of violence) by the person making the offer—this may not reflect much genuine "freedom of choice." If the only alternative is to starve in the street, most people would instead work even very long hours, under very bad conditions, for very low pay. Instead of seeing these workers as having "freely" accepted such agreements, however, one could view them as lacking any real freedom to *refuse* these conditions.

Radical economists, many of them inspired by the work of Karl Marx, argue that all workers fundamentally face these kinds of constraints on their choices. While the alternative for most workers in high-income countries might not be destitution or starvation, workers everywhere "choose" to work because they do not have another way to make a living or provide for their families. They do not have property of their own (such as a farm or business) that would allow them to make a living. That leaves one alternative—to work for someone else for pay.

Union contracts, minimum-wage laws, and other restraints on competition between workers do, indeed, restrict each individual worker's "freedom" to accept lower wages, worse conditions, and so on, just as neoclassical economists argue. However, this view ignores the benefit to each worker—that these institutions also constrain the agreements that other workers can make. Each worker is constrained from undercutting other workers (in order to get a job), but is also *protected* against other workers undercutting him or her. Instead of seeing restraints on labor competition as robbing workers of the freedom to accept lower wages or worse conditions, one can instead see them as giving workers the freedom to demand higher wages or better conditions.

Efficiency

We have already described one concept of efficiency used by neoclassical economists: The key idea is that resources are used if (and only if) the benefit to society is greater than the cost. If resources are used when the costs are greater than the benefit, this subtracts from the overall well-being of society. If resources are not used when the benefit would be greater than the costs, society is missing an opportunity to add to the overall well-being.

Neoclassical economists also use another concept of efficiency: An efficient condition is one in which nobody can be made better off without making someone worse off. This definition, pioneered by the Italian neoclassical economist Vilfredo Pareto, is known as "Pareto efficiency." The two definitions are connected: If resources were being wasted (used inefficiently), they could be used to make someone better off without making anyone worse off.

Neoclassical economists call a *change* that makes some people better off without making anyone worse off a "Pareto improvement." There are very few changes in public policies, however, that make some people better off while literally making nobody worse off. Most policy changes, potentially affecting millions of people, make some people better off and others worse off. In these cases, neoclassical economists apply what they call the "compensation test." They compare the benefits to the "winners" from some change in public policy to the losses to the "losers." It the total gains are greater than the total losses, neoclassical economists argue, the winners could compensate the losers—and leave everyone at least a little better off.

One problem with the compensation test is that it may be difficult to compare benefits and losses to different people, especially if not all the benefits or losses can be easily counted in dollars. For example, eliminating tariffs might reduce employment in the formerly protected industry. Suppose that a government eliminated agricultural tariffs and many farmers end up losing their farms. The loss of income is easy to count in dollars. For the farmers and their families, however, being farmers and having their own land may also have been important (for example, in terms of their self-image). That is very difficult to put in dollars-and-cents terms.

Even more important, in most cases where there are both winners and losers due to a change in public policy, the winners do not actually compensate the losers. These are not, then, actual efficiency improvements in the sense that some people are made better off while nobody is made worse off. Restraints on labor-market competition, for example, may benefit workers at the expense of their employers. (Eliminating such policies, meanwhile, has opposite effects—so it still benefits some people while harming others.) Judging whether these changes are for the better, then, involves weighing the benefits to some people against the losses to others. How one resolves such an issue depends on one's normative ideas, or values, about whose interests should take precedence. ❑

Article 1.4

AMERICA BEYOND CONSUMERISM
Has capitalist economic growth outlived its purpose?

BY THAD WILLIAMSON
May/June 2008

One of the great benefits of studying the history of economic ideas is coming to the recognition that the founding figures of capitalist economics, and in particular Adam Smith, author of the pivotal *Wealth of Nations*, were often deeply ambivalent about the acquisitive way of life. Consider the famous parable of the poor man's son, presented by Smith in his *Theory of Moral Sentiments*:

> The poor man's son, whom heaven in its anger has visited with ambition, when he begins to look around him, admires the condition of the rich. He finds the cottage of his father too small for his accommodation, and fancies he should be lodged more at his ease in a palace. He is displeased with being obliged to walk a-foot, or to endure the fatigue of riding on horseback. He sees his superiors carried about in machines, and imagines that in one of these he could travel with less inconveniency. ... He thinks if he had attained all these, he would sit still contentedly, and be quiet, enjoying himself in the thought of the happiness and tranquility of his situation. He is enchanted with the distant idea of this felicity. It appears in his fancy like the life of some superior rank of beings, and, in order to arrive at it, he devotes himself forever to the pursuit of wealth and greatness. To obtain the conveniencies which these afford, he submits in the first year, nay in the first month of his application, to more fatigue of body and more uneasiness of mind than he could have suffered through the whole of his life from want of them. He studies to distinguish himself in some laborious profession. With the most unrelenting industry he labours night and day to acquire talents superior to all his competitors. He endeavours next to bring those talents into public view, and with equal assiduity solicits every opportunity of employment. For this purpose he makes his court to all mankind; he serves those whom he hates, and is obsequious to those whom he despises. Through the whole of his life he pursues the idea of a certain artificial and elegant repose which he may never arrive at, for which he sacrifices a real tranquility that is at all times in his power, and which if in the extremity of old age, he should at last attain to it, he will find to be in no respect preferable to that humble security and contentment which he had abandoned for it. It is then ... that he begins at last to find that wealth and greatness are mere trinkets of frivolous utility, no more adapted for procuring ease of body or tranquility of mind than the tweezer-cases of the lover of toys; and like them too, more troublesome to the person who carries them about with him than all the advantages they can afford him...
>
> In his heart he curses ambition, and vainly regrets the ease and the indolence of youth, pleasures which are fled for ever, and which he has foolishly sacrificed for what, when he has got it, can afford him no real satisfaction.

Adam Smith, traditionally regarded as the patron saint of capitalist economics, here avers that the fundamental engines of the market economy—ambition and
acquisitiveness—rest on what he terms a "deception," the illusion that all the objects
we spend our days striving for will make us happy.

Fast forward over 200 years. Here is how a contemporary economist, Juliet
Schor of Boston College, describes "Greg," a sixth grader in a Boston suburb, in her
2004 book *Born to Buy: The Commercialized Child and the New Consumer Culture*:

> Greg is an avid consumer. He loves professional wrestling, Gameboy, Nintendo,
> television, movies, junk food, and CDs (especially those with parental advi-
> sories). Since he came to live with his [father and step-mother], they've had a
> succession of incidents, most of which resulted in Greg's losing privileges to
> one or another of these things. He isn't allowed to do wrestling moves on his
> younger sister, but he does, and he loses the right to watch wrestling. He's sup-
> posed to do his homework, but he has lied and said he doesn't have any so he
> can spend his time playing a new Gameboy. He's supposed to tell the truth,
> but he stole [his stepmom's] Snickers bar and denied it. He knows he's not
> allowed to have CDs with parental advisories, but he went behind [his par-
> ents]' back and asked his [biological] mother to buy them for him...
>
> Another couple described their son Doug as "the ultimate consumer." He
> wanted to buy every product he saw advertised on television. Doug was now
> in sixth grade, and they were fighting constant battles. He would stay on the
> computer all day if they let him. He has a weakness for fast food. He has a lot
> of trouble holding on to money. His mother even described trying to sneak
> out to the store without him to avoid conflicts about buying stuff.

Schor was stunned to find that persistent parent-child conflicts over money and
goods were widespread, not confined to a few severe cases like Greg and Doug. In
a survey of some 300 Boston-area fifth and sixth graders, Schor found strong evidence of a causal relationship between heavier involvement in consumer culture and
strained relationships with parents, greater feelings of boredom and physical pain,
higher levels of depression and anxiety, and lower self-esteem.

This finding is troubling precisely because corporate advertisers, as Schor and
others have amply documented, have become increasingly brazen in the past 10 to 15
years about marketing directly to children, with the explicit purpose of establishing
brand identifications and consumer loyalty as early as possible. By age ten, the average American kid is aware of over 300 specific brand names. A particular goal of this
marketing is to persuade children to nag their parents to buy them things. A recent
study reveals that the average American child aged three to eight now nags his or her
parents nearly five times a day for material goods. Furthermore, research shows that
over 80% of parents respond positively to such nagging at least some of the time,
and marketers have estimated that up to one-half of sales of popular products for
kids are a direct result of children nagging their parents. Probably not coincidentally,
since the 1970s, as the impact of commercial culture on childhood has increased, the
observed mental and physical health outcomes of American children, including levels of depression, obesity, and attention deficit disorder, have worsened.

So maybe it's not good to be obsessed with consumer goods, or to be, consciously or subconsciously, the slave of some advertising executive who knows how to play on your insecurities, self-image, and aspirations. But isn't money, at some level, necessary to make us happy?

Here the answer is slightly more complicated, but a large body of research—much of it usefully summarized by political scientist Robert Lane in his 2000 book *The Loss of Happiness in Market Democracies*—suggests it is not at all inconsistent with the view Aristotle expressed over 2,000 years ago: we need some material goods to be happy, but not an excess of them. Consider evidence from the Social Capital Community Benchmark Survey, a survey of some 33,050 Americans conducted by the Saguaro Center for Civic Engagement at Harvard in 2000. Among many other topics, this survey asked people how happy they are, allowing researchers to assess the most important predictors of greater happiness. How does income stack up in importance compared to having friends, confidantes, and close family relationships, and to being an active member of the community?

The survey data suggest that holding other demographic factors equal, an individual who earns $30,000 to $50,000 a year, visits with relatives three times a month, has at least ten "close friends" and at least three people he or she can confide in, and belongs to a religious congregation as well as three other organizations has a 47.5% likelihood of self-reporting as "very happy." In contrast, consider someone demographically alike in all other respects who earns over $100,000 a year, but visits with relatives just one time a month, has only one to two "close friends," has only one person to confide in, is not part of a religious congregation, and belongs to only one organization. That person—richer in income but poorer in social connections—is estimated to have just a 28.6% chance of feeling "very happy."

Now, it's true that higher income, while not connected at all to family visits, is somewhat correlated with having more friends and confidantes and even more strongly associated with increased group memberships. Nor can anyone deny that economic circumstances influence well-being: controlling for other factors, moving from $30,000-$50,000 to over $100,000 a year in income is associated with a substantial rise in the likelihood of being "very happy"—from 34.4% to 45.3%. But the projected increase in the likelihood of being "very happy" associated with moving from having just three to five friends and two confidantes to over ten friends and at least three confidantes is even more substantial (from 32.2% to 44.2%). For most people, making five new friends and developing one or two especially close friendships are more realistic goals than doubling their income. The evidence suggests that expanding social ties is also a better strategy for finding happiness—especially if the alternative, chasing after more income, comes at the cost of fewer friends and weaker social connections. Income matters in shaping subjective well-being, but social connections matter more.

It would be misleading to leave the story at that, however. So far we have only been discussing raw income figures. But a closer look reveals that what people value more than their raw income is a sense of being *satisfied* with their economic circumstances. When we include both measures in statistical models predicting individual happiness, economic satisfaction predominates; it's a far more powerful predictor of well-being than absolute income. *Controlling for income level*, individuals who are "very satisfied," "somewhat satisfied," or "not at all satisfied" with their economic circumstances have sharply divergent chances of being very happy: 48.7%, 33.3%, and 20.8% respectively. In contrast, if we control for people's level of economic satisfaction, more income does relatively little to promote happiness: a leap from the $30,000–$50,000 income bracket to the over-$100,000 bracket implies an increase of just four percentage points in the predicted likelihood of being "very happy," from 34.8% to 38.9%. Put another way, a person earning $30,000 to $50,000 who reports being "very satisfied" with her financial condition has, controlling for other factors, a 48.8% likelihood of being "very happy," whereas a person earning over $100,000 who is only "somewhat satisfied" with her financial condition has just a 37.5% likelihood of being "very happy." How much money one earns is, in itself, not an overwhelmingly decisive factor driving individual well-being, but being satisfied with what one has certainly is.

What is it that allows people to be happy with what they have? It could be that people who are psychologically disposed to be happier also tend to look more positively on whatever economic circumstances they find themselves in. But it's equally if not more plausible to think that two other factors drive economic satisfaction: a sense of economic security—in other words, knowing that you will be able to sustain your current lifestyle in the future—and freedom from the compulsion to compare your own versus others' income and consumption. But as scholars like Jacob Hacker and Robert Frank have pointed out, recent political-economic trends in the United States have had precisely the effect of weakening economic security and encouraging social comparisons. In his recent book *Falling Behind*, Frank insightfully discusses how the explosion in consumption by the super-rich in the last 20 years has shaped the behavior of middle- and upper-middle-class households, who feel that they too should have a bigger house or, to take Frank's favorite illustration, a more expensive barbecue grill.

If Consuming More Doesn't Make Us Happier, What's the Point of Capitalism?

This brings us back to Adam Smith, who anticipated much of this body of evidence when he described the poor man's son who forsakes enjoyment of life for a life of industry and self-advancement as suffering from a fundamental delusion. Yet this insight did not lead Smith to reject capitalism. On the contrary, he thought this deception had a socially productive purpose: namely, helping to fuel economic progress, the advancement of industry, and the gradual rise of living standards—not just the living standards of the rich, but the living standards of average working people as well.

Indeed, in the subsequent 200 years, capitalism—or more accurately, capitalism modified by a range of state interventions, public spending, social welfare programs, and labor laws—has been remarkably successful in lifting overall living standards in places like the United Kingdom and the United States (albeit with often enormous social costs borne by millions of nameless workers who labored for capitalist employers under horrific conditions, enforced by the threat of hunger, and in some cases literally at gunpoint). In the 20th century alone, per capita income in the United States increased eightfold and life expectancy rose from 49 to 77 years.

That's the good news. The bad news is, median wage growth has stalled in the United States in the last 30 years, and has gone backwards for the least educated Americans. Total hours worked per household have risen as women work longer hours without a corresponding reduction in men's work hours. The hope of a secure, stable job has all but disappeared—hence today's widespread feelings of economic insecurity and dissatisfaction across income brackets. More to the point, there is good reason to doubt that simply continuing to "grow the economy" is going to address any of these concerns—or make most people any happier.

Consider just how rich a society this is. The U.S. Gross Domestic Product now stands at $13.8 trillion. If it were divided equally, that would come to over $180,000 for a family of four, or about $125,000 in take-home pay assuming an effective tax rate of 30%. In other words, the U.S. economy is large enough to provide a very comfortable life for each and every American.

But it doesn't. Why not?

A skyrocketing degree of economic inequality is one reason. The median income for married couple households in 2006 was $70,000, with of course many families making far, far less. While the income and wealth of the top 1% spike to unimaginable levels, many Americans simply do not have enough money to get by. With inequality comes not just poverty, but also widening disparities in status which themselves help fuel ever-greater levels of consumption as people spend more and more to try to keep up with the (ever-richer) Joneses.

The second reason is the widespread fact of economic insecurity. People whose jobs, health coverage, wage levels, and pensions are fragile naturally feel pressure to accumulate and advance as far as they can, lest they fall behind and lose what they now have. And, every week, we read about workers and communities who do in fact lose what they have as layoffs and plant shutdowns are announced. As we have seen, survey data (as well Adam Smith's intuitions) suggest that what matters most for well-being is the sense that one has enough and can feel comfortable about the future—that is, the very thing that the American economy fails to provide to the vast majority of families.

This insecurity is most potent in blue-collar America, but the middle class does not escape it either. Consider the life pattern of the average white-collar American. To go to college and get ahead, you have to borrow money and incur debt; to pay off the debt, you're under pressure to land a high-paying job; when you start a family, financial responsibilities multiply: you take on a mortgage, begin paying for child care or else accept a drop in household income, and within a few years face the stark realization that unless you make enough to either pay for private education or live in a neighborhood with good public schools, your children's education will suffer; and by the time you are finally done paying your children's college costs, it's already past time to begin building a nest egg for retirement and a cushion against illness. At no point does it seem to most people prudent—or even possible—simply to get off the treadmill.

Little wonder, then, that the Harvard social capital survey found just 26% of Americans to be "very satisfied" with their economic status (including just 54% of those making over $100,000 a year). It is impossible to address the issue of runaway consumerism without also addressing the issue of economic security. Indeed, as Knox College psychologist Tim Kasser, author of *The High Price of Materialism*, notes, a host of studies by psychologists and others demonstrate a strong relationship between numerous kinds of insecurity, especially economic insecurity, and the development of a materialist outlook on life.

This brings us to the third major reason the U.S. economy fails to foster a comfortable life for most Americans: long hours and overwork. Stress, fatigue, and sleep deprivation have become hallmarks of the American way of life. Over three-quarters of Americans report feeling stressed at least "sometimes," with a full one-third saying they experience stress "frequently." (The figures are higher still for persons holding jobs and for parents.) Likewise, roughly one-half of all Americans—including three-fifths of employed workers, parents, and persons aged 18 to 49—say they do not have enough time to do what they would like to in daily life, such as spend time with friends. Harvard political scientist Robert Putnam reports that the percentage of Americans regularly eating dinner together declined by one-third between 1977 and 1999. Research by the Families and Work Institute indicates that almost two-thirds (63%) would like to work fewer hours. On average those questioned said they would reduce their work week by more than ten hours if they could. But what people want and what the political economy provides are two different things: in the past generation, the centuries-long trend towards reducing the length of the work week has come to a screeching halt.

So the U.S. economy, as presently constituted, produces tremendous inequality, insecurity, and overwork. Nor is there reason to think that growing from a $14 trillion to, say, a $20 or $25 trillion economy will change these destructive trends.

It doesn't have to be this way. There is no inherent reason why we could not cease to regard more income as a good in itself, but instead alter our political economy so that it provides what Americans really need and want: greater employment security, stronger protection against the pitfalls of poverty, and more free time. We could choose to have the public guarantee employment opportunities for every willing worker, to put a floor on income, to decommodify health care and education, to reduce the gross inequalities of income and status which themselves help fuel consumerism, and to take future productivity growth in the form of more time, not more stuff.

To be sure, doing so would not be easy, and would require substantial institutional changes, possibly even a shift to a system that, as economist Gar Alperovitz puts it, lies "beyond capitalism." Many careful analysts, including Alperovitz and Schor, have thought long and hard about just how that could happen; indeed, there has been a rich debate in the past 15 years about the long-term possibilities of alternative political-economic frameworks that would reshape the logic of our current system.

It would be very easy to dismiss these ideas as "crazy" or "utopian." But, I submit, the moral task Adam Smith set for capitalism—that of making it economically possible for each and every person to live a materially comfortable life—has been achieved, at least in the advanced industrialized countries. The acquisitive life that goes with capitalism Smith never endorsed as good in itself. Neither should we, especially given the unhealthy consequences of an excessive consumerism that is now warping children's lives from their earliest years, and given the potentially planet-melting consequences of a way of life based on continual increases in consumption and economic activity.

That wasn't what Adam Smith wanted. Nor was it what the most influential and pragmatic of 20th-century economists, John Maynard Keynes, the man many credit with saving capitalism from itself, wanted. In a famous but too often neglected essay called "Economic Possibilities for Our Grandchildren," Keynes looked to a time when at last it would be possible for humanity (at least in the affluent nations) to turn its attention away from acquisition and toward broader moral concerns—such as "how to use his freedom from pressing economic cares, how to occupy the leisure, which science and compound interest will have won for him, to live wisely and agreeably and well."

That time has not yet come. But the remaining barriers to it are political, not economic; and the great task of this century is to assure that our prodigious economic capacities are directed towards supplying the real goods of human life: material security, meaningful work, and plentiful time for the friends and family who are the most lasting source of human happiness. ❑

Sources: Adam Smith, *The Theory of Moral Sentiments* (1759) (Liberty Fund, 1984); Juliet Schor, *Born to Buy: The Commercialized Child and the New Consumer Culture* (Scribner, 2004); Tim Kasser, *The High Price of Materialism* (MIT Press, 2002); "Half of Americans are Pressed for Time; A Third Are Stressed Out," *Gallup News Svc*, May 3, 2004; "No time for R&R," *Gallup News Svc*, May 11, 2004; "Who Dreams, Perchance to Sleep?" *Gallup News Svc*, Jan. 25, 2005; Robert Putnam, *Bowling Alone: The Collapse and Revival of American Community* (Simon & Schuster, 2000); J. Bond, E. Galinsky, and J. Swanberg, *The 1997 National Study of the Changing Workforce*, Families and Work Institute, 1998; Gar Alperovitz, *America Beyond Capitalism: Reclaiming Our Wealth, Our Liberty, and Our Democracy* (Wiley, 2004); Jerome Segal, *Graceful Simplicity: Towards a Philosophy and Politics of Simple Living* (Henry Holt, 1999); Juliet Schor, *A Sustainable Economy for the 21st Century* (Open Media, 1995); John Maynard Keynes, *Essays in Persuasion* (W.W. Norton, 1963); Jacob S. Hacker, *The Great Risk Shift* (Oxford Univ. Press, 2006); Robert H. Frank, *Falling Behind: How Rising Inequality Harms the Middle Class* (Univ. of Calif. Press, 2007); Robert E. Lane, *The Loss of Happiness in Market Democracies* (Yale Univ. Press, 2000); Robert M. Biswas-Diener, "Material Wealth and Subjective Well-Being," in M. Eid and R. J. Larsen, eds., *The Science of Subjective Well-Being* (Guilford Press, 2008).

Article 1.5

BUBBLE TROUBLE

Talk about irrational exuberance. Housing is the new bull market.

BY DEAN BAKER
January/February 2005

As lukewarm as the economic recovery [from the 2001 recession] has been, it would have been far chillier if not for the housing market. Throughout the recession and recovery, overheated housing prices have kept the economy simmering.

Since late 1995, housing prices have risen nationwide by almost 35% after adjusting for inflation. In some regions, real home prices have risen by more than 50%. Such a steep run-up is abnormal. Prior to 1995, home prices had closely tracked the inflation rate.

By borrowing against the inflated values of their homes throughout the economic slowdown, families spurred consumption growth—despite the weak job market and stagnant wages—providing much of the lift for the current recovery. Since Bush took office in 2000, the amount of outstanding mortgage debt has risen a remarkable 50.4%. As a result, the ratio of mortgage debt to home equity hit a record high in 2003.

Some argue there's no need to worry; the rise in housing prices is not a bubble, but is founded on genuine factors such as scarce urban land, immigration, and income growth—but these explanations don't make sense. Vacant land in many urban areas has long been scarce, but this never before led to such a surge in prices. And most immigrants are not in the market for the half-million dollar homes that are driving the bubble in several regions. Income doesn't get us far in explaining the bubble, either; income growth during the late 1990s pales in comparison to the period between 1951 and 1973, when there was no bubble. Plus, the housing bubble has continued to grow over the past 3.5 years, when income growth was leveling off.

The housing bubble most likely has its origins in another bubble—the stock bubble of the late 1990s, when investors used their Wall Street returns to buy pricier homes. The increased demand began to drive up prices; soon, homebuyers came to expect continued price increases and based their purchase decisions on that expectation. Homebuyers who may otherwise have viewed a $200,000 home as too costly became willing to pay that much in the expectation that the home would sell for far more down the road. Expectations of ever-rising prices drive speculative bubbles.

Sound familiar? Indeed, the current housing bubble is not unlike the run-up in stock prices to which it owes its origins. If and when this bubble bursts, as the stock bubble did, the economy will likely find itself in another recession, and millions of families will see their net worth disappear as their homes, particularly those in over-inflated housing markets, plummet in value. With nearly 40% of new homebuyers choosing adjustable-rate mortgages, and interest rates on the rise, some homebuyers could face increased mortgage payments even as the values of their homes fall.

Those with high debt-to-equity balances could face negative equity, or the prospect of owing more than they own.

The recent rise in mortgage rates has begun to slow the four-year refinancing frenzy, but the middle class is now so laden with mortgage debt that the damage when the bubble bursts will be widely felt. ❑

Article 1.6

THE 99%, THE 1%, AND CLASS STRUGGLE

BY ALEJANDRO REUSS
November/December 2011

Between 1979 and 2007, the income share of the top 1% of U.S. households (by income rank) more than doubled, to over 17% of total U.S. income. Meanwhile, the income share of the bottom 80% dropped from 57% to 48% of total income. "We are the 99%," the rallying cry of the Occupy Wall Street movement, does a good job at calling attention to the dramatic increase of incomes for those at the very top—and the stagnation of incomes for the majority.

This way of looking at income distribution, however, does not explicitly focus on the different *sources* of people's incomes. Most people get nearly all of their incomes—wages and salaries, as well as employment benefits—by working for someone else. A few people, on the other hand, get much of their income not from work but from ownership of property—profits from a business, dividends from stock, interest income from bonds, rents on land or structures, and so on. People with large property incomes may also draw large salaries or bonuses, especially from managerial jobs. Executive pay, though treated in official government statistics as labor income, derives from control over business firms and really should be counted as property income.

Over the last forty years, the distribution of income in the United States has tilted in favor of capitalists (including business owners, stock- and bond-holders, and corporate executives) and against workers. Between the 1940s and 1960s, U.S. workers' hourly output ("average labor productivity") and workers' real hourly compensation both grew at about 3% per year, so the distribution of income between workers and capitalists changed relatively little. (If the size of a pie doubles and the size of your slice also doubles, your share of the pie does not change.) Since the 1970s,

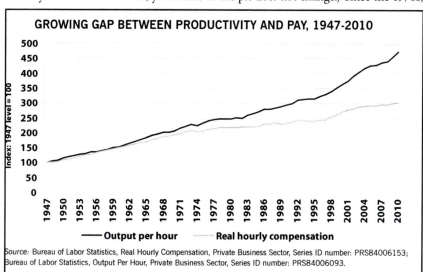

GROWING GAP BETWEEN PRODUCTIVITY AND PAY, 1947-2010

——Output per hour ······Real hourly compensation

Source: Bureau of Labor Statistics, Real Hourly Compensation, Private Business Sector, Series ID number: PRS84006153; Bureau of Labor Statistics, Output Per Hour, Private Business Sector, Series ID number: PRS84006093.

productivity has kept growing at over 2% per year. Average hourly compensation, however, has stagnated—growing only about 1% per year (see figure below). As the gap between what workers produce and what they get paid has increased, workers' share of total income has fallen, and capitalists' share has increased. Since income from property is overwhelmingly concentrated at the top of the income scale, this has helped fuel the rising income share of "the 1%."

The spectacular rise in some types of income—like bank profits or executive compensation—has provoked widespread outrage. Lower financial profits or CEO pay, however, will not reverse the trend toward greater inequality if the result is only to swell, say, profits for nonfinancial corporations or dividends for wealthy shareholders. Focusing too much on one or another kind of property income distracts from the fact that the overall property-income share has been growing at workers' expense.

Workers and employers—whether they like it or not, recognize it or not, prepare for it or not—are locked in a class struggle. Employers in the United States and other countries, over the last few decades, have recognized that they were in a war and prepared for it. They have been fighting and winning. Workers will only regain what they have lost if they can rebuild their collective fighting strength. In the era of globalized capitalism, this means not only building up labor movements in individual countries, but also creating practical solidarity between workers around the world.

A labor resurgence could end workers' decades-long losing streak at the hands of employers and help reverse the tide of rising inequality. Ultimately, though, this struggle should be about more than just getting a better deal. It should be—and can be—about the possibility of building a new kind of society. The monstrous inequalities of capitalism are plain to see. The need for an appealing alternative—a vision of a cooperative, democratic, and egalitarian way of life—is equally stark. ❑

Sources: Bureau of Labor Statistics, Real Hourly Compensation, Private Business Sector, Series ID number: PRS84006153; Bureau of Labor Statistics, Output Per Hour, Private Business Sector, Series ID number: PRS84006093; Congressional Budget Office, Trends in the Distribution of Household Income Between 1979 and 2007 (October 2011) (www.cbo.gov); James Heintz, "Unpacking the U.S. Labor Share," *Capitalism on Trial: A Conference in Honor of Thomas A. Weisskopf*, Political Economy Research Institute, University of Massachusetts-Amherst (September 2011).

CHAPTER 2

SUPPLY AND DEMAND

INTRODUCTION

Textbooks tell us that supply and demand work like a well-oiled machine. The Law of Supply tells us that as the price of an item goes up, businesses will supply more of that good or service. The Law of Demand adds that as the price rises, consumers will choose to buy less of the item. Only one equilibrium price can bring businesses' and consumers' intentions into balance. Away from this equilibrium point, surpluses or shortages tend to drive the price back toward the equilibrium. Of course, government actions such as taxation or setting a price ceiling or floor can move the economy away from its market equilibrium, and create what economists call a deadweight loss.

Our authors raise vexing issues about the mechanism of supply and demand. Chris Tilly and Marie Kennedy tell the complex story of a rise in the price of tortillas in Mexico, which turns out to be driven not by a shortage of corn, but by the multiple impacts of a nationwide shift towards free trade. The authors also go beyond an analysis of the causes of the price rise to explore its contribution to rising inequality in Mexico (Article 2.1). Marc Breslow argues that supply and demand do not always produce the best outcomes for society, noting that shortages lead to skyrocketing prices (Article 2.2). But he also suggests that government should make use of the Law of Demand, increasing taxes on fuel to drive down fuel consumption (Article 2.3).

Ellen Frank questions the mainstream textbook idea that rent controls (and other price ceilings) lead to permanent shortages. She maintains that rent control helps to equalize power between landlords and tenants and to assure a supply of affordable housing (Article 2.4). Does raising the minimum wage cause layoffs? Economist Paddy Quick says no. In "Don't Blame the Minimum Wage" (Article 2.5), Quick points out that the issue of employment in this sector of the economy is significantly more complex than the relative price of low-wage labor. She also brings up the Classical Theory of the Subsistence Wage, from which Adam Smith determined the wage level of English working men. This "Classical Theory" is still particularly germane to this topic today.

The chapter concludes with William Moseley's article, "Famine Myths: Five Misunderstandings of the 2011 Hunger Crisis in the Horn of Africa" (Article 2.6). It appears that mere supply and demand analysis is inadequate to explain what actually caused the crisis, which contines to wreak misery upon East Africa.

Taken together, these articles call into question the claims that markets always operate efficiently and lead to the best social allocation of resources. The articles also imply a role for the "visible hand" of government when markets persistently fail.

Discussion Questions

1) (General) Marc Breslow portrays a situation in which suppliers (energy companies) hold disproportionate power over buyers. Can you think of situations in which buyers have disproportionate power over suppliers? (Hint: Large corporations can be buyers as well as suppliers.)

2) (General) The authors of these articles call for a larger government role in regulating supply and demand. What are some possible results of expanded government involvement, positive and negative? On balance, do you agree that government should play a larger role?

3) (Article 2.1) What reasons do Tilly and Kennedy provide for the rise in the price of tortillas in Mexico? Would you classify these reasons as being on the "supply side" or "demand side"? Do you think the authors' analysis deviates in any way from standard economic analyses of changing market prices?

4) (Article 2.1) In Tilly and Kennedy's article, how does the government of Mexico react to the tortilla price rise? What is the reaction of different members of the tortilla industry? What do you think it might take to lower tortilla prices in Mexico?

5) (Article 2.2) One way of summarizing Breslow's article is "The Law of Demand guarantees that there will sometimes be price-gouging." Explain what this means. Do you agree?

6) (Article 2.2) Breslow says that shortages have different effects on prices in the short run and the long run. Explain the difference. How is this difference related to the concepts of elasticity of demand and elasticity of supply?

7) (Article 2.3) List a few factors that affect gasoline prices at the pump. What are some of the advantages and disadvantages (and for whom) of high gas prices?

8) (Article 2.3) What are two positive changes that would occur if SUVs and other gas-guzzlers were minimized on U.S. roads?

9) (Article 2.4) Ellen Frank states that because modern rent control laws are "soft," they do not lead to housing shortages. Explain. Do you agree with her reasoning?

10) (Article 2.5) What is Paddy Quick's argument against the claim that minimum wage laws create unemployment?

11) (Article 2.5) Why are all state-mandated minimum wages greater than the federal minimum wage? How does this relate to the Classical Theory of the Subsistence Wage?

12) (Article 2.6) What are William Moseley's five "myths" of the cause of the 2011 Horn of Africa famine?

Article 2.1

SUPPLY, DEMAND, AND TORTILLAS

BY CHRIS TILLY AND MARIE KENNEDY
March/April 2007

T he last year has been a fractious one in Mexico. Last May, in San Salvador Atenco in Mexico State, a group of street vendors and a wide range of allies protesting the vendors' expulsion from the central square were brutally repressed, with hundreds arrested, beaten, and sexually abused by police. To the south in Oaxaca, Governor Ulises Ruiz launched a similar police operation against striking teachers in June, sparking the formation of a broad front that occupied the center of the city for months despite constant attacks by police and armed goons, only to be swept out in November by a vicious federal-state police assault. Meanwhile, as the every-six-years presidential campaign heated up, a caravan of Zapatistas headed by *Subcomandante* Marcos toured the country arguing that only grassroots mobilization, not a vote for one of the three major-party candidates, would change Mexican politics. July's presidential election put the right-wing National Action Party (PAN) candidate, Felipe Calderón, ahead of the center-left Party of the Democratic Revolution's (PRD) Andrés Manuel López Obrador by a razor-thin margin, amid evidence of large-scale irregularities. Supporters of López Obrador (popularly known as AMLO) took to the streets, creating a festive tent city stretching miles along Mexico City's main boulevard, La Reforma, and coming together in animated rallies of up to two million. Failing to change the election result, they declared a parallel government.

In early 2007, all of these struggles have been heating up once again. Key Atenco leaders are getting out of jail. Activists are marching in Oaxaca city once again, and a major Triqui indigenous community in that state just declared itself autonomous from the state, federal, and "official" local governments. AMLO and allies across the country are gearing up for what they call the Democratic National Convention, with the aim of building a new politics and writing a new constitution. The Zapatistas held a four day forum—"Encounter with the Peoples of the World"—hosting some 2,000 delegates in their base communities.

And across Mexico, the hot topic of the moment is…the price of tortillas. Prices for this Mexican staple, just a few months ago selling at 5 pesos (about 50 cents) per kilo (2.2 pounds, about 40 tortillas), had by mid-January spiked up to 8, 10, and in some places even 12 or 15 pesos per kilo. It's hard to convey to a U.S. audience how central tortillas are to the Mexican diet, but suffice it to say that *tortillerías* are sprinkled every couple of blocks across urban Mexico, and the great majority of families anchor their main meal with a kilo or two of tortillas. (When we first went to a *tortillería* and asked for ten tortillas, the vendor assumed she had heard us wrong and asked, "Ten kilos?") Perhaps the closest U.S. equivalent in terms of breadth of impact would be if the price of gas doubled and in some places even tripled. Other prices are also climbing—milk, eggs, sugar, meat, and natural gas—but it's the tortilla price surge that has grabbed Mexicans by the throat.

A Peculiar Crisis

A number of things are odd about the tortilla crisis. For one thing, there is no shortage of corn. Mexico had the largest corn harvest ever last year, more than twice as much as in 1980 (the country's population grew 60% over the same period). However, the structure of corn production has changed dramatically. Millions of family farmers in central and southern Mexico once dominated the crop, but free-trade policies have driven many of them off the land. Today, northern Mexican agribusiness calls the tune. That plus NAFTA and other free trade agreements and the reduction of government subsidies mean that Mexico's corn price is now driven by the world price. The world price, in turn, increasingly responds to demand for ethanol as well as for food products. So the price has trended up as oil prices made ethanol more attractive—prompting *The Economist* to label corn "pure gold." Making matters worse, according to observers including the president of Mexico's central bank, speculation by large Mexican producers and traders is turbocharging the price hikes. Development expert Peter Rosset of the Center for the Study of Rural Change in Mexico points out that Mexican corn prices have spiked up far faster than those in the United States.

While one might expect the remaining small corn farmers in Mexico to benefit from rising prices, associations of small producers complain that they have not. Separated from consumers by layers of middlemen, they receive little or no trickle-down. The major beneficiaries are industry giants like Mexico's Maseca and U.S.-based Cargill, along with other large producers and traders. This pattern extends beyond Mexico. Guatemala's Institute for Agrarian and Rural Studies reports similar results of the Central American Free Trade Agreement in Guatemala: price increases for consumers, profits for the biggest corporations, and continued marginalization of small farmers.

Then there is the spectacle of a newly elected, pro-free trade president suddenly discovering the virtues of government intervention in the economy, at least to a limited extent. President Calderón speedily negotiated an 8.5 peso cap with major corn meal and tortilla producers and retailers, promising to boost corn supplies so as to underwrite this price and stock the 24,000-odd government-run rural DICONSA stores that sell staples at subsidized prices. Ironically, he's increasing the supply by importing corn from the United States. (Mexico, the birthplace of corn, currently imports almost one-third of its corn consumption!)

Of course, once the price agreement was concluded, the tortilla industry began backing away from it. The corn meal giants clarified that this was a goodwill gesture on their part, not an ironclad commitment. Spokespeople for neighborhood *tortillerías* pointed out that they didn't work for the big companies, so the agreement wasn't binding on them. A few days after Calderón's tortilla handshake, we spot-checked tortillas in Tlaxcala (central Mexico, where we are living for six months)—the two *tortillerías* we priced were both selling at 9. That same day, the state government of Tlaxcala announced with much fanfare that it had concluded a separate 8.5 peso agreement with *tortillerías*. So the next day we returned to the same two shops: one was closed (we stopped by too late); the other was still charging 9. Around the same time, federal government inspectors found prices over 8.5

at 53% of the *tortillerías* they visited nationwide. Still, two weeks after Calderón's pact, federal authorities had only managed to check prices at just over 3,000 shops out of an estimated 350,000. Even several weeks after the price *convenio*, tortilla sellers in the state of Aguascalientes announced that despite federal and state "agreements," they would not agree to a price ceiling under 10 pesos. On the other hand, the country's giant supermarket chains, including Wal-Mart, made a big show of discounting tortillas to 5 or 6 pesos (as a visit to our local Wal-Mart confirmed). Not a fair comparison, declared the *tortillería* industry: they mix all kinds of non-corn filler into their *nixtamal*, and besides, Mexicans prefer their tortillas fresh, hot, and local off a neighborhood *comal* (griddle).

"No to PAN, Yes to Tortillas!"

Naturally, Calderón's critics were not satisfied with his attempt to pull the tortillas out of the fire. AMLO and the PRD called for a 6-peso ceiling on tortilla prices and a 35% increase in the minimum wage (currently set at a laughably low $US5 a day). Not to be outdone, the Con-federation of Revolutionary Workers and Peasants (CROC —despite its fiery name, a mainstream union federation long affiliated with the Institutional Revolutionary Party [PRI] that ruled Mexico for seventy years until 2000) demanded price ceilings on 30 items in the *canasta básica* (the basket of basic consumer necessities tracked by the government). On January 31, these groups and more organized a peaceful *megamarcha* to protest the growing gap between prices and wages and to demand a "new social contract." Left-leaning daily *La Jornada* described the turnout in Mexico City as "tens of thousands" or "one hundred thousand"—numerically disappointing compared to other recent demonstrations—but what was significant was the presence of activists from the PRI, two smaller parties, and a large number of worker and peasant organizations that had not previously joined PRD-initiated mobilizations. They jointly issued the broad-ranging "Declaración del Zócalo," named after the central Mexico City square where the demonstration took place, announcing, "We are starting a new stage of struggle for the demands of the majority sectors in Mexico."

Particularly noteworthy is the active participation of peasant groupings such as the Permanent Agrarian Congress, the National Council of Peasant Organizations, and the National Peasant and Fisheries Council in the nationwide mobilizations. Thanks to their involvement, the protest movement has embraced a "food sovereignty" program that goes well beyond wage and price demands. Such a program would include government support for small Mexican producers of staple grains such as corn and beans through government-sponsored research and technology transfer. They also demand a renegotiation of the agricultural section of NAFTA, which is currently scheduled to remove all trade protection from Mexican corn and beans in 2008. A wave of cheaper, subsidized corn and beans from the United States would most likely lead to a temporary drop in Mexican corn prices, but the devastating effect on small Mexican farmers would leave the country far more dependent on imports and more vulnerable to future price fluctuations.

Although we were unable to attend the Tlaxcala branch of the action, we joined a smaller pre-march in Tlaxcala the weekend before. A cheerful crowd of a couple of hundred, including a large contingent from the local chapter of the Social Security Administration union, rallied to slogans like, "No to PAN, yes to tortillas!" (PAN is both the name of the ruling party and the word for bread.) José Roberto Pérez Luna, head of the union, told us, "The system is not meeting the needs of the majority. That's what leads to revolutions. I'd hate to think that our government is fertilizing a revolution."

The "Employment President" Says No

For three weeks after the rally, the government of Calderón, who campaigned as "the employment president" but so far has presided over job losses of 178,000, kept mum about the key demands, apart from some vague promises to help support Mexican corn producers and some noises about prosecuting speculators. Finally on February 21, the government gave its answer: No. No to mandatory price controls. No to an increase in the minimum wage, using the old argument, widely discredited by recent research, that minimum-wage increases destroy jobs. (Around the same time, Calderón announced a 46% increase in wages for the army, a move many see as designed to bolster the harsh repression the government has meted out to protestors in Oaxaca and elsewhere. "In this country, we will no longer confuse illegality with human rights," he remarked recently in a not-very-veiled warning.) And no to reopening NAFTA. Mexico "will not change the rules of the game," the president declared.

In the absence of further government action, Mexican consumers "voted" with their pocketbooks, reducing tortilla consumption by 20% to 30% during January, according to the National Chamber of Tortilla and Corn Flour Producers. Unfortunately, as Marie Antoinette learned to her regret a few centuries ago, for the poorest the alternative to eating unaffordable staples is simply not eating. Nearly one-fifth of Mexicans live in extreme poverty. Poor Mexicans get 40% of their protein from tortillas, and while statistics on short-term changes in nutritional intake are not available, it is safe to assume that more of these people are going hungry. Calderón's secretary of social development, Beatriz Zavala, stirred much outrage when she claimed that tortilla price hikes would not affect food consumption by the rural poor, since so many of them are self-sufficient peasants. The reality is that in rural areas—as in the United States—family farmers are increasingly compelled to reduce planting in order to supplement their income with non-agricultural jobs, or are being forced off their land outright.

The groups that launched the January 31 protests promise further mobilizations. One of the coalition members, the National Peasant and Fisheries Council, also proposes to set up a network of 5,000 small producers who will sell directly to consumers in six states, plus the federal district that includes Mexico City, working with popular organizations wherever possible.

Tlaxcala union leader Pérez Luna is right to warn of "fertilizing a revolution." Whatever happens next with tortilla prices, the issues of the widening gap between most Mexicans' salaries and the cost of living, and the other widening gap between the rich and the rest, are not going away. These are some of the same issues that fueled the Zapatista rebellion, the street vendors' protest in Atenco, the teachers' strike in Oaxaca, and the wave of anger at the elite that has made AMLO's protests much more than the sour grapes of a losing candidate. Calderón's strategy—continued free-market reforms sprinkled with crowd-pleasing tactical concessions like the tortilla pact, and the mailed fist when protests get out of hand—seems more likely to accelerate these trends than halt them. In the coming years, expect Mexican politics to heat up as hot as a *tortillería*'s *comal*. ❑

Resources: La Jornada (daily newspaper), www.jornada.unam.mx; "La declaración del Zócalo," www.jornada.unam.mx/2007/02/01/index.php?section=politica&article=006n1pol; Timothy Wise, "Policy space for Mexican maize," Global Development and Environment Institute, www. ase.tufts.edu/gdae/Pubs/wp/07-01MexicanMaize.pdf; Center for the Study of Rural Change in Mexico (CECCAM), "En defensa del maíz," www.ceccam.org.mx/ConclusionesDefensa.htm; Grassroots International, "Fixing the broken food system," grassrootsonline.org/food_is.html.

Article 2.2

PRICE GOUGING: IT'S JUST SUPPLY AND DEMAND

BY MARC BRESLOW
October 2000

- May 2000: Growing demand, along with supply cutbacks by OPEC, lead to soaring gasoline prices around the United States, especially in the upper Midwest, where they reach $2 a gallon, almost twice the levels of a year earlier.
- September 2000: Both presidential candidates, George W. Bush and Al Gore, offer plans to prevent dramatic increases in the price of heating oil during the coming winter, due to expected supply shortages.
- 1999 and 2000: red-hot high-tech economies in the San Francisco Bay and Boston areas draw in more professional workers, and raise the demand for housing. Vacancy rates dwindle to near zero, and prices for both rentals and house purchases rise out of sight. Moderate- and low-income renters are evicted for non-payment and forced to move into smaller quarters or out of these metropolitan areas.

Critics of the oil industry charge that the companies are conspiring to raise prices during shortages, ripping off consumers and gaining huge profits through illegal behavior. The industries respond that there is no conspiracy, prices are rising due to the simple functioning of supply and demand in the market. The media debate the question: can evidence be found of a conspiracy? Or are rising prices simply due to increased costs as supplies are short? Politicians ask whether companies are guilty of illegal activity, and demand that investigations be opened.

What's going on? In reality, critics of the industries are missing the point of how a capitalist "free market" operates during times of shortages. The industry spokespersons are more on target in their explanations—but that doesn't mean what the companies are doing is okay. In fact, they *are* profiting at the expense of everyone who is forced to pay outrageous prices.

Both the media and public officials want to know whether rising costs of operation are causing the high prices, and therefore the companies are justified. Why? Because simple textbook economics says that in a competitive market we should get charged according to costs, with companies only making a "normal" profit. But a careful reading of the texts shows that this is only in the "long run" when new supplies can come into the market. In the short run, when a shortage develops, "supply and demand" can force prices up to unbelievable levels, especially for any product or service that is really a necessity. It doesn't have any relationship to the cost of supplying the item, nor does it take a conspiracy. The industry spokespeople are right that market pressures are the cause.

What confuses consumers is why a relatively small shortage can cause such a huge price jump, as it did for gasoline and electricity. Why, if OPEC reduces world oil supplies by only 1% or 2%, can the price of gasoline rise by perhaps 50%? Why shouldn't prices rise by the 1% or 2%? The answer lies in a common-sense under-standing of what happens during a shortage. Everyone who owns a car, and still needs to get to work, drop the kids off at child care, and buy groceries, still needs to drive. In the short run, you can't sell your car for a more energy-efficient one, nor move someplace where public transit is more available, nor find a new day care center closer to home. Even if there are subways or buses available where you live, tight work and family time schedules probably make it difficult for you to leave the car at home.

So, as prices rise, everyone continues trying to buy as much gasoline as they did before (in technical terms, the "short run price elasticity of demand" is very low). But there is 2% less gas available, so not everyone can get as much as they want. Prices will continue rising until some people drop out of the market, cutting back on their purchases because they simply can't afford to pay the higher prices. For some-thing as essential to modern life as gasoline, this can take quite a price jump. If the price goes from $1.20 to $1.30 will you buy less? How about $1.50? Or $1.80? You can see the problem. Prices can easily rise by 50% before demand falls by the 2% needed for supply and demand to equalize.

Note that this situation has nothing to do with the costs of supplying gasoline, nor do oil companies in the United States have to conspire together to raise prices. All they have to do is let consumers bid for the available gasoline. Nothing illegal has taken place—OPEC is acting as a cartel, "conspiring," but the United States has no legal power over other countries. Profits can go up enormously, and they may be shared between OPEC, oil companies such as Exxon/Mobil and Royal Dutch Shell, and firms lower on the supply chain such as wholesalers and retail gas stations.

Housing is perhaps the worst of these situations, as no one should be forced to leave their home. But the "invisible hand" of the market will raise prices, and allo-cate housing, according to who has the greatest purchasing power, not who needs the housing. A highly-skilled computer programmer, moving into San Francisco from elsewhere, will get an apartment that some lesser-paid worker, maybe a public school teacher or a bus driver, has been living in, perhaps for many years.

In all these cases, the market has done what it does well—allocate sales to those who can afford to buy, without regard to need; and allocate profits to those who have a product in short supply, without regard to costs of production. The human costs to people of moderate- and low-incomes, who are priced out of the market, can be severe. But they can be prevented—by price controls that prevent price-gouging due to shortages. Such controls have been used many times in the United States—for rent in high-demand cities, for oil and gas during the "crises" of the 1970's, and for most products during World War II. Maybe it's time we made them a staple of sen-sible economic policy. ❑

Resources: "In Gas Prices, Misery and Mystery," Pam Belluck, *The New York Times*, 6/14/2000; "Federal action sought to cut power prices from May," Peter J. Howe, *The Boston Globe*, 8/24/2000; "Industry Blames Chemical Additives for High Gas Prices," Matthew L. Wald, *The New York Times*, 6/26/2000.

Article 2.3

WANT A COOL PLANET? RAISE GAS PRICES!

BY MARC BRESLOW
May/June 2000, revised June 2006

So gasoline prices have risen above $3.00 a gallon and threaten to go even higher. To hear many commentators and politicians talk, this is a tragedy rivaling the bubonic plague of the Middle Ages. How dare OPEC threaten Americans' god-given right to cheap gas! Why, after all, did we fight two Gulf Wars, if not to keep gas as cheap as bottled water?

No matter that even at $3.00 a gallon, gas is still not much more expensive, adjusted for inflation, than it was in the early 1970s, or that it is half the price that people pay in Britain, France, Germany, and Japan. It's still time to dip into the strategic oil reserve, cut the federal gas tax, and lift restrictions on oil drilling in environmentally-sensitive areas of Alaska.

I beg to differ. It's hard to think of another issue in which U.S. attitudes are more wrong-headed. The rest of the world knows that, because of global warming and because oil is eventually going to run out (unless we allow drilling to destroy every last bit of pristine environment anywhere), we have to reduce our burning of fossil fuels, including oil. Only the United States, under the political domination of the oil and auto companies, refuses to recognize reality.

Higher gas prices are one of the best things that could happen to this country. If we are lucky, they will start a trend toward smaller cars and away from SUVs. In the long run SUVs threaten to destroy the global environment. In the short run, they threaten to kill all of us foolish—or cash poor—enough to continue driving normal cars. Federal regulators have found that in a collision between an SUV and a car, car occupants are three times as likely to be killed as if they were hit by another car.

Just recently automakers have finally acknowledged this fact, and say they will redesign future SUV models with lower frames to make them less of a threat. But wouldn't it make more sense to just get rid of most of them? Doubling gas prices would be the surest way of making that happen.

Won't that hurt the U.S. economy? Well, yes. Unfortunately, once you have built an economy on wasting energy, rebuilding it in an energy-efficient manner will involve substantial costs. And that is a reason to make the transition gradual—perhaps raising gas prices 20 cents a year for the next ten years would be a reasonable schedule. By that time most people would be ready to get rid of their old gas guzzlers anyway. Not only could they downsize, but they could buy one of the new "hybrids," combination gas/electric vehicles (the engine charges the batteries) that Honda and Toyota are releasing this year. Just changing from SUVs (which get 15 or so miles to the gallon) to these hybrids (which get 60 or more), would go a long way toward meeting the United States' commitment to reduce carbon dioxide emissions in response to global warming.

What about the effects of higher fuel prices on moderate- and low-income people, who may be driving regular cars but still can't afford gas at $5 or $6 a gallon?

There is an answer here. Rather than let the Kuwaiti royal family get the benefits of oil scarcity, we should do what Europe and Japan do—tax the hell out of oil (and coal and natural gas, which also create carbon dioxide when burned). Then we should redistribute the tax revenues in a progressive manner, so that low-income people come out even or ahead.

Peter Barnes, creator of the Sky Trust Initiative, has perhaps the best proposal for how to do this. He suggests that rather than letting the federal government use the oil-tax revenue on anything it wants—which could be something horribly regressive like further cuts in income or capital-gains taxes—the money should go into a trust fund. Then it should be handed back to every U.S. resident on an equal per-capita basis. This method would mean low-income households getting back more than they pay for higher fuel costs—so we help the environment and economic equity at the same time. Not to mention sticking it to ExxonMobil. ❑

Resources: The Sky Trust Initiative, *www.skytrust.cfed. org*; the Union of Concerned Scientists, *www. ucsusa.org*; the Sierra Club, including its program on Transportation and Sprawl: *www.sierraclub.org.*

Article 2.4

DOES RENT CONTROL HURT TENANTS?

BY ELLEN FRANK
March/April 2003

> Dear Dr. Dollar,
> *What are the merits of the argument that rent control hurts tenants by limiting the incentives to create and maintain rental housing?*
> —Sarah Marxer, San Francisco, Calif.

The standard story of rent control, laid out in dozens of introductory economics textbooks, goes like this. In the housing market, landlords are willing to supply more rental units when prices are high, and tenants are willing to rent more units when prices are low. In an unregulated market, competition should result in a market-clearing price at which the number of apartments landlords are willing and able to provide just equals the number tenants are willing and able to rent. Thus, when prices are allowed to rise to their correct level, shortages disappear. Rent controls, in this story, disrupt the market mechanism by capping rents at too low a level. Artificially low rents discourage construction and maintenance, resulting in fewer available apartments than would exist without the controls. At the same time, low rents keep tenants in the area, searching for apartments that don't exist. The result: permanent housing shortages in rent-controlled markets.

What's wrong with this story? Just about everything.

First, the story ignores the unequal power that landlords and tenants exercise in an unregulated market. Boston College professor Richard Arnott notes that tenants are, for a number of reasons, averse to moving. This gives landlords inordinate pricing power even in a market where housing is not in short supply—and in areas where vacancy rates are low, land is scarce, and "snob zoning" commonplace, landlords can charge truly exorbitant prices. In Boston, rent controls were eliminated in 1997, and average apartment rents have since climbed nearly 100%. The city's spiraling rents show that without controls, landlords can—and do—gouge tenants.

Second, rent control opponents misrepresent the structure of controls. As practiced in the real world, rent control does not place fixed caps on rent. New York City enacted an actual rent freeze after World War II, and a small number of apartments still fall under this "old-law" rent control. But most rent-controlled apartments in New York and all controlled apartments in other U.S. cities fall under what Arnott calls "second generation" or "soft" controls, which simply restrict annual rent increases. Soft rent controls guarantee landlords a "fair return" on their properties and require that owners maintain their buildings. They allow landlords to pass along maintenance costs, and many allow improvement costs to be recouped on an accelerated schedule, making building upkeep quite lucrative.

Consequently, controlled apartments are not unprofitable. And as Occidental College professor and housing specialist Peter Dreier points out, landlords won't walk away as long as they are making a decent return. Residential landlords are not very mobile: they have a long-term interest in their properties, and only abandon them when *market* rents fall below even controlled levels as a result of poverty, crime, or economic depression. Rent controls themselves do not foster abandonment or poor maintenance.

Third, all second-generation rent control laws—enacted chiefly in the 1970s—exempted newly constructed buildings from controls. Thus, the argument that controls discourage new construction simply makes no sense. As for the oft-heard complaint that developers fear that rent controls, once enacted, will be extended to new buildings, the 1980s and 1990s construction booms in New York, Boston, San Francisco, and Los Angeles—all cities with controls—indicate that developers aren't all that worried. There is plenty of housing and construction in cities with and without rent controls.

Nevertheless, even in many cities with rent controls, there is a shortage of *affordable* apartments. Market housing costs have been rising faster than wages for at least two decades. That some apartments in New York and San Francisco are still affordable to low- and middle-income families is due primarily to rent control.

Indeed, limited as they might be, rent controls deliver real benefits. They prevent price-gouging and ration scarce apartments to existing tenants. The money tenants save in rent can be spent in the neighborhood economy, benefiting local businesses. Meanwhile, more secure tenants create neighborhoods that are stable, safe, and economically diverse. And rent controls are essential if tenants are to have credible legal protection against slumlords: the legal right to complain about lack of heat or faulty plumbing is meaningless if landlords can retaliate by raising rents.

There are many problems with the U.S. housing market. High prices, low incomes, and lack of public housing or subsidies for affordable housing all contribute to homelessness and housing insecurity in major American cities. Rent control is not the cause of these problems, nor is it the whole solution. But along with higher wages and expanded public housing, it is part of the solution. As Dreier puts it, "Until the federal government renews its responsibility to help poor and working-class people fill the gap between what they can afford and what housing costs to build and operate, rent control can at least help to keep a roof over their heads." ❏

Resources: Richard Arnott, "Time for Revisionism on Rent Control?" *Journal of Economic Perspectives*, Winter 1995. Dreier and Pitcoff, "I'm a Tenant and I Vote," *Shelterforce*, July/August 1997. Shelterforce website: <http://www.nhi.org/>.

Article 2.5

DON'T BLAME THE MINIMUM WAGE

Does raising the minimum wage cause layoffs? An economist says no

BY PADDY QUICK
January/February 2008

When businesses organize production, they figure out what different people they need to employ and in what numbers. A restaurant, for example, needs cooks, waiters/waitresses, dishwashers, cashiers and, sometimes, after-hours cleaning staff. It needs managers to keep track of who is doing what and when. Some of these people are paid a lot more than others, but they are all necessary. The lower-paid workers are as important as the higher-paid workers. Although the restaurant owner would like to pay them all less so that his profits would be higher, he needs them all.

This is important to understand. A bicycle needs two wheels, two pedals, a seat, a set of gears, and any number of parts that connect them all together. Which is most important? The front wheel? The rear wheel? The seat? The pedals? The fact that a pedal costs less than a wheel doesn't make it any less important. Similarly, all of the people who work in a restaurant play their part in the production of the meals, even though they "cost" their employer different amounts. If the pedal of a bicycle cost a bit more, it wouldn't be eliminated. Why then do people think their job would be eliminated if they had to be paid a little more?

People are laid off for many reasons. One possibility is that employers just want to shuffle people around so that everyone feels under pressure. There are always a lot of people unemployed, and it is pretty easy to lay one person off and hire another to replace her. The new person is now likely to work harder, even if the previous employee was doing a great job. There are also changes in the number of customers in different locations, and competition from other restaurants for these customers.

When the minimum wage increases, employers have to pay higher wages not only to those who received the old minimum, but also to those whose positions paid an extra dollar or more above that. If they decide to reorganize production, they may well decide to lay off these workers rather than the ones at the very bottom of the pay scale. Information technology, for example, may displace more highly paid workers who are responsible for inventory management at corporate headquarters, rather than the people who have direct contact with customers.

Corporations are, of course, always "crunching the numbers," figuring out whether they can save money by changing the combination of people and things they purchase in order to produce the pizzas and other things they sell. Sometimes they may be able to do so, but other times it may not be possible.

So let's look specifically at the fast-food restaurant business to see the effect on employment of an increase in the minimum wage. It turns out that there isn't much that fast-food restaurants can do when wages go up—other than hand over a small portion of their huge profits to their workforce!

Fast-food corporations, such as McDonald's, spend millions lobbying Congress in opposition to a raise in the minimum wage, pretending that their opposition has nothing to do with its effect on their profits. Instead they argue that it would break their hearts to have to lay off some of the poor people they employ. (Their employees are poor, of course, because of the low wages they receive!)

A famous study by two well-known economists, Alan Krueger of Princeton University and David Card of the University of California, Berkeley, looked very carefully at what happened to fast food employment in New Jersey in 1992 after that state raised its minimum wage. (This study is summarized in their 1997 book, *Myth and Measurement: The New Economics of the Minimum Wage*.) They compared New Jersey with its neighboring state, Pennsylvania, which did not raise its minimum wage. Fast food industry executives had argued that they would be "forced" to lay off workers if New Jersey raised its minimum wage, but the facts proved otherwise. New Jersey workers got higher wages, but they did not lose their jobs. So although it is possible that an increase in the minimum wage could lead restaurants to lay off workers, it turns out that this doesn't actually happen in the fast food industry.

After they studied minimum wages in the fast food industry, Krueger and Card went on to prove that increasing the minimum wage across the country as a whole has little or no effect on unemployment. This position was supported by a total of 650 economists, including five Nobel prize-winners, in a 2006 letter supporting the bill to raise the federal minimum wage to $7.15 an hour.

Production requires workers. Workers use tools and machinery, and businesses have the capital that is needed to buy these, but it is workers who turn the ovens, pizza dough, and tables into meals for their customers, and it is workers who make the computers that increasingly "mechanize" production. The big question, according to Adam Smith and other classical economists such as David Ricardo and Karl Marx, is how income is distributed, and in particular, how much of it goes to wage-earners.

Adam Smith, for example, believed that the level of wages depends on workers' bargaining power, and thought it obvious that the government was on the side of the employers. He did, however, think that if the rate of unemployment was low, wages could increase. Today, one part of the government, the Federal Reserve Board, takes this piece of theory very seriously, and makes sure that it keeps the rate of unemployment high enough to prevent wages from increasing! Smith's theory implies that we need to organize, both at the workplace and within the political system, to strengthen the power of labor against the power of capital.

Adam Smith also believed that wages could not sink below the minimum needed for workers to survive and bring up children. But unfortunately, when there is a lot of unemployment, workers find themselves in a "race to the bottom": "I'll work for whatever you're willing to pay me." "No, take me. I'll work for $1 less." "Please, please, I'll work for food." During the Great Depression, massive unemployment made this a terrifying possibility, and led to the enactment of minimum wage legislation. This was an important victory for an organized working class. But it is an ongoing struggle. With a decent minimum wage and low unemployment, we can get the higher wages that our hard work entitles us to. ❏

Sources: David Card & Alan B. Krueger, Myth and Measurement: The New Economics of the Minimum Wage, Princeton University Press, 1997; Adam Smith, Wealth of Nations, 1776 (Part I, Ch. 8).

Article 2.6

FAMINE MYTHS
Five Misunderstandings Related to the 2011 Hunger Crisis in the Horn of Africa

BY WILLIAM G. MOSELEY
March/April 2012

The 2011 famine in the horn of africa was one of the worst in recent decades in terms of loss of life and human suffering. While the UN has yet to release an official death toll, the British government estimates that between 50,000 and 100,000 people died, most of them children, between April and September of 2011. While Kenya, Ethiopia, and Djibouti were all badly affected, the famine hit hardest in certain (mainly southern) areas of Somalia. This was the worst humanitarian disaster to strike the country since 1991-1992, with roughly a third of the Somali population displaced for some period of time.

Despite the scholarly and policy community's tremendous advances in understanding famine over the past 40 years, and increasingly sophisticated famine early-warning systems, much of this knowledge and information was seemingly ignored or forgotten in 2011. While the famine had been forecasted nearly nine months in advance, the global community failed to prepare for, and react in a timely manner to, this event. The famine was officially declared in early July of 2011 by the United Nations and recently (February 3, 2012) stated to be officially over. Despite the official end of the famine, 31% of the population (or 2.3 million people) in southern Somalia remains in crisis. Across the region, 9.5 million people continue to need assistance. Millions of Somalis remain in refugee camps in Ethiopia and Kenya.

The famine reached its height in the period from July to September, 2011, with approximately 13 million people at risk of starvation. While this was a regional problem, it was was most acute in southern Somalia because aid to this region was much delayed. Figure 1 provides a picture of food insecurity in the region in the November-December 2011 period (a few months after the peak of the crisis).

The 2011 famine received relatively little attention in the U.S. media and much of the coverage that did occur was biased, ahistorical, or perpetuated long-held misunderstandings about the nature and causes of famine. This article addresses "famine myths"—five key misunderstandings related to the famine in the Horn of Africa.

Myth #1: Drought was the cause of the famine.

While drought certainly contributed to the crisis in the Horn of Africa, there were more fundamental causes at play. Drought is not a new environmental condition for much of Africa, but a recurring one. The Horn of Africa has long experienced erratic rainfall. While climate change may be exacerbating rainfall variability, traditional livelihoods in the region are adapted to deal with situations where rainfall is not dependable.

The dominant livelihood in the Horn of Africa has long been herding, which is well adapted to the semi-arid conditions of the region. Herders traditionally ranged widely across the landscape in search of better pasture, focusing on different areas depending on meteorological conditions.

The approach worked because, unlike fenced in pastures in America, it was incredibly flexible and well adapted to variable rainfall conditions. As farming expanded, including large-scale commercial farms in some instances, the routes of herders became more concentrated, more vulnerable to drought, and more detrimental to the landscape.

Agricultural livelihoods also evolved in problematic ways. In anticipation of poor rainfall years, farming households and communities historically stored surplus crop production in granaries. Sadly this traditional strategy for mitigating the risk of drought was undermined from the colonial period moving forward as households were encouraged (if not coerced by taxation) to grow cash crops for the market and store less excess grain for bad years. This increasing market orientation was also encouraged by development banks, such as the World Bank, International Monetary Fund, and African Development Bank.

FIGURE 1: FOOD INSECURITY IN THE HORN OF AFRICA REGION, NOVEMBER-DECEMBER 2011.

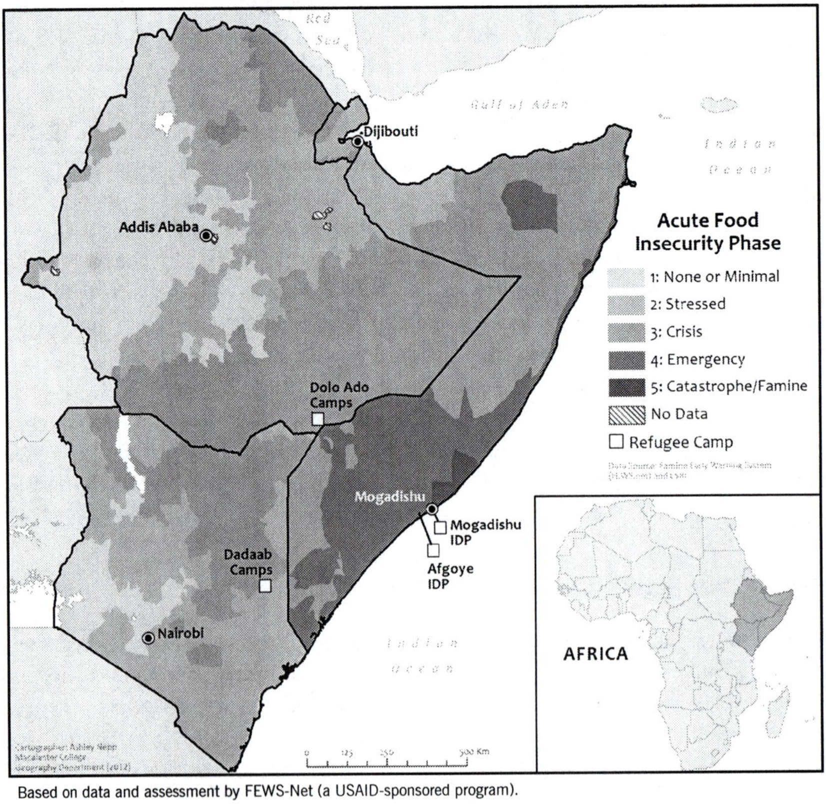

Based on data and assessment by FEWS-Net (a USAID-sponsored program).

Cartography by Ashley Nepp, Macalester College.

The moral of the story is that famine is not a natural consequence of drought (just as death from exposure is not the inherent result of a cold winter), but it is the structure of human society which often determines who is affected and to what degree.

Myth #2: Overpopulation was the cause of the famine.

With nearly 13 million people at risk of starvation last fall in a region whose population doubled in the previous 24 years, one might assume that these two factors were causally related in the Horn of Africa. Ever since the British political economist Thomas Malthus wrote "An Essay on the Principle of Population" in 1798, we have been concerned that human population growth will outstrip available food supply. While the crisis in Somalia, Ethiopia and Kenya appeared to be perfect proof of the Malthusian scenario, we must be careful not to make overly simplistic assumptions.

For starters, the semi-arid zones in the Horn of Africa are relatively lightly populated compared to other regions of the world. For example, the population density of Somalia is about 13 persons per sq. kilometer, whereas that of the U.S. state of Oklahoma is 21.1. The western half of Oklahoma is also semi-arid, suffered from a serious drought in 2011, and was the poster child for the 1930s Dust Bowl. Furthermore, if we take into account differing levels of consumption, with the average American consuming at least 28 times as much as the average Somali in a normal year, then Oklahoma's population density of 21.1 persons per sq. kilometer equates to that of 591 Somalis.

Despite the fact that Oklahoma's per capita impact on the landscape is over 45 times that of Somalia (when accounting for population density and consumption

Land Grabs in Africa

Long term leases of African land for export-oriented food production, or "land grabs," have been on the rise in the past decade. Rather than simply buying food and commodity crops from African farmers, foreign entities increasingly take control of ownership and management of farms on African soil. This trend stems from at least two factors. First, increasingly high global food prices are a problem for many Asian and Middle Eastern countries that depend on food imports. As such, foreign governments and sovereign wealth funds may engage in long-term leases of African land in order to supply their own populations with affordable food. Secondly, high global food prices are also seen as an opportunity for some Western investors who lease African land to produce crops and commodities for profitable global markets.

In the Horn of Africa, Ethiopia (which has historically been one of the world's largest recipients of humanitarian food aid) has made a series of long-term land leases to foreign entities. The World Bank estimates that at least 35 million hectares of land have been leased to 36 different countries, including China, Pakistan, India and Saudi Arabia. Supporters of these leases argue that they provide employment to local people and disseminate modern agricultural approaches. Critics counter that these leases undermine food sovereignty, or people's ability to feed themselves via environmentally sustainable technologies that they control.

levels), we don't talk about overpopulation in Oklahoma. This is because, in spite of the drought and the collapse of agriculture, there was no famine in Oklahoma. In contrast, the presence of famine in the Horn of Africa led many to assume that too many people was a key part of the problem.

Why is it that many assume that population growth is the driver of famine? For starters, perhaps we assume that reducing the birthrate, and thereby reducing the number of mouths to feed, is one of the easiest ways to prevent hunger. This is actually a difficult calculation for most families in rural Africa. It's true that many families desire access to modern contraceptives, and filling this unmet need is important. However, for many others, children are crucial sources of farm labor or important wage earners who help sustain the family. Children also act as the old-age social security system for their parents. For these families, having fewer children is not an easy decision. Families in this region will have fewer children when it makes economic sense to do so. As we have seen over time and throughout the world, the average family size shrinks when economies develop and expectations for offspring change.

Second, many tend to focus on the additional resources required to nourish each new person, and often forget the productive capacity of these individuals. Throughout Africa, some of the most productive farmland is in those regions with the highest population densities. In Machakos, Kenya, for example, agricultural production and environmental conservation improved as population densities increased. Furthermore, we have seen agricultural production collapse in some areas where population declined (often due to outmigration) because there was insufficient labor to maintain intensive agricultural production.

Third, we must not forget that much of the region's agricultural production is not consumed locally. From the colonial era moving forward, farmers and herders have been encouraged to become more commercially oriented, producing crops and livestock for the market rather than home consumption. This might have been a reasonable strategy if the prices for exports from the Horn of Africa were high (which they rarely have been) and the cost of food imports low. Also, large land leases (or "land grabs") to foreign governments and corporations in Ethiopia (and to a lesser extent in Kenya and Somalia) have further exacerbated this problem. These farms, designed solely for export production, effectively subsidize the food security of other regions of the world (most notably the Middle East and Asia) at the expense of populations in the Horn of Africa.

Myth #3: Increasing food production through advanced techniques will resolve food insecurity over the long run.

As Sub-Saharan Africa has grappled with high food prices in some regions and famine in others, many experts argue that increasing food production through a program of hybrid seeds and chemical inputs (a so-called "New Green Revolution") is the way to go.

While outsiders benefit from this New Green Revolution strategy (by selling inputs or purchasing surplus crops), it is not clear if the same is true for small farmers and poor households in Sub-Saharan Africa. For most food insecure households on the continent, there are at least two problems with this strategy. First, such an approach to farming is energy intensive because most fertilizers and pesticides are petroleum based. Inducing poor farmers to adopt energy-intensive farming methods is short sighted, if not unethical, if experts know that global energy prices are likely to rise. Second, irrespective of energy prices, the New Green Revolution approach requires farmers to purchase seeds and inputs, which means that it will be inaccessible to the poorest of the poor, i.e., those who are the most likely to suffer from periods of hunger.

If not the New Green Revolution approach, then what? Many forms of bio-intensive agriculture are, in fact, highly productive and much more efficient than those of industrial agriculture. For example, crops grown in intelligent combinations allow one plant to fix nitrogen for another rather than relying solely on increasingly expensive, fossil fuel-based inorganic fertilizers for these plant nutrients. Mixed cropping strategies are also less vulnerable to insect damage and require little to no pesticide use for a reasonable harvest. These techniques have existed for centuries in the African context and could be greatly enhanced by supporting collaboration among local people, African research institutes, and foreign scientists.

Myth #4: U.S. foreign policy in the Horn of Africa was unrelated to the crisis.

Many Americans assume that U.S. foreign policy bears no blame for the food crisis in the Horn and, more specifically, Somalia. This is simply untrue. The weakness of the Somali state was and is related to U.S. policy, which interfered in Somali affairs based on Cold War politics (the case in the 1970s and 80s) or the War on Terror (the case in the 2000s).

During the Cold War, Somalia was a pawn in a U.S.-Soviet chess match in the geopolitically significant Horn of Africa region. In 1974, the U.S. ally Emperor Haile Selassie of Ethiopia was deposed in a revolution. He was eventually replaced by Mengistu Haile Mariam, a socialist. In response, the leader of Ethiopia's bitter rival Somalia, Siad Barre, switched from being pro-Soviet to pro-Western. Somalia was the only country in Africa to switch Cold War allegiances under the same government. The U.S. supported Siad Barre until 1989 (shortly before his demise in 1991). By doing this, the United States played a key role in supporting a long-running dictator and undermined democratic governance.

More recently, the Union of Islamic Courts (UIC) came to power in 2006. The UIC defeated the warlords, restored peace to Mogadishu for the first time in 15 years, and brought most of southern Somalia under its orbit. The United States and its Ethiopian ally claimed that these Islamists were terrorists and a threat to the region. In contrast, the vast majority of Somalis supported the UIC and pleaded with the international community to engage them peacefully. Unfortunately, this peace did not last. The U.S.-supported Ethiopian invasion of Somalia begun in December 2006 and displaced more than a million people and killed close to 15,000 civilians. Those displaced then became a part of last summer and fall's famine victims.

The power vacuum created by the displacement of the more moderate UIC also led to the rise of its more radical military wing, al-Shabaab. Al-Shabaab emerged to engage the Transitional Federal Government (TFG), which was put in place by the international community and composed of the most moderate elements of the UIC (which were more favorable to the United States). The TFG was weak, corrupt, and ineffective, controlling little more than the capital Mogadishu, if that. A low-grade civil war emerged between these two groups in southern Somalia. Indeed, as we repeatedly heard in the media last year, it was al-Shabaab that restricted access to southern Somalia for several months leading up to the crisis and greatly exacerbated the situation in this sub-region. Unfortunately, the history of factors which gave rise to al-Shabaab was never adequately explained to the U.S. public. Until July 2011, the U.S. government forbade American charities from operating in areas controlled by al-Shabaab—which delayed relief efforts in these areas.

Myth #5: an austere response may be best in the long run.

Efforts to raise funds to address the famine in the Horn of Africa were well below those for previous (and recent) humanitarian crises. Why was this? Part of it likely had to do with the economic malaise in the U.S. and Europe. Many Americans suggested that we could not afford to help in this crisis because we had to pay off our own debt. This stinginess may, in part, be related to a general misunderstanding about how much of the U.S. budget goes to foreign assistance. Many Americans assume we spend over 25% of our budget on such assistance when it is actually less than one percent.

Furthermore, contemporary public discourse in America has become more inward-looking and isolationist than in the past. As a result, many Americans have difficulty relating to people beyond their borders. Sadly, it is now much easier to separate ourselves from them, to discount our common humanity, and to essentially suppose that it's okay if they starve. This last point brings us back to Thomas Malthus, who was writing against the poor laws in England in the late 18th century. The poor laws were somewhat analogous to contemporary welfare programs and Malthus argued (rather problematically) that they encouraged the poor to have more children. His essential argument was that starvation is acceptable because it is a natural check to over-population. In other words, support for the poor will only exacerbate the situation. We see this in the way that some conservative commentators reacted to last year's famine.

The reality was that a delayed response to the famine only made the situation worse. Of course, the worst-case scenario is death, but short of death, many households were forced to sell off all of their assets (cattle, farming implements, etc.) in order to survive. This sets up a very difficult recovery scenario because livelihoods are so severely compromised. We know from best practices among famine researchers and relief agencies in that you not only to detect a potential famine early, but to intervene before livelihoods are devastated. This means that households will recover more quickly and be more resilient in the face of future perturbations.

Preventing Famines

While the official famine in the horn of Africa region is over, 9.5 million people continue to need assistance and millions of Somalis remain in refugee camps in

Ethiopia and Kenya. While this region of the world will always be drought prone, it needn't be famine prone. The solution lies in rebuilding the Somali state and fostering more robust rural livelihoods in Somalia, western Ethiopia and northern Kenya. The former will likely mean giving the Somali people the space they need to rebuild their own democratic institutions (and not making them needless pawns in the War on Terror). The latter will entail a new approach to agriculture that emphasizes food sovereignty, or locally appropriate food production technologies that are accessible to the poorest of the poor, as well as systems of grain storage at the local level that anticipate bad rainfall years. Finally, the international community should discourage wealthy, yet food-insufficient, countries from preying on poorer countries in Sub Saharan African countries through the practice of land grabs. ❑

Sources: Alex de Waal, *Famine That Kills: Darfur, Sudan*, Oxford University Press, 2005; William G. Moseley, "Why They're Starving: The man-made roots of famine in the Horn of Africa," *The Washington Post*. July 29, 2011; William G. Moseley and B. Ikubolajeh Logan, "Food Security," in B. Wisner, C. Toulmin and R. Chitiga (eds)., *Toward a New Map of Africa*, Earthscan Publications, 2005; Abdi I. Samatar, "Genocidal Politics and the Somali Famine," Aljazeera English, July 30, 2011; Amartya Sen, *Poverty and Famines*, Oxford/Clarendon, 1981; Michael Watts and Hans Bohle, "The space of vulnerability: the causal structure of hunger and famine," *Progress in Human Geography*, 1993.

Chapter 3

CONSUMERS

Introduction

The "two economies" described in the introduction to this book—the textbook economy and the economy portrayed by critics of the status quo—come into sharp contrast when we consider the theory of consumer choice. In the textbook model of consumer choice, rational individuals seek to maximize their well-being by choosing the right mix of goods to consume and allocating their "scarce" time accordingly. They decide for themselves how much they would enjoy various things, and make their choices based on full information about their options. More of any good is always better, but diminishing marginal utility says that each additional unit of a good consumed brings less enjoyment than the one before. The theory attempts to assess the utility of each individual uniquely. Yet, we soon discover that it is difficult if not impossible to "measure pleasure" for a single individual and impossible to compare utility between individuals.

Critics launch a variety of challenges to this simplified model. The first three articles in this chapter contend that the idea of consumer sovereignty, that consumer wishes determine what gets produced, does not fit the facts.

The advertising that saturates our daily lives constantly creates new wants. This advertising has been increasingly targeting children in order to convince them to nag their parents into buying products they suddenly "need" (Article 3.1). In many transactions, consumers are also less than fully informed about what they are getting or even the price they are paying. For example, young children targeted by advertisers are unaware of the consequences of most of their consumption decisions. "Down with the Clown" (Article 3.2) further explores McDonald's marketing to children and the issue of childhood obesity.

The late Alan Durning, in his seminal piece "Enough is Enough: Why More is Not Necessarily Better Than Less," puts forward an even more radical critique of standard consumer theory. Durning argues that "more" is often "worse," not better, and that the accumulation of material goods in affluent societies threatens the environment (not sustainable), widens global inequalities, and hollows out our lives (Article 3.3).

In Jim Campen's article, "Update on Mortgage Lending Discrimination" (Article 3.4), we find that consumer markets are not a level playing field. Predatory lending, in which unscrupulous mortgage originators pressure home owners into mortgages that saddle them with hidden fees and high interest rates, is an extreme example of this problem of incomplete and asymmetric information. Communities of color are also routinely discriminated against, first with red-lining and then predatory lending (reverse red-lining) in the areas of housing and mortgages. The consequences of the recent sub-prime mortgage meltdown are being felt most heavily by black and Hispanic communities. Predatory lending has contributed to a new era of foreclosures, destroyed equity and wealth, and blighted communities.

Concluding the chapter, Jeannette Wicks-Lim addresses the destruction of wealth in black communities due to the sub-prime meltdown in her article, "The Great Recession in Black Wealth" (Article 3.5). One consequence of the sub-prime debacle was the effective reduction by half of median black household net worth (between 2004 and 2009), leading to an increasingly polarized distribution of wealth between black and white households. Unfortunately, this trend has actually accelerated since 2009.

Discussion Questions

1) (General) Standard consumer theory still applies if advertising is simply a way to inform consumers. But many of the authors in this chapter suggest that advertising manufactures and shapes our tastes and desires. Think of some of the purchases that you have made in the last six months. For which purchases was advertising primarily a source of information, and for which was it more of a taste-shaper?

2) (Article 3.1) According to Scharber, what are the negative impacts of advertising directed at children? Would you support a law banning advertising to young children? Why or why not?

3) (Articles 3.1 and 3.2) Mainstream economic theory depicts consumers as autonomous individuals making careful choices based on the preferences they themselves have developed. Scharber describes consumers as manipulated by crafty advertisers and dishonest businesses. In what areas of consumer choice is each picture more accurate? Which do you think is more accurate overall?

4) (Article 3.2) Do you believe that McDonald's should retire Ronald McDonald? What are the arguments pro and con? Why do you suppose that medical professionals (doctors and nurses) are leading this corporate campaign?

5) (Article 3.2) Is marketing to children problematic for rational choice models of consumer behavior? Who bears the responsibility for childhood obesity?

6) (Article 3.3) Durning says that it's wrong for people in rich countries to consume so much when others in the world live in poverty. His viewpoint could be summarized as, "Live simply, so that others may simply live." Do you agree with this outlook?

7) (Article 3.3) Durning's argument implies that rather than seeking pleasure by consuming material goods, we should seek enjoyment through family, friends, and community. How could you use standard utility theory to describe this kind of choice? (Hint: Can family, friends, and community be "goods"?) What are some possible problems in using the theory in this way?

8) (Articles 3.4 and 3.5) Predatory lenders often target African-American borrowers. Why would they do this? More generally, why would businesses discriminate (by race, gender, or other categories) in which consumers they seek out and are willing to sell to?

9) (Articles 3.4 and 3.5) Explain in detail why the predatory lending and the subprime mortgage debacle effectively reduced by half the median household net worth of Blacks between 2004 and 2009. What are the future consequences of this dramatic reduction in Black household wealth?

Article 3.1

THE 800-POUND RONALD McDONALD IN THE ROOM

BY HELEN SCHARBER

January 2007

When your child's doctor gives you advice, you're probably inclined to take it. And if 60,000 doctors gave you advice, ignoring it would be even more difficult to justify. Last month, the American Academy of Pediatrics (AAP) issued a policy statement advising us to limit advertising to children, citing its adverse effects on health. Yes, banning toy commercials might result in fewer headaches for parents ("Please, please, pleeeeeeease, can I have this new video game I just saw 10 commercials for????"), but the AAP is more concerned with other health issues, such as childhood obesity. Advertising in general—and to children specifically—has reached astonishingly high levels, and as a country, we'd be wise to take the doctors' orders.

Advertising to kids is not a new phenomenon, but the intensity of it is. According to Juliet Schor, author of *Born to Buy*, companies spent around $100 million in 1983 on television advertising to kids. A little more than 20 years later, the amount earmarked for child-targeted ads in a variety of media has jumped to at least $12 billion annually. That's over $150 per boy and girl in the U.S. And it's not as though kids only see ads for action figures and sugary cereal; the other $240 billion spent on advertising each year ensures that they see ads for all kinds of products, everywhere they go. According to the AAP report, "the average young person views more than 3,000 ads per day on television, on the Internet, on billboards, and in magazines." Ads are also creeping into schools, where marketers have cleverly placed them in "educational" posters, textbook covers, bathroom stalls, scoreboards, daily news programs, and bus radio programming.

If advertising to children is becoming increasingly ubiquitous, it's probably because it's becoming increasingly profitable. Once upon a time, kids didn't have as much market power as they do today. The AAP report estimates that kids under 12 now spend $25 billion of their own money annually, teenagers spend another $155 billion, and both groups probably influence around $200 billion in parental spending. Not too surprising, considering that 62 percent of parents say their children "actively participate" in car-buying decisions, according to a study by J.D. Power & Associates. Marketers are also becoming more aware of the long-term potential of advertising to children. While they may not be the primary market now, they will be someday. And since researchers have found that kids as young as two can express preferences for specific brands, it's practically never too early to begin instilling brand loyalty.

But while small children have an incredible memory for commercial messages, they may not have developed the cognitive skills necessary to be critical of them. In 2004, the American Psychological Association (APA) also called for setting limits on advertising to kids, citing research that "children under the age of eight are unable to critically comprehend televised advertising messages and are prone to accept advertiser messages as truthful, accurate and unbiased." Many people take offense at the idea that we might be manipulated by marketing. Aren't we, after all, intelligent enough to make up our own minds about what to buy? The research cited by the APA, however, shows that children are uniquely vulnerable to manipulation by advertising. Marketers therefore should not be allowed to prey on them in the name of free speech.

Such invasive advertising to children is not only an ethical problem. The American Academy of Pediatrics cited advertising's effects on health through the promotion of unhealthy eating, drinking and smoking as the main motivation for setting limits. Children's health issues certainly merit attention. The Center for Disease Control, for example, has found that the prevalence of overweight children (ages 6 to 11) increased from 7 percent in 1980 to about 19 percent in 2004, while the rate among adolescents (ages 12 to 19) jumped from 5 percent to 17 percent. In addition to physical health problems, Schor argues that extensive marketing has negative effects on children's emotional well being. In her research for Born to Buy, Schor found links between immersion in consumer culture and depression, anxiety, low self esteem and conflicts with parents. The big push to consume can also lead to financial health problems, as many Americans know all too well, with credit card debt among 18 to 24-year-olds doubling over the past decade.

Not even the staunchest critics of marketing to children would argue that advertisements are completely at fault for these trends. Yet, the commercialization of nearly everything is negatively affecting children's well being in rather profound ways. Why, then, is hardly anyone paying attention to the 800-pound Ronald McDonald in the room? Perhaps it's because advertising appears to be a necessary evil or a fair tradeoff—maybe little Emma's school couldn't afford a soccer team without Coke on the scoreboard, for example. Or perhaps some would argue that parents who don't approve of the commercial culture should limit their kids' exposure to it. Increasingly invasive marketing techniques make it practically impossible to simply opt out of commercial culture, though. Thus, decisions to limit marketing to children must be made by the country as a whole. Sweden, Norway, Greece, Denmark, and Belgium have already passed laws curbing kid-targeted advertising, and according to 60,000 pediatricians, if we care about the health of our kids, we should too. ❑

Sources: American Association of Pediatrics, Policy Statement on Children, Adolescents, and Advertising, December 2006 (pediatrics.aappublications.org/cgi/content/full/118/6/2563); American Psychological Association, "Television Advertising Leads to Unhealthy Habits in Childen" February 2004 (releasees/childrenads.html); Jennifer Saranow, "Car makers direct more ads at kids," *Wall Street Journal*, November 9th, 2006 (www.commercialexploitation.org/news/carmakers.html); David Burke, "Two-year olds branded by TV advertising" (www.whitedot.org/issue/isssory.aps?slug=Valkenburg); Center for a New American Dream, *Kids and Commercialism* (www.newdream.org/kids/);; Juliet Schor, Born to Buy: The Commercialized Child and the New Consumer Culture (New York: Scribner, 2004); Center for Disease Control, "Facts about Childhood Overweight" www.cdc.gov/Healthy Youth/overweight/index.html).

Article 3.2

DOWN WITH THE CLOWN
It's time for Ronald McDonald to retire.

BY RAJ PATEL
May/June 2010

When Ronald Reagan ended his presidential debate with Jimmy Carter in 1979 with "Are you better off than you were four years ago?", his media savvy changed politics forever.

But long before that, another Ronald messed with mass communications no less indelibly. In 1963, Ronald McDonald broke every rule in advertising when he began speaking to children directly.

It seems impossible that there might have been a time when kids were considered anything other than shorter, louder, more pestering versions of adult consumers. But it wasn't always thus. It took a canny cabal of ad-men to tap the pockets of a newly affluent generation of youngsters. They wanted to redefine the frontiers of what advertising in the television age could be. And they succeeded.

Today, the McDonald's corporation boasts that their frontman is more recognizable than Santa Claus. He's the champion of a $32 billion brand. With a wink and a smile, Ronald has charged into neighborhoods around and inside schools, plumbing every depth to keep his parent company's arches golden and bright in the minds of impressionable young eaters.

McDonald's and other fast-food corporations hide behind the fact that their advertising is "free speech" and that, in any case, the corporations clearly declare their commercial intentions. This isn't terribly helpful. When it comes to children, advertising is far closer to brainwashing.

From the moment they are exposed to TV, our children are subject to Ronald's manipulations. Corporations spend $17 billion a year turning children into consumers. Globally, for every dollar spent promoting healthy food, $500 is spent promoting junk. For parents wanting their kids to eat well, those are tough odds, especially for parents on restricted incomes.

Ronald isn't just a clown—he's also an architect. Here and around the world, the way food is grown, subsidized, processed, and eaten has been fashioned by the needs of the McDonald's corporation. More sales for the clown mean bigger returns for Cargill and Tyson's factory farms, Archer Daniels Midland's high-fructose corn-syrup processing plants, and Monsanto's pesticide production facilities. And it's our tax dollars that go into everything from the cheap commodities they depend on to the small-business loans and tax credits that allow fast-food franchises to breed in and around our schools. For these subsidies, and for the lax regulations around health and advertising to children, the fast-food industry has spent millions in lobbying fees. Ronald McDonald may have a big smile, but his shoes are steel-tipped.

Ultimately, McDonald's cheap food is cheat food. Ronald is more of a Hamburglar, dipping into our pockets with our children's fingers, and leaving us with bills for long afterward. The cost of diabetes in the United States alone is $700 for every man, woman, and child. For people of color, diet-related disease is incredibly important—one in two children of color born in 2000 will develop diabetes.

Times are changing, though. A new survey shows that most parents who have kids under 18 want Ronald to go. Corporate Accountability International has released a terrific report entitled *Clowning with Kid's Health: The Case for Ronald McDonald's Retirement*, which makes some tight legal and epidemiological arguments against him. The report is part of Corporate Accountability's "Value [the] Meal" campaign, which aims to "challenge fast food corporations to stop driving the global epidemic of diet-related disease."

This isn't some curmudgeonly attack on fun. For those who want to watch clowns, there'll always be circuses and cable news. There are bigger questions here. Why is junk food cheaper than healthy food? Why is persistent poverty driving people into the arms of the junk-food industry? Why isn't there real choice in the U.S. diet?

But as a matter of public health, as a way to give parents the chance to get their children eating well, as a way of making it possible to have fun with food without spending scarce cash on unhealthy food, the clown's gotta go. There's a lot to do to transform how we eat, but for starters, it's time to Retire Ronald. ❏

Sources: Corporate Accountability International's "Value [the] Meal" campaign (stopcorporateabuse.org/value-meal); Retire Ronald (www.retireronald.org).

Article 3.3

ENOUGH IS ENOUGH
Why more is not necessarily better than less.

BY ALAN DURNING
June 1991, updated May 2009

> "Our enormously productive economy ... demands that we make consumption our way of life, that we convert the buying and use of goods into rituals, that we seek our spiritual satisfaction, our ego satisfaction, in consumption... We need things consumed, burned up, worn out, replaced, and discarded at an ever increasing rate."
>
> —*Victor Lebow, U.S. retailing analyst, 1955*

Across the country, Americans have responded to Victor Lebow's call, and around the globe, those who could afford it have followed. And many can: Worldwide, on average, a person today is four-and-a-half times richer than were his or her great-grandparents at the turn of the last century.

Needless to say, that new global wealth is not evenly spread among the earth's people. One billion live in unprecedented luxury; one billion live in destitution. Overconsumption by the world's fortunate is an environmental problem unmatched in severity by anything except perhaps population growth. Surging exploitation of resources threatens to exhaust or unalterably disfigure forests, soils, water, air, and climate. High consumption may be a mixed blessing in human terms, too. Many in the industrial lands have a sense that, hoodwinked by a consumerist culture, they have been fruitlessly attempting to satisfy social, psychological, and spiritual needs with material things.

Of course, the opposite of overconsumption—poverty—is no solution to either environmental or human problems. It is infinitely worse for people and bad for the natural world. Dispossessed peasants slash and burn their way into Latin American rain forests, and hungry nomads turn their herds out onto fragile African range land, reducing it to desert. If environmental destruction results when people have either too little or too much, we are left to wonder how much is enough. What level of consumption can the earth support? When does having more cease to add appreciably to human satisfaction?

The Consuming Society

Consumption is the hallmark of our era. The headlong advance of technology, rising earnings, and cheaper material goods have lifted consumption to levels never dreamed of a century ago. In the United States, the world's premier consuming society, people today on average own twice as many cars, drive two-and-a-half times as far, and travel 25 times further by air than did their parents in 1950. Air conditioning spread from 15% of households in 1960 to 64% in 1987, and color televisions from 1% to 93%. Microwave ovens and video cassette recorders reached almost two-thirds of American homes during the 1980s alone.

Japan and Western Europe have displayed parallel trends. Per person, the Japanese today consume more than four times as much aluminum, almost five times as much energy, and 25 times as much steel as they did in 1950. They also own four times as many cars and eat nearly twice as much meat. Like the Japanese, Western Europeans' consumption levels are only one notch below Americans'.

The late 1980s saw some poor societies begin the transition to consuming ways. In China, the sudden surge in spending on consumer durables shows up clearly in data from the State Statistical Bureau: Between 1982 and 1987, color televisions spread from 1% to 35% of urban Chinese homes, washing machines quadrupled from 16% to 67%, and refrigerators expanded their reach from 1% to 20%. By 2002 there were 126 color televisions, 93 washing machines, and 87 refridgerators for every 100 urban Chinese households.

Few would begrudge anyone the simple advantages of cold food storage or mechanized clothes washing. The point, rather, is that even the oldest non-Western nations are emulating the high-consumption lifestyle. Long before all the world's people could achieve the American dream, however, we would lay waste the planet.

The industrial world's one billion meat eaters, car drivers, and throwaway consumers are responsible for the lion's share of the damage humans have caused common global resources. Over the past century, the economies of the wealthiest fifth of humanity have pumped out two-thirds of the greenhouse gases threatening the earth's climate, and each year their energy use releases three-fourths of the sulfur and nitrogen oxides causing acid rain. Their industries generate most of the world's hazardous chemical wastes, and their air conditioners, aerosol sprays, and factories release almost 90% of the chlorofluorocarbons destroying the earth's protective ozone layer. Clearly, even one billion profligate consumers is too much for the earth.

Beyond the environmental costs of acquisitiveness, some perplexing findings of social scientists throw doubt on the wisdom of high consumption as a personal and national goal: Rich societies have had little success in turning consumption into fulfillment. Regular surveys by the National Opinion Research Center of the University of Chicago reveal, for example, that no more Americans report they are "very happy" now than in 1957.

Likewise, a landmark study by sociologist Richard Easterlin in 1974 revealed that Nigerians, Filipinos, Panamanians, Yugoslavians, Japanese, Israelis, and West Germans all ranked themselves near the middle of a happiness scale. Confounding any attempt to correlate affluence and happiness, poor Cubans and rich Americans were both found to be considerably happier than the norm.

If the effectiveness of consumption in providing personal fulfillment is questionable, perhaps environmental concerns can help us redefine our goals.

In Search of Sufficiency

By examining current consumption patterns, we receive some guidance on what the earth can sustain. For three of the most ecologically important types of consumption—transportation, diet, and use of raw materials—the world's people are distributed unevenly over a vast range. Those at the bottom clearly fall below the "too little" line, while those at the top, in the cars-meat-and-disposables class, clearly consume too much.

Approximately one billion people do their traveling, aside from the occasional donkey or bus ride, on foot. Unable to get to jobs easily, attend school, or bring their complaints before government offices, they are severely hindered by the lack of transportation options.

Another three billion people travel by bus and bicycle. Kilometer for kilometer, bikes are cheaper than any other vehicle, costing less than $100 new in most of the Third World and requiring no fuel.

The world's automobile class is relatively small: Only 8% of humans, about 400 million people, own cars. The automobile makes itself indispensable: Cities sprawl, public transit atrophies, shopping centers multiply, workplaces scatter.

The global food consumption ladder has three rungs. According to the latest World Bank estimates, the world's 630 million poorest people are unable to provide themselves with a healthy diet. On the next rung, the 3.4 billion grain eaters of the world's middle class get enough calories and plenty of plant-based protein, giving them the world's healthiest basic diet.

The top of the ladder is populated by the meat eaters, those who obtain close to 40% of their calories from fat. These 1.25 billion people eat three times as much fat per person as the remaining four billion, mostly because they eat so much red meat. The meat class pays the price of its diet in high death rates from the so-called diseases of affluence—heart disease, stroke, and certain types of cancer.

The earth also pays for the high-fat diet. Indirectly, the meat-eating quarter of humanity consumes nearly 40% of the world's grain—grain that fattens the livestock they eat. Meat production is behind a substantial share of the environmental strains induced by agriculture, from soil erosion to overpumping of underground water.

In consumption of raw materials, such as steel, cotton, or wood, the same pattern emerges. A large group lacks many of the benefits provided by modest use of nonrenewable resources—particularly durables like radios, refrigerators, water pipes, tools, and carts with lightweight wheels and ball bearings. More than two billion people live in countries where per capita consumption of steel, the most basic modern material, falls below 50 kilograms a year.

Roughly 1.5 billion live in the middle class of materials use. Providing each of them with durable goods every year uses between 50 and 150 kilograms of steel. At the top of the heap is the industrial world or the throwaway class. A typical resident of the industrialized fourth of the world uses 15 times as much paper, 10 times as much steel, and 12 times as much fuel as a Third World resident.

In the throwaway economy, packaging becomes an end in itself, disposables proliferate, and durability suffers. Americans toss away 180 million razors annually, enough paper and plastic plates and cups to feed the world a picnic six times a year, and enough aluminum cans to make 6,000 DC-10 airplanes. Similarly, the Japanese use 30 million "disposable" single-roll cameras each year, and the British dump 2.5 billion diapers.

The Cultivation of Needs

What prompts us to consume so much? "The avarice of mankind is insatiable," wrote Aristotle 23 centuries ago. As each of our desires is satisfied, a new one appears in its place. All of economic theory is based on that observation.

What distinguishes modern consuming habits, some would say, is simply that we are much richer than our ancestors, and consequently have more ruinous effects on nature. While a great deal of truth lies in that view, five distinctly modern factors play a role in cultivating particularly voracious appetites: the influence of social pressures in mass societies, advertising, the shopping culture, various government policies, and the expansion of the mass market into households and local communities.

In advanced industrial nations, daily interactions with the economy lack the face-to-face character prevailing in surviving local communities. Traditional virtues such as integrity, honesty, and skill are too hard to measure to serve as yardsticks of social worth. By default, they are gradually supplanted by a simple, single indicator—money. As one Wall Street banker put it bluntly to the *New York Times,* "Net worth equals self-worth."

Beyond social pressures, the affluent live completely enveloped in pro-consumption advertising messages. The sales pitch is everywhere. One analyst estimates that the typical American is exposed to 50 to 100 advertisements each morning before nine o'clock. Along with their weekly 22-hour diet of television, American teenagers are typically exposed to three to four hours of TV advertisements a week, adding up to at least 100,000 ads between birth and high school graduation.

Advertising has been one of the fastest-growing industries during the past half-century. In the United States, ad expenditures rose from $198 per capita in 1950 to $498 in 1989 to $930 for every man, woman, and child in the country in 2007. Worldwide, over the same period, per person advertising expenditures grew from $15 in 1950 to $46 in 1989 and $71 in 2002. In developing countries, the increases have been astonishing. Advertising billings in India jumped fivefold in the 1980s; newly industrialized South Korea's advertising industry grew 3540% annually in the late 1980s.

Government policies also play a role in promoting consumption and in worsening its ecological impact. The British tax code, for example, encourages businesses to buy thousands of large company cars for employee use. Most governments in North and South America subsidize beef production on a massive scale.

Finally, the sweeping advance of the commercial mass market into realms once dominated by family members and local enterprise has made consumption far more wasteful than in the past. More and more, flush with cash but pressed for time, households opt for the questionable "conveniences" of prepared, packaged foods, miracle cleaning products, and disposable everything—from napkins to shower curtains. All these things cost the earth dearly.

Like the household, the community economy has atrophied—or been dismembered—under the blind force of the money economy. Shopping malls, superhighways, and strips have replaced corner stores, local restaurants, and neighborhood theaters—the very places that help create a sense of common identity and community. Traditional Japanese vegetable stands and fish shops are giving way to supermarkets and convenience stores, and styrofoam and plastic film have replaced yesterday's newspaper as fish wrap.

All these things nurture the acquisitive desires that everyone has. Can we, as individuals and as citizens, act to confront these forces?

The Culture of Permanence

The basic value of a sustainable society, the ecological equivalent of the Golden Rule, is simple: Each generation should meet its own needs without jeopardizing the prospects of future generations to meet theirs.

For individuals, the decision to live a life of sufficiency—to find their own answer to the question "how much is enough?"—is to begin a highly personal process. Social researcher Duane Elgin estimated in 1981—perhaps optimistically—that 10 million adult Americans were experimenting "wholeheartedly" with voluntary simplicity. India, the Netherlands, Norway, Western Germany, and the United Kingdom all have small segments of their populations who adhere to a nonconsuming philosophy. Motivated by the desire to live justly in an unjust world, to walk gently on the earth, and to avoid distraction, clutter, and pretense, their goal is not ascetic self-denial but personal fulfillment. They do not think consuming more is likely to provide it.

Realistically, voluntary simplicity is unlikely to gain ground rapidly against the onslaught of consumerist values. And, ultimately, personal restraint will do little if not wedded to bold political and social steps against the forces promoting consumption. Commercial television, for example, will need fundamental reorientation in a culture of permanence. As religious historian Robert Bellah put it, "That happiness is to be attained through limitless material acquisition is denied by every religion and philosophy known to humankind, but is preached incessantly by every American television set."

Direct incentives for overconsumption are also essential targets for reform. If goods' prices reflected something closer to the environmental cost of their production, through revised subsidies and tax systems, the market itself would guide consumers toward less damaging forms of consumption. Disposables and packaging would rise in price relative to durable, less-packaged goods; local unprocessed food would fall in price relative to prepared products trucked from far away.

The net effect might be lower overall consumption as people's effective purchasing power declined. As currently constituted, unfortunately, economies penalize the poor when aggregate consumption contracts: Unemployment skyrockets and inequalities grow. Thus arises one of the greatest challenges for sustainable economics in rich societies—finding ways to ensure basic employment opportunities for all without constantly stoking the fires of economic growth. ❏

Article 3.4

UPDATE ON MORTGAGE LENDING DISCRIMINATION

After a disastrous detour, we're back where we started.

BY JIM CAMPEN
November/December 2010

In the 1980s and early 1990s, racial discrimination in mortgage lending resulted in less access to home loans for predominantly black and Latino borrowers and neighborhoods. Home mortgages were a fairly standardized product, and the problem was that banks avoided lending in minority neighborhoods (redlining) and denied applications from blacks and Latinos at disproportionately high rates compared to equally creditworthy white applicants (lending discrimination).

Soon afterwards, however, a different form of lending discrimination rose to prominence as high-cost subprime loans became increasingly common. Precisely because borrowers and neighborhoods of color had limited access to the traditional prime loans, they were vulnerable for exploitation by predatory lenders pushing the new product.

Redlining was soon over-shadowed by "reverse redlining." Instead of being ignored, borrowers and neighborhoods of color were now aggressively targeted for high-cost subprime loans. Community groups documented and aggressively publicized the problem, and the U.S. Department of Housing and Urban Development (HUD) reported in 2000 that "subprime loans are five times more likely in black neighborhoods than in white neighborhoods." By the final year of the Clinton administration, government regulators were mobilizing to take action against this plague. But once the Bush administration took over in 2001, predatory lenders had nothing to fear from the federal government.

In the early 2000s, predatory lending began to take on a new and more explosive form. Mortgage brokers earned high fees for persuading borrowers to take on high-cost loans from lenders, who then sold the loans to big Wall Street firms, who in turn packaged them into "mortgage-backed securities" that were sold to investors. Everybody earned big fees along the way—in fact, the worse the deal was for borrowers, the bigger the fees for everyone else—and so the system gathered incredible momentum. Wall Street's demand for loan volume led ultimately to a complete lack of lending standards and millions upon millions of loans were made to borrowers who had no realistic prospect of repaying them.

For present purposes, the most important aspect of this appalling story is that these exploitative high-cost loans were strongly targeted to borrowers and neighborhoods of color. My own research on lending in Greater Boston during 2006, the peak year of the subprime lending boom, found that 49% of all home-purchase loans to blacks, and 48% of all home-purchase loans to Latinos, were high-cost loans, compared to just 11% of all loans to whites—and that the share of high-cost loans in predominantly minority neighborhoods was 4.4 times greater than it was in predominantly white neighborhoods. Similar racial and ethnic disparities were documented in numerous studies all across the country. Echoing work by researchers at the Federal

Reserve Bank of Boston fifteen years earlier, the Center for Responsible Lending made use of industry data to demonstrate that these disparities could be only partially accounted for by differences in credit scores and other legitimate measures of borrower risk. In other words, they again provided statistical proof that racial discrimination was at least partly responsible for the observed racial disparities.

Nevertheless, federal regulators again did virtually nothing in response to the abundant evidence of violations of fair housing laws. Their most vigorous action was when the Comptroller of the Currency, the principal regulator of the nation's largest banks, actually went to court to stop New York's attorney general from enforcing that state's anti-discrimination laws against big national banks.

Finally, in 2007, the housing bubble popped and subprime lenders collapsed. Millions of homeowners who had received high-cost subprime loans either lost their homes to foreclosure or are in danger of being foreclosed upon soon. Because they were targeted by the predatory lenders, blacks and Latinos have been hit the hardest by this foreclosure tsunami. For example, researchers at the Center for Responsible Lending estimated that among recent mortgage borrowers, "nearly 8% of both African Americans and Latinos have lost their homes to foreclosures, compared to just 4.5% of whites."

By 2008, borrowers and neighborhoods of color were no longer being targeted by predatory lenders, as that industry had all but disappeared in the aftermath of the subprime meltdown. Instead, the more traditional form of discrimination again rose to the foreground. A recent report by a group of community-based organizations from seven cities across the country found that between 2006 and 2008 prime mortgage lending decreased 60.3% in predominantly minority neighborhoods while falling less than half that much (28.4%) in predominantly white neighborhoods. Home Mortgage Disclosure Act data for 2009, as tabulated by the Federal Reserve, showed that the denial rate for black applicants for conventional mortgage loans was 2.48 times greater than the denial rate for their white counterparts (45.7% vs. 18.4%; the denial rate for Latinos was 35.9%). This denial rate disparity ratio is actually greater than those that created widespread outrage when denial rate data first became public in the early 1990s.

Geoff Smith, senior vice president of Chicago's Woodstock Institute, summed up the new situation this way: "After inflicting harm on neighborhoods of color through years of problematic subprime loans, banks are now pulling back at a time when these communities are most in need of responsible loans and investment. We are concerned that we have gone from a period of reverse redlining to a period of re-redlining." ❏

Sources: U.S. Dept. of Housing and Urban Development, Unequal Burden: Income & Racial Disparities in Subprime Lending in America, 2000; Jim Campen, Changing Patterns XIV: Mortgage Lending to Traditionally Underserved Borrowers & Neighborhoods in Boston, Greater Boston, and Massachusetts, 2006, Massachusetts Community and Banking Council; Center for Responsible Lending, "Unfair Lending: the Effect of Race and Ethnicity on the Price of Subprime Mortgages," 2006, and "Foreclosures by Race and Ethnicity: The Demographics of a Crisis," 2010 (both available at www.responsiblelending.org); California Reinvestment Coalition and six other groups, "Paying More for the American Dream IV: The Decline of Prime Mortgage Lending in Communities of Color," 2010 (available at www.woodstockinst.org).

Article 3.5

THE GREAT RECESSION IN BLACK WEALTH

BY JEANNETTE WICKS-LIM
January/February 2012

The Great Recession produced the largest setback in racial wealth equality in the United States over the last 25 years. In 2009 the average white household's wealth was 20 times that of the average black household, nearly double that in previous years, according to a 2011 report by the Pew Research Center.

Driving this surge in inequality is a devastating drop in black wealth. The typical black household in 2009 was left with less wealth than at any time since 1984 after correcting for inflation.

It's important to remember wealth's special role—different from income—in supporting a household's economic well-being. Income pays for everyday expenses— groceries, clothes, and gas. A family's wealth, or net worth, includes all the assets they've built up over time (e.g., savings account, retirement fund, home, car) minus any money they owe (e.g., school loans, credit card debt, mortgage). Access to such wealth determines whether a layoff or medical crisis creates a bump in the road, or pushes a household off a financial cliff. Wealth can also provide families with financial stepping-stones to advance up the economic ladder—such as money for college tuition, or a down payment on a house.

Racial wealth inequality in the United States has always been severe. In 2004, for example, the typical black household had just $1 in net worth for every $11 of a typical white household. This is because families slowly accumulate wealth over their lifetime and across generations. Wealth, consequently, ties the economic fortunes of today's households to the explicitly racist economic institutions in America's past—especially those that existed during key phases of wealth redistribution. For example, the Homesteading Act of 1862 directed the large-scale transfer of government-owned land nearly exclusively to white households. Also starting in the 1930s, the Federal Housing Authority made a major push to subsidize home mortgages— for primarily white neighborhoods. On top of that, Jim Crow Laws—in effect until the mid-1960s—and racial violence severely curtailed efforts by the black community to start their own businesses to generate their own wealth.

The housing market crisis and the Great Recession made racial wealth inequality yet worse for two reasons. First, the wealth of blacks is more concentrated in their

MEDIAN HOUSEHOLD NET WORTH (2009 DOLLARS)

	1984	1988	1991	1993	1995	2004	2009
White	$76,951	$75,403	$68,203	$67,327	$68,520	$111,313	$92,000
Black	$6,679	$7,263	$7,071	$6,503	$9,885	$9,823	$4,900
Ratio of White to Black	12	10	10	10	7	11	19

Source: Taylor et al., *Twenty-to-One: Wealth Gaps to Rise to Record High Between Whites, Blacks and Hispanics,* Pew Research Center.

homes than the wealth of their white counterparts. Homes of black families make up 59% of their net worth compared to 44% among white families. White households typically hold more of other types of assets like stocks and IRA accounts. So when the housing crisis hit, driving down the value of homes and pushing up foreclosure rates, black households lost a much greater share of their wealth than did white households.

Second, mortgage brokers and lenders marketed subprime mortgages specifically to black households. Subprime mortgages are high-interest loans that are supposed to increase access to home financing for risky borrowers—those with a shaky credit history or low income. But these high-cost loans were disproportionately peddled to black households, even to those that could qualify for conventional loans. One study estimated that in 2007 nearly double the share of upper-income black households (54%) had high-cost mortgages compared to low-income white households (28%).

Subprime mortgages drain away wealth through high fees and interest payments. Worse, predatory lending practices disguise the high-cost of these loans with initially low payments. Payments then shoot up, often leading to default and foreclosure, wiping out a family's home equity wealth. In 2006, Mike Calhoun, president of the Center for Responsible Lending, predicted that the surge of subprime lending within the black community would "…likely be the largest loss of African-American wealth that we have ever seen, wiping out a generation of home wealth building." It was a prescient prediction.

To reverse the rise in racial wealth inequality, we need policies that specifically build wealth among black households, such as the "baby bonds" program proposed by economists William Darity of Duke University and Darrick Hamilton of The New School. Baby bonds would be federally managed, interest-bearing trusts given to the newborns of asset-poor families, and could be as large as $50,000 to $60,000 for the most asset-poor. By using a wealth means-test, this program would disproportionately benefit black communities, while avoiding the controversy of a reparations policy. When recipients reach age 18, they could use the funds for a house down payment, tuition, or to start a business. This program would cost about $60 billion per year, which could easily be covered by letting the Bush-era tax cuts expire for the top 1% of income earners. ❑

Sources: Amaad Rivera, Brenda Cotto-Escalera, Anisha Desai, Jeannette Huezo, and Dedrick Muhammad, *Foreclosed: State of the Dream 2008*, United for a Fair Economy, 2008; Citizens for Tax Justice, "The Bush Tax Cuts Cost Two and a Half Times as Much as the House Democrats' Health Care Proposal," CTJ Policy Brief, September 9, 2009; Darrick Hamilton and William Darity, Jr., "Can 'Baby Bonds' Eliminate the Racial Wealth Gap in Putative Post-Racial America?" *Review of Black Political Economy*, 2010; Paul Taylor, Rakesh Kochhar, Richard Fry, Gabriel Velasco, and Seth Motel, *Twenty-to-One: Wealth Gaps to Rise to Record High Between Whites, Blacks and Hispanics*, Washington DC: Pew Research Center, 2011.

Chapter 4

FIRMS, PRODUCTION, AND PROFIT MAXIMIZATION

Introduction

How do producers make decisions? Textbooks describe a process that is rational, benign, and downright sensible. There is one best, that is, least costly and most profitable, way to produce any given amount of goods or services. Given a particular scale of operations, there is one most profitable amount to produce. Businesses adjust their total output and the mix of inputs at the margin until they achieve these most profitable outcomes. They pay the going wage for labor, just as they pay the going price for any input. And when businesses have achieved the lowest possible costs, market competition ensures that they pass on savings to consumers.

This chapter describes a reality that is a bit more complicated, and in some ways uglier than the textbook model. Very large companies are not the passive price-takers of neoclassical lore but do in fact "affect" the market-wide level of prices, profits, and wages, and manufacture their own demand. Thus, large corporations are the very embodiment of the Tilly Assumption of "Market Power."

Alejandro Reuss opens the discussion with a "Primer on Corporations" (Article 4.1). He describes the ways that corporations are "special"—that is, different from other capitalist enterprises—and why they have become the dominant form of business organization. He concludes by discussing how corporations' economic power—their control over investment and employment—can translate into political power.

Next, John Miller provides a particularly salient example of firms' market power (Article 4.2). He suggests that there may not be just "one best way" for retail businesses, but rather two: a "high road" based on high levels of service, skilled, decently-paid employees, and higher prices, as exemplified by the business model at Costco; and a "low road" that offers low prices, no frills, and a low-paid, high-turnover workforce, which is Wal-Mart's business model. Despite Wal-Mart's growth and its position as the world's largest retailer (third largest global employer of 2.1 million workers—only 200,000 draftees behind China's People's Liberation Army), the author questions whether the business model has in fact proven beneficial for the U.S. economy as a whole.

Arthur MacEwan then looks inside large companies and asks how they set CEO salaries (Article 4.3). He concludes that executive pay does not fit with the "one best way" analysis of business decision-making. According to MacEwan, corporate directors set executive pay at high levels not because of profit-maximizing principles, but because they themselves are top executives and are peers and often buddies of the CEOs whose compensation they are deciding. Thus we find a mutually enriching system of inflated salaries for a very small and rarified group of corporate managers. But more fundamentally, the much higher CEO pay in the United States than elsewhere reflects the fact that work is organized differently in different countries—again, a departure from the idea of "one best way".

The metal giant ASARCO provides another example of a corporation pursuing a particularly perverse "low road" profit maximization strategy (Article 4.4). Fischel, et al. describe ASARCO's history of evading and actively violating worker and environmental safety laws. This history recently culminated in a successful bankruptcy declaration that released the corporation from its legal liabilities towards the affected communities. This bankruptcy has allowed ASARCO to re-emerge as a "healthy" new corporation even as its former workers and their families struggle with mounting medical bills. The authors also point out the regulatory failures of the American government along the way. Amongst the most striking is the failure of Congress to reinstate "polluter pays" fees to finance the so-called "superfund" that the government uses to pay for environmental clean-up projects. As a result, corporations like ASARCO can find ever more creative ways to evade their financial obligations.

Jonathan Latham documents the selling of "indulgences" by "Big Conservation" to global agribusiness corporations over the issue of habitat destruction, in "Way Beyond Greenwashing" (Article 4.5). Market Power is evident in that these massive agribusiness companies can silence their critics through "greenwashed" contributions. The net effect is to co-opt the very non-governmental organizations that claim to be protecting habitat for wildlife, allowing global agribusiness to effectively destroy rainforest in order to increase soybean production.

John Miller next provides an example of a "Principal-Agent Problem" leading to "moral hazard." His article, "A Dirty Job No One Should Do" (Article 4.6), is the story of Steve Eckhaus, a Wall Street lawyer who negotiated astronomical pay packages for banking/finance executives and sees no connection between those inflated salaries and benefits and the financial crisis. Miller describes the self-dealing and risk-taking behavior that damaged the American financial system.

The final essay is a timely manifesto from Richard Wolff, "Turning Toward Solutions" (Article 4.7). Arguing that the current capitalist economic system and model of production is irretrievably broken, Wolff suggests that it is time to "reorganize production from the ground up." He suggests a number of areas to be democratically transformed.

Discussion Questions

1) (General) Do you agree that the use and purchase of labor raises different issues than the use of other inputs for production (i.e., that labor is a "unique" factor input)? Why or why not?

2) (General) Miller suggests that we should change the rules of the competitive game to steer businesses toward better treatment of workers. Current-day

capitalism already has some such rules (such as those forbidding slavery), so it makes sense to think through what rules would best meet our goals as a society. What rule changes do each of these articles propose? What do you think of these proposals?

3) (General) The authors in this chapter present various corporate strategies as a choice, rather than an imperative. How does this compare with the standard microeconomic analysis of business decision-making?

4) (Article 4.2) Given the comparatively low wages at Wal-Mart, why do you think there is still strong demand for Wal-Mart jobs? Would you characterize this labor market as being "free"?

5) (Article 4.2) According to Cervantes (sidebar), how does Costco keep prices low while following very different labor practices?

6) (Article 4.3) MacEwan maintains that in the case of CEO compensation, boards of directors pay high salaries rather than minimizing costs because they see it as the "right" thing to do. Do companies do this in areas other than executive pay? Why doesn't competition drive out such practices?

8) (Articles 4.2 and 4.4) John Miller implies that there is more than one "best" way to organize production. Do you agree? If other ways of organizing production are equally good, why are certain ways dominant, at least in particular industries? In the case of ASARCO, what are some factors that may have enabled a "low road" rather than "high road" strategy?

9) (Articles 4.2 and 4.4) Fischel, et al., and Miller both discuss formally legal ways used by corporations to cut costs. When does aggressive cost-cutting cross the line? Would you draw the line at law-breaking, or are there some legal business practices—in addition to illegal ones—that you consider unacceptable?

10) (Article 4.5) What is "greenwashing?" What advantage do large corporations find in greenwashing? What is an "indulgence?" Do you find any similarity between the Vatican and the WWF in the issuing of such things?

12) (Article 4.6) Explain, in the context of Steve Eckhaus's clients, what a "Principal-Agent Problem" is. How does the Principal-Agent Problem contribute to a "moral hazard" problem? Do you agree with Eckhaus that Wall Street bears no responsibility for the recent financial crisis and subsequent Great Recession?

13) (Article 4.7) Richard Wolff writes: "For the last half-century, it was taboo in the United States to criticize, debate, or propose changes to the economic system." Do you agree that it is no longer taboo to do so? If so, what has happened to cause this change?

Article 4.1

CORPORATIONS

BY ALEJANDRO REUSS
April 2012

When people use the word "corporation," they are usually referring to certain private, for-profit businesses, especially the largest businesses in the United States or other capitalist economies. When we think of corporations, we usually think of "big business." Besides size, people often picture other features of corporations when they hear the word. A corporation can have many shareholders—all part-owners of the company—instead of being owned by a single owner or a couple of partners. A corporation has a board of directors, elected by some or all of the shareholders, which may direct the overall way the corporation is managed. The board usually hires a few top executives, who then make decisions about how the corporation in managed on a day-to-day basis.

Many different kinds of organizations are, legally, corporations. Nonprofit organizations, like charities, churches, or private schools, for example, can be corporations, just as for-profit businesses can be. This just means that the organization is recognized under the law, and may both have legal obligations and enjoy legal protections. A corporation may take in money but, depending on what type of corporation it is, it may have to pay taxes. If a corporation harms some individual, the person who has been harmed can sue the corporation, just as one individual can sue another. Meanwhile, a corporation can also sue an individual or another corporation.

Corporations do not have to be large. There are corporations of all different sizes. Even a small company with a few employees could be a corporation. There are some large companies that are not corporations, but the very largest companies, which may have hundreds of thousands of employees and may sell billions of dollars of goods each year, are almost always corporations. Various different kinds of businesses can be corporations, including manufacturing companies (such as General Motors), retail companies (like Wal-Mart), or financial companies (like Bank of America or Liberty Mutual).

Even though some corporations are not private, for-profit businesses, people usually use the word "corporation" as shorthand for this particular kind of corporation. A corporation, in this sense, is a particular type of capitalist enterprise. We can also refer to this kind of business as a "capitalist corporation."

What Is a Capitalist Enterprise?

Capitalist corporations are a particular kind of capitalist enterprise. By "capitalist enterprise," we just mean a private, for-profit business whose owners employ other people in exchange for wages. By this definition, a private business where a "self-employed" owner works, but which does not hire other people for wages, is not a capitalist enterprise.

In the United States and other similar economies, relatively few people are business owners (either of capitalist enterprises or of small "individual proprietorships" which employ nobody but the owner). Farm workers do not usually own the farms where the work. Miners do not usually own the mines. Factory workers usually do not own the factories. People who work in shops or offices usually do not own those businesses. Most workers do not own the businesses where the work, the buildings where they go to work, the materials or tools they use, or the products they produce. Instead, they work for pay at capitalist enterprises that are owned by others.

Workers get paid a wage or salary by the owner of the business, who in turn owns whatever the worker produces using the materials and tools provided. The owners of a business, of course, do not usually want the goods that employees produce, but want to sell these goods. If a capitalist enterprise cannot sell these goods for more than what it cost to produce them, it cannot make a profit. Companies that do not make a profit usually go out of business. Business owners do not have unlimited funds, and so cannot go on forever pouring money into a loss-producing business. Many will conclude, long before they run out of money, that the business will never turn a profit and is not worth running.

Even a business that makes a profit may not stay in business for very long if the profit is less than "normal" (whatever that may be in a particular society at a particular time). The owners may decide that it is not worth investing in that business, if it is possible for them to make a larger profit in another business, or just by lending out their money. In addition, a business that makes less than the normal profit may not be able to compete in the long run with other, more successful businesses. Those that make higher profits can reinvest these profits to expand and modernize, and may put the less profitable business at a competitive disadvantage in the future. Therefore, owners of capitalist enterprises are under competitive pressure to make the most profit they can.

How Are Corporations Special?

In many ways, capitalist corporations are like other capitalist enterprises. However, corporations are also defined by their special legal status, which makes them different from other capitalist enterprises. Corporations are granted a "charter" by the government, which means that the corporation exists as a legal entity. (In the United States, state governments grant corporate charters.) This is different from other kinds of businesses. An individual can start a business without getting a charter from the government. Two people can form a business as a partnership by coming to some kind of agreement (or "contract") between themselves, again without a government charter. Corporations, however, do not exist until the government permits them to exist.

All the things that make corporations different from other capitalist enterprises are determined by government policy (in particular, the set of laws governing corporations). "Corporate law" creates certain special privileges for corporations that other businesses do not have. It also imposes special obligations on corporations (especially those whose shares are bought and sold on the stock market). The most important of these special characteristics are "limited liability," the "fiduciary responsibility" of management to the corporation's shareholders, "public disclosure" requirements, and the corporate "governance" structure.

Limited Liability

Suppose that a corporation borrows a huge sum of money, or that it has harmed many people who sue it for damages and win (as in the case of the tobacco companies a few years back, or as is happening with BP, the company responsible for the Gulf of Mexico oil spill). If the corporation cannot pay its debts, it can declare bankruptcy, and the people it owes can get paid off from the sale of its assets, like the buildings or machinery it owns. A bankrupt business can even sell off "intangible" assets, like brand names or trademarks, to raise money to pay off its debts. If the money from the sale of assets is not enough to pay off all the debts, however, the shareholders are not responsible (not "liable") to pay the rest. This is what we mean by the term "limited liability." Someone who buys stock in a corporation is risking whatever they paid for the stock, but cannot lose more than this amount. If the corporation goes bankrupt, the shareholders' stock becomes worthless, but the shareholders cannot lose any more money since they cannot be forced, legally, to pay whatever debts the corporation has left unpaid.

The justification usually given for the legal principle of limited liability is that it promotes economic growth and development. The idea is that, if companies were limited to what an individual or family, or perhaps a couple of partners, could scrape together to start a business, they would not be able to operate at the scale that modern corporations do. They would not have enough money to buy expensive machinery, let alone buy large factories or put together huge assembly lines.

Even if the reason given for limited liability is to fuel economic growth, however, we should remember that this is also a big favor from the government for the people who own shares in corporations. (Most people, even in the United States, do not own any shares of stock. If we look at all the shares of stock owned by members of the public, we find that most are owned by a very small percentage of the U.S. population.) First, limited liability means that the government gives the shareholders of a corporation a certain kind a protection from other people's claims against it. The corporation they own, and whose management they have a say in selecting, may owe someone a debt, but the shareholders are not legally obligated to pay it. Second, it means that corporations can afford to take bigger risks in order to make a bigger profit. The shareholders may select a management that is willing to take risks that could result in big profits, knowing that they are not on the hook for all the corporation's liabilities if these risks do not pay off.

Fiduciary Responsibility

The management of a corporation has a legal responsibility to act in the interests of the corporation's shareholders, who are its legal owners. They cannot legally put anyone's interests, including their own, ahead of the shareholders'. It may sound surprising, given what we are accustomed to hearing about corporate executives' lavish salaries and perks, but the legal doctrine of fiduciary responsibility means that they cannot treat the company coffers like their own personal bank account. Rather, their decisions must be guided by the objective of enhancing "shareholder value" (in effect, the profitability of the corporation, of which the shareholders are the legal owners, and therefore the value of an ownership stake in the corporation).

A single person who fully owns an entire company (known as a "privately held" company) can use the company's funds for whatever he or she likes, whether that is expanding the company's operations or buying luxury cars. In contrast, corporate executives receive a salary and other compensation (often lavish, in the case of large companies) decided by the board of directors or a committee of the board. They are legally free to spend this income as they wish. Corporate executives also control how company funds are spent, but are not free to treat corporate funds as their own. This means that the chief executive of a company is not legally entitled to use company funds to remodel his or her house, buy fancy cars, take expensive vacations, and so on. Of course, executives still fly on private jets, take "business trips" to exotic locales, enjoy fancy "business dinners," and so on, but they have to justify these as necessary costs of doing business. If shareholders think that executives have failed in their fiduciary responsibility, they can actually sue the company.

Since fiduciary responsibility means that corporate managers are legally obligated to the shareholders and only the shareholders, it also means that they cannot put other people's interests ahead of those of the shareholders. Corporate managers have no legal duty to workers, besides abiding by contracts and labor law. It is not their job to further workers' interests. In fact, their fiduciary responsibility to the shareholders can be interpreted as meaning that they are obligated to get as much work for as little pay as possible. If they pay workers more than they really have to, they are giving away the company's (that is, the shareholders') money. Likewise, corporate managers have no legal duty to the broader community, beyond abiding by the law. They do not have to "give back," say, by funding schools, libraries, or parks in the communities where they operate. When corporations engage in philanthropic giving, they do justify this as helping to promote the business and its reputation— and therefore enhancing shareholder value.

Public Disclosure

Corporations that sell shares of stock on the stock market are called "publicly traded corporations." Each time a corporation sells a share of its stock to an individual or another company, it raises some money. This is one way the company can finance its operations. Once a member of the public buys a share of stock, he or she can sell it to someone else. Stocks in many different companies are bought and sold in stock markets, like the New York Stock Exchange, NASDAQ, and many other markets around the world. Most stock sales do not involve a corporation selling stock to a member of the public, but one member of the public selling shares to another (that is, the resale of shares that a corporation had previously sold). Therefore, most stock sales do not result in any money going to the corporation that originally issued the stock.

By law, publicly traded companies have to disclose certain business information. They have to file forms with the government (in particular, the Securities and Exchange Commission, or SEC) listing their officers (board members and top executives), the officers' compensation (salaries and other benefits), the company's profits or losses, and other information. (If someone purchases all the shares of a corporation, which is known as "taking it private," the corporation no longer has to disclose this kind of information.) The idea behind disclosure requirements is to protect shareholders or people who might consider purchasing shares in a company, often referred to as the "investing public." In effect, this is like the nutritional information labels on packaged foods. Corporate disclosures are supposed to tell the buyers (or potential buyers) of stock in a company important information about what they are thinking about buying.

In practice, corporate "insiders" (board members, top executives, etc.) have much more information about the financial condition of a corporation than members of the public. This has led to well-publicized scandals in recent years, such as the Enron case. Corporate executives sold the stock they owned when the price was high, knowing that in reality the company was not as profitable as the public thought, and that the stock price would soon plummet.

Corporate Governance

When an individual buys a share (or many shares) of a corporation, he or she gets certain property rights. Shareholders are not legally entitled to receive a share of the company's profits each year. Suppose that, at the end of the year, a corporation has made a profit—in the case of the largest U.S. corporations, this could be billions or tens of billions of dollars. The company management decides how much of this money to pay out to shareholders and how much to keep. A corporation might keep cash reserves, use profits to buy existing businesses, use them to expand its existing operations (for example, by buying or renting additional factory or office buildings, buying new machinery, hiring additional workers, etc.). The profits that corporations pay out to shareholders are called "dividends." Generally, if a corporation's management decides to issue a dividend, this is a certain amount of money per share of stock. This means that someone who owns ten shares gets 10 times the total dividend money as someone who owns a single share. Someone who owns 100 shares gets 100 times the dividend money, and so on. The rest of the profits are called "retained profits." It is not necessarily preferable for shareholders to receive all or most of the company's profit for a year in the form of dividends. By using retained earnings to expand, a corporation may increase in overall value. This increases the value of an ownership share in the company (the value of the stock that shareholders own).

Shareholders have the right to sell their shares if and when they wish. This gives them a stake in the profitability of the corporation, since the price of a share (on the stock exchange) is likely to go higher the more profitable the company is. This share price is what the shareholder will get per share if he or she decides to sell. Note that the corporation does not have to give shareholders their money back if they decide they do not want the shares anymore. The company does not even have to buy the shares back at whatever might be their going price at the time. Rather, a shareholder can sell the shares to whoever will buy them on the stock market. A shareholder who does not want to be a part owner of the company anymore does not get to take "their" piece of the company with them. The corporation is not required to give the shareholder any tangible asset—the shareholder cannot claim any particular thing owned by the corporation—nor is the corporation forced to sell off tangible assets in order to pay a shareholder who does not want his or her shares anymore. This way, shareholders come and go (people who are shareholders today can decide to sell all their shares, and no longer be shareholders, tomorrow), but the corporation itself stays intact.

Shareholders also have a say in the governance structure of the corporation. You can think of a corporation as a political entity, like a small (or, in some cases, not so small) country. Shareholders are like the citizens. They are entitled to attend annual shareholder meetings, where they can address questions or comments to the corporation's directors (board members) and executives. Shareholders are entitled to vote in elections to the board of directors (except for those holding certain classes of "nonvoting" or "preferred" stock). They can even run for election to the board of directors, if they so wish.

Corporate elections are different from government elections. First, in corporate elections, only shareholders are allowed to vote. The decisions made by a corporation's management may affect many other people—workers, people in communities where the corporation has operations, etc.—all around the world. However, if they are not shareholders in the corporation, they are not entitled to vote. In addition, in corporate elections, different shareholders do not get the same number of votes. Rather, each shareholder gets a number of votes equal to the number of shares he or she owns (excluding nonvoting stock). Someone who owns one share gets one vote; 10 shares, 10 votes; 100 shares, 100 votes.

Even in the United States, most people do not own stock in any corporation. Among those who do, many do not own very much stock. Even people (mostly very affluent people) who own a great deal of stock may own relatively small amounts of stock in many different companies. This means that a shareholder does not have to own 50% of the shares in a company to effectively control the company. A very large shareholder may own only a few percent of the shares of a company. If the other shares are spread out among many people, these other shareholders are unlikely to organize as a group to control the management of the company. If small shareholders get really disgruntled with the way the corporation in run, they are more likely to just sell their shares than to devote a lot of time and energy to getting the management replaced. Relatively small shareholders, in fact, usually just sign away their voting rights to other, larger shareholders (with the view that very large shareholders are likely to have more information about how the company should be run, and will have a strong incentive to make sure that it is profitable). This way a very wealthy individual may have effective control of a company even though he or she "only" owns, say, 5% of the total shares. Keep in mind that 5% of the stock in the largest corporate giants could be worth billions of dollars.

Corporations, Economic Power, and Political Power

Large corporations are certainly among the most powerful entities in the U.S. economy and politics. We can start by classifying the power of large corporations into economic power, on the one hand, and political power, on the other. Economic power has to do with the ability of large corporations to dictate to others (other businesses, workers, etc.) the conditions under which they will do business. Political power has to do with their ability to get what they want from the government, including both favors they can get from the government and influence over the overall direction of government policy.

Mainstream or "neoclassical" economists do not talk about economic power very much. Mostly, they talk about "market" economies as if nobody exercised any power over anyone else—buyers and sellers engaging in voluntary exchanges, each free from any kind of coercion from other buyers or sellers. The main form of economic power neoclassical economists do talk about is "market power." Sellers have market power if they can charge more than what the price would be under "perfect competition" (with a very, very large number of sellers all competing with each other to sell the same product). Sellers are most likely to have market power when there is just one seller ("monopoly") or a few sellers ("oligopoly") of a particular product or kind of product. Buyers have market power if they can pay less than what the price would be under "perfect competition." Likewise, buyers are most likely to have market power when there is just one buyer ("monopsony") or a few buyers ("oligopsony") of a particular product or type of product.

Radical political economists, on the other hand, focus a great deal of their attention on economic power. When they look at the U.S. economy, or other capitalist economies, they do not see a bunch of individuals freely engaging in exchanges that leave both parties better off. Rather, they see dramatic differences in resources and power that allow the wealthy and powerful to dominate and exploit others. A neoclassical economist looks at labor relations and figures that, however low a worker's wages or however difficult their conditions of work, they must be better off than they would have been otherwise, or they would not have accepted the job. A radical political economist, on the other hand, looks at the same situation and says that, if the worker had no other way to make a living or to provide for his or her family, this was not really a free choice. The individual employer is not responsible for the worker's lack of another way to make a living, besides working for someone else for pay. This does, however, give the employer power over the workers. The employer dominates the workers. If workers want to keep their jobs, they cannot do what they want, but must do what the employer (or a boss hired by the employer) says. The employer also exploits the workers. The workers must accept a wage that is low enough for the employer to make a profit, or the employer will not hire them. Because the employer owns means of production and the workers do not, the employer can take some of the value that the workers produce.

In the view of radical political economists, employers as a group also have economic power in a different sense. Most people in a capitalist economy are employed by capitalist enterprises. If capitalist employers decide not to hire people to produce goods and services, many people will be unemployed. The government depends on private economic activity (production and sale of goods by capitalist enterprises) to bring in revenue and therefore to be able to run at all. If workers are not employed, the government does not get payroll taxes. If people are not buying goods, the government does not get sales taxes. If people do not have incomes, the government does not collect income taxes. Moreover, if capitalist enterprises are not hiring, many people are unemployed, and many others are afraid of losing their jobs, the party in power probably will not survive the next election. Most of the economic activity in capitalist economies depends on the economic decisions made by capitalist enterprises, such as how much output to produce, how many people to hire, whether to buy new machines or new buildings (this is what economists mean by "investment"), and so on.

This leads us into the political power of large corporations and other capitalist enterprises. Sometimes, large corporations use their power over hiring and investment to get special favors from governments. This is often especially clear at the state level. State governments may offer corporations tax breaks, government-financed facilities, and other favors if they decide to locate their facilities in the state. States compete with each other, keeping business taxes low and offering other benefits, to lure business there. The same thing also happens on the national level. Some radical political economists argue that the ability of companies to locate facilities anywhere in the world, in the age of "globalization," has created a "race to the bottom." The governments of different countries, they say, are forced to cut taxes on business, slash public spending, adopt policies to keep wages low, and so on, to attract investment by large multinational corporations.

If the owners and managers of capitalist enterprises do not like the kinds of economic policies the government is putting in place, they may decide not to hire or invest. In some cases, where capitalists feel very threatened by government policies, they may actually do this with the conscious political aim of bringing down the government. More often, a decline in employment and investment can arise from a simple decline in "business confidence." The owners and managers of capitalist enterprises become pessimistic about being able to sell their goods at a profit in the short run, and make a business decision to cut back on production, employment, and investment. The effect, however, can still be to force the government to bend over backwards to maintain profitable conditions for business, in order to avoid an economic downturn. This way, the economic power of capitalist enterprises over the state of the whole economy can result in their getting the kinds of government policies that favor them. ❏

Article 4.2

WHAT'S GOOD FOR WAL-MART . . .

BY JOHN MILLER
January/February 2006

"Is WAL-MART GOOD FOR AMERICA?"

It is a testament to the public relations of the anti-Wal-Mart campaign that the question above is even being asked.

By any normal measure, Wal-Mart's business ought to be noncontroversial. It sells at low costs, albeit in mind-boggling quantities. ...

The company's success and size ... do not rest on monopoly profits or price-gouging behavior. It simply sells things people will buy at small markups and, as in the old saw, makes it up on volume. ... You may believe, as do service-workers unions and a clutch of coastal elites—many of whom, we'd wager, have never set foot in Wal-Mart—that Wal-Mart "exploits" workers who can't say no to low wages and poor benefits. You might accept the canard that it drives good local businesses into the ground, although both of these allegations are more myth than reality.

But even if you buy into the myths, there's no getting around the fact that somewhere out there, millions of people are spending billions of dollars on what Wal-Mart puts on its shelves. No one is making them do it. ... Wal-Mart can't make mom and pop shut down the shop anymore than it can make customers walk through the doors or pull out their wallets.

What about the workers? ... Wal-Mart's average starting wage is already nearly double the national minimum of $5.15 an hour. The company has also recently increased its health-care for employees on the bottom rungs of the corporate ladder.

—*Wall Street Journal* editorial, December 3, 2005

"Who's Number One? The Customer! Always!" The last line of Wal-Mart's company cheer just about sums up the *Wall Street Journal* editors' benign view of the behemoth corporation. But a more honest answer would be Wal-Mart itself: not the customer, and surely not the worker.

The first retail corporation to top the Fortune 500, Wal-Mart trailed only Exxon-Mobil in total revenues last year. With 1.6 million workers, 1.3 million in the United States and 300,000 offshore, Wal-Mart is the largest private employer in the nation and the world's largest retailer.

Being number one has paid off handsomely for the family of Wal-Mart founder Sam Walton. The family's combined fortune is now an estimated $90 billion, equal to the net worth of Bill Gates and Warren Buffett combined.

But is what's good for the Walton family good for America? Should we believe the editors that Wal-Mart's unprecedented size and market power have redounded not only to the Walton family's benefit but to ours as well?

Low Wages and Meager Benefits

Working for the world's largest employer sure hasn't paid off for Wal-Mart's employees. True, they have a job, and others without jobs line up to apply for theirs. But that says more about the sad state of today's labor market than the quality of Wal-Mart jobs. After all, less than half of Wal-Mart workers last a year, and turnover at the company is twice that at comparable retailers.

Why? Wal-Mart's oppressive working conditions surely have something to do with it. Wal-Mart has admitted to using minors to operate hazardous machinery, has been sued in six states for forcing employees to work off the books (i.e., unpaid) and without breaks, and is currently facing a suit brought by 1.6 million current and former female employees accusing Wal-Mart of gender discrimination. At the same time, Wal-Mart workers are paid less and receive fewer benefits than other retail workers.

Wal-Mart, according to its own reports, pays an average of $9.68 an hour. That is 12.4% below the average wage for retail workers even after adjusting for geography, according to a recent study by Arindrajit Dube and Steve Wertheim, economists at the University of California's Institute of Industrial Relations and long-time Wal-Mart researchers. Wal-Mart's wages are nearly 15% below the average wage of workers at large retailers and about 30% below the average wage of unionized grocery workers. The average U.S. wage is $17.80 an hour; Costco, a direct competitor of Wal-Mart's Sam's Club warehouse stores, pays an average wage of $16 an hour.

Wal-Mart may be improving its benefits, as the *Journal*'s editors report, but it needs to. Other retailers provide health care coverage to over 53% of their workers, while Wal-Mart covers just 48% of its workers. Costco, once again, does far better, covering 82% of its employees. Moreover, Wal-Mart's coverage is far less comprehensive than the plans offered by other large retailers. Dube reports that according to 2003 IRS data, Wal-Mart paid 59% of the health care costs of its workers and dependents, compared to the 77% of health care costs for individuals and 68% for families the average retailer picks up.

A recent internal Wal-Mart memo leaked to the *New York Times* confirmed the large gaps in Wal-Mart's health care coverage and exposed the high costs those gaps impose on government programs. According to the memo, "Five percent of our Associates are on Medicaid compared to an average for national employees of 4 percent. Twenty-seven percent of Associates' children are on such programs, compared to a national average of 22 percent. In total, 46 percent of Associates' children are either on Medicaid or are uninsured."

A considerably lower 29% of children of all large-retail workers are on Medicaid or are uninsured. Some 7% of the children of employees of large retailers go uninsured, compared to the 19% reported by Wal-Mart.

Wal-Mart's low wages drag down the wages of other retail workers and shutter downtown retail businesses. A 2005 study by David Neumark, Junfu Zhang, and Stephen Ciccarella, economists at the University of California at Irvine, found that Wal-Mart adversely affects employment and wages. Retail workers in a community with a Wal-Mart earned 3.5% less because Wal-Mart's low prices force other businesses to lower prices, and hence their wages, according to the Neumark study. The same study also found that Wal-Mart's presence reduces retail employment by 2% to 4%. While other studies have not found this negative employment effect, Dube's research also reports fewer retail jobs and lower wages for retail workers in metropolitan counties with a Wal-Mart. (Fully 85% of Wal-Mart stores are in metropolitan counties.) Dube figures that Wal-Mart's presence costs retail workers, at Wal-Mart and elsewhere, $4.7 billion a year in lost earnings.

In short, Wal-Mart's "everyday low prices" come at the expense of the compensation of Wal-Mart's own employees and lower wages and fewer jobs for retail workers in the surrounding area. That much remains true no matter what weight we assign to each of the measures that Wal-Mart uses to keep its costs down: a just-in-time inventory strategy, its ability to use its size to pressure suppliers for large discounts, a routinized work environment that requires minimal training, and meager wages and benefits.

How Low are Wal-Mart's Everyday Low Prices?

Even if one doesn't subscribe to the editors' position that it is consumers, not Wal-Mart, who cause job losses at downtown retailers, it is possible to argue that the benefit of Wal-Mart's low prices to consumers, especially low-income consumers, outweighs the cost endured by workers at Wal-Mart and other retailers. Jason Furman, New York University economist and director of economic policy for the 2004 Kerry-Edwards campaign, makes just such an argument. Wal-Mart's "staggering" low prices are 8% to 40% lower than people would pay elsewhere, according to Furman. He calculates that those low prices on average boost low-income families' buying power by 3% and more than offset the loss of earnings to retail workers. For Furman, that makes Wal-Mart "a progressive success story."

But exactly how much savings Wal-Mart affords consumers is far from clear. Estimates vary widely. At one extreme is a study Wal-Mart itself commissioned by Global Insight, an economic forecasting firm. Global Insight estimates Wal-Mart created a stunning savings of $263 billion, or $2,329 per household, in 2004 alone.

At the other extreme, statisticians at the U.S. Bureau of Labor Statistics found no price savings at Wal-Mart. Relying on Consumer Price Index data, the BLS found that Wal-Mart's prices largely matched those of its rivals, and that instances of lower prices at Wal-Mart could be attributed to lower quality products.

Both studies, which rely on the Consumer Price Index and aggregate data, have their critics. Furman himself allows that the Global Insight study is "overly simplistic" and says he "doesn't place as much weight on that one." Jerry Hausman, the M.I.T. economist who has looked closely at Wal-Mart's grocery stores, maintains that the CPI data that the Bureau of Labor Statistics relies on systematically miss the savings offered by "supercenters" such as Wal-Mart. To show the difference between prices at Wal-Mart and at other grocers, Hausman, along with Ephraim Leibtag, USDA Economic Research Service economist, used supermarket scanner data to examine the purchasing patterns of a national sample of 61,500 consumers from 1988 to 2001. Hausman and Leibtag found that Wal-Mart offers many identical food items at an average price about 15%-25% lower than traditional supermarkets.

The Costco Alternative?

Wall Street Prefers Wal-Mart

In an April 2004 online commentary, *BusinessWeek* praised Costco's business model but pointed out that Costco's wages cause Wall Street to worry that the company's "operating expenses could get out of hand." How does Costco compare to low-wage Wal-Mart on overhead expenses? At Costco, overhead is 9.8% of revenue; at Wal-Mart, it is 17%. Part of Costco's secret is that its better paid workers are also more efficient: Costco's operating profit per hourly employee is $13,647; each Wal-Mart employee only nets the company $11,039. Wal-Mart also spends more than Costco on hiring and training new employees: each one, according to Rutgers economist Eileen Appelbaum, costs the company $2,500 to $3,500. Appelbaum estimates that Wal-Mart's relatively high turnover costs the company $1.5 to $2 million per year.

Despite Costco's higher efficiency, Wall Street analysts like Deutsche Bank's Bill Dreher complain that "Costco's corporate philosophy is to put its customers first, then its employees, then its vendors, and finally its shareholders. Shareholders get the short end of the stick." Wall Street prefers Wal-Mart's philosophy: executives first, then shareholders, then customers, then vendors, and finally employees.

Average Hourly Wage		Percentage of U.S. Workforce in Unions		Employees Covered by Company Health Insurance		Employees Who Leave After One Year	
Wal-Mart	Costco	Wal-Mart	Costco	Wal-Mart	Costco	Sam's Club*	Costco
$9.68	$16.00	0.0%	17.9%	48%	82%	21%	6%
* Sam's Club is the Wal-Mart unit that competes directly with Costco.							

In 2004, Wal-Mart paid CEO Lee Scott $5.3 million, while a full-time employee making the average wage would have received $20,134. Costco's CEO Jim Senegal received $350,000, while a full-time average employee got $33,280. And *BusinessWeek* intimates that the top job at Costco may be tougher than at Wal-Mart. "Management has to hustle to make the high-wage strategy work. It's constantly looking for ways to repackage goods into bulk items, which reduces labor, speeds up Costco's just-in-time inventory, and boosts sales per square foot. Costco is also savvier ... about catering to small shop owners and more affluent customers, who are more likely to buy in bulk and purchase higher-margin goods."

Costco's allegedly more affluent clientele may be another reason that its profit per employee is higher than Wal-Mart's and its overhead costs a lower percentage of revenue. However, Costco pays its employees enough that they could afford to shop there. As the *BusinessWeek* commentary noted, "the low-wage approach cuts into consumer spending and, potentially, economic growth."

—*Esther Cervantes*

While Hausman and Leibtag report substantial savings from shopping at Wal-Mart, they fall far short of the savings alleged in the Global Insight study. The Hausman and Leibtag study suggests a savings of around $550 per household per year, or about $56 billion in 2004, not $263 billion. Still, that is considerably more than the $4.7 billion a year in lost earnings to retail workers that Dube attributes to Wal-Mart.

But if "Wal-Mart hurts wages, not so much in retail, but across the whole country," as economist Neumark told *BusinessWeek*, then the savings to consumers from Wal-Mart's everyday low prices might not outweigh the lost wages to all workers. (Retail workers make up just 11.6% of U.S. employment.)

Nor do these findings say anything about the sweatshop conditions and wages in Wal-Mart's overseas subcontractors. One example: A recent Canadian Broadcasting Corporation investigative report found that workers in Bangladesh were being paid less than $50 a month (below even the United Nation's $2 a day measure of poverty) to make clothes for the Wal-Mart private label, Simply Basic. Those workers included ten- to thirteen-year-old children forced to work long hours in dimly lit and dirty conditions sewing "I Love My Wal-Mart" t-shirts.

Making Wal-Mart Do Better

Nonetheless, as Arindrajit Dube points out, the relevant question is not whether Wal-Mart creates more savings for consumers than losses for workers, but whether the corporation can afford to pay better wages and benefits.

Dube reasons that if the true price gap between Wal-Mart and its retail competitors is small, then Wal-Mart might not be in a position to do better—to make up its wage and benefit gap and still maintain its price advantage. But if Wal-Mart offers consumers only minor price savings, then its lower wages and benefits hardly constitute a progressive success story that's good for the nation.

If Wal-Mart's true price gap is large (say, the 25% price advantage estimated by Hausman), then Wal-Mart surely is in a position to do better. For instance, Dube calculates that closing Wal-Mart's 16% overall compensation gap with other large retailers would cost the company less than 2% of sales. Raising prices by two cents on the dollar to cover those increased compensation costs would be "eminently absorbable," according to Dube, without eating away much of the company's mind-boggling $10 billion profit (2004).

Measures that set standards to force Wal-Mart and all big-box retailers to pay decent wages and provide benefits are beginning to catch on. Chicago, New York City, and the state of Maryland have considered or passed laws that would require big-box retailers to pay a "living wage" or to spend a minimum amount per worker-hour for health benefits. The Republican board of Nassau County on Long Island passed an ordinance requiring that all big-box retailers pay $3 per hour toward health care. Wal-Mart's stake in making sure that such proposals don't become law or spread nationwide goes a long way toward explaining why 80% of Wal-Mart's $2 million in political contributions in 2004 went to Republicans.

Henry Ford sought to pay his workers enough so they could buy the cars they produced. Sam Walton sought to pay his workers so little that they could afford to shop nowhere else. And while what was good for the big automakers was probably never good for the nation, what is good for Wal-Mart, today's largest employer, is undoubtedly bad for economic justice. ❑

Sources: "Is Wal-Mart Good for America?" *Wall Street Journal*, 12/3/05; "Gauging the Wal-Mart Effect," *WSJ*, 12/03/05; Arindrajit Dube & Steve Wertheim, "Wal-Mart and Job Quality—What Do We Know, and Should We Care?" 10/05; Jason Furman, "Wal-Mart: A Progressive Success Story," 10/05; Leo Hindery Jr., "Wal-Mart's Giant Sucking Sound," 10/05; A. Bernstein, "Some Uncomfortable Findings for Wal-Mart," *BusinessWeek* online, 10/26/05, and "Wal-Mart: A Case for the Defense, Sort of," *BusinessWeek* online, 11/7/05; Dube, Jacobs, and Wertheim, "The Impact of Wal-Mart Growth on Earnings Throughout the Retail Sector in Urban and Rural Counties," *Institute of Industrial Relations Working Paper*, UC Berkeley, 10/05; Dube, Jacobs, and Wertheim, "Internal Wal-Mart Memo Validates Findings of UC Berkeley Study," 11/26/05; Jerry Hausman and Ephraim Leibtag, "Consumer Benefits from Increased Competition in Shopping Outlets: Measuring the Effect of Wal-Mart," 10/05; Hausman and Leibtag, "CPI Bias from Supercenters: Does the BLS Know that Wal-Mart Exists?" *NBER Working Paper No. 10712*, 8/04; David Neumark, Junfu Zhang, and Stephen Ciccarella, "The Effects of Wal-Mart on Local Labor Markets," *NBER Working Paper No. 11782*, 11/05; Erin Johansson, "Wal-Mart: Rolling Back Workers' Wages, Rights, and the American Dream," American Rights at Work, 11/05; Wal-Mart Watch, "Spin Cycle"; CBC News, "Wal-Mart to cut ties with Bangladesh factories using child labour," 11/30/05; National Labor Committee, "10 to 13-year-olds Sewing 'I Love My Wal-Mart' Shirts," 12/05; Global Insight, "The Economic Impact of Wal-Mart," 2005.

Article 4.3

WHY CEO SALARIES SKYROCKET

BY ARTHUR MacEWAN
November/December 1998

> Dear Dr. Dollar:
> *Why do companies compensate CEOs with such high salaries and bonuses? Do the CEOs themselves decide on their pay? Isn't it always said that no one is indispensable?*
> — Gwen Nottingham, Laurel, Montana

CEOs and other top executives of large corporations do not *formally* decide on their own salaries—that's the job of the board of directors. The board members, however, are generally high level executives of other corporations, who by supporting the big pay packages of others, win support for big pay packages for themselves.

For example, top executives of industrial companies with over $250 million in sales were compensated an average of $870,000 in 1997, according to *Forbes*. Consider Frank Newman, who runs Bankers Trust, one of the banks that fueled the current crisis in Asia with ill-conceived loans. His 1997 salary and bonuses added up to $10.9 million. Or Harvey Golub, who oversaw the layoffs of 3,300 workers from American Express in 1997, and was compensated $33.4 million—that's about $10,000 for each layoff.

Yet the huge salaries are not only a result of executives taking good care of each other. Other countries also have "interlocking directorates" of top executives serving on other companies' boards, yet CEO salaries are not nearly so high as in the United States. Top executives in Canada, Japan, the United Kingdom, and Germany are paid only half as much as their U.S. peers (with pay including salaries, bonuses, perks, and long-term incentives). You can find individual executives in those countries who take home millions, but nowhere do top executives as a group come close to the U.S. corporate elite.

So what's the difference? Are U.S. executives more valuable than European or Japanese executives in producing profits? The answer lies not in their productivity, but in their power.

Over many decades, U.S. companies have created a highly unequal corporate structure that relies heavily on management control while limiting workers' authority. Large numbers of bureaucrats work to maintain the U.S. system. While in the United States about 13% of nonfarm employees are managers and administrators, that figure is about 4% in Japan and Germany. So U.S. companies rely on lots of well-paid managers to keep poorly paid workers in line, and the huge salaries of the top executives are simply the tip of an iceberg.

This highly unequal corporate system is buttressed by an unequal political and social structure. Without a powerful union movement, for example, there is little pressure on Washington to adopt a tax code that limits corporate-generated inequality. Several other high-income countries have a wealth tax, but not the United States. In addition, U.S. laws governing the operation of unions and their role in corporate decision making are relatively weak (and often poorly enforced). Without powerful workers' organizations, direct challenges to high CEO pay levels are very limited (as is the power to raise workers' wages). So income distribution in the United States is among the most unequal within the industrialized world, and high executive salaries and low wages can be seen as two sides of the same coin. ❑

Article 4.4

BANKRUPTCY AS CORPORATE MAKEOVER
ASARCO demonstrates how to evade environmental responsibility.

BY ANNE FISCHEL, MARA KARDAS-NELSON, AND LIN NELSON
May/June 2010

> *"At around noon [every] July and August … our folks would bring us into the house, because the smoke, the pollution, the sulfur, would settle into our commu-nity for about two or three hours … when there was no breeze to take that away. When we would breathe that, we could not be outside because we were constantly coughing. So nobody can tell me that there was no ill effect on the majority of the folks that lived in Smeltertown."*
>
> —Daniel Solis, resident of Smeltertown, a Mexican-American neighborhood in El Paso, Texas, located next to an ASARCO smelter

After five long years in court, the bankruptcy of the American Smelting and Refining Company, or ASARCO, has finally been determined.

Hailed as one of the earliest and largest multinational corporations and responsible for the employment of hundreds of thousands, ASARCO has a long history of polluting both the environment and the workplace. After rack-ing up billions in environmental damages, the company filed for bankruptcy in 2005.

It is billed as the largest environmental bankruptcy in United States history; 90 communities from 21 states will share a $1.79 billion settlement to cover the costs of environmental monitoring and cleanup and limited compensation to some of its workers. This figure, however, represents less than one percent of the funds origi-nally identified as needed by claimants.

The ASARCO case emerged in the context of a diminished and disabled "Superfund," as the federal environmental program established to deal with haz-ardous waste sites is known. The fund was originally created by Congress to hold companies accountable for environmental damage and to ensure that communi-ties are not left with large bills and no means to pay them. But years of corporate pressure on Capitol Hill has depleted Superfund, placing the financial burden of environmental cleanups on taxpayers, rather than on corporations.

This use of bankruptcies to avoid responsibility, coupled with a cash-strapped Superfund, offers a chilling glimpse into the world of corporate irresponsibility allowable under U.S. bankruptcy provisions and environmental policy. As the case closes, ASARCO is transforming from an aging corporation weighed down by shuttered factories and contaminated communities into a lean and profitable company. This is setting a precedent for how others can use legal loopholes to evade liability and undermine government protections.

Damaging Health and Environment, Yet Shaping Environmental Policy

ASARCO began operations in the late 1890s, mining, smelting, and refining essential ores (first lead, then copper) in order to provide base materials for industrial production. By the mid-20th century, the company had expanded to include holdings and operations in Latin America, Australia, Canada, Africa, and the Philippines. In 1914 company workers unionized through the Western Federation of Miners, which later became the Mine, Mill & Smelterworkers, eventually merging with the United Steelworkers in the 1960s. In its heyday, ASARCO operated in close to 90 U.S. communities in 22 states, employing thousands.

By the mid-1970s, employees and communities were growing concerned about environmental and public health risks resulting from company operations. Researchers, health departments, unions, and workers began tracking the impact of exposure to arsenic, lead, cadmium, and sulfur dioxide, all byproducts of the smelting process. In Tacoma, WA, site of one of ASARCO's largest smelting operations, dissident workers launched "The Smelterworker" newsletter, one of the first union-based occupational health efforts in the country. The Puget Sound Air Pollution Control Agency began to voice similar concerns when ASARCO's lobbying regarding federal laws and regulations successfully slowed development of a federal arsenic standard.

Health concerns also emerged in El Paso, Texas, site of a large ASARCO smelter that had polluted both sides of the U.S.-Mexico border. In 1970, following passage of the Clean Air Act, the City of El Paso sued ASARCO over its sulfur dioxide emissions. During the process of discovery, ASARCO submitted documentation of its emissions to the City for the first time. These reports showed that between 1969 and 1971, 1,012 metric tons of lead, 508 metric tons of zinc, eleven metric tons of cadmium, and one metric ton of arsenic had been released during operations.

By 1969 the city had a higher concentration of airborne lead than any other in the state. In the early 1970s a research team from the Centers for Disease Control (CDC), led by Dr. Philip Landrigan, confirmed a pattern of smelter-sourced lead threatening the children on the U.S. side.

The studies conducted by the CDC linked the high levels of lead in air, soil, and dust to the ASARCO smelter. They also linked the lead in soil and dust to elevated lead levels in children's blood. Landrigan's research team administered IQ tests and reaction time tests, and found significant differences in performance between lead-impacted children and those with lower blood levels. This pathbreaking research transformed scientific thinking about the impact of lead on children's development, and confirmed numerous dangers, even in children without obvious clinical symptoms.

At the time of research the threshold for lead in blood was 40 micrograms per deciliter. Today it is 10 micrograms per deciliter, and many health researchers and physicians want to see it set even lower. Yet some researchers had asserted that lead from smelters was not harmful to humans, and an El Paso pediatrician, in a study funded by an organization connected to the industry, claimed that levels of 40 to 80 micrograms were acceptable, as long as the children were properly nourished. As a result of the CDC studies, however, "it is now widely accepted in the scientific community that lead is toxic at extremely low levels," according to Landrigan.

Some of the affected children were treated with painful chelation therapy. Daniel Solis, a Smeltertown resident, recalls his siblings' reaction to the treatment:

> They would get hysterical because of how much the treatment would hurt, they would literally go underneath their cribs and they would hold on to the bottom of the bed. I would literally have to go underneath and drag them out… It was excruciating. My mom would cry to see… the pain that her kids would be going through. But we had no other choice, you know, my siblings were that infected with lead that they had to get that treatment.

In 1991, through its subsidiary Encycle, ASARCO received highly hazardous waste, sourced from a Department of Defense site at Rocky Mountain Arsenal in Colorado. Napalm, sarin nerve gas, cluster bombs, and white phosphorous had all been produced at this site, and private pesticide companies also rented space in the facility. At Encycle, hazardous waste labels were removed and materials were shipped to ASARCO facilities in El Paso and in East Helena, Mont. Neither facility was licensed to manage hazardous waste; it is possible that the waste was shipped to other sites as well. In El Paso, workers were not informed of the risks of such incineration and were not trained to deal with these hazardous materials. This lack of protection and withholding of information violates the federal right-to-know workplace law.

The Government Accountability Office (GAO) has verified that from 1991 to 1999, the El Paso and East Helena plants received and incinerated waste meant only for licensed hazardous waste facilities. This illegal disposal potentially exposed hundreds of workers and both communities. In 1998, the federal government fined ASARCO $50 million for these violations and problems at other ASARCO sites. The settlement did not include provisions for testing workers, soil, air, water, or community members for exposure to potential contaminants. The El Paso community was not informed about these illegal activities; the extent of knowledge in East Helena is unclear. The wrist-slap against the company—and the actions that provoked it—became public only through the investigative work of citizen activists in El Paso, leading to a *New York Times* exposé in 2006.

Although many communities endure severe health effects and environmental problems, ASARCO's ties to powerful politicians gave it substantial influence on public health policy. During the George W. Bush years, James Connaughton, one of ASARCO's key attorneys, served as head of the White House Council for Environmental Quality. A key ASARCO scientist was positioned for the federal Lead Advisory Board, while other prominent, independent scientists were pushed to the margins. ASARCO has also promoted the corporate "audit privilege," allowing companies to self-monitor hazards.

Superfund: Hope and Disappointment for Polluted Communities

ASARCO was hardly the only company polluting communities throughout the industrial boom of the 20th century. As research linked contamination to birth defects, higher cancer rates, and other serious illnesses, community advocates and municipal and state leaders took collective action. In 1980, in response to the discovery of hazardous waste at Love Canal, N.Y., Congress passed the Comprehensive Environmental Response, Compensation & Liability Act (CERCLA), better known as "Superfund." The Act made companies legally and financially responsible for environmental degradation that occurred as a result of their operations. Additionally, cleanup costs for "orphan sites" where specific companies could not be identified or held responsible would draw money from the Superfund, made of a series of corporate taxes, or "polluter-pays fees," and supported by government revenue. The legislation authorized the Environmental Protection Agency (EPA) to place heavily contaminated sites on the National Priorities List. If identified as a "Superfund site," a community qualified for enforced cleanup and funds. Since the inception of Superfund, the EPA has identified over 1,200 sites, including 20 ASARCO operations. One in four Americans lives within four miles of a Superfund site.

In 1995, under the watch of President Clinton and a Republican Congress, Superfund's polluter-pays fees expired, thus shifting most of the financial burden onto taxpayers. As of 2010, these fees have yet to be reinstated. By 2003, all corporate funds were exhausted and the Superfund now relies solely on taxpayer-funded government revenues. According to the U.S. Public Interest Research Group, in 1995 taxpayers paid only 18% ($300 million) of the Superfund, but by 2005, they contributed 100%—approximately $1.2 billion.

As a result of under-financing and lack of political will, the number of Superfund sites undergoing cleanup has diminished. While the EPA averaged 87 completed cleanups a year from 1997 to 2000, in 2008 only 30 sites were processed, representing a drop of over 50% in the pace of cleanups. Without polluter-pays fees and in light of the bankruptcy, the affected communities at ASARCO sites are left with few options to ensure comprehensive cleanup and reparations.

Penny Newman of the Center for Community Action & Environmental Justice calls the fund "impotent" without corporate contributions: "It's disingenuous to pretend a program exists without the funding." In spring 2009, the Obama administration directed $600 million in stimulus money to 50 Superfund sites—including the ASARCO site in Tacoma—that have shown significant progress in their cleanups. Obama and the EPA call this a "stopgap measure," setting the restoration of the polluter-pays tax as an important environmental health goal.

The Bankruptcy "Solution"

As environmental and community health concerns mounted, public pressure increased, and projected cleanup costs skyrocketed, ASARCO closed most of its operations. All of ASARCO's sites—operating, shuttered, or in remediation—were affected by the 2005 Chapter 11 bankruptcy filing. The company cited environmental liabilities as a primary explanation for the action.

The bankruptcy was not a last-minute act of desperation. On the contrary, the company had been rearranging itself for some time, shedding liabilities and cutting costs through sales and mergers. In 1999, ASARCO was "bought" by its major subsidiary, Grupo México, a Mexican-based company that is one of the largest metal producers in the world. This sale is significant because ASARCO's assets and records were shifted outside of the United States and therefore no longer under U.S. government jurisdiction; citizens requesting records and remediation from the company now had difficulty doing so. In 2002, ASARCO sold one of its most valuable mining complexes, Southern Peru Copper, to its new parent company, transferring even more valuable resources beyond national boundaries. Fearing a potential bankruptcy, the Department of Justice forced ASARCO to set up a $100 million trust to cover liabilities for impacted U.S. communities.

Chapter 11 of the U.S. Bankruptcy Code permits corporate reorganization and invokes "automatic stay," in which most litigation is put on hold until it can be resolved in court, with creditors ceasing collection attempts. This status allowed ASARCO to legally avoid paying for environmental damage at sites that required it for the duration of the bankruptcy. Additionally, pension payments and other monies owed to workers as negotiated by the United Steelworkers, which represents most employees, were threatened and delayed. As a result of the bankruptcy, the Steelworkers, a member of the bankruptcy creditors' committee, settled with a one-year extension of their collective bargaining agreement.

Complexities stemming from ASARCO's multinational status became more apparent during the 2005-2009 bankruptcy proceedings. During the case, Grupo México, by court ruling, was removed as the controlling agent of ASARCO. As such, Grupo México battled with another corporate suitor, India-based Sterilite/Vedanta Corporation, for control; Grupo México eventually prevailed. This competition prolonged proceedings, as the judge assessed competing purchase offers and changing promises to affected communities and workers.

Through bankruptcy negotiations, ASARCO significantly reduced its debts to damaged communities. The *Tacoma News Tribune* reported that more than a dozen states and the federal government originally collectively filed $6 billion in environmental claims involving 20 ASARCO sites. Other estimates placed cleanup and liability costs as high as $25.2 billion. This figure was subsequently reduced to $3.6 billion in early bankruptcy court proceedings, which was later sliced to the final settlement of $1.79 billion.

In the days following the announcement of the settlement, government spokespeople and community members expressed a mix of relief and disappointment. According to U.S. Associate Attorney General Tom Perrelli, "The effort to recover this money was a collaborative and coordinated response by the states and federal government. Our combined efforts have resulted in the largest recovery of funds to pay for past and future cleanup of hazardous materials in the nation's history. Today is a historic day for the environment and the people affected across the country."

But activists and affected communities insist the ruling did not go far enough. In addition to paying less than originally projected, ASARCO's parent company, Grupo México, faces fewer responsibilities than it did before the bankruptcy. While the company had previously been pegged with penalty payments for the transfer of Southern Peru Copper, the bankruptcy decision, which reinstated Grupo México control, nullified this.

The $1.79 billion settlement will also be unevenly split between affected communities. While Washington State celebrated the perseverance of their attorneys and coordinated work of departments, Texas, which had relatively little sustained support and attention by federal authorities, will not be as well served. The El Paso area has a modest $52 million to address complex and hazardous contamination.

ASARCO's Legacy and Communities' Call for Responsibility

Throughout the bankruptcy proceedings, U.S. Senator Maria Cantwell (D-WA) warned that ASARCO's use of bankruptcy will be imitated by other companies aiming to minimize their liability for environmental and health damages. The *Tacoma News Tribune* has reported that companies in eight of the ten regions under EPA jurisdiction have considered bankruptcy in order to elude responsibility. A 2007 study identified six companies connected to approximately 120 Superfund sites in 28 states filing for bankruptcy, with four of these companies successfully avoiding over half a billion dollars in cleanup costs. In 2009, eleven states involved in the ASARCO bankruptcy and the Justice Department reaffirmed the warning that more companies will follow suit.

Twice Cantwell has introduced bills to curtail companies' use of bankruptcies and other "legal" techniques to avoid responsibility; twice the bills have failed.

Texas State Senator Shapleigh has witnessed the city of El Paso's struggle with the high cost of environmental cleanup and jeopardized public health. Commenting on the bankruptcy and echoing Cantwell's concerns, he warns, "This is a strategy that will be used over and over again in the United States. The corporations will play out this environmental saga…this is the first one."

A Familiar Story

The story of ASARCO is a complicated one. It is a story of environmental degradation, of countless hidden occupational health hazards, of a corporation comfortably connected to federal and state administrations, and of a broken safety net that offers little compensation for communities impacted by a century of industrial operations.

Yet the story of ASARCO is not an unfamiliar one. The company's evasion of corporate responsibility in the face of weakened federal regulations demonstrates how companies can shift billions of dollars of environmental cleanup costs onto affected communities.

The special brew of corporate bankruptcies and an under-funded Superfund leaves us extremely vulnerable to industrial contamination. ASARCO's bankruptcy left thousands of exposed workers and family members, 21 states, two Indian tribal communities, and unions in limbo for years, and now with very limited reparation for life-altering health effects and degraded environments. Despite the company's responsibility for extensive environmental and health damage, the settlement holds them accountable for only a sliver of originally projected cleanup costs. A lack of political will from Congress to ensure corporate funding for Superfund and to pass legislation that tightens legal loopholes has left communities who believed they were protected by the 1980 CERCLA legislation strapped for cash and with few legal protections to enforce corporate responsibility.

Current and former ASARCO employees, affected communities, and allies are organizing to push for corporate accountability and government regulations. In El

Paso, as a result of the bankruptcy, the Superfund dysfunction, and the special burden of illegal hazardous waste incineration, community advocates are working to shape a strategy for activating workplace right-to-know for former employees at high risk for illness. They are further insisting on transparency in the cleanup and corporate accountability for public health.

In February 2010, a group of over two dozen organizations and individuals, including current and former ASARCO employees and several Mexican government officials, wrote to the EPA with concerns that the cleanup plan for the El Paso site is "inadequate to protect the health of the [El Paso] community and does not address offsite-pollution in [New Mexico], Mexico and Texas." The current plan only addresses hazards in El Paso, but according to Mariana Chew of the Sierra Club, "Cuidad Juárez in Mexico and Sunland Park in [New Mexico] are the communities most affected by ASARCO's legal and illegal operations and yet are not taken in account." Chew and others are especially concerned about the health of children at an elementary school in Cuidad Juárez that sits just 400 feet downwind from the smelter.

The group demands larger payments from ASARCO, specifically for its illegal incineration of hazardous waste. In the interim, the group claims that federal monies from the Superfund should be used.

The 2010 National Latino Congress has also condemned ASARCO's contamination of the border region and the company's bankruptcy. The Congress, supported by hundreds of organizations and over 40 elected U.S. officials, demanded full disclosure of the illegal incineration of hazardous waste, and comprehensive testing and treatment for workers and community members who may have been exposed.

Meanwhile, in Hayden, Ariz., site of the company's only operating U.S. smelter, ASARCO officials have reassured residents that blowing dust from mine tailings is not a hazard. According to ASARCO vice president Thomas Aldrich, "Across the board these are very low in metals, about what you'd expect here, comparable to the background levels in soil."

Such statements offer little comfort for communities still struggling for information, protection, and accountability. ❏

This article is based on the project "No Borders: Communities Living and Working with Asarco" based at Evergreen State College and guided by Fischel and Nelson. The project examines the occupational and environmental health and social justice implications of ASARCO's operations with a focus on three communities: Ruston/Tacoma, Wash., Hayden, Ariz., and El Paso, Texas. A documentary film, "Borders of Resistance," to be released in the summer of 2010, documents the El Paso story of community and labor advocates pressing for accountability and health protections. Other films and writing are forthcoming.

Sources: Office of Texas Senator Eliot Shapleigh, "Asarco in El Paso," September 2008; Les Blumenthal, "Asarco Mess Reveals Superfund Failings," *Tacoma News Tribune*, March 21, 2006; Les Blumenthal, "Lawyers Dissect Asarco's cleanup obligation in the US," *Tacoma News Tribune*, May 20, 2006; Les Blumenthal, "Grupo México wins Asarco back in court ruling," *Tacoma News Tribune*, September 3, 2009; Joel Millman, "Asarco Bankruptcy Leaves Many Towns with Cleanup Mess," *Wall Street Journal*, May 24, 2006; Office of U.S. Senator Maria Cantwell,

"Cantwell Introduces Legislation to Prevent Corporate Polluters from Evading Toxic Cleanup Responsibilities," June 15, 2006; Center for Health, Environment and Justice, "Superfund: In the Eye of the Storm," March 2009; Center for Health, Environment and Justice, "America's Safety Net in Crisis: 25th Anniversary of Superfund," 2005; The Smelterworker rank-and-file union newsletter, circa 1970-75, Tacoma Wash.; Marianne Sullivan, "Contested Science and Exposed Workers: ASARCO and the Occupational Standard for Inorganic Arsenic," Public Health Chronicles, July 2007; Ralph Blumenthal, "Copper Plant Illegally Burned Hazardous Waste, EPA Says," *New York Times*, October 11, 2006; Government Accountability Office, "Environmental Liabilities: EPA Should Do More to Ensure That Liable Parties Meet Their Cleanup Obligations," August 2005; Government Accountability Office, "Hazardous Waste: Information about How DOD and Federal and State Regulators Oversee the Off-site Disposal of Waste from DOD Installations," November 2007; Department of Justice, "Largest Environmental Bankruptcy in US History Will Result in Payment of $1.79 Billion Towards Environmental Cleanup and Restoration," December 10, 2009; Seattle and King County Department of Public Health, Arsenic Facts, 2010; The Center for Health, Environment & Justice, "Letter to the Environmental Protection Agency," February 16 2010; The Center for Health, Environment & Justice, "News Release," February 16 2010; The 2010 National Latino Congress, "Draft Amended ASARCO Resolution," 2010; Interview, Dr. Philip Landrigan, Mt Sinai Medical School, August 27 2009; Interview, Daniel Solis, El Paso, Tex, August 2007.

Article 4.5

WAY BEYOND GREENWASHING

Have corporations captured "Big Conservation"?

BY JONATHAN LATHAM
March/April 2012

Imagine an international mega-deal. The global organic food industry agrees to support international agribusiness in clearing as much tropical rainforest as they want for farming. In return, agribusiness agrees to farm the now-deforested land using organic methods, and the organic industry encourages its supporters to buy the resulting timber and food under the newly devised "Rainforest Plus" label. There would surely be an international outcry.

Virtually unnoticed, however, even by their own membership, the world's biggest wildlife conservation groups have agreed to exactly such a scenario, only in reverse. Led by the World Wide Fund for Nature (WWF, still known as the World Wildlife Fund in the United States), many of the biggest conservation nonprofits including Conservation International and the Nature Conservancy have already agreed to a series of global bargains with international agribusiness. In exchange for vague promises of habitat protection, sustainability, and social justice, these conservation groups are offering to greenwash industrial commodity agriculture.

The big conservation nonprofits don't see it that way, of course. According to WWF's "Vice President for Market Transformation" Jason Clay, the new conservation strategy arose from two fundamental realizations.

The first was that agriculture and food production are the key drivers of almost every environmental concern. From issues as diverse as habitat destruction to over-use of water, from climate change to ocean dead zones, agriculture and food production are globally the primary culprits. To take one example, 80-90% of all fresh water extracted by humans is for agriculture, according to the UN Food and Agriculture Organization's "State of the World's Land and Water" report.

This point was emphasized once again in an analysis published in the scientific journal *Nature* in October 2011. The lead author of this study was Professor Jonathan Foley. Not only is Foley the director of the University of Minnesota-based Institute on the Environment, but he is also a science board member of the Nature Conservancy.

The second crucial realization for WWF was that forest destroyers typically are not peasants with machetes but national and international agribusinesses with bulldozers. It is the latter who deforest tens of thousands of acres at a time. Land clearance on this scale is an ecological disaster, but Claire Robinson of Earth Open Source points out it is also "incredibly socially destructive," as peasants are driven off their land and communities are destroyed. According to the UN Permanent Forum on Indigenous Issues, 60 million people worldwide risk losing their land and means of subsistence from palm plantations.

By about 2004, WWF had come to recognize the true impacts of industrial agriculture. Instead of informing their membership and initiating protests and boycotts, however, they embarked on a partnership strategy they call "market transformation."

Market Transformation

With WWF leading the way, the conservation nonprofits have negotiated approval schemes for "Responsible" and "Sustainable" farmed commodity crops. According to WWF's Clay, the plan is to have agribusinesses sign up to reduce the 4-6 most serious negative impacts of each commodity crop by 70-80%. And if enough growers and suppliers sign up, then the Indonesian rainforests or the Brazilian Cerrado will be saved.

The ambition of market transformation is on a grand scale. There are schemes for palm oil (the Roundtable on Sustainable Palm Oil; RSPO), soybeans (the Round Table on Responsible Soy; RTRS), biofuels (the Roundtable on Sustainable Biofuels), Sugar (Bonsucro) and also for cotton, shrimp, cocoa and farmed salmon. These are markets each worth many billions of dollars annually and the intention is for these new "Responsible" and "Sustainable" certified products to dominate them.

The reward for producers and supermarkets will be that, reinforced on every shopping trip, "Responsible" and "Sustainable" logos and marketing can be expected to have major effects on public perception of the global food supply chain. And the ultimate goal is that, if these schemes are successful, human rights, critical habitats, and global sustainability will receive a huge and globally significant boost.

The role of WWF and other nonprofits in these schemes is to offer their knowledge to negotiate standards, to provide credibility, and to lubricate entry of certified products into international markets. On its UK website, for example, WWF offers its members the chance to "Save the Cerrado" by emailing supermarkets to buy "Responsible Soy." What WWF argues will be a major leap forward in environmental and social responsibility has already started. "Sustainable" and "Responsible" products are already entering global supply chains.

Reputational Risk

For conservation nonprofits these plans entail risk, one of which is simple guilt by association. The Round Table on Responsible Soy (RTRS) scheme is typical of these certification schemes. Its membership includes WWF, Conservation International, Fauna and Flora International, the Nature Conservancy, and other prominent nonprofits. Corporate members include repeatedly vilified members of the industrial food chain. As of January 2012, there are 102 members, including Monsanto, Cargill, ADM, Nestle, BP, and UK supermarket ASDA.

That is not the only risk. Membership in the scheme, which includes signatures on press-releases and sometimes on labels, indicates approval for activities that are widely opposed. The RTRS, for example, certifies soybeans grown in large-scale chemical-intensive monocultures. They are usually GMOs. They are mostly fed to animals. And they originate in countries with hungry populations. When, according to an ABC News poll, 52% of Americans think GMOs are unsafe and 93% think genetically modified organisms (GMOs) ought to be labeled, for example, this is a risk most organizations dependent on their reputations probably would not consider.

The remedy for such reputational risk is high standards, rigorous certification, and watertight traceability procedures. Only credibility at every step can deflect the seemingly obvious suspicion that the conservation nonprofits have been hood-winked or have somehow "sold out."

So, which one is it? Are "Responsible" and "Sustainable" certifications indicative of a genuine strategic success by WWF and its fellows, or are the schemes nothing more than business as usual with industrial-scale greenwashing and a social-justice varnish?

Low and Ambiguous Standards

The first place to look is the standards themselves. The language from the RTRS standards (see sidebar), to stick with the case of soy, illustrates the tone of the RTRS principles and guidance.

There are two ways to read these standards. The generous interpretation is to recognize that the sentiments expressed are higher than what is actually practiced in many countries where soybeans are grown, in that the standards broadly follow common practice in Europe or North America. Nevertheless, they are far lower than organic or fair-trade standards; for example, they don't require crop rotation, or prohibit pesticides. Even a generous reading also needs to acknowledge the crucial point that adherence to similar requirements in Europe and North America has contaminated wells, depleted aquifers, degraded rivers, eroded the soil, polluted the oceans, driven species to extinction, and depopulated the countryside—to mention only a few well-documented downsides.

There is also a less generous interpretation of the standards. Much of the content is either in the form of statements, or it is merely advice. Thus section 4.2 reads: "Pollution is minimized and production waste is managed responsibly." Imperatives, such as: "must," "may never," "will," etc., are mostly lacking from the document. Worse, key terms such as "pollution," "minimized," "responsible," and "timely" (see sidebar) are left undefined. This chronic vagueness means that both certifiers and producers possess effectively infinite latitude to implement or judge the standards. They could never be enforced, in or out of court.

The Rountable on Responsible Soy Standards

RTRS standards (version 1, June 2010) cover five "principles." Principle 1: Legal Compliance and Good Business Practices. Principle 2: Responsible Labour Conditions. Principle 3: Responsible Community Relations. Principle 4: Environmental Responsibility. Principle 5: Good Agricultural Practice.

Language typical of the standards includes, under Principle 2 (Responsible Labour Conditions), section 2.1.1 states: "No forced, compulsory, bonded, trafficked, or otherwise involuntary labor is used at any stage of production," while section 2.4.4 states, "Workers are not hindered from interacting with external parties outside working hours."

Under Principle 3 (Responsible Community Relations), section 3.3.3 states: "Any complaints and grievances received are dealt with in a timely manner."

Under Principle 4 (Environmental Responsibility), section 4.2 states: "Pollution is minimized and production waste is managed responsibly," and section 4.4 states: "Expansion of soy cultivation is responsible."

Under Principle 5 (Good Agricultural Practice), Section 5.9 states: "Appropriate measures are implemented to prevent the drift of agrochemicals to neighboring areas."

Dubious Verification and Enforcement

Unfortunately, the flaws of RTRS certification do not end there. They include the use of an internal verification system. The RTRS uses professional certifiers, but only those who are members of RTRS. This means that the conservation nonprofits are relying on third parties for compliance information. It also means that only RTRS members can judge whether a principle was adhered to. Even if they consider it was not, there is nothing they can do, since the RTRS has no legal status or sanctions.

The "culture" of deforestation is also important to the standards. Rainforest clearance is often questionably legal, or actively illegal, and usually requires removing existing occupants from the land. It is a world of private armies and bribery. This operating environment makes very relevant the irony under which RTRS members, under Principle 1, volunteer to obey the law. The concept of volunteering to obey the law invites more than a few questions. If an organization is not already obeying the law, what makes WWF suppose that a voluntary code of conduct will persuade it? And does obeying the law meaningfully contribute to a marketing campaign based on responsibility?

Of equal concern is the absence of a clear certification trail. Under the "Mass Balance" system offered by RTRS, soybeans (or derived products) can be sold as "Responsible" that were never grown under the system. Mass Balance means vendors can transfer the certification quantity purchased, to non-RTRS soybeans. Such an opportunity raises the inherent difficulties of traceability and verification to new levels.

How Will Certification Save Wild Habitats?

A key stated goal of WWF is to halt deforestation through the use of maps identifying priority habitat areas that are off-limits to RTRS members. There are crucial questions over these maps, however. First, even though soybeans are already being traded, the maps have yet to be drawn up. Secondly, the maps are to be drawn up by RTRS members themselves. Thirdly, RTRS maps can be periodically redrawn. Fourthly, RTRS members need not certify all of their production acreage. This means they can certify part of their acreage as "Responsible," but still sell (as "Irresponsible"?) soybeans from formerly virgin habitat. This means WWF's target for year 2020 of 25% coverage globally and 75% in WWF's "priority areas" would still allow 25% of the Brazilian soybean harvest to come from newly deforested land. And of course, the scheme cannot prevent non-members, or even non-certified subsidiaries, from specializing in deforestation.

These are certification schemes, therefore, with low standards, no methods of enforcement, and enormous loopholes. Pete Riley of UK GM Freeze dubs their instigator the "World Wide Fund for naïveté" and believes "the chances of Responsible soy saving the Cerrado are zero." Claire Robinson of Earth Open Source agrees: "The RTRS standard will not protect the forests and other sensitive ecosystems. Additionally, it greenwashes soy that's genetically modified to survive being sprayed with quantities of herbicide that endanger human health and the environment." There is even a website (www.toxicsoy.org) dedicated to exposing the greenwashing of GMO soy.

Many other groups apparently share that view. More than 250 large and small sustainable farming, social justice, and rainforest preservation groups from all over the world signed a "Letter of Critical Opposition to the RTRS" in 2009. Signatories included the Global Forest Coalition, Friends of the Earth, Food First, the British Soil Association and the World Development Movement.

Other commodity certifications involving WWF have also received strong criticism. The Mangrove Action Project in 2008 published a "Public Declaration Against the Process of Certification of Industrial Shrimp Aquaculture" while the World Rainforest Movement issued "Declaration against the Roundtable on Sustainable Palm Oil (RSPO)," signed by 256 organizations in October 2008.

What Really Drives Commodity Certification?

Commodity certification is in many ways a strange departure for conservation nonprofits. In the first place the big conservation nonprofits are more normally active in acquiring and researching wild habitats. Secondly, these are membership organizations, yet it is hard to envisage these schemes energizing the membership. How many members of the Nature Conservancy will be pleased to find that their organization has been working with Monsanto to promote GM crops as "Responsible"? Indeed, one can argue that these programs are being actively concealed from their members, donors, and the public. From their advertising, their websites, and their educational materials, one would presume that poachers, population growth and ignorance are the chief threats to wildlife in developing countries. It is not true, however, and as WWF's Jason Clay and the very existence of these certification schemes make clear, senior management knows it well.

In public, the conservation nonprofits justify market transformation as cooperative; they wish to work with others, not against them. However, they have chosen to work preferentially with powerful and wealthy corporations. Why not cooperate instead with small farmers' movements, indigenous groups, and already successful standards, such as fair-trade, organic and non-GMO? These are causes that could use the help of big international organizations. Why not, with WWF help, embed into organic standards a rainforest conservation element? Why not cooperate with your membership to create engaged consumer power against habitat destruction, monoculture, and industrial farming? Instead, the new "Responsible" and "Sustainable" standards threaten organic, fair-trade, and local food systems—which are some of the environmental movement's biggest successes.

One clue to the enthusiasm for "market transformation" may be that financial rewards are available. According to Nina Holland of Corporate Europe Observatory, certification is "now a core business" for WWF. Indeed, WWF and the Dutch nonprofit Solidaridad are currently receiving millions of euros from the Dutch government (under its Sustainable Trade Action Plan) to support these schemes. According to the plan, 67 million euros have already been committed, and similar amounts are promised.

The Threat From the Food Movement

Commodity-certification schemes like RTRS can be seen as an inability of global conservation leadership to work constructively with the ordinary people who live in and around wild areas of the globe; or they can be seen as a disregard for fair-trade and organic labels; or as a lost opportunity to inform and energize members and potential members as to the true causes of habitat destruction; or even as a cynical moneymaking scheme. These are all plausible explanations of the enthusiasm for certification schemes and probably each plays a part. None, however, explains why conservation nonprofits would sign up to schemes whose standards and credibility are so low. Especially when, as never before, agribusiness is under pressure to change its destructive social and environmental practices.

The context of these schemes is that we live at an historic moment. Positive alternatives to industrial agriculture, such as fair trade, organic agriculture, agro-ecology, and the System of Rice Intensification, have shown they can feed the planet, without destroying it, even with a greater population. Consequently, there is now a substantial international consensus of informed opinion that industrial agriculture is a principal cause of the current environmental crisis and the chief obstacle to hunger eradication.

This consensus is one of several roots of the international food movement. As a powerful synergism of sustainability, social-justice, sustainability, food-quality, and environmental concerns, the food movement is a clear threat to the long-term existence of the industrial food system. Incidentally, this is why big multinationals have been buying up ethical brands.

Under these circumstances, evading the blame for the environmental devastation of the Amazon, Asia, and elsewhere, undermining organic and other genuine certification schemes, and splitting the environmental movement must be a dream come true for members of the industrial food system. A true cynic might surmise that the food industry could hardly have engineered it better had they planned it themselves.

Who Runs Big Conservation?

To guard against such possibilities, nonprofits are required to have boards of directors whose primary legal function is to guard the mission of the organization and to protect its good name. In practice, for conservation nonprofits this means overseeing potential financial conflicts and preventing the organization from lending its name to greenwashing.

So, who are the individuals guarding the mission of global conservation nonprofits? U.S.-WWF boasts (literally) that its new vice-chair was the last CEO of Coca-Cola, Inc. (a member of Bonsucro) and that another board member is Charles O. Holliday Jr., the current chairman of the board of Bank of America, who was formerly CEO of DuPont (owner of Pioneer Hi-Bred International, a major player in the GMO industry). The current chair of the executive board at Conservation International is Robert Walton, better known as chair of the board of Wal-Mart (which now sells "sustainably sourced" food and owns the supermarket chain ASDA). The boards of WWF and Conservation International do have more than a sprinkling of members with conservation-related careers. But they are heavily outnumbered by business representatives. On the board of Conservation International, for example, are GAP, Intel, Northrop Grumman, JP Morgan, Starbucks, and UPS, among others.

The Nature Conservancy's board of directors has only two members (out of 22) who list an active affiliation to a conservation organization in their board CV (Prof. Gretchen Daly and Cristian Samper, head of the U.S. Museum of Natural History). Only one other member even mentions among his qualifications an interest in the subject of conservation. The remaining members are like Shona Brown, who is an employee of Google and a board member of Pepsico, or Meg Whitman, the current president and CEO of Hewlett-Packard, or Muneer A. Satter, a managing director of Goldman Sachs.

So, was market transformation developed with the support of these boards or against their wishes? The latter is hardly likely. The key question then becomes: Did these boards in fact instigate market transformation? Did it come from the very top?

Never Ending

Leaving aside whether conservation was ever their true intention, it seems highly unlikely that WWF and its fellow conservation groups will leverage a positive transformation of the food system by bestowing "Sustainable" and "Responsible" standards on agribusiness. Instead, it appears much more likely that, by undermining existing standards and offering worthless standards of their own, habitat destruction and human misery will only increase.

Market transformation, as envisaged by WWF, nevertheless might have worked. However, WWF neglected to consider that successful certification schemes start from the ground up. Organic and fair-trade began with a large base of committed farmers determined to fashion a better food system. Producers willingly signed up to high standards and clear requirements because they believed in them. Indeed, many already were practicing high standards without certification. But when big players in the food industry have tried to climb on board, game the system and manipulate standards, problems have resulted, even with credible standards like fair-trade and organic. At some point big players will probably undermine these standards. They seem already to be well on the way, but if they succeed their efforts will only have proved that certification standards can never be a substitute for trust, commitment and individual integrity.

The only good news in this story is that it contradicts fundamentally the defeatist arguments of the WWF. Old-fashioned activist strategies, of shaming bad practice, boycotting products, and encouraging alternatives, do work. The market opportunity presently being exploited by WWF and company resulted from the success of these strategies, not their failure. Multinational corporations, we should conclude, really do fear activists, non-profits, informed consumers, and small producers all working together. ❑

Sources: Jonathan A. Foley et al. "Solutions for a Cultivated Planet" *Nature*, October 2011 (Nature.com); Jason Clay, "Economics, Behavior and Biodiversity Loss: Sustainability as a Pre-competitive Issue," March 25, 2011 (youtube.com); Food and Agriculture Organization of the United Nations, "Scarcity and degradation of land and water: growing threat to food security," November 28, 2011 (fao.org); State of the World's Land and Water Resources for Food and Agriculture (SOLAW), November 28, 2011 (fao.org); Mat McDermott, "More Dirty Deforestation: 55% of Indonesia's Logging Illegal + Cargill's Two Hidden Palm Oil Plantations," May 6, 2010 (treehugger.com); Earth Open Source (earthopensource.org); United Nations (UN; un.org); Roundtable on Sustainable Palm Oil (RSPO; rspo.org); Round Table on Responsible Soy (RTRS; responsiblesoy.org); Roundtable on Sustainable Biofuels (rsb.epfl.ch); Bonsucro (Bonsucro.com); WWF, "Save the Cerrado: What's happening in the Cerrado?" (wwf.org. uk); Gary Langer, "Behind the Label, Many Skeptical of Bio-engineered Food," June 19, 2001 (abcnews.com); Round Table on Responsible Soy, "Why certifying under the RTST Standard?" (responsiblesoy.org); Natural Resources Defense Council, "Atrazine: Poisoning the Well," May 2010 (nrdc.org); The *Capital-Journal* Editorial Board, "Time for action on rural depopulation," July 28, 2011 (cjonline.com); "State of the World's Indigenous Peoples Report, Chapter 7: Emerging Issues," January 2010 (un.org); "A Brief History of Rubber" (rainforests.mongabay.com); "Letter of critical opposition to the Round Table on Responsible Soy," April 2009 (bangmfood. org); Global Forest Coalition (globalforestcoalition.org); Public Declaration Against the Process of Certification of Industrial Shrimp Aquaculture, November 3, 2008 (mangroveactionproject. org); World Rainforest Movement, "Declarations against the Roundtable on Sustainable Palm Oil (RSPO) in Defence of Human Rights, Food Sovereignty," September 2008 (wrm.org); System of Rice Intensification (SRI-Rice; sri.ciifad.cornell.edu); Sarah Hills, "Coca-Cola snaps up first Bonsucro certified sugarcane," June 22, 2011 (foodnavigator.com); "Wal-Mart Unveils Global Sustainable Agriculture Goal," October 14, 2010 (walmartstores.com); "Largest Corporate Dairy, Biotech Firm and USDA Accused of Conspiring to Corrupt Rulemaking and Pollute Organics," January 23, 2012 (cornucopia.org); Dutch Ministry of Agriculture, "Nature and Food Quality Sustainable Food: Public Summary of Policy Document" (government.nl); Jonathan Latham and Allison Wilson, "How the Science Media Failed the IAASTD," April 7, 2008 (independentsciencenews.org).

Article 4.6

A DIRTY JOB NO ONE SHOULD DO

A lawyer's self-serving defense of Wall Street pay doesn't add up.

BY JOHN MILLER
May/June 2011

WALL STREET LAWYER: DON'T BLAME PAY

Steve Eckhaus just wanted to get some deals done. He has negotiated hundreds of high-profile pay packages, some of which were met with scorn and scrutiny in Washington and beyond.

"I hate to say it, but I have friends who blame me for the financial crisis," says Mr. Eckhaus, who estimates he has negotiated well over $5 billion in banker pay over the years, including several $100 million pay deals.

"It was understandable why there was anger," says Mr. Eckhaus, but "the crisis was not caused by Wall Street fat cats." In general, he said his clients are "pure as the driven snow" and doing work that supports the economy and justifies their pay.

"There's nothing helpful or healing in the midst of a financial crisis to talk about Wall Street 'fat cats,' " added Mr. Eckhaus. "To blame Wall Street for the financial meltdown is absurd."

—Steve Eder, "Wall Street Lawyer: Don't Blame Pay," *Wall Street Journal*, February 5, 2011

Pure as the driven snow? How about as dirty as what remains of the Northeast's snow piles, covered with filth a month after record storms? Eckhaus and his fat-cat clients richly deserve the scorn that even his friends have heaped upon them. The pay packages Eckhaus negotiated are obscene. They cushioned financial fat cats from the often-disastrous consequences of their actions. And Eckhaus's protestations notwithstanding, the finance industry's compensation structures lie at the heart of the financial crisis. Banking execs and other key decision-makers all along the mortgage securitization process were induced to take excessive risks because of the way they were compensated.

Let's start with the first link in the process—the people who made the mortgage loans to homebuyers. It's standard practice to pay mortgage brokers based on the volume of loans they originate, not the performance or quality of those loans. And since the banks and mortgage companies who employ the brokers bundled up the loans and sold them off as mortgage-backed securities, they too had little interest in the quality of the loans.

The fees garnered by the financial-services industry from home mortgage lending and mortgage securitization were enormous, as much as $2 trillion in the six years from 2003 to 2008, according to estimates by economist James Crotty. That figure includes the fees paid to mortgage brokers as well as the fees collected by investment bankers who packaged the loans into securities, the fees paid to the ratings agencies who gave the securities their seal of approval, and the fees paid to yet others who serviced the securities. Those massive sums were paid out for short-term success even when the decisions those sums rewarded resulted in long-term losses or failures, a point Securities and Exchange Commission chair Mary Schapiro confirmed for the Financial Crisis Inquiry Commission, the ten-member panel appointed by Congress to examine the causes of the financial crisis.

That the compensation system has "no rhyme or reason" is the conclusion Andrew Cuomo, then attorney general of New York, reached in his 2009 report on compensation practices in the U.S. banking system. The record of Bank of America, for Cuomo, shows just how little compensation had to do with bank performance. In 2006, as the bank raked in profits during the housing bubble, it paid out $18 billion in compensation. In 2008, after the bubble had burst, Bank of America continued to make compensation payments at the $18 billion level—even as its net income plummeted from $14 billion to $4 billion. That fall Bank of America took over Merrill Lynch, which had just brought a new investment banking chief on board—Mr. Eckhaus's client Tom Montag—by guaranteeing him a $39.4 million bonus.

Those giant bonuses paid out to Wall Street high rollers provoked the ire of many, especially when they came from financial firms that received TARP (Troubled Asset Relief Program) bailout funds from the federal government, as was the case with Mr. Montag's millions. The Cuomo report pays special attention to the bonuses paid out by the original TARP recipients. For two of the nine, Citigroup and Merrill Lynch, the disconnect between the banks' earnings and executive bonuses was especially alarming. Together, these two corporations in 2008 lost $54 billion, paid out nearly $9 billion in bonuses, and then received TARP bailouts totaling $55 billion. At Merrill Lynch, 700 employees received bonuses in excess of $1 million in 2008. The top four recipients alone received a total of $121 million. Merrill's reported losses for 2007 and 2008, as Crotty points out, were enough to wipe out 11 years of earnings previously reported by the company.

The Cuomo report rails against this "heads I win, tails you lose" bonus culture. As Cuomo put it, when banks did well, executives and traders were showered with bonuses. When the banks lost money, taxpayers bailed them out, and bonuses and overall compensation remained sky-high.

The consequences of such a perverse compensation system are disastrous, as Crotty explains:

> It becomes rational for top financial firm operatives to take excessive risk in the bubble even if they understand that their decisions are likely to cause a crash in the intermediate future. Since they do not have to return their bubble-year bonuses when the inevitable crisis occurs and since they continue to receive substantial bonuses even in the crisis, they have a powerful incentive to pursue high-risk, high-leverage strategies.

So go ahead and blame Wall Street for the crisis. Not to would indeed be absurd. The bonuses Eckhaus's clients and others took home were the most deformed element of a compensation system that enabled the risk-taking that pushed the financial industry into crisis. Those bonus babies deserve your scorn. Throwing them out with their dirty bathwater, the whole compensation system, is the first step toward curbing the destructive behavior they helped to perpetuate. ❑

Sources: Steve Eder, "Wall Street Lawyer: Don't Blame Pay," Wall Street Journal, February 5, 2011; James Crotty, "The Bonus-Driven 'Rainmaker' Financial Firm," Political Economy Research Institute Working Paper 209, revised August 2010 (www.peri.umass.edu/236/hash/468a9ba021/ publication/386/); Andrew Cuomo, No Rhyme Or Reason: The Heads I Win, Tails You Lose Bank Bonus Culture, State of New York, 2009 (www.scribd.com/doc/17849813/Andrew-Cuomos-Bonus-Report); The Financial Crisis Inquiry Report: Final Report of the National Commission on the Causes of the Financial and Economic Crisis in the United States, January 2011 (www.fcic.gov/report).

Article 4.7

TURNING TOWARD SOLUTIONS
It's time to occupy and reorganize production.

BY RICHARD WOLFF
January/February 2012

Since last September, the 99% have been wielding the weapon of criticism against the 1%. They are effective because they act in a new, collective, and organized way. Occupy Wall Street (OWS) and its many offshoots expose basic truths and demand basic changes. They struggle peacefully to reach, inform, and mobilize public opinion. They keep winning huge numbers of hearts and minds. In reaction, the U.S. 1% copied their counterparts in Tunisia, Egypt, Syria, and Bahrain. They limited media access needed by the movement to reach its growing audience. That failed. Their police intimidated, but that failed. Democratic Party operatives tried to convert Occupiers into Obama enthusiasts for the 2012 election. That failed, too.

Then, the 99%'s weapon of criticism suffered the counter-criticism of weapons. The 1%—frequent preachers of non-violence to others—resorted to coordinated police violence in cities across the country. As elsewhere, to cover up its failure to win hearts and minds, the U.S. government resorted to violence. Chickens raised abroad returned home to roost. Internet images flashed of New York Police Department machines and personnel bulldozing the free library in Zuccotti Park. Many recalled the famous 1930s photographs of police burning the books of those the Nazis feared or hated and therefore demonized.

New York's newly renamed billionaire mayor—*Mubarak* Bloomberg—gave the order to "clear and clean" Zuccotti Park. Having presided over some of the world's filthiest subway tunnels and stations, Bloomberg suddenly became obsessed with cleanliness. In New York, where income distribution is even more unequal than in the nation as a whole, the 1% mayor tried to silence OWS criticisms of that inequality and its capitalist roots. As OWS matures into a national movement, will that lead to renaming the President—as *Mubarak* Obama?

The conditions causing OWS include deepening economic inequality, the money-eyed corruption of politics, and the collapsing fortunes and prospects of the mass of Americans. Neither Bloomberg nor Obama are changing them. The U.S. Census Bureau recalculated poverty last November (as requested and reported by the *New York Times,* November 19, 2011). The new calculation divided poverty into three types: "deep" (earning 50% or less of the official poverty level), "poor" (earning 50-100% of the poverty level) and "near poor" (earning 100-150% of the poverty level). The new calculation took into account regional cost of living differences, government benefits (transfer payments) and income lost to taxation, health care and work expenses.

The Census Bureau's conclusion: *one-third of the United States population was in or near poverty.* Over 100 million of our fellow citizens live at poverty levels hard to imagine, let alone endure. What this capitalist system delivers contradicts most Americans' notions of fairness, expectations of "middle-class" rewards for hard work, and hopes for their children. Business and political leaders had refused to see, debate, or change these conditions for decades. Most mainstream media and academics were similarly in denial. The system thus kept reproducing the causes of poverty (unemployment that precluded wage increases, "deficit reductions" that cut government transfer payments to the needy, foreclosures yielding more homeless people alongside more abandoned homes, etc.). The capitalist system became increasingly intolerable to increasing numbers of people. It produced a mass movement like OWS that shook and disrupted the national consensus on denial. Today, the criticism of weapons (police) risks losing to the weapon of criticism (OWS).

For the last half-century, it was taboo in the United States to criticize, debate, or propose changes to the economic system. We could question and alter our educational, transportation, health and other basic systems. However, Cold War anxieties and hysterical anti-communism dictated that the economic system be celebrated. Criticism of capitalism was branded as disloyalty to the United States. Journalists and academics followed the politicians in giving capitalism a free pass. Behind that celebratory veil, a protected capitalism performed ever more poorly for ever more people. As average real wages stopped rising since the 1970s, Americans borrowed more than they could sustain. As flat real wages and rising worker productivity made for huge profits, executives paid themselves astronomical salaries, stock options, and bonuses. Inequality has mushroomed since the 1970s and has contributed considerably to this crisis's depth and duration.

American capitalists took full advantage of their exemption from basic criticism. They widened the distance between employers and employees to produce a new "Gilded Age" now targeted by the 99% vs. 1% slogan. It is stunningly effective because it rings so true to most Americans.

The Occupy movement keeps developing and now turns increasingly toward finding solutions for the problems it exposed. One emerging perspective holds that the capitalist economic system itself is the problem and movement to another system is the solution. The goal is not to transition to traditional socialist alternatives (e.g., the old Soviet Union or modern China). Rather, these alternatives too seem flawed systems needing basic change.

The solution for them too is to reorganize production *from the ground up*. Wherever production of goods or services occurs, the workers there should collectively and democratically function as their own board of directors. An exploitative and conflicted capitalism (employer versus employee) should be abolished much as our ancestors abolished slavery (master versus slave) and feudalism (lord versus serf). The solution is a system of *workers' self-directed enterprises*—where those who do the work also design and direct it and distribute its fruits. The basic goal of democracy—that all those affected by any decision participate equally in making it—would finally arrive inside production itself. No longer would a tiny elite minority—major shareholders and the corporate boards of directors they choose—make all the basic decisions: what, how and where to produce and how to use the surpluses/profits. Instead, the workers themselves—in shared democratic partnership with the residential communities interdependent with their enterprises—would make all those decisions.

Only then could we avoid repeating capitalist cycles. Those begin when capital accumulation and competition generate a crisis. When sustained mass suffering follows, movements for reform arise and sometimes succeed. Capitalists use their profits to block reforms and, when unsuccessful, to undo the reforms. This sets the stage for the next period of accumulation and competition and the next crisis: the U.S. pattern since the 1929 crash.

To break such truly vicious cycles, we need now to transform capitalism by internally reorganizing enterprises. Then, those who most need and benefit from reforms would be the self-directed workers who dispose of as well as create the profits of enterprises. No separate class of employers will exist and use the profits to undo the reforms won by workers. Self-directing workers would pay taxes to a state only insofar as it secures those reforms. More basically, our best hope of ending history's legacy of 99% against 1% lies in establishing new enterprises where democratically self-directed workers would no longer distribute incomes in capitalism's grotesquely unequal ways.

Workers' self-directed enterprises are a solution to problems shared by both capitalism and socialism. Establishing workers' self-directed enterprises moves further in the modern democratic movement beyond monarchies and autocracies. Democratizing production in this way can finally take political democracy beyond being merely an electoral ritual facilitating the same old rule by the 1% over the 99%. ❑

Chapter 5

MARKET STRUCTURE AND MONOPOLY

INTRODUCTION

With monopoly, we finally encounter a situation in which most economists, orthodox and otherwise, agree that unfettered markets lead to an undesirable outcome. If a firm is able to create a monopoly, it faces a downward-sloping demand curve—that is to say, if it reduces output, it can charge a higher price. The monopolist has a profit incentive to restrict output in order to charge consumers that higher price. The result is a dead-weight loss—a loss to consumers that is not fully offset by the gains to the monopolist. Economists argue that competitive forces tend to undermine any monopoly, but failing this, they support antitrust policy as a backstop. The concept of monopoly not only points to an important failing of markets, but it opens the door to thinking about many possible market structures other than perfect competition, including oligopoly, in which a small group of producers dominate the market. This market domination is through the very "visible hand" of a firm having "market power" (Tilly Assumption No. #1—see Article 1.2), which is the ability of a firm to affect the market-wide level of prices, profits and wages. Market power alters how markets function from the ideal of perfect competition and delivers significantly less optimal results.

We begin this chapter with a seminal article by Chris Tilly, "Is Small Beautiful? Is Bigger Better? Small and Big Businesses Both Have Their Drawbacks" (Article 5.1). This article walks through the pluses and minuses of large and small businesses, and finds both wanting. Tilly also observes that in "real world" markets, firms typically display unique traits associated with both competitive and concentrated markets.

In "Drug Prices in Crisis: The Case Against Protectionism" (Article 5.2), Dean Baker describes how large pharmaceutical companies use monopoly power to wring extra profits from consumers, creating a variety of problems along the way. But there's a twist! The source of these monopolies' profits are intellectual property rights—in particular, patents, which standard economic analysis sees as necessary to provide the incentive to innovate. In the pharmaceutical business, significant public funding and resources go into the research and development of these new drugs, yet the property rights and profits are privatized. From this public stake in the drug

119

business, Baker offers a novel market-driven strategy for reducing the prices of pharmaceuticals using the market mechanism itself.

The current financial crisis has provided particularly egregious examples of what happens when we institute laissez-faire regulatory regimes, especially in the area of finance. In "A Brief History of Mergers and Antitrust Policy" (Article 5.3), Edward Herman provides a historical context for the discussion of this issue by reviewing the history of U.S. antitrust law. He also criticizes economists for justifying this hands-off policy toward big business mergers over the last few decades. With the repeal of the Glass-Steagall Act of 1933, banks rapidly transformed themselves from agents of finance to high-flying casinos, and corporations from risk-adverse, stable agents of production to speculative entities "too big to fail."

Dollars & Sense's "Dr. Dollar," Arthur MacEwan, answers a letter inquiring about the relevance of the concept of "monopoly capital" in the present day (Article 5.4). MacEwan finds that firm size and market concentration have continued to grow throughout the era of globalization and that large firms still exhibit extraordinary market power.

Completing the chapter is Rob Larson's piece, "Not Too Big Enough" (Article 5.5). This timely article explores the phenomenon of the "too big to fail" banks as an expression of "market power."

Discussion Questions

1) (Article 5.1) List the pros and cons of large and small businesses that Tilly discusses. How does this compare with the problems associated with market structure that your textbook mentions? Be sure to compare Tilly's list of small business flaws with what your textbook has to say about small business.

2) (Articles 5.1 and 5.2) Baker says that a company with a monopoly on a drug has "an enormous incentive to overstate the benefits and understate the risks." Tilly says that in the case of oligopoly, the incentive is for a business to pour huge amounts of money into advertising and other ways to make its brand stand out. Explain why even though both companies have an incentive to spin the truth about their products, the incentives are somewhat different in the cases of monopoly versus oligopoly.

3) (Article 5.2) Baker sharply criticizes the monopoly effects of the patent system. But others argue that patents are necessary for innovation—they give companies a monopoly for a limited time so that they can recoup their research investment. How should this clash be resolved? Should patents be granted in some industries but not others? If so, how should we encourage research in areas with no patent protection?

4) (Articles 5.1, 5.2, and 5.3) Tilly describes how corporations fund so-called "citizens'" (or, in the view of critics, "astroturf"—phony grassroots) groups to push policies that the corporations want. Baker says that giant drug companies fund scientists to prove that the companies' drugs work. Herman states that large

businesses hired economists to come up with theories demonstrating why huge businesses and mega-mergers can be beneficial (or at least not harmful). What are some likely results if corporations control "the marketplace of ideas?" What, if anything, should be done about it?

5) (Article 5.5) What does it mean to say a company is "too big to fail?" Does the sheer size of a company change the rules as to how that company operates in the economy? Reread the definition of "market power" in Article 1.2 (box); might that definition have to be expanded? If so, how?

6) (Article 5.5) What is "moral hazard?" How does this concept relate to "too big to fail?" Is the "freedom to fail" vital for "efficient" markets?

Article 5.1

IS SMALL BEAUTIFUL? IS BIG BETTER?
Small and big businesses both have their drawbacks.

BY CHRIS TILLY
July/August 1989, revised April 2002

Beginning in the late 1980s, the United States has experienced a small, but significant boom in small business. While big businesses have downsized, small enterprises have proliferated. Should we be glad? Absolutely, declare the advocates of small business. Competition makes small businesses entrepreneurial, innovative, and responsive to customers.

Not so fast, reply big business's boosters. Big corporations grew big because they were efficient, and tend to stay efficient because they are big—and thus able to invest in research and upgrading of technology and workforce skills.

But each side in this debate omits crucial drawbacks. Small may be beautiful for consumers, but it's often oppressive for workers. And while big businesses wield the power to advance technology, they also often wield the market power to bash competitors and soak consumers. In the end, the choices are quite limited.

Big and Small

Is the United States a nation of big businesses, or of small ones? There are two conventional ways to measure business size. One is simply to count the number of employees per firm. By this measure, small businesses (say, business establishments with less than 20 employees) make up the vast majority of businesses (Table 1). But they provide only a small fraction of the total number of jobs.

The other approach gauges market share—each firm's share of total sales in a given industry. Industries range between two extremes: what economists call "perfect competition" (many firms selling a standardized product, each too tiny to affect the market price) and monopoly (one business controls all sales in an industry). Economy-wide, as with employment, small businesses are most numerous, but control only a small slice of total sales. Sole proprietorships account for 73% of established businesses, far outnumbering corporations, which are 20% of the total (the remainder are partnerships). But corporations ring up a hefty 90% of all sales, leaving sole proprietors with only 6%. It takes a lot of mom and pop stores to equal General Motors' 1999 total of $177 billion in sales.

Industry by industry, the degree of competition varies widely. Economists consider an industry concentrated when its top four companies account for more than 40% of total sales in the industry (Table 2). At the high end of the spectrum are the cigarette, beer, and aircraft industries, where four firms account for the bulk of U.S. production.

No market comes close to meeting the textbook specifications for perfect competition, but one can still find industries in which a large number of producers compete for sales. The clothing and restaurant industries, for example, remain relatively competitive. Overall, about one-third of U.S. goods are manufactured in concentrated industries, about one fifth are made in competitive industries, and the rest fall somewhere in between.

Beating the Competition

Those who tout the benefits of small, competitive business make a broad range of claims on its behalf. In addition to keeping prices low, they say the quality of the product is constantly improving, as companies seek a competitive edge. The same desire, they claim, drives firms toward technological innovations, leading to productivity increases.

The real story is not so simple. Competition does indeed keep prices low. Believe it or not, clothing costs us less—in real terms—than it cost our parents. Between 1960 and 1999, while the overall price level and hourly wages both increased nearly sixfold, apparel prices didn't even triple. And small businesses excel at offering variety, whether it is the ethnic restaurants that dot cities or the custom machine-tool work offered by small shops. Furthermore, however powerful small business lobbies may be in Washington, they do not influence the legislative process as blatantly as do corporate giants.

TABLE 1: SMALL BUSINESS NATION?

Most businesses are small, but most employees work for big businesses

Company size (number of employees)	Percent of all firms	Percent of all workers
1–4	54%	6%
5–9	20%	8%
10–19	13%	11%
20–49	8%	16%
50–99	3%	13%
100–249	2%	16%
250–499	0.4%	10%
500–999	0.2%	7%
1,000 or more	0.1%	13%

Note: "Businesses" refers to establishments, meaning business locations.

Source: County Business Patterns, 1998.

TABLE 2: WHO COMPETES, WHO DOESN'T

Industry	Percent of sales by top four firms
Light truck and utility vehicle manufacturing	96%
Breweries	91%
Home center stores	91%
Breakfast cereal manufacturing	78%
General book stores	77%
Credit card issuing	77%
Lawn equipment manufacturing	62%
Cable providers	63%
Computer and software stores	51%
Sock manufacturing	30%
Hotels and motels (excl. casinos)	22%
Gas stations	9%
Real estate	4%
Bars	2%

Source: 2002 Economic Census.

But those low prices often have an ugly underside. Our sportswear is cheap in part because the garment industry increasingly subcontracts work to sweatshops—whether they be export assembly plants in Haiti paying dollar-a-day wages, or the "underground" Los Angeles stitcheries that employ immigrant women in virtual slavery. Struggling to maintain razor-thin profit margins, small businesses cut costs any way they can—which usually translates into low wages and onerous working conditions.

"There is a rule of survival for small business," Bill Ryan, president of Ryan Transfer Corporation, commented some years ago. "There are certain things you want to have [in paying workers] and certain things you can afford. You had better go with what you can afford." Bottom line, workers in companies employing 500 or more people enjoy average wages 30% higher than their counterparts in small businesses.

Part of this wage gap results from differences other than size—unionization, the education of the workforce, the particular jobs and industries involved. But University of Michigan economist Charles Brown and his colleagues controlled for all these differences and more, and still found a 10% premium for big business's employees. A note of caution, however: Other recent research indicates that this wage bonus is linked to long-term employment and job ladders. To the extent that corporations dissolve these long-term ties—as they seem to be rapidly doing—the pay advantage may dissolve as well.

Small business gurus make extravagant claims about small businesses' job-generation capacity. An oft-quoted 1987 report by consultant David Birch claimed that businesses with fewer than 20 employees create 88% of new jobs. The reality is more mundane: over the long run, businesses with 19 or fewer workers account for about one quarter of net new jobs. One reason why Birch's statistics are misleading is that new small businesses are created in great numbers, but they also fail at a high rate. The result is that the *net* gain in jobs is much smaller than the number created in business start-ups.

For companies in very competitive markets, the same "whip of competition" that keeps prices down undermines many of competition's other supposed benefits. The flurry of competition in the airline industry following deregulation, for example, hardly resulted in a higher quality product. Flying became temporarily cheaper, but also less comfortable, reliable, and safe.

Technological innovation from competition is also more myth than reality. Small firms in competitive industries do very little research and development. They lack both the cash needed to make long-term investments and the market power to guarantee a return on that investment. In fact, many of them can't even count on surviving to reap the rewards: only one-third to one-half of small business startups survive for five years, and only about one in five makes it to ten years. A 1988 Census Bureau survey concluded that in manufacturing, "technology use is positively correlated with plant size." Agriculture may be the exception that proves the rule. That highly competitive industry has made marked productivity gains, but its research is supported by the taxpayer, and its risks are reduced by government price supports.

Of course, the biggest myth about competition is that it is in any way a "natural state" for capitalism. In fact, in most markets the very process of competing for high profits or a bigger market share tends to create a concentrated, rather than a competitive, market structure. This process occurs in several ways. Big firms sometimes drive their smaller competitors out of business by selectively cutting prices to the bone. The smaller firms may lack the financial resources to last out the low prices. In the 1960s, several of IBM's smaller competitors sued it for cutting prices in a pattern that was designed to drive the smaller firms out of the market. Large corporations can also gain a lock on scarce resources: for example, large airlines like United and American operate the comprehensive, computerized information and reservation systems that travel agents tap into—and you can bet that each airline's system lists their own flights first. Or businesses may exploit an advantage in one market to dominate another, as Microsoft used its control of the computer operating system market to seize market share for its Internet browser.

Other firms eliminate competitors by buying them out—either in a hostile takeover or a friendly merger. Either way, a former competitor is neutralized. This strategy used to be severely limited by strict antitrust guidelines that prohibited most horizontal mergers—those between two firms that formerly competed in the same market. The Reagan administration's team at the Justice Department, however, loosened the merger guidelines significantly in the early 1980s. Since that time, many large mergers between former competitors have been allowed to go through, most notably in the airline industry.

The Power of Concentration

Concentration, then, is as natural to market economies as competition. And bigness, like smallness, is a mixed bag for us as consumers and workers. For workers, bigness is on the whole a plus. Whereas competition forces small businesses to be stingy, big firms are on average more generous, offering employees higher wages, greater job security, and more extensive fringe benefits. In 1993, 97% of businesses with 500 or more workers provided health insurance; only 43% of businesses with 25 or fewer employees did so. Large firms also provide much more employee training. The strongest unions, as well, have historically been in industries where a few firms control large shares of their markets, and can pass along increased costs to consumers—auto, steel, and tires, for example. When profits are threatened, though, firms in concentrated markets also have more resources with which to fight labor. They are better able to weather a strike, oppose unionization, and make agreements with rivals not to take advantage of each other's labor troubles. In addition, large companies, not surprisingly, score low on workplace autonomy.

What about consumers? Corporations in industries where there are few competitors may compete, but the competitive clash is seldom channeled into prolonged price wars. The soft drink industry is a classic example. David McFarland, a University of North Carolina economist, likens soft drink competition to professional wrestling. "They make a lot of sounds and groans and bounce on the mat, but they know who is going to win," he remarked.

Coke and Pepsi introduce new drinks and mount massive ad campaigns to win market share, but the net result is not lower prices. In fact, because competition between industry giants relies more on product differentiation than price, companies pass on their inflated advertising expenses to consumers. In the highly concentrated breakfast cereal market, the package frequently costs more than the contents. And of every dollar you pay for a box, nearly 20 cents goes for advertising.

It takes resources to develop and market a new idea, which gives large corporations distinct advantages in innovation. The original idea for the photocopier may have come from a patent lawyer who worked nights in his basement, but Xerox spent $16 million before it had a product it could sell. RCA invested $65 million developing the color television. RCA could take this gamble because its dominance in the television market ensured that it would not be immediately undercut by some other firm.

But market dominance can also translate into complacency. The steel industry illustrates the point. A few major producers earned steady profits through the 1950s and 1960s but were caught off-guard when new technologies vaulted foreign steel-makers to the top of the industry in the 1970s. Similarly, when IBM dominated the computer industry in the 1960s and early 1970s, innovation proceeded quite slowly, particularly compared to the frantic scramble in that industry today. With no competitors to worry about, it was more profitable for IBM to sit tight, since innovation would only have made its own machines obsolete.

And large corporations can also put their deep pockets and technical expertise to work to short-circuit public policy. In the 1980s, when Congress changed corporate liability laws to make corporate executives criminally liable for some kinds of offenses, General Electric's lobbyists and legal staff volunteered to help draft the final regulations, in order to minimize the damage.

Big businesses sometimes hide their lobbying behind a "citizen" smokescreen. The largest-spending lobby in Washington in 1986 was Citizens for the Control of Acid Rain. These good citizens had been organized by coal and electric utility companies to oppose tighter pollution controls. Along the same lines, the Coalition for Vehicle Choice (now, who could be against that?) was set up by Ford and General Motors in 1990 to fight higher fuel efficiency standards.

Concentration or Conglomeration

Over the last couple of decades, the mix of big and small businesses has changed, but the changes are small and—at first glance—contradictory. Over time, employment has shifted toward smaller firms, though the shift has been subtle, not revolutionary. Meanwhile, the overall level of industry-by-industry sales concentration in the economy has increased, but only slightly. As older industries become more concentrated, newer, more competitive ones crop up, leaving overall concentration relatively steady. In his book *Lean and Mean*, economist Bennett Harrison points out that there is actually no contradiction between the small business employment boomlet and big firms' continued grip on markets. Big businesses, it turns out, are orchestrating much of the flowering of small business, through a variety of outsourcing and subcontracting arrangements.

But if industry-by-industry concentration has changed little over the decades, conglomeration is a different matter. Corporate ownership of assets has become much more concentrated over time, reflecting the rise in conglomerates—corporations doing business in a variety of industries. Five decades ago, the top 200 manufacturing firms accounted for 48% of all sales in the U.S. economy. By 1993, the 200 biggest industrial businesses controlled 65% of sales.

Most mainstream economists see these groupings as irrelevant for the competitive structure of the economy. Antitrust laws place no restrictions on firms from different industries banding together under one corporate roof. But sheer size can easily affect competition in the markets of the individual firms involved. A parent company can use one especially profitable subsidiary to subsidize start-up costs for a new venture, giving it a competitive edge. And if one board of directors controls major interests in related industries, it can obviously influence any of those markets more forcefully.

A case in point is the mega-merger of Time Inc. and Warner, which will soon be joining with America Online. The resulting conglomerate will control massive sections of the home entertainment business, bringing together Time's journalists, film and television producers, and authors, Warner's entertainment machine, which includes Home Box Office, the nation's largest pay television channel, and AOL's huge share of the Internet access market. The conglomerate can influence the entertainment business from the initial point—the actors, writers, and directors—up to the point where the finished products appear on people's televisions or computers. Conglomeration also multiplies the political clout of large corportions. No wonder Disney and other entertainment giants have also hopped on the conglomeration bandwagon.

Choose your Poison

Competition, concentration, or conglomeration: The choice is an unsavory one indeed. Opting for lots of tiny, competing firms leaves labor squeezed and sacrifices the potential technological advantages that come with concentrated resources. Yet the big monopolies tend to dominate their markets, charge high prices, and waste countless resources on glitzy ad campaigns and trivial product differentiation. And the big conglomerate firms, while not necessarily dominant in any single market, wield a frightening amount of political and economic power, with budgets larger than those of most countries.

Of course, we don't have much to say about the choice, no matter how much "shopping for a better world" we engage in. Market competition rolls on—sometimes cutthroat, other times genteel. Industries often start out as monopolies (based on new inventions), go through a competitive phase, but end up concentrating as they mature. As long as bigness remains profitable and the government maintains a hands-off attitude, companies in both competitive and concentrated industries will tend to merge with firms in other industries. This will feed a continuing trend toward conglomeration. Since bigness and smallness both have their drawbacks, the best we can do is to use public policies to minimize the disadvantages of each. ❏

Resources: Lean and Mean: The Changing Landscape of Corporate Power in the Age of Flexibility, Bennett Harrison, 1994; *Employers Large and Small*, Charles Brown, James Hamilton, and James Medoff, 1990.

Article 5.2

DRUG PRICES IN CRISIS
The Case Against Protectionism

BY DEAN BAKER
May/June 2001

In recent years, drug prices have risen to astronomical levels. In the United States, senior citizens are increasingly unable to afford prescription medication, while in developing nations, life-saving drugs are being priced out of reach for tens of millions of people with AIDS. In both cases, there is a single explanation for soaring drug prices: patent protection. If the pharmaceutical industry's patent monopolies were eliminated, most drugs would sell for only a fraction of their current cost.

Remarkably, however, the issue of drug patent monopolies rarely arises in public debate. Patent protection is a form of protectionism, but that's problematic terminology in a political climate where support for "free trade" is considered the only respectable opinion. So the pharmaceutical industry has managed to frame patent protection as a matter of "intellectual property rights" instead. Rarely has an industry been so successful in controlling the language of debate.

The industry has had a lot of help from the economics profession. Mainstream economists have developed an extensive body of research on the expected consequences of protection or monopoly pricing. If they were really as committed to efficiency and free trade as they pretend to be, they would be screaming about drug patents at the top of their lungs. The reason they don't is that they hold the drug industry in much higher esteem than manufacturing workers who might benefit from other forms of protectionism.

Of course, patent protection for prescription drugs, like all forms of protectionism, does serve a purpose—to provide industry with an incentive to research new drugs. If any firm could produce and sell every new drug that was developed, then no company would ever have a reason to spend money on research. However, the fact that drug patents *can* provide an incentive for research does not mean that they are the only or best way to support research. In fact, most biomedical research is currently supported by the federal government or private foundations, charities, and universities—not undertaken by private companies in anticipation of future sales.

We can only assess the full costs of patent protection if we recognize it as a form of protectionism, and look for all of the distortions that economists would expect protectionism to create. Once we do that, we'll see that the benefits derived from state-sanctioned monopoly protection are not justified by the quality and quantity of research that the pharmaceutical industry undertakes.

The Economics of Protectionism

Patent monopolies are a windfall for the pharmaceutical industry. Under the present system, a single firm gets to control the sale of a drug for the duration of its patent. Evidence from countries without effective protection for patents, or for drug prices after patents expire, indicates that most drugs would only sell for 25% of their patent protected price. In some cases, the difference is much greater. For example, the current state-of-the-art combination of anti-viral AIDS drugs sells in the United States for approximately $10,000 a year, according to the pharmaceutical industry. By contrast, a leading Indian manufacturer of generic drugs believes that it can sell the same combination profitably for $350 per year.

Why the huge gap between the monopoly patent protected price and the competitive market price? Because most drugs are relatively cheap to produce. Drugs are expensive because the government gives the industry a monopoly, not because they cost a lot to manufacture.

The costs of patent protection to consumers are enormous. The industry, which includes such giants as GlaxoSmithKline, Pfizer, and Bristol-Myers Squibb, estimates that it sold $106 billion worth of drugs in 2000. If eliminating patent protection had reduced the price of these drugs by 75%, then consumers would have saved $79 billion. This figure, to put it in perspective, is 30% more than what the federal government spends on education each year. It's more than ten times the amount that the federal government spends on Head Start. And it roughly equals the nation's annual bill for foreign oil.

What do we get for this money? Last year, the pharmaceutical industry, according to its own figures, spent $22.5 billion on domestic drug research (and another $4 billion on research elsewhere). For tax purposes, the industry claimed research expenditures of just $16 billion. Since these expenditures qualify for a 20% tax credit, the federal government directly covered $3.2 billion of the industry's research spending (20% of the $16 billion reported on tax returns). Even if we accept the $22.5 billion figure as accurate, this still means that the industry, after deducting the government contribution, spent just over $19 billion of its own money on drug research.

In other words, consumers (and the government, through Medicaid and other programs) spent an extra $79 billion on drugs because of patent protection, in order to get the industry to spend $19 billion of its own money on research. This comes out to more than four dollars in additional spending on drugs for every dollar that the industry spent on research. The rest of the money went mainly to:

- *Marketing*: The industry spends tens of billions each year to convince us (or our doctors) that its new drugs are absolutely essential and completely harmless.
- *Protecting patent monopolies*: Pharmaceutical companies regularly stand near the top in contributing to political campaigns. It's no accident that so many politicians are willing to push their cause.
- *Profits*: The pharmaceutical industry consistently ranks at the top in return on investment. It pulled in more than $20 billion in profits for 1999.

If spending an extra four dollars on drugs in order to persuade the industry to spend one dollar on research doesn't sound like a good deal, don't worry. It gets worse.

The Inefficiencies of Protectionism

Mainstream economists, who usually love to recite the evils of government protection, have been mostly silent on the issue of patent protection for drugs. But the evils are visible for all to see.

One major source of waste is research spending on imitation or "copycat" drugs. When a company gets a big hit with a new drug like Viagra or Claritin, its competitors will try to patent comparable drugs in order to get a slice of the market. In a world with patent protection, this can be quite beneficial to consumers, since a second drug creates some market competition. However, in the absence of patent protection, the incentive for copycat research would be unnecessary, since anyone who wanted to produce Viagra or Claritin would be free to do so, thereby pushing prices down.

How much do drug companies spend on copycat research? The industry won't say. But the Food and Drug Administration (FDA), in evaluating "new" drugs, considers only one third of them to be qualitatively new or better than existing drugs, while classifying the other two thirds as comparable to existing drugs. This doesn't mean that two thirds of research spending goes to copycat drugs; after all, the breakthrough drugs probably require more research spending, on average, than copycats. But suppose the industry wasted just 20% of its $19 billion in research spending on copycat drugs. This would bring the value of that spending down to $15 billion. That means consumers and the government are paying more than five dollars on drugs for each dollar of useful research.

The evils of protectionism don't end there. Prescription drugs present a classic case of asymmetric information: The drug companies know more about their drugs than the doctors who prescribe them, and far more than the patients who take them. The lure of monopoly profits gives the industry an enormous incentive to overstate the benefits and understate the risks of the newest wonder drugs. A June 2000 *New England Journal of Medicine* study found that the media consistently offered glowing accounts of drug breakthroughs. According to the study, the main villains in distorting the news were the public-relations departments of the drug manufacturers.

Still more serious is evidence that published research findings may be influenced by the drug industry's support. Last summer, the *New York Times* cited data showing that drugs, when tested by researchers who were supported by the drug's manufacturer, were found to be significantly more effective than existing drugs 89% of the time. By contrast, drugs tested by neutral researchers were found to be significantly more effective only 61% of the time.

Even if the industry's research could be completely trusted, there is still another problem created by the patent system—secrecy. The industry generally maintains the right to control the dissemination of findings from the research it supports. In some cases, this can mean a delay of months or even years before a researcher can disclose her findings at a conference or in a journal. In April 1996, for example, the *Wall Street Journal* reported on a British drug company's efforts to suppress a study showing that Synthroid, a drug to control thyroid problems, was no more effective than much cheaper alternatives.

In other cases, the secrecy is even more extreme. When the industry funds studies designed to prove that drugs are safe and effective enough to win FDA approval, it routinely keeps the results secret as proprietary information. This research may contain important clues about how best to use the new drug, or even about other factors affecting patients' health. Generally, however, the scientific community will not have access to it.

By creating incentives to misrepresent, falsify, or conceal research findings, patent monopolies are harmful to our pocketbooks as well as our health. At the very least, consumers may waste money on new, patent-protected drugs that are no more effective than existing drugs whose patents have expired. For example, a recent study estimated that consumers were spending $6 billion a year on a patented medication for patients with heart disease, which was no more effective than generic alternatives in preventing heart problems. As a result of industry propaganda, consumers might also spend money on drugs that could be less effective than cheaper alternatives—or on drugs that could even be hazardous to their health.

Another byproduct of monopoly drug pricing—the underground market—also has detrimental effects. When drugs can be sold profitably at prices that are much lower than their patent protected prices, consumers may seek underground sources for drugs. The most obvious way to do this is to purchase drugs in countries that either impose price controls or don't have the same patent protection as the United States. In recent years, there has been a much-publicized flow of senior citizens to Canada and Mexico in search of lower cost drugs. In the case of people traveling to Canada, the major cost to consumers is the waste of their time. However, when people buy drugs in countries with less stringent safety regulations, the health consequences may be severe.

The Proven Alternative

Listing the problems associated with drug patents would be an empty intellectual exercise—unless there were alternative ways to support research. Fortunately, there are. The federal government currently supports $18 billion a year in biomedical research through the National Institutes of Health (NIH) and the Centers for Disease Control (CDC). (The vast majority of NIH-funded research is carried out at universities and research centers across the country; less than 20% is conducted on the campus of the Institutes themselves.) In addition, universities, private foundations, and charities fund a combined total of approximately $10 billion worth of research annually. Added together, these institutions spend 25% more on research than the pharmaceutical industry claims to spend, and nearly twice as much as the industry reports on tax returns.

Over the years, the research supported by government and non-profit institutions has led to numerous medical breakthroughs, including the discovery and development of penicillin and the polio vaccine. More recently, NIH-supported research has played a central role in developing AZT as an AIDS drug, and in developing Taxol, a leading cancer drug. The NIH's impressive list of accomplishments over the last five decades proves that the government can support effective research.

Traditionally, the NIH has focused on basic research and early phases of drug testing, while the pharmaceutical industry has engaged primarily in the later phases of drug testing—which include conducting clinical trials and carrying drugs through the FDA approval process. However, there is not a sharp division between the type of research done by the NIH and that undertaken by the pharmaceutical industry; the NIH has conducted research in all areas of drug development. There is no reason to believe that, given enough funding, the NIH could not effectively carry out all phases of drug research.

While the idea of a panel of government-supported scientists (most of whom would probably be affiliated with universities and other research institutions) deciding which drugs should be researched may seem scary, consider the current situation. Drug-company executives make their research decisions based on their assessment of a drug's profitability. In turn, that assessment depends on whether the company can get insurance companies to pay for the drug, whether it can effectively lobby legislators to have Medicaid and other government programs pay for it, and whether it can count on the courts to fully enforce its patents against competitors. It is these factors—not consideration of what will benefit the public's health—that dominate the industry's decisions about research. It is hard to believe that publicly accountable bodies that are charged with directing research for the general good would not produce better results.

The arithmetic behind a proposed switch is straightforward. If the federal government spent an additional $20 billion a year to support research at the NIH and various non-profit and educational institutions, it would more than fully replace the useful research conducted by the pharmaceutical industry. The cost to the federal government would be less than the cost of the prescription drug plan that Al Gore advocated in last year's presidential campaign. If patent protection for drugs were eliminated, consumers would save more than $79 billion a year. These savings would increase with each passing year, since spending on drugs is currently rising at more than twice the rate of inflation.

Even assuming that the United States continues to rely on patent protection to support drug research for the immediate future, interim steps can be taken. First, it will be important to sharply restrict the worst abuses of the patent system. At the top of the list, the U.S. government should not be working with the pharmaceutical

THE USES OF DRUG MONEY

Drug Company Revenues, Profits, and Spending, 1999

Company	($ millions) Revenues	Profits (as % of revenue)	Mrktg Costs (as % of revenue)	R&D (as % of revenue)
Merck	$32,714	18.0%	15.9%	6.3%
Pfizer	$16,204	19.6%	39.2%	17.1%
Eli Lilly	$10,003	27.2%	27.6%	17.8%
Schering-Plough	$9,176	23.0%	37.4%	13.0%
Pharmacia & Upjohn	$7,253	11.1%	38.6%	19.8%

Source: Families USA

industry to impose its patents on developing countries. This is especially important in the case of AIDS drugs, since patent protection in sub-Saharan Africa may effectively be sentencing tens of million of people to death. There should also be pressure to allow the importation of drugs from nations where they are sold at lower prices, or even better, the imposition of domestic price controls.

A second priority is to create a greater opening for alternative sources of research. There should be more support for the NIH to carry some of its research through to the actual testing and approval of new drugs. The patents for these drugs should then be placed in the public domain, so that the industry can compete to supply the drugs at the lowest cost. In addition to bringing immediate benefits to consumers, this would allow for a clear test of the patent system's value as a means of supporting research, as compared with direct public support.

Back in the Middle Ages, the guild system was established to protect the secrets of masters from their apprentices. If you tried to make and sell hats but didn't belong to the hatmakers' guild, you'd be subject to arrest. Patents (and their cousin, copyrights) come out of this tradition. While most medieval restrictions have long since been discarded, patents have managed to survive and are now deeply enmeshed in our economic system. Not all forms of patent protection cause the problems associated with drug patents; in some areas, such as industrial processes, it may be reasonable to keep patent protection intact. But the case of drug patents cries out for the free market that economics say they favor, to wipe this feudal relic away. ❏

Sources: Annals of Thoracic Surgery (September 2000): 883-888; *Wall Street Journal,* 25 April 1996, p. A1; Pharmaceutical Research and Manufacturers of America <www.phrma.org>; Families USA (familiesusa.org).

Article 5.3

A BRIEF HISTORY OF MERGERS AND ANTITRUST POLICY

BY EDWARD HERMAN
May/June 1998

Government efforts to prevent or break up monopolies are called antitrust policy. They assume that when a few companies dominate an industry, this weakens competition and hurts the public by reducing production, raising prices, and slowing technical advance. Antitrust has gone through cycles during this century. In some years, strongly pro-business presidencies (usually Republican) have allowed businesses to merge at will. These have often been followed by "reform" administrations, which tend to restrain, but not to reverse, concentrations of corporate power.

The federal government first took on a strong antitrust role with the Sherman Act of 1890, which outlawed monopoly and efforts to obtain it. In 1914 the Clayton Act also put restrictions on stock purchases and interlocking directorates that would reduce competition. This legislation responded to public anger and fears about "trusts," which brought separate firms under common control. Most notorious were Rockefeller's Standard Oil Trust and James Duke's American Tobacco Company, which employed ruthless tactics to drive their competitors out of business.

Early on the antitrust laws also treated organized labor as a "monopoly," and were used in breaking the Pullman strike in 1892. In 1908, the Supreme Court awarded damages to an employer against whom unions had organized a secondary boycott. This led to the Clayton Act exempting unions from its restrictions.

Otherwise, the federal government only minimally enforced the Sherman Act until Theodore Roosevelt was elected in 1900. Then in 1911 the Supreme Court decided that both the Standard Oil and American Tobacco trusts were "bad trusts," and ordered their dismantling. But in 1920 the Court refused to condemn the U.S. Steel consolidation, because it was a "good trust" that didn't attack its smaller rivals. This began a long period when the Antitrust Division and the courts approved mergers that produced industries with a few dominant firms, but which were "well-behaved." And in the 1920s, Republicans virtually ended antitrust enforcement.

The Golden Age

Franklin Roosevelt revived antitrust during 1938 to 1941, and antitrust law had its golden age from 1945 to 1974, fueled by a liberal Supreme Court, anti-merger legislation passed in 1950, and mildly progressive enforcement (though less so in the Republican years). During this period Alcoa's monopoly over aluminum production was broken (1945), and the Court found the tobacco industry guilty of "group monopoly" (1946), although the companies were only assessed a modest fine.

During the 1960s, when antitrust law blocked mergers among companies in the same industry, businesses adapted by acquiring firms in unrelated industries. Many such "conglomerate" mergers took place during 1964-68, when Lyndon Johnson was president. Companies like International Telephone and Telegraph, Ling-Temco-Vought, Gulf & Western, Tenneco, and Litton Industries grew rapidly.

The Reagan-Bush Collapse

Antitrust policy went into recession around 1974, then plunged during the presidencies of Ronald Reagan and George H. W. Bush. They aggressively dismantled antitrust, imposing drastic cuts in budgets and manpower, installing officials hostile to the antitrust mission, and failing to enforce the laws. During 1981-89, the Antitrust Division of the Justice Dept. challenged only 16 of over 16,000 pre-merger notices filed with them.

Despite his high-profile contest with Microsoft, Bill Clinton largely accepted the conservative view that most mergers are harmless. During his two terms, federal authorities approved or ignored many giant mergers. These included Westinghouse's buyout of CBS, the joining of "Baby Bells" Bell Atlantic and Nynex, and the combination of Chemical Bank and Manufacturers Hanover. During 1997 alone, 156 mergers of $1 billion or more, and merger transactions totalling more than *$1 trillion*, passed antitrust muster.

Clinton's failure to attack giant mergers rests nominally on the alleged efficiency of large firms and the belief that globalized markets make for competition. FTC head Robert Pitofsky said, "this is an astonishing merger wave," but not to worry because these deals "should be judged on a global market scale, not just on national and local markets."

But the efficiency of large size—as opposed to the profit-making advantages that corporations gain from market power and cross-selling (pushing products through other divisions of the same company)—is eminently debatable. And many markets are not global—hospitals, for example, operate in local markets, yet only some 20 of 3,000 hospital mergers have been subjected to antitrust challenge. Even in global markets a few firms are often dominant, and a vast array of linkages such as joint ventures and licensing agreements increasingly mute global competition.

The Clinton administration's failure to contest many giant mergers did not rest only on intellectual arguments. It also reflected political weakness and an unwillingness to oppose powerful people who fund elections and own or dominate the media. This was conspicuously true of the great media combinations—Disney and Cap-Cities/ABC, and TimeWarner and Turner—and the merger of Boeing and McDonnell-Douglas, which involved institutions of enormous power, whose mergers the stock market greeted enthusiastically.

The Economists Sell Out

Since the early 1970s, powerful people and corporations have funded not only elections but conservative economists, who are frequently housed in think-tanks such as the American Enterprise, Hoover, and Cato Institutes, and serve as corporate consultants in regulatory and anti-trust cases. Most notable in hiring economic consultants have been AT&T and IBM, which together spent hundreds of millions of dollars on their antitrust defenses. AT&T hired some 30 economists from five leading economics departments during the 1970s and early 1980s.

Out of these investments came models and theories downgrading the "populist" idea that numerous sellers and decentralization were important for effective competition (and essential to a democratic society). They claimed instead that the market can do it all, and that regulation and antitrust actions are misconceived. First, theorists showed that efficiency gains from mergers might reduce prices even more than monopoly power would cause them to rise. Economists also stressed "entry," claiming that if mergers did not improve efficiency any price increases would be wiped out eventually by new companies entering the industry. Entry is also the heart of the theory of "contestable markets," developed by economic consultants to AT&T, who argued that the ease of entry in cases where resources (trucks, aircraft) can be shifted quickly at low cost, makes for effective competition.

Then there is the theory of a "market for corporate control," in which mergers allow better managers to displace the less efficient. In this view, poorly-managed firms have low stock prices, making them easy to buy. Finally, many economists justified conglomerate mergers on three grounds: that they function as "mini capital markets," with top managers allocating capital between divisions of a single firm so as to maximize efficiency; that they reduce transaction costs; and that they are a means of diversifying risk.

These theories, many coming out of the "Chicago School" (the economics department at the University of Chicago), suffer from over-simplification, a strong infusion of ideology, and lack of empirical support. Mergers often are motivated by factors other than enhancing efficiency—such as the desire for monopoly power, empire building, cutting taxes, improving stock values, and even as a cover for poor management (such as when the badly-run U.S. Steel bought control of Marathon Oil).

Several researchers have questioned the supposed benefits of mergers. In theory, a merger that improves efficiency should increase profits. But one study by Dennis Mueller, and another by F. W. Scherer and David Ravenscraft, showed that mergers more often than not have reduced returns to stockholders. A study by Michael Porter of Harvard University demonstrated that a staggering 74% of the conglomerate acquisitions of the 1960s were eventually sold off (divested)—a good indication that they were never based on improving efficiency. William Shepherd of the University of Massachusetts investigated the "contestable markets" model, finding that it is a hypothetical case with minimal applicability to the real world.

Despite their inadequacies, the new apologetic theories have profoundly affected policy, because they provide an intellectual rationale for the agenda of the powerful. ❑

Sources: "Competition Policy in America: The Anti-Antitrust Paradox," James Brock, *Antitrust Bulletin*, Summer 1997; "The Promotional-Financial Dynamic of Merger Movements: A Historical Perspective," Richard DuBoff and Edward Herman, *Journal of Economic Issues*, March 1989; "Antimerger Policy in the United States: History and Lessons," Dennis C. Mueller, *Empirica*, 1996; "Dim Prospects: effective competition in telecommunications, railroads and electricity," William Shepherd, *Antitrust Bulletin*, 1997.

Article 5.4

MONOPOLY CAPITAL AND GLOBAL COMPETITION

BY ARTHUR MACEWAN
September/October 2011

Dear Dr. Dollar:
Is the concept of monopoly capital relevant today, considering such things as global competition?
—Paul Tracy, Oceanside, Calif.

In 1960, the largest 100 firms on *Fortune* magazine's "annual ranking of America's largest corporations" accounted for 15% of corporate profits and had revenues that were 24% as large as GDP. By the early 2000s, each of these figures had roughly doubled: the top 100 firms accounted for about 30% of corporate profits and their revenues were over 40% as large as GDP.*

The banking industry is a prime example of what has been going on: In 2007 the top ten banks were holding over 50% of industry assets, compared with about 25% in 1985.

If by "monopoly capital" we mean that a relatively small number of huge firms play a disproportionately large role in our economic lives, then monopoly capital is a relevant concept today, even more so than a few decades ago.

Global competition has certainly played a role in reshaping aspects of the economy, but it has not altered the importance of very large firms. Even while, for example, Toyota and Honda have gained a substantial share of the U.S. and world auto markets, this does not change the fact that a small number of firms dominate the U.S. and world markets. Moreover, much of the rise in imports, which looks like competition, is not competition for the large U.S. firms themselves. General Motors, for example, has established parts suppliers in Mexico, allowing the company to pay lower wages and hire fewer workers in the states. And Wal-Mart, Target, and other large retailers obtain low-cost goods from subcontractors in China and elsewhere.

Economics textbooks tell us that in markets dominated by a few large firms, prices will be higher than would otherwise be the case. This has generally been true of the auto industry. Also, this appears to be the case in pharmaceuticals, telecommunications, and several other industries.

Wal-Mart and other "big box" stores, however, often do compete by offering very low prices. They are monopsonistic (few buyers) as well as monopolistic (few sellers). They use their power to force down both their payments to suppliers and the wages of their workers. In either case—high prices or low prices—large firms are exercising their market power to shift income to themselves from the rest of us.

Beyond their operation within markets, the very large firms shift income to themselves by shaping markets. Advertising is important in this regard, including, for example, the way pharmaceutical firms effectively create "needs" in pushing their products. Then there is the power of large firms in the political sphere. General

Electric, for example, maintains huge legal and lobbying departments that are able to affect and use tax laws to reduce the firm's tax liability to virtually nothing. Or consider the success of the large banks in shaping (or eliminating) financial regulation, or the accomplishments of the huge oil companies and the military contractors that establish government policies, sometimes as direct subsidies, and thus raise their profits. And the list goes on.

None of this is to say that everything was fine in earlier decades when large firms were less dominant. Yet, as monopoly capital has become more entrenched, it has generated increasingly negative outcomes for the rest of us. Most obvious are the stagnant wages and rising income inequality of recent years. The power of the large firms (e.g., Wal-Mart) to hold down wages is an important part of the story. Then there is the current crisis of the U.S. economy—directly a result of the way the very large financial firms were able to shape their industry (deregulation). Large firms in general have been prime movers over recent decades in generating deregulation and the free-market ideology that supports deregulation.

So, yes, monopoly capital is still quite relevant. Globalization does make differences in our lives, but globalization has in large part been constructed under the influence and in the interest of the very large firms. In many ways globalization makes the concept of monopoly capital even more relevant. ❑

* The profits of the top 100 firms (ranked by revenue) were quite low in 2010, back near the same 15% of total profits as in 1960, because of huge losses connected to the financial crisis incurred by some of the largest firms. Fannie Mae, Freddie Mac, and AIG accounted for combined losses of over $100 billion. Also, the revenues of all firms are not the same as GDP; much of the former is sales of intermediate products, but only sales of final products are included in GDP. Thus, the largest firms' revenues, while 40% as large as GDP, do not constitute 40% of GDP.

Article 5.5

NOT TOO BIG ENOUGH
Where the big banks come from.

BY ROB LARSON
April 2010

The government bailout of America's biggest banks set off a tornado of public anger and confusion. When the House of Representatives initially rejected the bailout bill, the *Wall Street Journal* attributed it to "populist fury," and since then the public has remained stubbornly resentful over the bailout of those banks considered "too big to fail." Now, the heads of economic policy are trying to gracefully distance themselves from bailouts, claiming that future large-scale bank failures will be avoided by stronger regulation and higher insurance premiums.

Dealing with the collapse of these "systemically important banks" is a difficult policy issue, but the less-discussed issue is how the banking industry came to this point. If the collapse of just one of our $100 billion megabanks, Lehman Brothers, was enough to touch off an intense contraction in the supply of essential credit, we must know how some banks became "too big to fail" in the first place. The answer lies in certain incentives for bank growth, which after the loosening of crucial industry regulations drove the enormous waves of bank mergers in the last thirty years.

Geographical Growth

Prior to the 1980s, American commercial banking was a small-scale affair. State-chartered banks were prohibited by state laws from running branches outside their home state, or sometimes even outside their home county. Nationally chartered banks were likewise limited, and federal law allowed interstate acquisitions only if a state legislature specifically decided to permit out-of-state banks to purchase local branches. No states allowed such acquisition until 1975, when Maine and other states began passing legislation allowing at least some interstate banking. The trend was capped in 1994 by the Riegle-Neal Act, which removed the remaining restrictions on interstate branching and allowed direct cross-state banking mergers.

This geographic deregulation allowed commercial banks to make extensive acquisitions, in state and out. When Wells Fargo acquired another large California bank, Crocker National, in 1986 it was the largest bank merger in U.S. history. Since "the regulatory light was green," a single banking company could now operate across the uniquely large U.S. market, opening up enormous new opportunities for economies of scale in the banking industry.

Economies of scale are savings that companies enjoy when they grow larger and produce more output. The situation is similar to a cook preparing a batch of cookies for a Christmas party, and then preparing a batch for New Year's while all the ingredients and materials are already out. Producing more output (cookies) in one afternoon is more efficient than taking everything out again later to make the New Year's batch separately. In enterprise, this corresponds to spreading the large costs of startup investment over more and more output, and is often thought of as lower per-unit costs as the level of production increases. In other words, there's less effort per cookie if you make them all at once. Economies of scale, when present in an industry, create a strong incentive for firms to grow larger, since profitability will improve. But they also give larger, established firms a valuable cost advantage over new competitors, which can put the brakes on competition.

Once unleashed by the policy changes, these economies of scale played a major role in the industry's seemingly endless merger activity. "In order to compete, you need scale," said a VP for Chemical Bank when buying a smaller bank in 1994. Of course, in 1996 Chemical would itself merge with Chase Manhattan Bank.

Economies of Scale in Banking and Finance

Economies of scale are savings that companies benefit from as they grow larger and produce more output. While common in many industries, in banking and finance, these economies drove bank growth after industry deregulation in the 1980s and 90s. Some of the major scale economies in banking are:

- **Spreading investment over more output.** With the growth in importance of large-scale computing power and sophisticated systems management, the costs of setting up a modern banking system are very large. However, as a firm grows it can "spread out" the cost of that initial investment over more product, so that its cost per unit decreases as more output is produced.

- **Consolidation of functions.** The modern workforce is no stranger to the mass firings of "redundant" staff after mergers and acquisitions. If one firm's payroll staff and computer systems can handle twice the employees with little additional expense, an acquired bank may see its payroll department harvest pink slips while the firm's profitability improves. When Citicorp merged with the insurance giant Travelers Group in 1998, the resulting corporation laid off over 10,000 workers—representing 6% of the combined company's total workforce and over $500 million in reduced costs for Citigroup. This practice can be especially lucrative in a country like the United States, with a fairly unregulated labor market where firms are quite free to fire. Despite the economic peril inflicted on workers and their families, this consolidation is key to increasing company efficiency post-merger. Beyond back-office functions, core profit operations may also benefit from consolidation. When Bank of America combined its managed mutual funds into a single fund, it experienced lower total costs, thanks to trimming overhead from audit and prospectus mailing expenses. Consolidating office departments in this fashion can yield savings of 40% of the cost base of the acquired bank.

- **Funding mix.** The "funding mix" used by banks refers to where banks get the capital they then package into loans. Smaller institutions, having only limited deposits from savers, must "purchase funds" by borrowing from other institutions. This increases the funding cost of loans for banks, but larger banks will naturally have access to larger pools of deposits from which to arrange loans. This funding cost advantage for larger banks relative to smaller ones represents another economy of scale.

- **Advertising.** The nature of advertising requires a certain scale of operation to be viable. Advertising can reach large numbers of potential customers, but if a firm is small or local, many of those customers will be too far afield to act on the marketing. Large firm size, and especially geographic reach, can make the returns on ad time worth the investment.

Spreading big investment costs over more output is the main source of generic economies of scale, and in banking, the large initial investments are in sophisticated computer systems. The cost of investing in new computer hardware and systems development is now recognized as a major investment obstacle for new banks, although once installed by banks large enough to afford them, they are highly profitable. The *Financial Times* describes how "the development of bulk computer processing and of electronic data transmission…has allowed banks to move their back office operations away from individual branches to large remote centers. This had helped to bring real economies of scale to banking, an industry which traditionally has seen diseconomies set in at a very modest scale."

Economies of scale are common in manufacturing, and in the wake of deregulation the banking industry was also able to exploit a number of them. Besides spreading out the cost of computer systems, economies of scale may be present in office consolidation, in the funding mix used by banks, and in advertising (see sidebar).

Industry-to-Industry Growth

BusinessWeek's analysis is that the banking industry "has produced large competitors that can take advantage of economies of scale…as regulatory barriers to interstate banking fell," although not until the banks could "digest their purchases." The 1990s saw hundreds of bank purchases annually and hundreds of billions in acquired assets.

But an additional major turn for the industry came with the Gramm-Leach-Bliley Act of 1999 (GLB), which further loosened restrictions on bank growth, this time not geographically but industry-to-industry. After earlier moves in this direction by the Federal Reserve, GLB allowed for the free combination of commercial banking, insurance, and the riskier field of investment banking. These had been separated by law for decades, on the grounds that the availability of commercial credit was too important to the overall economy to be tied to the volatile world of investment banking.

GLB allowed firms to grow further, through banks merging with insurers or investment banks. The world of commercial credit was widened, and financial mergers this time exploited economies of scope—where production of multiple products jointly is cheaper than producing them individually. As commercial banks, investment banks, and insurers have expanded into each others' fields in the wake of GLB, their different lines of business can benefit from single expenses—for example, banks perform research on loan recipients that can also be used to underwrite bond issues. Scope economies such as these allow the larger banks to both run a greater profit on a per-service basis and attract more business. Thanks to the convenience of "one stop shopping," Citigroup now does more business with big corporations, like IT giant Unisys, than its component firms did pre-merger.

Exploiting economies of scope to diversify product lines in this fashion can also help a firm by reducing its dependence on any one line of business. Bank of America weathered the stock market downturn of 2001 in part because its corporate debt underwriting business was booming. Smaller, more specialized banks can become "one-trick ponies" as the *Wall Street Journal* put it—outdone by larger competitors with low-cost diversification thanks to scope economies.

These economies of scope are parallel to the scale economies, since both required deregulatory policy changes to be unleashed. Traditionally, banking wasn't seen as an industry with the strong economies of scale seen in, say, manufacturing. But the deregulation and computerization of the industry have allowed these firms to realize returns to greater scale and wider scope, and this has been a main driver of the endless acquisitions in the industry in recent decades.

Market Power

The enormous proportions that the banking institutions have taken on following deregulation have meant serious consequences for market performance. A number of banks have reached sufficient size to exercise market power—the ability of firms to influence prices and to engage in anticompetitive behavior. The market power of our enormous banks allows them to take positions as price leaders in local markets, where large firms use their dominance to elevate prices (i.e., increase fees and rates on loans, and decrease interest rates on deposits). Large firms can do this because smaller firms may perceive that lowering their prices to take market share could be met by very drastic reductions in prices from the larger firm in retaliation. Large firms, having deeper pockets, may be able to withstand longer periods of operating at a loss than the smaller firms.

Small banks are likely to perceive that the colossal size and resources of the megabanks make them unprofitable to cross—better to follow along and charge roughly what the dominant, price-leading firm does. Empirical research by Federal Reserve Board senior economist Steven Pilloff supported this analysis, finding that the arrival of very large banks in local markets tended to increase bank profitability for reasons of price leadership, due to the larger banks' economies of scale and scope, financial muscle, and diversification.

Examples of the use of banking industry market power are easy to find. Several bills now circulating in Congress deal with the fees retail businesses pay to the banks and the credit card companies. When consumers make purchases with their Visas or MasterCards, an average of two cents of each dollar goes not to the retailer but to the credit card companies that run the payment network and the banks that supply the credit. These "interchange fees" bring in over $35 billion in profit in the United States alone, and they reflect the strong market power of the banks and credit card companies over the various big and small retailers. The 2% charge comes to about $31,000 for a typical convenience store, just below the average per-store yearly profit of $36,000, and this has driven a coalition of retailers to press for congressional action.

Visa has about 50% of the credit card market (including debit cards), and MasterCard has 25%, which grants them profound market power and strong bargaining positions. Federal Reserve Bank of Kansas City economists found the United States "maintains the highest interchange fees in the world, yet its costs should be among the lowest, given economies of scale and declining cost trends." The *Wall Street Journal*'s description was that "these fees…have also been paradoxically tending upward in recent years when the industry's costs due to technology and economies of scale have been falling." Of course, there's only a paradox if market power is omitted from the picture. The dominant size and scale economies of the banks and the credit card oligopoly allow for high prices to be sustained—bank muscle in action against a less powerful sector of the economy. The political action favored by the retailers includes proposals for committees to enact price ceilings or (interestingly) collective bargaining by the retailers. As is often the case, the political process is the reflection of the different levels and positions of power of various corporate institutions, and the maneuvering of their organizations.

Market power brings with it a number of other advantages. A powerful company is likely to have a widespread presence, make frequent use of advertising, and be able to raise its profile by contributing to community organizations like sports leagues. This allows the larger banks to benefit from stronger brand identity—their scale and resources make customers more likely to trust their services. This grants a further advantage in the form of customer tolerance of higher prices due to brand loyalty.

Political Clout

Crucially, large firms with market power are free to participate meaningfully in politics—using their deep pockets to invest in electoral campaigns and congressional lobbying. The financial sector is among the highest-contributing industries in the United States, with total 2008 campaign contributions approaching half a billion dollars, according to the Center For Public Integrity. So it's unsurprising that they receive so many favors from the government, since they fund the careers of the decision-making government personnel. This underlying reality is why influential Senator Dick Durbin said of Congress, "The banks own the place."

Finally, banks may grow so large by exploiting scale economies and market power that they become "systemically important" to the nation's financial system. In other words, the scale and interconnectedness of the largest banks is considered to have reached a point where an abrupt failure of one or more of them may have "systemic" effects—meaning the broader economic system will be seriously impaired. These "too big to fail" banks are the ones that were bailed out by act of Congress in the fall 2008. Once a firm becomes so enormous that the government must prevent its collapse for the good of the economy, it has the ultimate advantage of being free to take far greater risks. Riskier investments come with higher returns and profits, but the greater risk of collapse that accompanies them will be less intimidating to huge banks that have an implied government insurance policy.

Some analysts have expressed doubt that such firms truly are too large to let fail, and that the banks have pulled a fast one. It might be pointed out in this connection that in the past the banks themselves have put their money where their mouths are—they have paid out of pocket to rescue financial institutions they saw as too large and connected to fail. An especially impressive episode took place in 1998, when several of Wall Street's biggest banks and financiers agreed to billions in emergency loans to rescue Long Term Capital Management. LTCM was a high-profile hedge fund that borrowed enormous sums of capital to make billion-dollar gambles on financial markets.

America's biggest banks aren't in the habit of forking over $3.5 billion of good earnings, but they had loaned heavily to LTCM and feared losing their money if the fund went under. The Federal Reserve brought the bankers together, and in the end, they paid up to bail out their colleagues, and the *Wall Street Journal* reported that it was the Fed's "clout, together with the self-interest of several big firms that already had lent billions of dollars to Long-Term Capital, that helped fashion the rescue." Interestingly, the banks insisted on real equity in the firm they were pulling out of the fire, and they gained a 90% stake in the hedge fund. Comparing this to the less-valuable "preferred stock" the government settled for in its 2008 bailout package of the large banks is instructive. The banks also got a share of control in the firm they rescued, again in stark contrast to the public bailout of some of the same banks.

Even Bigger?

In fact, the financial crisis and bailout led only to further concentration of the industry. The crisis gave stronger firms an opportunity to pick up sicker ones in another "wave of consolidation," as *BusinessWeek* put it. And a large part of the government intervention itself involved arranging hasty purchases of failing giants by other giants, orchestrated by the Federal Reserve. For example, the Fed helped organize the purchase of Bear Stearns by Chase in March 2008 and the purchase of Wachovia by Wells Fargo in December 2008. Even the bailout's "capital infusions" were used for further mergers and acquisitions by several recipients. The Treasury Department was "using the bailout bill to turn the banking system into the oligopoly of giant national institutions," as the *New York Times* reported.

The monumental growth of the largest banks owes a lot to the industry's economies of scale and scope, once regulations were relaxed so firms could exploit them. While certainly not unique to finance, these dynamics have brought the banks to such enormous size that their bad bets can put the entire economy in peril. Banking therefore offers an especially powerful case for the importance of these economies and the role of market power, since it's left the megabanks holding all the cards.

In fact, many arguments between defenders of the market economy and its critics center on the issue of competition vs. power—market boosters reliably insist that markets mean efficient competition, where giants have no inherent advantage over small, scrappy firms. However, the record in banking clearly shows that banks have enjoyed a variety of real benefits from growth. The existence of companies of great size and power is a quite natural development in many industries, due to the appeal of returns to scale and power. This is why firms end up with enough power to influence government policy, or such absurd size that they can blackmail us for life support.

And leave us crying all the way to the bank. ❑

Sources: Judith Samuelson and Lynn Stout, "Are Executives Paid Too Much?" *Wall Street Journal*, February 26, 2009; Tom Braithwaite, "Geithner Presses Congress for Action on Reform," *Financial Times*, September 23, 2009; Phillip Zweig, "Intrastate Mergers Between Banking Giants Might Not Be Out of the Question Anymore," *Wall Street Journal*, March 25, 1986; Bruce Knecht, "Chemical Banking plans acquisition of Margaretten," *Wall Street Journal*, May 13, 1994;

Eric Weiner, "Banks Will Post Good Quarterly Results," *Wall Street Journal*, January 10, 1997; Gabriella Stern, "Four Big Regionals To Consolidate Bank Operations," *Wall Street Journal*, July 22, 1992; "Pressure for change grows," *Financial Times*, September 27, 1996; Tracy Corrigan and John Authers, "Citigroup To Take $900 million charge: Cost-cutting Program to Result in Loss of 10,400 Jobs," *Financial Times*, December 16, 1998; Eleanor Laise, "Mutual-Fund Mergers Jump Sharply," *Wall Street Journal*, March 9, 2006; Steven Pilloff, "Banking, commerce and competition under the Gramm-Leach-Bliley Act," *The Antitrust Bulletin*, Spring 2002; David Humphrey, "Why Do Estimates of Bank Scale Economies Differ?" *Economic Review* of Federal Reserve Bank of Richmond, September/October 1990, note four; Michael Mandel and Rich Miller, "Productivity: The Real Story," *BusinessWeek*, November 5, 2001; John Yang, "Fed Votes to Give 7 Bank Holding Firms Additional Power in Securities Sector," *Wall Street Journal*, July 16, 1987; "Banking Behemoths—What Happens Next: Many companies Like to Shop Around For Their Providers of Financial Services," *Wall Street Journal*, September 14, 2000; Carrick Mollenkamp and Paul Beckett, "Diverse Business Portfolios Boost Banks' Bottom Lines," *Wall Street Journal*, July 17, 2001; *Journal of Financial Services Research*, "Does the Presence of Big Banks Influence Competition in Local Markets?" May 1999; "Credit-Card Wars," *Wall Street Journal*, March 29, 2008; *Economic Review* of the Federal Reserve Bank of Kansas City, "Interchange Fees in Credit and Debit Card Markets: What Role for Public Authorities," January-March 2006; "Credit Where It's Due," *Wall Street Journal*, January 12, 2006; Keith Bradsher, "In One Pocket, Out the Other," *New York Times*, November 25, 2009; Center For Public Integrity, Finance/Insurance/Real Estate: Long-Term Contribution Trends, opensecrests.org; Dean Baker, "Banks own the U.S. government," *Guardian*, June 30, 2009; Anita Raghavan and Mitchell Pacelle, "To the Rescue? A Hedge Fun Falters, So the Fed Persuades Big Banks to Ante Up," *Wall Street Journal*, September 24, 1998; Theo Francis, "Will Bank Rescues Mean Fewer Banks?" *BusinessWeek*, November 25, 2008; Joe Nocera, "So When Will Banks Give Loans?" *New York Times*, October 25, 2008.

Chapter 6

LABOR MARKETS

INTRODUCTION

Mainstream economics textbooks emphasize the ways that labor markets are similar to other markets. In the standard model, labor suppliers (workers) decide how much to work in the same way that producers decide how much to supply, by weighing the revenues against the costs—in this case, the opportunity costs of foregone leisure, and other potential costs of having a job, like physical injury. Labor demand is derived demand: Consumer demands for goods and services drive firms' production decisions, which in turn dictate the amount of labor to use. Workers are paid their marginal product, i.e. the amount that they contribute, per hour, to output. Thus, workers earn different wages because they contribute different marginal products to output. Of course, economists of every stripe acknowledge that in reality, many non-market factors, such as government assistance programs, unionization, and discrimination, affect labor markets. But in most economics textbooks, these produce only limited deviations from the basic laws of supply and demand. Discriminating employers are assumed to be hurt, not helped, by their discrimination because the color- and gender-blind market is assumed to punish such behavior.

The authors in this chapter focus on these "deviations." In the first article, Amy Gluckman points out the persistent wage gap between men and women, and outlines "comparable worth" policies that compensate female-dominated jobs equally with male-dominated ones (Article 6.1). As her article suggests, the analyses in this chapter demand ambitious public policy. This public policy should not simply ensure the smooth operation of markets for labor and other inputs, but also create a better set of rules for all involved in these markets (this will be evident in Article 6.7).

"Nike to the Rescue?" (Article 6.2) offers John Miller's response to several articles by New York Times columnist Nicholas Kristof praising sweatshops. Miller addresses the issue of sweatshops within the context of the causal link between globalization and growth, and finds that here, too, mainstream economists are on shaky ground.

Arthur MacEwan responds to an inquiry concerning the merits of international labor standards and whether labor and progressive groups should support the inclusion of such standards in trade agreements (Article 6.3). MacEwan points out that the same critics of labor standards who claim to be advocates for workers in developing countries regularly deny workers' demands for better working conditions within their own countries. Ultimately, he argues, we should take our cues from workers themselves, which is only possible if we make it easier for them to organize and unionize.

The remaining articles in the chapter address the impact of the Great Recession upon labor markets in the United States. Miller and Jeannette Wicks-Lim take apart the argument, increasingly heard in policy circles, that a large share of unemployment today is a result not of the generalized lack of demand caused by the recession, but of workers not having the skills that employers desire (Article 6.4). In this article, Miller and Wicks-Lim show that this argument has little empirical support and this line of argument also shifts the blame for unemployment onto workers themselves.

In the current regime of persistent high unemployment, the only safety net available to the unemployed is an unemployment insurance system that Marianne Hill describes as "broken" (Article 6.5). As Hill points out, the system today covers both shrinking numbers of those in need, as well as a shrinking percentage of the incomes workers earn when employed.

Job losses in the Great Recession hit male-dominated jobs especially hard, as economist Heather Boushey documents ("Women Breadwinners, Men Unemployed," Article 6.6). While the economic recovery has put men back to work more quickly than women, her call for more support for female workers who increasingly find themselves in the role of family breadwinners remains timely. As elevated unemployment has persisted, the number of long-term unemployed—job-seekers who have gone more than half a year without work—has reached unprecedented levels and has hit older workers and black workers especially hard.

Dr. Dollar (Arthur MacEwan) returns to address a reader's question about the current "race to the bottom" of globalization and the assumed inevitability of a future of low wages and high unemployment ("Are Low Wages and Job Loss Inevitable?," Article 6.7). Dr. Dollar does not think these are inevitable, and suggests a number of ways to reverse this trend.

In the chapter's final article, "Wal-Mart Makes the Case for Affirmative Action" (Article 6.8), Wicks-Lim reviews the class-action lawsuit against Wal-Mart and the Supreme Court decision against Wal-Mart's female employees. The case can be made for affirmative action at both of these institutions.

Discussion Questions

1) (Articles 6.1 and 6.7) "Equal pay for equal work" has not proven sufficient to equalize women's and men's pay. Why not? Contrast the explanations of mainstream economic commentators with those of comparable worth advocates. Where do you come down in this debate?

2) (Article 6.1) Gender discrimination means that women workers (like workers from other marginalized groups) are "underpriced" relative to their true marginal products. If this is so, why don't rational, cost-minimizing businesses snap up these low-cost workers, bidding their wages back up to their marginal product?

3) (Article 6.1) At the close of her article, Amy Gluckman contrasts comparable worth with a "far more radical" revaluation of different types of work. Explain the difference between the two. How does each of these reform programs relate to the idea that wages are set to equal marginal product?

4) (Article 6.2) According to Nicolas Kristof, the "anti-sweatshop movement hurts the very workers it intends to benefit." Why does John Miller believe Kristof is wrong? Who do you find more convincing and why?

5) (Article 6.3) What is MacEwan's argument for supporting international labor standards in trade agreements?

6) (Article 6.4) Explain the difference between structural unemployment and cyclical unemployment? How would emphasizing the former absolve policymakers of responsibility to do something about unemployment?

7) (Article 6.4) What is the evidence that a "skills mismatch" is not the primary cause of unemployment today?

8) (Article 6.5) The current system of unemployment insurance is based upon a combination of tax and subsidy. How would your textbook analyze the effect of such a system on unemployment? Does Marianne Hill's analysis differ from that?

9) (Article 6.5) In what way is the U.S. unemployment insurance system "broken," according to Hill? As a society, what do you think should be our responsibility toward the unemployed?

10) (Article 6.6) Why did men's unemployment increase more quickly than women's unemployment during the Great Recession and why have more men than women found jobs in the economic recovery that followed? What are some possible policy responses that could address this gender disparity in unemployment levels?

11) (Article 6.6) What is long-term unemployment? How much of a problem is long-term unemployment in today's economy?

12) (Article 6.7) Judging from the number of ways MacEwan suggests to reverse the "race to the bottom" of globalization, is the determination of wages, income and employment more complex than simply the supply and demand of labor allocated through the market mechanism? Will lowering Americans' wages bring back ("in-source") industrial and manufacturing jobs? Would we even want those industrial and manufacturing jobs back?

13) (Article 6.8) How does Wal-Mart profit from systematically discriminating against its female employees? How has the company been able to get away with this for so long?

Article 6.1

COMPARABLE WORTH

BY AMY GLUCKMAN
September/October 2002

There must be something to an idea that the business press has recently labeled "crackpot," "more government humor," an attempt "to Sovietize U.S. wage scales," and one of ten "dumbest ideas of the century." The idea is comparable worth (or "pay equity"), a broad term for a range of policies aimed at reducing the pay gap between occupations traditionally filled by women and those traditionally filled by men.

Comparable worth proposals first appeared in the 1970s, when women's rights campaigners began to recognize that much of the pay gap between men and women occurred not because women were paid less for doing the exact same work, but because women workers were concentrated in occupations that paid less than male-dominated occupations.

Consider a nurse who earns less than a maintenance worker working for the same employer. (This is typical of the pay gaps researchers uncovered in studies of municipal pay scales in several U.S. cities in the 1970s.) The nurse is responsible for the well-being and even the lives of her patients, and the job typically requires at least two years of postsecondary education. The maintenance worker may have far less serious responsibilities and probably did not even need a high-school diploma to get the job. Why might he earn more? His job may be physically demanding and may entail unpleasant or risky working conditions (although so may hers!). But in many cases, any reasonable evaluation of the two jobs supports the nurse's claim that she should earn the higher salary.

Comparable worth advocates argue that this kind of pay gap is the result of gender bias. Historically, they claim, employers set wages in various occupations based on mistaken stereotypes about women—that women had little to contribute, that they were just working for "pin money." These wage differences have stuck over time, leaving the 60% of women who work in female-dominated occupations (as well as the small number of men who do) at a disadvantage. Studies show that even after other factors affecting wages are accounted for, the percentage of women in an occupation has a net downward effect on that occupation's average wage.

Mainstream economists take issue with this view. How do they explain the persisting wage gap between male-dominated and female-dominated occupations? The market, of course. Wages are not set by evaluating the requirements of each job, they claim, but rather by shifts in the supply of and demand for labor. In this view, the nurse-janitor pay gap represents the outcome of past employment discrimination against women. Discrimination in hiring kept women out of many occupations, resulting in an oversupply of women entering the traditionally-female jobs such as nursing. This oversupply kept wages in those fields low. Not to worry: as gender bias against women wanes and women are able to enter the full range of occupations, some economists argue, this situation will resolve itself and the pay gap between female- and male-dominated occupations will disappear.

As it turns out, the majority of women workers continue to labor within the confines of the "pink-collar" ghetto. Women have indeed entered certain professions in significant numbers over the past thirty years. Physicians were 10% female in 1972, but 27.9% female in 2000. Lawyers and judges were 3.8% female in 1972, but 29.7% female in 2000. But the extent of sex segregation in a wide range of occupations has barely budged during this time. Teachers (K-12) were 70% female in 1972; 75.4% female in 2000. Secretaries were 99.1% female in 1972; 98.9% female in 2000. Hairdressers were an identical 91.2% female in 1972 and in 2000! Retail sales clerks were 68.9% female in 1972; 63.5% female in 2000. On the other side, automobile mechanics were 0.5% female in 1972; 1.2% female in 2000. Plumbers were 0.3% female in 1972; 1.9% female in 2000. (Women moved into a few blue-collar jobs in greater—but still relatively low—numbers. For example, telephone installers were 0.5% female in 1972, but 13.1% female in 2000.) So either employers are still discriminating directly against women to a significant degree, or else the mainstream economists' predictions about the effects of waning job discrimination are wrong—or both.

Another analysis points to the lower wages women earn as the price they pay for choosing jobs that give them the flexibility to fulfill parenting responsibilities. For example, many women (and a few men) choose to become teachers so that they can be home with their children in the late afternoon and during school vacations. But leaving gender aside, do employees typically trade off lower wages for greater flexibility? Higher-paid jobs tend to have more flexibility, not less. If this argument has some relevance for women in female-dominated professions such as teaching, it ignores entirely the vast number of women in low-wage, female-dominated occupations: retail clerk, direct care worker, waitress, beautician. These jobs certainly don't offer their occupants flexibility in return for their low wages.

Conservative commentators also stress that the overall wage gap between men and women—women employed full time, year round earn about 74% as much as men—is reasonable because women on average have fewer years of work experience and less seniority. That's true, but accounts for only about 40% of the gap. That leaves about 15 to 16 cents on every dollar unaccounted for. (Ironically, it is deindustrialization and the resulting decline in men's wages—not growth in women's wages—that has been primarily responsible for the shrinking of the gender wage gap, down from 59% in 1970.)

So the work force continues to be segregated by sex, and women's wages continue to lag behind men's, if not as much as in the past. What can be done? Comparable worth advocates have used a variety of strategies: legislation, lawsuits, collective bargaining agreements. Typically, advocates call for employers to use job evaluation instruments that rate different jobs according to several criteria such as skill, responsibility, and working conditions. Job evaluation instruments like these are not new; many large corporations already use them in their ordinary personnel procedures.

Of course, a job rating scale does not automatically indicate how to weight different factors in determining compensation, and so does not in itself determine how much a job should pay. Usually, this piece of the puzzle comes from information about what employers actually do pay. In other words, these instruments don't exclude the market from consideration. Instead, they usually take market wages for various occupations as baseline data to determine how much value to assign to different job characteristics. Then, however, employees and employers can recognize jobs that fall off the curve—jobs that pay much more or much less than the broad average of jobs with the same rating. On this basis, workers can then push employers to raise the wages of "underpaid" jobs.

The comparable worth movement made a lot of headway in the 1970s and early 1980s, primarily in unionized, public-sector workplaces. However, comparable worth barely made a dent in the private sector. Even in the public sector, the movement's momentum slowed by the late 1980s. Today, Congress is again considering legislation authorizing workers to sue their employers in order to correct pay inequities between male- and female-dominated job titles and also between race-segregated job titles.

Comparable worth legislation, if enacted, could potentially give an enormous boost to low-wage women workers. One study estimates that "among those currently earning less than the federal poverty threshold for a family of three, nearly 50% of women of color and 40% of white women would be lifted out of poverty" by a national comparable worth policy that addressed both race-segregated and sex-segregated occupations.

However, comparable worth is not a cure-all. Since comparable worth typically addresses wage gaps within a single workplace, it does not help workers whose employers pay everyone the minimum wage. Without strong unions, comparable worth won't get very far even if new legislation were enacted; for one thing, it is unions that are most likely to be able to fund the expensive litigation necessary to force companies to revise their pay scales. At a deeper level, existing comparable worth policies largely accept how the U.S. economic system has typically rewarded different job factors. It is one thing to even out pay inequities between jobs that rate the same on existing job-evaluation instruments. It would be far more radical to rebuild our notions of fair compensation in a way that values the skills of caring, communication, and responsibility for people's emotional well-being that are critical to many female-dominated occupations. ❑

Sources: Deborah M. Figart and Heidi I. Hartmann, "Broadening the Concept of Pay Equity: Lessons for a Changing Economy" in Ron Baiman, Heather Boushey, Dawn Saunders, eds., *Political Economy and Contemporary Capitalism: Radical Perspectives on Economic Theory and Policy* (M. E. Sharpe, 2000); "In Pursuit of Pay Equity" in *Women at Work: Gender and Inequality in the '80s,* Economic Affairs Bureau, 1985; Paula England, "The case for comparable worth," *Quarterly Review of Economics and Finance* 39:3, Fall 1999; *Forbes,* December 27, 1999; *Statistical Abstract of the United States.*

Article 6.2

NIKE TO THE RESCUE?
Africa needs better jobs, not sweatshops.

BY JOHN MILLER
September/October 2006

"In Praise of the Maligned Sweatshop"

WINDHOEK, Namibia—Africa desperately needs Western help in the form of schools, clinics and sweatshops.

On a street here in the capital of Namibia, in the southwestern corner of Africa, I spoke to a group of young men who were trying to get hired as day laborers on construction sites.

"I come here every day," said Naftal Shaanika, a 20-year-old. "I actually find work only about once a week."

Mr. Shaanika and the other young men noted that the construction jobs were dangerous and arduous, and that they would vastly prefer steady jobs in, yes, sweatshops. Sure, sweatshop work is tedious, grueling and sometimes dangerous. But over all, sewing clothes is considerably less dangerous or arduous—or sweaty—than most alternatives in poor countries.

Well-meaning American university students regularly campaign against sweatshops. But instead, anyone who cares about fighting poverty should campaign in favor of sweatshops, demanding that companies set up factories in Africa.

The problem is that it's still costly to manufacture in Africa. The headaches across much of the continent include red tape, corruption, political instability, unreliable electricity and ports, and an inexperienced labor force that leads to low productivity and quality. The anti-sweatshop movement isn't a prime obstacle, but it's one more reason not to manufacture in Africa.

Imagine that a Nike vice president proposed manufacturing cheap T-shirts in Ethiopia. The boss would reply: "You're crazy! We'd be boycotted on every campus in the country."

Some of those who campaign against sweatshops respond to my arguments by noting that they aren't against factories in Africa, but only demand a "living wage" in them. After all, if labor costs amount to only $1 per shirt, then doubling wages would barely make a difference in the final cost.

One problem … is that it already isn't profitable to pay respectable salaries, and so any pressure to raise them becomes one more reason to avoid Africa altogether.

One of the best U.S. initiatives in Africa has been the African Growth and Opportunity Act, which allows duty-free imports from Africa—and thus has stimulated manufacturing there.

—Op-ed by Nicholas Kristof, *New York Times*, June 6, 2006

Nicholas Kristof has been beating the pro-sweatshop drum for quite a while. Shortly after the East Asian financial crisis of the late 1990s, Kristof, the Pulitzer Prize-winning journalist and now columnist for the *New York Times*, reported the story of an Indonesian recycler who, picking through the metal scraps of a garbage dump, dreamed that her son would grow up to be a sweatshop worker. Then, in 2000, Kristof and his wife, *Times* reporter Sheryl WuDunn, published "Two Cheers for Sweatshops" in the *Times Magazine*. In 2002, Kristof's column advised G-8 leaders to "start an international campaign to promote imports from sweatshops, perhaps with bold labels depicting an unrecognizable flag and the words 'Proudly Made in a Third World Sweatshop.'"

Now Kristof laments that too few poor, young African men have the opportunity to enter the satanic mill of sweatshop employment. Like his earlier efforts, Kristof's latest pro-sweatshop ditty synthesizes plenty of half-truths. Let's take a closer look and see why there is still no reason to give it up for sweatshops.

A Better Alternative?

It is hardly surprising that young men on the streets of Namibia's capital might find sweatshop jobs more appealing than irregular work as day laborers on construction sites.

The alternative jobs available to sweatshop workers are often worse and, as Kristof loves to point out, usually involve more sweating than those in world export factories. Most poor people in the developing world eke out their livelihoods from subsistence agriculture or by plying petty trades. Others on the edge of urban centers work as street-hawkers or hold other jobs in the informal sector. As economist Arthur MacEwan wrote a few years back in *Dollars & Sense*, in a poor country like Indonesia, where women working in manufacturing earn five times as much as those in agriculture, sweatshops have no trouble finding workers.

But let's be clear about a few things. First, export factory jobs, especially in labor-intensive industries, often are just "a ticket to slightly less impoverishment," as even economist and sweatshop defender Jagdish Bhagwati allows.

Beyond that, these jobs seldom go to those without work or to the poorest of the poor. One study by sociologist Kurt Ver Beek showed that 60% of first-time Honduran *maquila* workers were previously employed. Typically they were not destitute, and they were better educated than most Hondurans.

Sweatshops don't just fail to rescue people from poverty. Setting up export factories where workers have few job alternatives has actually been a recipe for serious worker abuse. In *Beyond Sweatshops*, a book arguing for the benefits of direct foreign investment in the developing world, Brookings Institution economist Theodore Moran recounts the disastrous decision of the Philippine government to build the Bataan Export Processing Zone in an isolated mountainous area to lure foreign investors with the prospect of cheap labor. With few alternatives, Filipinos took jobs in the garment factories that sprung up in the zone. The manufacturers typically paid less than the minimum wage and forced employees to work overtime in factories filled with dust and fumes. Fed up, the workers eventually mounted a series of crippling strikes. Many factories shut down and occupancy rates in the zone plummeted, as did the value of exports, which declined by more than half between 1980 and 1986.

Kristof's argument is no excuse for sweatshop abuse: that conditions are worse elsewhere does nothing to alleviate the suffering of workers in export factories. They are often denied the right to organize, subjected to unsafe working conditions and to verbal, physical, and sexual abuse, forced to work overtime, coerced into pregnancy tests and even abortions, and paid less than a living wage. It remains useful and important to combat these conditions even if alternative jobs are worse yet.

The fact that young men in Namibia find sweatshop jobs appealing testifies to how harsh conditions are for workers in Africa, not the desirability of export factory employment.

Oddly, Kristof's desire to introduce new sweatshops to sub-Saharan Africa finds no support in the African Growth and Opportunity Act (AGOA) that he praises. The Act grants sub-Saharan apparel manufacturers preferential access to U.S. markets. But shortly after its passage, U.S. Trade Representative Robert Zoellick assured the press that the AGOA would not create sweatshops in Africa because it requires protective standards for workers consistent with those set by the International Labor Organization.

Antisweatshop Activism and Jobs

Kristof is convinced that the antisweatshop movement hurts the very workers it intends to help. His position has a certain seductive logic to it. As anyone who has suffered through introductory economics will tell you, holding everything else the same, a labor standard that forces multinational corporations and their subcontractors to boost wages should result in their hiring fewer workers.

But in practice does it? The only evidence Kristof produces is an imaginary conversation in which a boss incredulously refuses a Nike vice president's proposal to open a factory in Ethiopia paying wages of 25 cents a hour: "You're crazy! We'd be boycotted on every campus in the country."

While Kristof has an active imagination, there are some things wrong with this conversation.

First off, the antisweatshop movement seldom initiates boycotts. An organizer with United Students Against Sweatshops (USAS) responded on Kristof's blog: "We never call for apparel boycotts unless we are explicitly asked to by workers at a particular factory. This is, of course, exceedingly rare, because, as you so persuasively argued, people generally want to be employed." The National Labor Committee, the largest antisweatshop organization in the United States, takes the same position.

Moreover, when economists Ann Harrison and Jason Scorse conducted a systematic study of the effects of the antisweatshop movement on factory employment, they found no negative employment effect. Harrison and Scorse looked at Indonesia, where Nike was one of the targets of an energetic campaign calling for better wages and working conditions among the country's subcontractors. Their statistical analysis found that the antisweatshop campaign was responsible for 20% of the increase in the real wages of unskilled workers in factories exporting textiles, footwear, and apparel from 1991 to 1996. Harrison and Scorse also found that "antisweatshop activism did not have significant adverse effects on employment" in these sectors.

Campaigns for higher wages are unlikely to destroy jobs because, for multinationals and their subcontractors, wages make up a small portion of their overall costs. Even Kristof accepts this point, well documented by economists opposed to sweatshop labor. In Mexico's apparel industry, for instance, economists Robert

Pollin, James Heintz, and Justine Burns from the Political Economy Research Institute found that doubling the pay of nonsupervisory workers would add just $1.80 to the production cost of a $100 men's sports jacket. A recent survey by the National Bureau of Economic Research found that U.S. consumers would be willing to pay $115 for the same jacket if they knew that it had not been made under sweatshop conditions.

Globalization in Sub-Saharan Africa

Kristof is right that Africa, especially sub-Saharan Africa, has lost out in the globalization process. Sub-Saharan Africa suffers from slower growth, less direct foreign investment, lower education levels, and higher poverty rates than most every other part of the world. A stunning 37 of the region's 47 countries are classified as "low-income" by the World Bank, each with a gross national income less than $825 per person. Many countries in the region bear the burdens of high external debt and a crippling HIV crisis that Kristof has made heroic efforts to bring to the world's attention.

But have multinational corporations avoided investing in sub-Saharan Africa because labor costs are too high? While labor costs in South Africa and Mauritius are high, those in the other countries of the region are modest by international standards, and quite low in some cases. Take Lesotho, the largest exporter of apparel from sub-Saharan Africa to the United States. In the country's factories that subcontract with Wal-Mart, the predominantly female workforce earns an average of just $54 a month. That's below the United Nations poverty line of $2 per day, and it includes regular forced overtime. In Madagascar, the region's third largest exporter of clothes to the United States, wages in the apparel industry are just 33 cents per hour, lower than those in China and among the lowest in the world. And at Ramatex Textile, the large Malaysian-owned textile factory in Namibia, workers only earn about $100 per month according to the Labour Resource and Research Institute in Windhoek. Most workers share their limited incomes with extended families and children, and they walk long distances to work because they can't afford better transportation.

On the other hand, recent experience shows that sub-Saharan countries with decent labor standards *can* develop strong manufacturing export sectors. In the late 1990s, Francis Teal of Oxford's Centre for the Study of African Economies compared Mauritius's successful export industries with Ghana's unsuccessful ones. Teal found that workers in Mauritius earned ten times as much as those in Ghana—$384 a month in Mauritius as opposed to $36 in Ghana. Mauritius's textile and garment industry remained competitive because its workforce was better educated and far more productive than Ghana's. Despite paying poverty wages, the Ghanaian factories floundered.

Kristof knows full well the real reason garment factories in the region are shutting down: the expiration of the Multifiber Agreement last January. The agreement, which set national export quotas for clothing and textiles, protected the garment industries in smaller countries around the world from direct competition with China. Now China and, to a lesser degree, India, are increasingly displacing other garment producers. In this new context, lower wages alone are unlikely to sustain the sub-Saharan garment industry. Industry sources report that sub-Saharan Africa suffers from several other drawbacks as an apparel producer, including relatively high utility and transportation costs and long shipping times to the United States. The region also has lower productivity and less skilled labor than Asia, and it has fewer sources of cotton yarn and higher-priced fabrics than China and India.

If Kristof is hell-bent on expanding the sub-Saharan apparel industry, he would do better to call for sub-Saharan economies to gain unrestricted access to the Quad markets—the United States, Canada, Japan, and Europe. Economists Stephen N. Karingi, Romain Perez, and Hakim Ben Hammouda estimate that the welfare gains associated with unrestricted market access could amount to $1.2 billion in sub-Saharan Africa, favoring primarily unskilled workers.

But why insist on apparel production in the first place? Namibia has sources of wealth besides a cheap labor pool for Nike's sewing machines. The *Economist* reports that Namibia is a world-class producer of two mineral products: diamonds (the country ranks seventh by value) and uranium (it ranks fifth by volume). The mining industry is the heart of Namibia's export economy and accounts for about 20% of the country's GDP. But turning the mining sector into a vehicle for national economic development would mean confronting the foreign corporations that control the diamond industry, such as the South African De Beers Corporation. That is a tougher assignment than scapegoating antisweatshop activists.

More and Better African Jobs

So why have multinational corporations avoided investing in sub-Saharan Africa? The answer, according to international trade economist Dani Rodrik, is "entirely due to the slow growth" of the sub-Saharan economies. Rodrik estimates that the region participates in international trade as much as can be expected given its economies' income levels, country size, and geography.

Rodrik's analysis suggests that the best thing to do for poor workers in Africa would be to lift the debt burdens on their governments and support their efforts to build functional economies. That means investing in human resources and physical infrastructure, and implementing credible macroeconomic policies that put job creation first. But these investments, as Rodrik points out, take time.

In the meantime, international policies establishing a floor for wages and safeguards for workers across the globe would do more for the young men on Windhoek's street corners than subjecting them to sweatshop abuse, because grinding poverty leaves people willing to enter into any number of desperate exchanges. And if Namibia is closing its garment factories because Chinese imports are cheaper, isn't that an argument for trying to improve labor standards in China, not lower them in sub-Saharan Africa? Abusive labor practices are rife in China's export factories, as the National Labor Committee and *BusinessWeek* have documented. Workers put in 13- to 16-hour days, seven days a week. They enjoy little to no health and safety enforcement, and their take-home pay falls below the minimum wage after the fines and deductions their employers sometimes withhold.

Spreading these abuses in sub-Saharan Africa will not empower workers there. Instead it will take advantage of the fact that they are among the most marginalized workers in the world. Debt relief, international labor standards, and public investments in education and infrastructure are surely better ways to fight African poverty than Kristof's sweatshop proposal. ❑

Sources: Arthur MacEwan, "Ask Dr. Dollar," *Dollars & Sense*, Sept–Oct 1998; John Miller, "Why Economists Are Wrong About Sweatshops and the Antisweatshop Movement," *Challenge*, Jan–Feb 2003; R. Pollin, J. Burns, and J. Heintz, "Global Apparel Production and Sweatshop Labor: Can Raising Retail Prices Finance Living Wages?" Political Economy Research Institute, Working Paper 19, DATE; N. Kristof, "In Praise of the Maligned Sweatshop,"*New York Times*, June 6, 2006; N. Kristof, "Let Them Sweat," *NYT* , June 25, 2002; N. Kristof, "Two Cheers for Sweatshops," *NYT* , Sept 24, 2000; N. Kristof, "Asia'[s Crisis Upsets Rising Effort to Confront Blight of Sweatshops," *NYT,* June 15, 1998; A. Harrison and J. Scorse, "Improving the Conditions of Workers? Minimum Wage Legislation and Anti-Sweatshop Activism," *Calif. Management Review*, Oct 2005; Herbert Jauch, "Africa's Clothing and Textile Industry: The Case of Ramatex in Namibia," in *The Future of the Textile and Clothing Industry in Sub-Saharan Africa*, ed. H. Jauch and R. Traub-Merz (Friedrich-Ebert-Stiftung, 2006); Kurt Alan Ver Beek, "Maquiladoras: Exploitation or Emancipation? An Overview of the Situation of Maquiladora Workers in Honduras," *World Development,* 29(9), 2001; Theodore Moran, *Beyond Sweatshops: Foreign Direct Investment and Globalization in Developing Countries* (Brookings Institution Press, 2002); "Comparative Assessment of the Competitiveness of the Textile and Apparel Sector in Selected Countries," in *Textiles and Apparel: Assessment of the Competitiveness of Certain Foreign Suppliers to the United States Market*, Vol. 1, U.S. International Trade Commission, Jan 2004; S. N. Karingi, R. Perez, and H. Ben Hammouda, "Could Extended Preferences Reward Sub-Saharan Africa's Participation in the Doha Round Negotiations?," *World Economy*, 2006; Francis Teal, "Why Can Mauritius Export Manufactures and Ghana Can Not?," *The World Economy*, 22 (7), 1999; Dani Rodrik, "Trade Policy and Economic Performance in Sub-Saharan Africa," Paper prepared for the Swedish Ministry for Foreign Affairs, Nov 1997.

Article 6.3

INTERNATIONAL LABOR STANDARDS

BY ARTHUR MacEWAN
September/October 2008

Dear Dr. Dollar:
U.S. activists have pushed to get foreign trade agreements to include higher labor standards. But then you hear that developing countries don't want that because cheaper labor without a lot of rules and regulations is what's helping them to bring industries in and build their economies. Is there a way to reconcile these views? Or are the activists just blind to the real needs of the countries they supposedly want to help?
—Philip Bereaud, Swampscott, Mass.

In 1971, General Emilio Medici, the then-military dictator of Brazil, commented on economic conditions in his country with the infamous line: "The economy is doing fine, but the people aren't."

Like General Medici, the government officials of many low-income countries today see the well-being of their economies in terms of overall output and the profits of firms—those profits that keep bringing in new investment, new industries that "build their economies." It is these officials who typically get to speak for their countries. When someone says that these countries "want" this or that—or "don't want" this or that—it is usually because the countries' officials have expressed this position.

Do we know what the people in these countries want? The people who work in the new, rapidly growing industries, in the mines and fields, and in the small shops and market stalls of low-income countries? Certainly they want better conditions—more to eat, better housing, security for their children, improved health and safety. The officials claim that to obtain these better conditions, they must "build their economies." But just because "the economy is doing fine" does not mean that the people are doing fine.

In fact, in many low-income countries, economic expansion comes along with severe inequality. The people who do the work are not getting a reasonable share of the rising national income (and are sometimes worse off even in absolute terms). Brazil in the early 1970s was a prime example and, in spite of major political change, remains a highly unequal country. Today, in both India and China, as in several other countries, economic growth is coming with increasingly severe inequality.

Workers in these countries struggle to improve their positions. They form—or try to form—independent unions. They demand higher wages and better working conditions. They struggle for political rights. It seems obvious that we should support those struggles, just as we support parallel struggles of workers in our own country. The first principle in supporting workers' struggles, here or anywhere else, is supporting their right to struggle—the right, in particular, to form independent unions without fear of reprisal. Indeed, in the ongoing controversy over the U.S.-

Colombia Free Trade Agreement, the assassination of trade union leaders has rightly been a major issue.

Just how we offer our support—in particular, how we incorporate that support into trade agreements—is a complicated question. Pressure from abroad can help, but applying it is a complex process. A ban on goods produced with child labor, for example, could harm the most impoverished families that depend on children's earnings, or could force some children into worse forms of work (e.g., prostitution). On the other hand, using trade agreements to pressure governments to allow unhindered union organizing efforts by workers seems perfectly legitimate. When workers are denied the right to organize, their work is just one step up from slavery. Trade agreements can also be used to support a set of basic health and safety rights for workers. (Indeed, it might be useful if a few countries refused to enter into trade agreements with the United States until we improve workers' basic organizing rights and health and safety conditions in our own country!)

There is no doubt that the pressures that come through trade sanctions (restricting or banning commerce with another country) or simply from denying free access to the U.S. market can do immediate harm to workers and the general populace of low-income countries. Any struggle for change can generate short-run costs, but the long-run gains—even the hope of those gains—can make those costs acceptable. Consider, for example, the Apartheid-era trade sanctions against South Africa. To the extent that those sanctions were effective, some South African workers were deprived of employment. Nonetheless, the sanctions were widely supported by mass organizations in South Africa. Or note that when workers in this country strike or advocate a boycott of their company in an effort to obtain better conditions, they both lose income and run the risk that their employer will close up shop.

Efforts by people in this country to use trade agreements to raise labor standards in other countries should, whenever possible, take their lead from workers in those countries. It is up to them to decide what costs are acceptable. There are times, however, when popular forces are denied even basic rights to struggle. The best thing we can do, then, is to push for those rights—particularly the right to organize independent unions—that help create the opportunity for workers in poor countries to choose what to fight for. ❑

Article 6.4

UNEMPLOYMENT: A JOBS DEFICIT OR A SKILLS DEFICIT?

BY JOHN MILLER AND JEANNETTE WICKS-LIM
January/February 2011

Millions of Americans remain unemployed nearly a year and a half after the official end-date of the Great Recession, and the nation's official unemployment rate continues at nearly 10%.

Why? We are being told that it is because—wait for it—workers are not qualified for the jobs that employers are offering.

Yes, it's true. In the aftermath of the deepest downturn since the Great Depression, some pundits and policymakers—and economists—have begun to pin persistently high unemployment on workers' inadequate skills.

The problem, in this view, is a mismatch between job openings and the skills of those looking for work. In economics jargon, this is termed a problem of "structural unemployment," in contrast to the "cyclical unemployment" caused by a downturn in the business cycle.

The skills-gap message is coming from many quarters. Policymaker-in-chief Obama told Congress in February 2009: "Right now, three-quarters of the fastest-growing occupations require more than a high school diploma. And yet, just over half of our citizens have that level of education." His message: workers need to go back to school if they want a place in tomorrow's job market.

The last Democrat in the White House has caught the bug too. Bill Clinton explained in a September 2010 interview, "The last unemployment report said that for the first time in my lifetime, and I'm not young ... we are coming out of a recession but job openings are going up twice as fast as new hires. And yet we can all cite cases that we know about where somebody opened a job and 400 people showed up. How could this be? Because people don't have the job skills for the jobs that are open."

Economists and other "experts" are most likely the source of the skills-gap story. Last August, for instance, Narayana Kocherlakota, president of the Federal Reserve Bank of Minneapolis, wrote in a Fed newsletter: "How much of the current unemployment rate is really due to mismatch, as opposed to conditions that the Fed can readily ameliorate? The answer seems to be a lot." Kocherlakota's point was that the Fed's monetary policy tools may be able to spur economic growth, but that won't help if workers have few or the wrong skills. "The Fed does not have a means to transform construction workers into manufacturing workers," he explained.

The skills-mismatch explanation has a lot to recommend it if you're a federal or Fed policymaker: it puts the blame for the economic suffering experienced by the 17% of the U.S. workforce that is unemployed or underemployed on the workers themselves. Even if the Fed or the government did its darndest to boost overall spending, unemployment would be unlikely to subside unless workers upgraded their own skills.

The only problem is that this explanation is basically wrong. The weight of the evidence shows that it is not a mismatch of skills but a lack of demand that lies at the heart of today's severe unemployment problem.

High-Skill Jobs?

President Obama's claim that new jobs are requiring higher and higher skill levels would tend to support the skills-gap thesis. His interpretation of job-market trends, however, misses the mark. The figure that Obama cited comes from the U.S. Department of Labor's employment projections for 2006 to 2016. Specifically, the DOL reports that among the 30 fastest growing occupations, 22 of them (75%) will typically require more than a high school degree. These occupations include network systems and data communications analysts, computer software engineers, and financial advisors. What he fails to say, however, is that these 22 occupations are projected to represent less than 3% of all U.S. jobs.

What would seem more relevant to the 27 million unemployed and underemployed workers are the occupations with the *largest* growth. These are the occupations that will offer workers the greatest number of new job opportunities. Among the 30 occupations with the largest growth, 70%—21 out of 30—typically do not require more than a high school degree. To become fully qualified for these jobs, workers will only need on-the-job training. The DOL projects that one-quarter of all jobs in 2016 will be in these 21 occupations, which include retail salespeople, food-preparation and food-service workers, and personal and home care aides.

In fact, the DOL employment projections estimate that more than two-thirds (68%) of the jobs in 2016 will be accessible to workers with a high school degree or less. Couple this with the fact that today, nearly two-thirds (62%) of the adult labor force has at least some college experience, and an alleged skills gap fails to be convincing as a driving force behind persistent high unemployment.

LABOR MARKET MUSICAL CHAIRS

To understand the data discussed here, try picturing the U.S. labor market as a game of musical chairs, with a few twists. At any time, chairs (job openings) can be added to the circle and players can sit down (get hired). When the music stops at the end of the month, not all the chairs are filled. Still, many people—far more people than the number of empty chairs—are left standing.

Each month, the Bureau of Labor Statistics reports on what happened in that month's game of labor market musical chairs in its various measures of unemployment and in the Job Openings and Labor Turnover Survey (JOLTS). Here's how the BLS scorecard for labor market musical chairs works.

- **Job openings** is a snapshot of the number of jobs available on the last day of the month—the number of empty chairs when the music stops.

- **Hires** are all the new additions to payroll during the month—the number of people who found a chair to sit in while the music was playing. Because many chairs are added to the circle and filled within the same month, the number of hires over a month is typically greater than the number of openings available on the last day of that month.

- **Unemployed persons** are those who looked for a job that month but couldn't find one—the number of people who played the game but were left standing when the music stopped at the end of the month.

Low-Skill Workers?

If employers were having a hard time finding qualified workers to fill job openings, you'd think that any workers who are qualified would be snapped right up. But what the unemployment data show is that there remains a substantial backlog of experienced workers looking for jobs or for more hours in their existing part-time jobs in those major industries that have begun hiring—including education, healthcare, durable goods manufacturing, and mining.

Most telling are the *underemployed*—those with part-time jobs who want to work full-time. Today there are more underemployed workers in each of the major industries of the private economy than during the period from 2000 to 2007, as Arjun Jayadev and Mike Konczal document in a 2010 paper published by the Roosevelt Institute. Even in the major industries with the highest number of job openings— education and health services, professional and business services, transportation and utilities, leisure and hospitality, and manufacturing—underemployment in 2010 remains at levels twice as high or nearly twice as high as during the earlier period (measured as a percentage of employed workers).

Purveyors of the mismatch theory would have a hard time explaining how it is that underemployed workers who want full-time work do not possess the skills to do the jobs full time that they are already doing, say, 20 hours a week.

More broadly, workers with a diverse set of skills—not just construction workers—lost jobs during the Great Recession. Workers in manufacturing, professional and business services, leisure and hospitality, transportation and utilities, and a host of other industries were turned out of their jobs. And many of these experienced workers are still looking for work. In each of the 16 major industries of the economy unemployment rates in September 2010 were still far higher than they had been at the onset of the Great Recession in December 2007. In the industries with a large number of (cumulative) job openings during the recovery—education and health services, professional and business services, and manufacturing—experienced workers face unemployment rates twice what they were back in December 2007.

There are plenty of experienced workers still looking for work in the industries with job openings. To be faithful to the data, Kocherlakota and the other mismatch proponents would need to show that experienced workers no longer possess the skills to work in their industry, even though that industry employed them no more than three years ago. That seems implausible.

Statistical Errors

Still, the statistical oddity that Bill Clinton and many economists have pointed to does seem to complicate the picture. If the number of job openings is rising at a good clip yet the number of new hires is growing more slowly and the unemployment rate is stagnant, then maybe employers *are* having trouble finding qualified folks to hire.

Once you take a closer looks at the numbers, though, there is less here than meets the eye.

First, the *rate* at which job openings and new hires numbers change over time is not the right place to look. What we really need to know is how the number of unfilled job posts compares to the number of qualified workers employers hire over the same month. If employers in today's recovery are having a hard time finding workers, then the job openings left unfilled at the end of the month should be relatively high compared to the number of newly hired workers that month. In other words, if the number of positions left unfilled at the end of the month relative to the number of new hires rises *above* what we've seen during past recoveries, this would mean that employers are finding it harder to fill their positions with the right workers this time around.

But it turns out that the ratio of unfilled job openings to new hires is approximately the same during this recovery as in the recovery from the 2001 recession. In September 2010, fifteen months into the current economic recovery, the ratio of job posts left unoccupied at the end of the month to the number of monthly new hires stood at 69%—very close to its 67% level in February 2003, fifteen months into the last recovery. In other words, today's employers are filling their job openings with the same rate of success as yesterday's employers.

Comparisons that focus on the unemployment rate rather than on the number of new hires are even less meaningful. As hiring picks up at the beginning of an economic recovery, workers who had given up the job search start looking again. This brings them back into the official count of the unemployed, keeping the unemployment rate from dropping even as both job openings and new hires rise.

WHERE MISMATCHES MAY MATTER

The skills-mismatch theory does not go very far toward explaining stubbornly high U.S. unemployment. Still, there are unquestionably some unemployed and underemployed workers whose job prospects are limited by "structural" factors.

One kind of structural unemployment that does seem to fit the contours of the Great Recession to at least some degree is that caused by a mismatch of geography: the workers are in one part of the country while the jobs they could get are in another. The housing crisis surely has compromised the ability of unemployed workers to unload their single largest asset, a house, and move to another part of the country. Plus, job losses have been particularly heavy in regions where the housing crisis hit hardest.

But at the same time, lost jobs have been widespread across industries and there is little real evidence of geographic mismatch between job openings and unemployed workers. As labor economist Michael Reich reports, "economic decline and the growth of unemployment have been more widespread than ever before, making it unclear where the unemployed should migrate for greater job opportunities."

Even where there is a skills mismatch, that doesn't mean the government shouldn't get involved. On the contrary, government policies to boost economic demand can help significantly. When demand is high, labor markets become very tight and there are few available workers to hire. Workers previously viewed as "unemployable" get hired, get experience and on-the-job training, and see their overall career prospects brighten.

And, of course, government can fund expanded job-training programs. If the economy continues to slog along with low growth rates and persistent unemployment, the ranks of the long-term unemployed will rise. As they go longer and longer without work, their skills will atrophy or become obsolete and they will face a genuine skills-mismatch problem that will make job-training programs more and more necessary.

Not Enough Jobs

The reality of the situation—the widespread job losses and the long, fruitless job searches of experienced workers—make it clear that today's employment problem is a jobs deficit across the economy, not a skills deficit among those looking for work.

While it's true that any given month ends with some number of unfilled job openings, the total number of jobs added to the economy during this recovery has simply been inadequate to put the unemployed back to work. In fact, if every job that stood open at the end of September 2010 had been filled, 11.7 million officially unemployed workers would still have been jobless.

This recovery has seen far fewer job openings than even the so-called "jobless" recovery following the 2001 recession. Economists Lawrence Mishel, Heidi Shierholz, and Kathryn Edwards of the Economic Policy Institute report that cumulative job openings during the first year of this recovery were roughly 25% lower than during the first year of the recovery following the 2001 recession—that's 10 million fewer jobs. Even in the industries generating the most job openings in the current recovery—education and health services, professional and business services, leisure and hospitality, and manufacturing—the cumulative number of job openings has lagged well behind the figure for those industries during the first year of the recovery from the 2001 recession. (Only the mining and logging category, which accounted for just 0.5% of employment in 2007, has had more job openings during the first year of this recovery than during the first year of the 2001 recovery.)

Why has the pick-up in jobs following the Great Recession been worse than usual? The simple answer is that the recession was worse than usual. The sharp and extreme decline of output and employment in the Great Recession has severely dampened demand—that is, people have not had money to buy things. With the resulting lack of sales, businesses were not willing to either invest or hire; and this in turn has meant a continuing lack of demand.

If businesses have barely resumed hiring, it has not been for lack of profits. By the middle of 2010, corporate profits (adjusted for inflation) were about 60% above their low point at the end of 2008, well on their way back to the peak level of mid-2006. Also, in early 2010 non-financial firms were sitting on almost $2 trillion in cash. There was no lack of ability to invest and hire, but there was a lack of incentive to invest and hire, that is, a lack of an expectation that demand (sales) would rise. As is well known, small businesses have generally accounted for a disproportionately large share of job growth. Yet, since the onset of the Great Recession, small business owners have consistently identified poor sales as their single most important problem—and thus, presumably, what has prevented them from expanding employment.

The Role of Demand

Regardless of the lack of evidence to support it, the skills-mismatch story has seeped into media coverage of the economy. Take, for example, National Public Radio's recent Morning Edition series titled "Skills gap: holding back the labor market." In one segment, reporter Wendy Kaufman presents anecdotes about employers turning down record numbers of applicants and leaving job openings unfilled. Economist Peter Capelli then comes on and remarks, "You know, a generation ago you'd never expect that somebody could come into a reasonably skilled, sophisticated position in your organization and immediately make a contribution. That's a brand new demand." Now, that comment does not point to today's workers possessing fewer skills or qualifications. Rather, it suggests that employers have raised the bar: they are pickier than in the past.

That makes sense. We've seen that employers are successfully filling positions at about the same rate as in the recent past. What's different this time around is that employers have had up to six unemployed workers competing for every job opening left vacant at the close of the month. This is by far the highest ratio on record with data back to 2000. During the 2001 recession, that ratio rose to just over two unemployed workers for each opening. (In the first years of the "jobless recovery" following the 2001 recession, the ratio continued to rise, but it remained below three to one.) Clearly, these numbers favor the alternative explanation. Unfortunately, Kaufman doesn't even consider it.

That's too bad. Recognizing that a lack of demand for goods and services is to blame for the severe crisis of unemployment puts the focus squarely back on the federal government and on the Fed, which could help to remedy the problem —*if* they had the political will to do so. Millions of unemployed workers, organized and armed with an accurate diagnosis of the problem, could create that political will— unless they are distracted by a wrong-headed diagnosis that tries to blame them for the problem. ❑

Sources: Bureau of Labor Statistics Table A-14, Unemployed persons by industry and class of workers, not seasonally adjusted, historical data (bls.gov); Lawrence Mishel, Heidi Shierholz, and Kathryn Anne Edwards, "Reasons for Skepticism About Structural Unemployment," Economic Policy Institute, Briefing Paper #279, September 22, 2010 (epi.org); Arjun Jayadev and Mike Konczal, "The Stagnating Labor Market," The Roosevelt Institute, September 19, 2010 (rooseveltinstitute. org); Bureau of Labor Statistics, Job Openings and Labor Turnover (JOLTS) Highlights, September 2010 (bls.gov); Michael Reich, "High Unemployment after the Great Recession: Why? What Can We Do?," Policy Brief from the Center on Wage and Employment Dynamics, Institute for Research on Labor and Employment, University of California, Berkeley, June 2010 (irle.berkeley.edu/cwed); Narayana Kocherlakota, President Federal Reserve Bank of Minneapolis, "Inside the FOMC," Marquette, Michigan, August 17, 2010 (minneapolisfed.org); Lawrence Mishel and Katherine Anne Edwards, "Bill Clinton Gets It Wrong," Economic Policy Institute, Economic Snapshot, September 27, 2010 (epi.org); "Remarks of President Barack Obama—Address to Joint Session of Congress," February 24, 2009 (whitehouse.gov); "The Skills Gap: Holding Back the Labor Market," Morning Edition, National Public Radio, November 15, 2010 (npr.org).

Article 6.5

UNEMPLOYMENT INSURANCE: A BROKEN SYSTEM

BY MARIANNE HILL

September/October 2009

Millions of workers have lost their jobs in the current recession. Employment is down 12% in manufacturing, 7% in professional and business services, and more than 5% overall in the private sector compared to last year. Over 5.6 million people have lost their jobs since June 2009. The ranks of the unemployed are continuing to grow; the unemployment rate in June hit 9.5%. Good thing that unemployment insurance provides income to help tide these workers over this rough patch, right? Not so fast.

The share of unemployed workers receiving benefits has gradually shrunk since the 1970s. In 1975, over half of unemployed workers received regular benefits. But in 2008, only 37% of the unemployed did; in some states the figure was less than 25%. And so-called "discouraged workers," those who want but are not actively seeking employment, are not considered part of the labor force and so are not even included in these figures.

Unemployment insurance, in short, is not a benefit that everyone who loses a job can count on. Several groups are working to change this. The American Recovery and Reinvestment Act (ARRA), better know as the Obama stimulus package, provides temporary funding for states that expand their unemployment coverage, and so far this year 25 states have done so. Others, however, are resisting even a temporary expansion of coverage that would be fully federally funded.

Why Unemployment Compensation?

When unemployment insurance was established as a nationwide program in 1935, it was hailed as a means of enabling workers to protect their standard of living between jobs. With it, workers are better able to keep their homes and their health. It helps to stabilize family well-being and maintain the labor force in a region. By enabling workers to engage in longer job searches, unemployment compensation also improves workers' job choices. It even enhances employers' flexibility in hiring by making lay-offs less painful.

Unemployment insurance is also an important countercyclical tool: it bolsters consumer spending during economic downturns and then automatically drops off as the economy recovers and unemployment falls. Because it reduces the need for other forms of government intervention to raise demand in a downturn, the program has supporters across the ideological spectrum.

Coverage and benefits vary by state. The average weekly benefit in 2008 was $300—about 35% of the average weekly wage. Benefits are paid from state funds that are financed by a payroll tax on employers. This tax is levied on anywhere from the first $7,000 to the first $35,300 of each worker's annual earnings depending on the state; the national average is $11,482. The tax rate ranges from 0.83% to 5% of the taxable portion of wages, with a national average of 2.42%. (Who bears the cost of this tax is debated: economists have shown that whether or not a company is able to pass the cost of payroll taxes forward to customers or back to employees depends on conditions in its particular product and labor markets.)

Shifts in employment patterns and a tightening of eligibility requirements are behind the nationwide reduction in effective unemployment insurance coverage. Today almost 30% of the U.S. work force is employed in nonstandard work arrangements, including part-time, temporary, contract or on-call work, and self-employment. Most of these jobs are subject to the payroll tax that funds unemployment benefits—yet these workers often find they are ineligible. For instance, persons who are seeking only part-time employment do not qualify for unemployment benefits in many states. This affects women in particular, including heads of households, who often work part time due to dependent care responsibilities. People who work full time but only for part of the year may also find it difficult to qualify for unemployment benefits.

Many workers who are not eligible for benefits provide income that is critical to their families. In 2007, 41% of workers worked only part-time or part-year. Among heads of households, this figure, though lower, is still sizeable: in 2007, it was 32% overall and 42% for female family heads. Besides child care, elder care can also mean part-time or part-year work for many. Nearly one-third of working adults with older parents report missing some work to care for them.

Who Are the Unemployed?

Certain industries, regions, and workers are being hit harder than others this recession. In June, 15 states and the District of Columbia had unemployment rates of over 10%, but only one, North Dakota, had an unemployment rate below 5%. Michigan, Oregon, South Carolina and Rhode Island all had seasonally adjusted jobless rates of 12% or more.

Unemployment hits some population groups much harder than others—young people, people of color, and anyone with relatively few years of education. Among workers over 20 years of age, black men had the highest jobless rate in June at 16.4%. The rate for Hispanic women was 11.5%, for black women 11.3%, and for Hispanic men 10.7%. In contrast, the jobless rate was under 10% for both white men (9.2%) and white women (6.8%).

A combination of factors including occupational segregation, lower educational levels, and discrimination result in lower incomes for women and for black and Latino men, exacerbating the impact of higher unemployment. Data from 2005-2007 show that black women working year-round, full-time earned $15,900 a year less than white men; for Hispanic women the wage gap was $21,400. Lower-income families have fewer assets to see them through rough economic times, and their extended families are also hard-pressed as demands upon them increase. Nonprofits, another part of the social safety net, suffer from increased demand for services and decreased donations during recession. As a result, families of blacks, women and Hispanics suffer severe setbacks during a period of recession, and unemployment insurance can be especially critical to them.

Families in which one or more wage earners lose their jobs bear costs greater than just the lost wages. Savings are exhausted; rates of illness, both mental and physical, increase; debt levels often rise (inadequate medical insurance coverage is a major factor—in 2008, 60% of the unemployed lacked health insurance); and the pursuit of a college education or other training may be postponed. Studies have documented a rise in suicide rates, mental and physical illnesses, and domestic and other violence among the unemployed. These problems become widespread during recessions and become a burden on society, not just on individual families.

Promising Initiatives

Under the Obama stimulus package, states that elect to expand their programs in certain ways receive federal funds to finance these changes for at least two to three years. States can make unemployment benefits more available in a number of ways:

- Changing the base period used to determine whether a worker qualifies for benefits and if so, the amount he or she will receive.
- Making unemployment insurance available to certain individuals who are seeking only part-time work and/or to those who lost or left their jobs due to certain compelling family reasons (for example, domestic violence or a spouse relocating).
- Providing an additional 26 weeks of compensation to workers who have exhausted regular unemployment benefits and are enrolled in and making satisfactory progress in certain training programs.
- Paying an additional dependents' allowance of at least $15 per dependent per week to eligible beneficiaries.

Another potential reform relates to the extension of benefits beyond the regular 13- to 26-week period. States are required to offer extended benefits during periods of especially high unemployment (with half the cost covered by the federal government) only if certain trigger requirements are met—and that does not happen often. The ARRA offers states the option of adopting a new, less stringent trigger requirement. As of mid-July 2009, 29 of the 30 states adopting the new trigger requirements have had extended benefits go into effect, compared with only six of the 20 states that have kept earlier triggers. Last year Congress authorized a separate program, Emergency Unemployment Compensation, to provide federally funded benefits after regular benefits are exhausted. The National Employment Law Project estimated that about 1.2 million workers would exhaust their benefits under *this* program before July 2009 and so become eligible for extended benefits.

A permanent expansion of coverage to a larger share of the unemployed, with or without an increase in benefit levels, would cost more than the average $23 per month in unemployment insurance taxes currently paid per worker. This could be achieved by expanding the portion of wages on which the tax is levied. To reduce the negative impact on low-income workers, this could be accompanied by adjustments to the earned income tax credit.

Even if the reforms contained in the Obama administration's stimulus package were fully enacted, benefits and coverage would be low in the United States in comparison to Europe. Much remains to be done to ensure minimal income security here. As the unemployment rate approaches 10%, it is time to revamp our broken system. ❑

Sources: U.S. Department of Labor, especially www.ows.doleta.gov/unemploy/finance.asp; U.S. Bureau of Labor Statistics; National Employment Law Project, www.nelp.org; William Conerly, "European Unemployment: Lessons for the United States," National Center for Policy Analysis, May 26, 2004; National Institutes of Health, www.pubmedcentral.nih.gov; Marcus Walker and Roger Thurow, "U.S., Europe Are an Ocean Apart on Human Toll of Joblessness," *Wall Street Journal,* May 7, 2009.

Article 6.6

WOMEN BREADWINNERS, MEN UNEMPLOYED

BY HEATHER BOUSHEY

July 2009; updated March 2012

The employment situation over the past 19 months has dramatically changed for millions of American families. Since the Great Recession began in December 2007, there has been a sharp rise in the number of married couples where a woman is left to bring home the bacon because her husband is unemployed. What is striking is not only how many more families are experiencing unemployment among husbands, but also how this loss of the traditional breadwinner has occurred across a variety of demographic groups.

The reason that more married couples now boast women as the primary breadwinners is because men have experienced greater job losses than women over the course of this recession, losing three out of every four jobs lost. This puts a real strain on family budgets since women typically earn only 78 cents for every dollar men earn. In the typical married-couple family where both spouses work, the wife brings home just over a third—35.6%—of the family's income.

What's equally worrisome is that most families receive health insurance through the employers of their husbands. So when husbands lose their jobs, families are left struggling to find ways to pay for health insurance at the same time they are living on just a third of their prior income. These new health insurance costs can be crushing if families have to turn to the individual insurance market, where coverage is limited and expensive, or pay for continued coverage through their husbands' old insurance policies, which is possible because of federal law but is also expensive—though the American Recovery and Reinvestment Act subsidized that cost for many workers. Still, many families with an unemployed worker simply have to go without health insurance.

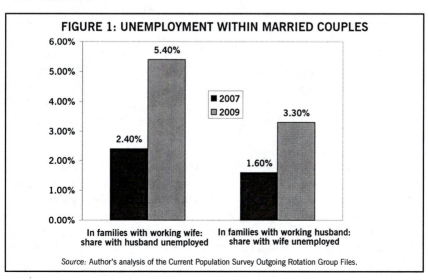

FIGURE 1: UNEMPLOYMENT WITHIN MARRIED COUPLES

Source: Author's analysis of the Current Population Survey Outgoing Rotation Group Files.

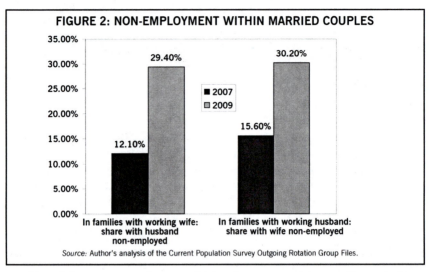

FIGURE 2: NON-EMPLOYMENT WITHIN MARRIED COUPLES

Source: Author's analysis of the Current Population Survey Outgoing Rotation Group Files.

The job losses mounting among husbands are acute this year. Figure 1 shows that the share of families where women hold down a job while men are unemployed jumped sharply in 2009 compared to 2007 at the peak of the last economic cycle. In the first five months of 2009, 5.4% of working wives had an unemployed husband at home—that is, a husband who was actively searching for work, but could not find a job—compared to an average of 2.4% over the first five months of 2007. This means that there are about 2 million working wives today with an unemployed husband.

In contrast, working husbands continue to be less likely to have an unemployed wife. In the first five months of 2009, an average of only 3.3% of husbands had an unemployed wife at home, up from 1.6%. Importantly, the difference in the shares of unemployed husbands and wives is not due to women telling the surveyor that they are "out of the labor force" rather than report they are out of a job, willing to work, and actively seeking employment. Figure 2 examines non-working spouses and shows not only a sharp rise in the share of working wives who have a non-working husband but also the share of both husbands and wives who are either unavailable to work or are not looking for a job.

So far this year, 15.6% of working wives have a husband who is not working, up a stunning 3.5 percentage points from early 2007, when 12.1% of working wives had a husband who did not work. But working husbands did not see a similarly large increase in their chances of having a non-working wife. In 2007, 29.4% of husbands had a non-working wife, up only 0.8 percentage points to 30.2% in 2009.

Families with children have been hit especially hard hit by unemployment. Among working wives in families with a small child—under age six—at home, 5.9% have an unemployed husband. This is higher than among families with a working wife but with no child under age six at home, where 5.3% have an unemployed husband.

Among families with a working wife and a child under age 18, the share with an unemployed husband is 5.7%, compared to 5.0% among those with no children. This means that there are 1 million working wives with children at home, but an unemployed husband. The numbers are smaller for families with a working husband and an unemployed wife. The share with a child under age 18 is 3.2%—compared to 3.4% among those with no children.

The share of workers with an unemployed spouse is lower than the overall unemployment rate of 9.5%. Typically, married workers have lower unemployment rates compared to single workers and they stay unemployed for shorter periods of time. There are many reasons why this is the case, but one is that married workers may have more of an incentive to find work as quickly as possible—if possible—because there are more people relying on their earnings, compared to single workers—at least single workers without children. Of course, single mothers, who typically have higher unemployment than other workers, do have children relying on their earnings and are under similar pressures to find employment.

Especially striking in the recently released data is the sharp increase in breadwinner wives and unemployed husbands across demographic groups. The table below shows, for example, that among young (ages 18 to 24) families with a working wife, one in ten married women (9.9%) has an unemployed husband, up 5.5

UNEMPLOYMENT AMONG FAMILIES WITH A WORKING SPOUSE					
	In families with working wife: Share with husband unemployed			In families with working husband: Share with wife unemployed		
	January - May 2007	January - May 2009	Percentage point change	January - May 2007	January - May 2009	Percentage point change
All families	2.4	5.4	3	1.6	3.3	1.7
Ages 18 to 24	4.4	9.9	5.5	4.8	6	1.2
Ages 25 to 54	2.4	5.5	3.1	1.6	3.3	1.7
Ages 55 to 64	1.9	4.1	2.2	1.4	3	1.6
Less than highschool	4.3	8.3	4	2.7	5.8	3.1
High school	2.7	6.8	4.1	2	3.9	1.9
Some college	2.6	5.5	2.9	1.4	2.8	1.4
College	1.7	3.9	2.2	1.2	2.4	1.2
White, non-Hispanic	2.1	4.7	2.6	1.4	2.8	1.4
Black, non-Hispanic	4.1	7.8	3.7	2.9	3.9	1
Hispanic, any race	3.4	7.7	4.3	2.2	5.1	2.9
Other race, non-Hispanic	2.5	6.3	3.8	1.9	3.2	1.3
No children under age 18	2.3	5	2.7	1.6	3.4	1.8
Children under age 18	2.4	5.7	3.3	1.7	3.2	1.5
No children under age six	2.3	5.3	3	1.6	3.4	1.8
Children under age six	2.5	5.9	3.4	1.7	3	1.3

Source: Author's analysis of the Current Population Survey Outgoing Rotation Group Files.

percentage points from early 2007. Among working women without a high school degree, slightly less than one in ten (8.3%) have an unemployed husband, up four percentage points since 2007. This share of women with unemployed husbands has increased 2.2 percentage points among wives with a college degree.

There has also been a sharp rise in the share of families where both the husband and wife are unemployed. Between the first five months of 2007 and of 2009, the share of married-couple families with both spouses unemployed rose to 0.5% from 0.1%, meaning that one in 500 families is struggling with dual unemployment. The share of families with a child under age 18 with both parents unemployed is 0.6%, meaning that one in 165 families with children have both parents looking for work.

Long-Term Unemployment Rises Even After the Recession Ends

Record job losses and persistent unemployment have left the U.S. economy out of order and forced those looking for a job to longer and longer without work.

When the Great Recession hit at the end of 2007 jobs disappeared, unemployment rose, and its duration lengthened. By the official end of the recession in midyear 2009 the unemployed who had gone 27 weeks or longer without work, what economists call long-term unemployment, had nearly doubled to 29% of those job seekers.

But as the anemic economic recovery that followed did little to put people back to work, long term unemployment rate continued to climb reaching a peak of 45% of the unemployed in April 2010. In February 2012, more than two and half years into this "97 pound weakling of a recovery," as Time Magazine called it, more than 5.4 million job-seekers had gone more than a half of year without work and the long term unemployment rate still stood at 42.6% of the unemployed.

Long-term unemployment in the current period is more pervasive than any time on record, with data available in 1948. During the typical downturn of the last 60 years less than one fifth of the unemployed went more than 27 weeks without a job.

As long-term unemployment increases so too does the economic suffering inflicted on those without work and their families. At the beginning of 2012, more than 2 million of the unemployed had gone 99 weeks or more without work exhausting their unemployment benefits. Also, as the Congressional Research Service confirms, when unemployment spells lengthen the prospects for finding employment diminishes. Finally the long-term unemployed are at increasing risk of drop out the labor force (by not actively searching for a job) and joining those without work who go uncounted in this data even though they want a job.

Long-term unemployment hits older workers and black workers especially hard. While the official unemployment rates for older workers are lower than those of younger workers, older workers who loose their jobs find it particularly difficult to find another. In February 2012, more than half (52.4%) of the unemployed 55 to 64 year olds had gone more than 27 weeks without a job. For black workers conditions are considerably worse. Nearly the same share of the black unemployed had been out of work for 27 months or more as for older workers. (In February 2012 the long-term unemployment stood at 46.7% for unemployed black men and 51.8% for unemployed black women.) But the official unemployment rate for blacks was 14.1% in February 2012, while the rate for workers 55 and older was 5.9%.   —John Miller

Sources: Bureau of Labor Statistics, "The Employment Situation – February 2012," Table A-2, Table A-12, Table A-36; The 97-lb. Recovery," by Rana Foroohar and Bill Saporito. *Time Magazine*, April 12, 2012; "The Trend in Long-Term Unemployment and Characteristics of Workers Unemployed for More than 99 Weeks," by Gerald Mayer, Congressional Research Service, December 20, 2010; and, "Long-Term Hardship in the Labor Market," by John Schmitt and Janelle Jones, Center for Economic and Policy Research, March 2012.

Among some demographic groups dual unemployment rises to one in 100: young couples (with a spouse between 18 and 24), less-educated couples (where either spouse has no more than a high-school degree), and African-American families (0.9% of African-American wives in the labor force are unemployed and have an unemployed husband, while 0.8% of African-American husbands in the labor force are unemployed with an unemployed wife).

The Great Recession that began in December 2007 has now lasted 19 months. The unemployment picture remains tough: Unemployment rose to 9.5% in June and 29.0% of unemployed workers have been out of work for at least six months—a shocking fact given that 3.4 million of the 6.5 million people who have lost their jobs since the recession began were laid off only within the past six months. There are now more than five unemployed workers available for every job opening and the employment prospects for men seem especially challenging given the continued lay-offs in manufacturing and construction. Families will continue to rely on the earnings of a working woman for a long time to come.

As families need the earnings of wives more than ever, policymakers should focus their attention on ensuring that women—including mothers—have access to good jobs with benefits that will support their families. There could not be a more important moment to pass legislation ensuring pay equity for all workers. Nor could there be a more important time to ensure that caregivers are not discriminated against by employers.

The Paycheck Fairness Act, which passed the House in January, would go a long way toward eradicating pay inequalities, but it is languishing in the Senate. The Equal Employment Opportunity Commission issued new guidelines in 2007 to help employers avoid caregiver discrimination, but more could be done to use develop this guidance to ensure that every caregiver has the same access to good jobs as other workers. These and other policy solutions to the crisis facing women breadwinners need to be acted upon swiftly. ❑

Source: Bureau of Labor Statistics, "Women in the Labor Force: A Databook," (Washington, DC: U.S. Department of Labor, 2008), Table 24.

The data analysis for this report was conducted by Jeff Chapman. The analysis compares the experiences of married couples from the first five months of 2007 to the first five months of 2009. Note that data are only for married heterosexual couples and do not include cohabiting heterosexual couples or lesbian or gay couples, married or otherwise.

Update, March 2012

The Great Recession had just come to an end when Heather Boushey published her article "Women Breadwinners, Men Unemployed. " Nearly three years into the anemic recovery that followed fewer men are unemployed. The "man-covery," as it has been called, has done more to put men to work than to put women to work, bringing the adult (20 and older) men's unemployment rate down to that of adult women. Still, as of February 2012, both rates remain quite elevated at 7.7%. The "man-covery" was the sequel to the "man-cession," the moniker the press gave the

Great Recession because twice as many men as women lost their jobs. But as the economy recovered fitfully, women continued to lose jobs well into 2011, largely because the public sector, especially state and local government, which disproportionately employs women, cut jobs instead of adding them.

Still there is little reason to believe that women breadwinners are any less important for families. According to the latest data, wives' earning accounted for 37% of family earnings in 2009, and nearly 4 out 10 (38%) of working wives earned more than their husbands. *—John Miller*

Sources: "The 'Man-covery': Women Gaining Jobs Recovery at a Slower Pace than Men," by Heather Boushey, Center for American Progress, March 9, 2012; "Women in the Labor Force: A Data Book" (2011 Edition), Bureau of Labor Statistics, Tables 24 and 25.

Article 6.7

ARE LOW WAGES AND JOB LOSS INEVITABLE?

BY ARTHUR MacEWAN
May/June 2011

Dear Dr. Dollar:

The main narrative that I hear in mainstream press is that U.S. workers are being undercut and eventually displaced by global competition. I think this narrative has a tone of inevitability, that low wages and job loss are driven by huge impersonal forces that we can't do much about. Is this right?
—— Vicki Legion, San Francisco, Calif.

Yes, that is the main narrative. But, no, it's not right.

Globalization, in the sense of increasing international commerce over long distances, has been going on since human beings made their way out of Africa and spread themselves far and wide. Trade between China and the Mediterranean seems to have been taking place at least 3,000 years ago. (We know this through chemical analysis of silk found in the hair of an Egyptian mummy interred around 1000 BCE; the silk was identified as almost certainly from China.) The long history of long-distance commerce does cast an aura of inevitability over globalization.

But the spread of international commerce has not taken shape outside of human control. Globalization takes many forms; its history has variously involved colonial control, spheres of influence, and forms of regulated trade.

The current era of globalization was quite consciously planned by the U.S. government and U.S. business during and after World War II. They saw the United States replacing the British Empire as the dominant power among capitalist countries. But in place of 19th century-style colonial control, they looked to a "free trade" regime to give U.S. firms access to resources and markets around the world. While U.S. business and the U.S. government did not achieve the "free trade" goal immediately, this has been what they have promoted over the last 65 years.

This U.S.-sponsored form of globalization has given great advantage to U.S. business. And it has put many U.S. workers in direct competition with more poorly paid workers elsewhere in the world, who are often denied the right to organize and have little choice but to work long hours in often unsafe conditions. U.S. business can make its profits off these workers elsewhere—often by sub-contracting to local firms. But there is nothing inevitable about this set-up.

Furthermore, there are ways to counter these developments. Just as the current global economic arrangements were created by political decisions, they can be altered by political decisions. Two examples:

- The development of better social programs in the United States would put workers here in a stronger bargaining position, regardless of global competition. With universal health care (a "single-payer" system), for instance, U.S. workers would be in a better position to leave a bad job or turn down a bad offer.

- Rebuilding the labor movement is essential for placing U.S. workers in a stronger bargaining position in relation to their employers. Equally important, stronger unions would give workers more leverage in the political arena, where many decisions about the nature of global commerce are made.

No, we may not be able to create the same labor movement of decades past. However, lest one think that the decline of the labor movement has been itself inevitable in the face of globalization, consider some of the political decisions that have undermined labor's strength:

- The National Labor Relations Board has not done its job. In the 50s, 60s, and early 1970s, fewer than one in ten union elections were marred by illegal firings of union organizers. By the early 1980s, over 30% of union elections involved illegal firings. While the figure declined to 16% by the late 1990s, it was back up to 25% in the early 2000s.

- Or consider the minimum wage. Even with the recent increase of the federal minimum wage to $7.25 per hour, adjusted for inflation it is still below what it was in the 1960s and 1970s.

These are crucial political decisions that have affected organized labor, wage rates, and jobs. But they were not inevitable developments.

It would be folly to think that the changes in the global economy have not affected economic conditions in the United States, including the position of organized labor. But it would also be folly to assume that conditions in the United States are inevitably determined by the global economy. Political action matters.

(Caveat: Advocating a "different shape" for globalization is not a call for protectionism. It is possible to engage in world commerce and protect the interest of U.S. workers without resorting to traditional protectionism. But that is a topic for another day.) ❑

Article 6.8

WAL-MART MAKES THE CASE FOR AFFIRMATIVE ACTION

Lessons from the Supreme Court's ruling on sex discrimination.

BY JEANNETTE WICKS-LIM

September/October 2011

On June 20, 2011, the Supreme Court put an end to what would have been the largest class-action lawsuit in U.S. history. The lawsuit, filed on behalf of more than 1.5 million current and former female Wal-Mart employees, alleged that Wal-Mart supervisors routinely discriminated against female workers by promoting and paying them less than their male counterparts.

That's too bad, because the facts presented by the plaintiffs describe a situation that surely calls out for redress.

Wal-Mart has a bare-bones policy telling managers how to dole out promotions. Eligible workers need only meet three basic criteria: 1) an above-average performance rating, 2) at least one year of job tenure, and 3) a willingness to relocate. Among these candidates, local supervisors have full discretion over whom to promote.

With the door wide open for supervisors to act on their subjective preferences, it may be no surprise that men dominate the company's management team. In 2001 women made up only 33% of Wal-Mart's managers, according to labor economist Richard Drogin, even though they made up 70% of its hourly workforce. Compare that with Wal-Mart's peer companies, where 57% of managers were women.

Wal-Mart also gives its (mostly male) managers significant wiggle room in setting their supervisees' wages. The result? Drogin reported that in 2001, Wal-Mart women earned consistently less than their male counterparts even after controlling for such factors as job performance and job tenure. He concluded that "... there are statistically significant disparities between men and women at Wal-Mart ... [and] these disparities ... can be explained only by gender discrimination."

The trouble is that these disparities exist even though no part of Wal-Mart's wage or promotion policy directs managers to make biased decisions. In fact, Wal-Mart has an anti-discrimination policy on its books.

With no "smoking gun" corporate policy, the Supreme Court blocked the women of Wal-Mart from lodging a collective complaint against the company. In the majority opinion, Justice Antonin Scalia writes: "Other than the bare existence of delegated discretion, respondents have identified no 'specific employment practice' ... Merely showing that Wal-Mart's policy of discretion has produced an overall sex-based disparity does not suffice."

In other words, the majority of Supreme Court justices intend to take a narrow view of which employment practices justify class-action discrimination lawsuits. Potential plaintiffs will have to show exactly how an employer discriminated. And as the Wal-Mart case demonstrates, this can boil down to the murky business of trying to expose employers' unspoken intentions.

What this means is that the traditional, complaint-driven approach to enforcing the 1964 Civil Rights Act cannot protect workers from discrimination. Deprived of class-action lawsuits as a tool, the women behind the Wal-Mart case and other workers in plainly discriminatory workplaces will now have to pursue their claims individually—at best putting them into a much weaker position with fewer resources.

To eliminate workplace discrimination and achieve true equality, policies have to focus squarely on the pattern of outcomes of employers' decisions. In a phrase, on the question of whether an employer discriminates, "the proof is in the pudding." President Lyndon Johnson recognized this more than 40 years ago when his administration first put such policies into action under the rubric of affirmative action.

What does affirmative action require? First, the employer keeps a record of whether the race and gender make-up of its workforce is proportional to the wider pool of eligible workers. If not, the employer develops a plan to act "affirmatively"—with goals and timetables—to improve female and minority representation.

Affirmative action plans may include sexual harassment awareness training for supervisors, for instance, or directing recruitment efforts toward minority and women's organizations. Rigid quotas—the most controversial aspect of affirmative action policies—can only be used in the context of a court-ordered or -approved plan in response to a discrimination suit.

The Wal-Mart case demonstrates why workers need affirmative action policies to eradicate discrimination. As President Johnson put it in 1965, affirmative action represents "… the next and more profound stage of the battle for civil rights. We seek … not just equality as a right and a theory, but equality as a fact and as a result." ❑

Sources: "Statistical analysis of gender patterns in Wal-Mart workforce," Expert testimony by Richard Drogin, Ph. D., February 2003 (walmartclass.com); "The representation of women in store management at Wal-Mart Stores, Inc.," Expert testimony by Marc Bendick, Jr., Ph.D., January 2003 (walmartclass.com); Supreme Court of the United States, Wal-Mart Stores, Inc., petitioner v. Betty Dukes et al. (No. 10–277) June 20, 2011.

Chapter 7

THE DISTRIBUTION
OF INCOME

INTRODUCTION

For many mainstream economists, inequality in the distribution of income is a natural outcome of the functioning of markets. If workers get paid based on productivity, wage differences simply reflect underlying differences in their productivity.

People who supply other inputs—investors or lenders supplying capital, landowners supplying land—are similarly rewarded according to the marginal products of those inputs. Even poverty is largely seen as a result of low productivity, which can be interpreted more compassionately as the consequence of a lack of education and training, or, at an extreme, as a result of shirking and a whole host of moral failings. President Reagan's deliberate use of the term "welfare queen" to cast poor, black women as undeserving of society's support is perhaps the most famous example of the latter. Indeed, in this view, a high degree of equality (or measures aimed at reducing inequality) would reduce the incentives for increasing productivity, slowing overall growth. Economists also argue that because the rich tend to save more (thus swelling the pool of resources available for investment), the larger the share of the economic pie that goes to them, the better the entire economy does. Trickle on down!

The authors in this section, however, see increasing inequality as neither natural, nor inevitable, nor beneficial for growth. Ellen Frank ("Measures of Poverty," Article 7.1) provides some context for the discussion of poverty and inequality by explaining how poverty is measured in the United States. Of particular importance for students is how the federal poverty threshold is measured, thus setting a lower boundary for determining that illusive, yet all encompassing concept, "the middle class."

Chris Tilly, in his remarkable essay "Geese, Golden Eggs, and Traps" (Article 7.2), lays out the arguments for and against income equality and then takes on the rosy view of the economic benefits of inequality. His analysis shows how economies such as the United States' can end up in an "inequality trap" where high inequality leads to low growth, which in turn can lead to even higher inequality.

For anyone who wants to explore questions of inequality and fairness, Gar Alperovitz and Lew Daly's article "The Undeserving Rich" (Article 7.3) provides some fascinating grist for the mill with their view that growth is built on a base of collectively produced knowledge that each generation inherits—not merely on the efforts of individuals.

Alejandro Reuss ("Cause of Death: Inequality," Article 7.4) illustrates how increased inequality can even more directly undermine the quality of life by reducing life expectancy.

The United States has the most unequal distribution of income and wealth of any advanced industrialized nation. How did we get this way? In the best narrative on the subject, James Cypher ("Slicing Up at the Long Barbeque," Article 7.5) traces the rise in income inequality in the United States and points to some of the causes for this trend.

A key example of "zombie economics" (dead economic ideas that still walk among us) is "trickle-down economics." Alejandro Reuss ("No Thanks to the Super-Rich," Article 7.6) shows yet again that heaping added wealth upon the wealthy does not contribute to job creation and economic growth. Such "zombie" policies might in fact have the opposite effect.

Our last article in this chapter is an exceptional piece by Randy Albelda, "New Welfare Policy, Same Single-Mother Poverty" (Article 7.7). Albelda brings us up to date on the current collection of anti-poverty programs and evaluates their relative success or lack thereof. The "feminization of poverty" continues with the Great Recession, adding extra burden on single mothers. Albelda suggests solutions to single-mother poverty if the country is serious about addressing the problem as opposed to stigmatizing the poor and powerless.

Discussion Questions

1) (Article 7.1) Consult the Census Bureau website (www.census.gov) to find the current federal poverty line for an individual. Did you expect it to be higher or lower? In your opinion, what are the "basic necessities" that should be included in the calculation of the poverty line?

2) (Article 7.1) Why might the federal poverty rate understate poverty in the United States? In what way might it overstate poverty in the United States?

3) (Article 7.2) According to Tilly, many of the mechanisms linking equality and growth are political. Should economic models incorporate political behavior as well as economic behavior? What are some ideas about how they could do that?

4) (Article 7.2) Explain Tilly's metaphor about the "Goose that Laid the Golden Eggs." How is "equality" the Goose? Explain in great detail.

5) (Article 7.3) Consider the following quotation:

> "I think we've been through a period where too many people have been given to understand that if they have a problem, it's the government's job to cope with it. 'I have a problem, I'll get a grant.' 'I'm homeless, the government must house me.' They're casting their problem

on society. And, you know, there is no such thing as society. There are individual men and women, and there are families. And no government can do anything except through people, and people must look to themselves first. It's our duty to look after ourselves and then, also to look after our neighbor. People have got the entitlements too much in mind, without the obligations. There's no such thing as entitlement, unless someone has first met an obligation."

    —British Prime Minister Margaret Thatcher, talking to *Women's Own* magazine, October 31, 1987

After reading Gar Alperovitz and Lew Daly's article "The Undeserving Rich," how do you think they would respond to Thatcher?

6) (Article 7.4) Death rates are higher where inequality is higher. These mortality differences apply at all income levels, even after taking into account differences in poverty. How can this be explained?

7) (Article 7.5) According to James Cypher, how has globalization increased economic inequality in the United States?

8) (Article 7.5) Explain why mainstream economists believe that increases in "millionairism" can stimulate economic growth. How does Cypher respond to this argument?

9) (Article 7.5) Cypher argues that "we all do better when we all do better." What does he mean? What economic policies would you propose to reduce inequality in the United States?

10) (Article 7.6) How do U.S. productivity and inequality levels compare with those in other industrialized countries? What does Reuss conclude from those two comparisons? Do you think he is right?

11) (Article 7.7) Are "the rich" the "job creators?" Will tax cuts on capital gains spur job creation? If not, why not?

12) (Article 7.8) Can you solve the problem of poverty by simply insisting that the poor "work their way out" of poverty? Why is this work your way out of poverty burden especially hard for single mothers? Why do we stigmatize poor single mothers? Is there a greater social cost in doing so?

Article 7.1

MEASURES OF POVERTY

BY ELLEN FRANK
January/February 2006, updated March 2011

Dear Dr. Dollar:
Can you explain how poverty is defined in government statistics? Is this a realistic definition?
—Susan Balok, Savannah, Ga.

Each February, the Census Bureau publishes the federal poverty thresholds—the income levels for different sized households below which a household is defined as living "in poverty." Each August, the bureau reports how many families, children, adults, and senior citizens fell below the poverty threshold in the prior year. For 2009, the federal poverty thresholds were as follows:

HOUSEHOLD SIZE	FEDERAL POVERTY THRESHOLD
1 person	$11,201
2 people	14,417
3 people	17,330
4 people	21,834
5 people	25,694

Using these income levels, the Census Bureau reported that 14.3% percent of U.S. residents and 20.7% of U.S. children lived in poverty in 2009. Black Americans experienced poverty at nearly double these rates: 25.8% of all Blacks and 35.7% of Black children lived in households with incomes below the poverty line in 2009.

The poverty threshold concept was originally devised by Social Security analyst Mollie Orshansky in 1963. Orshansky estimated the cost of an "economy food plan" designed by the Department of Agriculture for "emergency use when funds are low." Working from 1955 data showing that families of three or more spent one-third of their income on food, Orshansky multiplied the food budget by three to calculate the poverty line. Since the early 1960s, the Census Bureau has simply recalculated Orshansky's original figures to account for inflation.

The poverty line is widely regarded as far too low for a household to survive on in most parts of the United States. For one thing, as antipoverty advocates point out, since 1955 the proportion of family budgets devoted to food has fallen from one-third to one-fifth. Families expend far more on nonfood necessities such as child care, health care, transportation, and utilities today than they did 50 years ago, for obvious reasons: mothers entering the work force, suburbanization and greater dependence on the auto, and soaring health care costs, for example. Were

Orshansky formulating a poverty threshold more recently, then, she would likely have multiplied a basic food budget by five rather than by three.

Furthermore, costs—particularly for housing and energy—vary widely across the country, so that an income that might be barely adequate in Mississippi is wholly inadequate in Massachusetts. Yet federal poverty figures make no adjustment for regional differences in costs.

A number of state-level organizations now publish their own estimates of what it takes to support a family in their area, in conjunction with the national training and advocacy group Wider Opportunities for Women. Using local data on housing costs, health care premiums, taxes, and child care costs as well as food, transportation and other necessities, these "self-sufficiency standards" estimate that a two-parent two-child family needs between $40,000 and $70,000 a year, depending on the region, to cover basic needs.

State and federal officials often implicitly recognize that official poverty thresholds are unrealistically low by setting income eligibility criteria for antipoverty programs higher than the poverty level. Households with incomes of 125%, 150%, or even 185% of the federal poverty line are eligible for a number of federal and state programs. In addition, the Census Bureau publishes figures on the number of households with incomes below 200% of the federal poverty line—a level many social scientists call "near poor" or "working poor."

Poverty calculations also have critics on the right. Conservative critics contend that the official poverty rate overstates poverty in the United States. While the Census Bureau's poverty-rate calculations include Social Security benefits, public assistance, unemployment and workers' compensation, SSI (disability) payments, and other forms of cash income, they exclude noncash benefits from state and federal antipoverty programs like Food Stamps, Medicaid, and housing subsidies. If the market value of these benefits were counted in family income, fewer families would count as "poor." On the other hand, by not counting such benefits, policy makers have a better grasp of the numbers of Americans in need of such transfer programs. ❏

Resources: For background information on poverty thresholds and poverty rate calculations, see aspe.hhs.gov/poverty/papers/hptgssiv.htm and http://www.census.gov/hhes/www/poverty/. Self-sufficiency standards for different states can be found at www.sixstrategies.org/states/states.cfm. In addition, the Economic Policy Institute has calculated family budgets for the 435 metropolitan areas: www.epi.org/content/budget_calculator.

Article 7.2

GEESE, GOLDEN EGGS, AND TRAPS

Why inequality is bad for the economy.

BY CHRIS TILLY
July/August 2004

Whenever progressives propose ways to redistribute wealth from the rich to those with low and moderate incomes, conservative politicians and economists accuse them of trying to kill the goose that lays the golden egg. The advocates of unfettered capitalism proclaim that inequality is good for the economy because it promotes economic growth. Unequal incomes, they say, provide the incentives necessary to guide productive economic decisions by businesses and individuals. Try to reduce inequality, and you'll sap growth. Furthermore, the conservatives argue, growth actually promotes equality by boosting the have-nots more than the haves. So instead of fiddling with who gets how much, the best way to help those at the bottom is to pump up growth.

But these conservative prescriptions are absolutely, dangerously wrong. Instead of the goose-killer, equality turns out to be the goose. Inequality stifles growth; equality gooses it up. Moreover, economic expansion does not necessarily promote equality—instead, it is the types of jobs and the rules of the economic game that matter most.

Inequality: Goose or Goose-Killer?

The conservative argument may be wrong, but it's straightforward. Inequality is good for the economy, conservatives say, because it provides the right incentives for innovation and economic growth. First of all, people will only have the motivation to work hard, innovate, and invest wisely if the economic system rewards them for good economic choices and penalizes bad ones. Robin Hood-style policies that collect from the wealthy and help those who are worse off violate this principle. They reduce the payoff to smart decisions and lessen the sting of dumb ones. The result: people and companies are bound to make less efficient decisions. "We must allow [individuals] to fail, as well as succeed, and we must replace the nanny state with a regime of self-reliance and self-respect," writes conservative lawyer Stephen Kinsella in *The Freeman: Ideas on Liberty* (not clear how the free woman fits in). To prove their point, conservatives point to the former state socialist countries, whose economies had become stagnant and inefficient by the time they fell at the end of the 1980s.

If you don't buy this incentive story, there's always the well-worn trickle-down theory. To grow, the economy needs productive investments: new offices, factories, computers, and machines. To finance such investments takes a pool of savings. The rich save a larger fraction of their incomes than those less well-off. So to spur growth, give more to the well-heeled (or at least take less away from them in the form of taxes), and give less to the down-and-out. The rich will save their money and then invest it, promoting growth that's good for everyone.

Unfortunately for trickle-down, the brilliant economist John Maynard Keynes debunked the theory in his *General Theory of Employment, Interest, and Money* in 1936. Keynes, whose precepts guided liberal U.S. economic policy from the 1940s through the 1970s, agreed that investments must be financed out of savings. But he showed that most often it's changes in investment that drive savings, rather than the other way around. When businesses are optimistic about the future and invest in building and retooling, the economy booms, all of us make more money, and we put some of it in banks, 401(k)s, stocks, and so on. That is, saving grows to match investment. When companies are glum, the process runs in reverse, and savings shrink to equal investment. This leads to the "paradox of thrift": if people try to save too much, businesses will see less consumer spending, will invest less, and total savings will end up diminishing rather than growing as the economy spirals downward. A number of Keynes's followers added the next logical step: shifting money from the high-saving rich to the high-spending rest of us, and not the other way around, will spur investment and growth.

Of the two conservative arguments in favor of inequality, the incentive argument is a little weightier. Keynes himself agreed that people needed financial consequences to steer their actions, but questioned whether the differences in payoffs needed to be so huge. Certainly state socialist countries' attempts to replace material incentives with moral exhortation have often fallen short. In 1970, the Cuban government launched the Gran Zafra (Great Harvest), an attempt to reap 10 million tons of sugar cane with (strongly encouraged) volunteer labor. Originally inspired by Che Guevara's ideal of the New Socialist Man (not clear how the New Socialist Woman fit in), the effort ended with Fidel Castro tearfully apologizing to the Cuban people in a nationally broadcast speech for letting wishful thinking guide economic policy.

But before conceding this point to the conservatives, let's look at the evidence about the connection between equality and growth. Economists William Easterly of New York University and Gary Fields of Cornell University have recently summarized this evidence:

- Countries, and regions within countries, with more equal incomes grow faster. (These growth figures do not include environmental destruction or improvement. If they knocked off points for environmental destruction and added points for environmental improvement, the correlation between equality and growth would be even stronger, since desperation drives poor people to adopt environmentally destructive practices such as rapid deforestation.)
- Countries with more equally distributed land grow faster.
- Somewhat disturbingly, more ethnically homogeneous countries and regions grow faster—presumably because there are fewer ethnically based inequalities.
- In addition, more worker rights are associated with higher rates of economic growth, according to Josh Bivens and Christian Weller, economists at two Washington think tanks, the Economic Policy Institute and the Center for American Progress.

These patterns recommend a second look at the incentive question. In fact, more equality can actually strengthen incentives and opportunities to produce.

Equality as the Goose

Equality can boost growth in several ways. Perhaps the simplest is that study after study has shown that farmland is more productive when cultivated in small plots. So organizations promoting more equal distribution of land, like Brazil's Landless Workers' Movement, are not just helping the landless poor—they're contributing to agricultural productivity!

Another reason for the link between equality and growth is what Easterly calls "match effects," which have been highlighted in research by Stanford's Paul Roemer and others in recent years. One example of a match effect is the fact that well-educated people are most productive when working with others who have lots of schooling. Likewise, people working with computers are more productive when many others have computers (so that, for example, email communication is widespread, and know-how about computer repair and software is easy to come by). In very unequal societies, highly educated, computer-using elites are surrounded by majorities with little education and no computer access, dragging down their productivity. This decreases young people's incentive to get more education and businesses' incentive to invest in computers, since the payoff will be smaller.

Match effects can even matter at the level of a metropolitan area. Urban economist Larry Ledebur looked at income and employment growth in 85 U.S. cities and their neighboring suburbs. He found that where the income gap between those in the suburbs and those in the city was largest, income and job growth was slower for everyone.

"Pressure effects" also help explain why equality sparks growth. Policies that close off the low-road strategy of exploiting poor and working people create pressure effects, driving economic elites to search for investment opportunities that pay off by boosting productivity rather than squeezing the have-nots harder. For example, where workers have more rights, they will place greater demands on businesses. Business owners will respond by trying to increase productivity, both to remain profitable even after paying higher wages, and to find ways to produce with fewer workers. The CIO union drives in U.S. mass production industries in the 1930s and 1940s provide much of the explanation for the superb productivity growth of the 1950s and 1960s. (The absence of pressure effects may help explain why many past and present state socialist countries have seen slow growth, since they tend to offer numerous protections for workers but no right to organize independent unions.) Similarly, if a government buys out large land-holdings in order to break them up, wealthy families who simply kept their fortunes tied up in land for generations will look for new, productive investments. Industrialization in Asian "tigers" South Korea and Taiwan took off in the 1950s on the wings of funds freed up in exactly this way.

Inequality, Conflict, and Growth

Inequality hinders growth in another important way: it fuels social conflict. Stark inequality in countries such as Bolivia and Haiti has led to chronic conflict that hobbles economic growth. Moreover, inequality ties up resources in unproductive uses such as paying for large numbers of police and security guards—attempts to prevent individuals from redistributing resources through theft.

Ethnic variety is connected to slower growth because, on the average, more ethnically diverse countries are also more likely to be ethnically divided. In other words, the problem isn't ethnic variety itself, but racism and ethnic conflict that can exist among diverse populations. In nations like Guatemala, Congo, and Nigeria, ethnic strife has crippled growth—a problem alien to ethnically uniform Japan and South Korea. The reasons are similar to some of the reasons that large class divides hurt growth. Where ethnic divisions (which can take tribal, language, religious, racial, or regional forms) loom large, dominant ethnic groups seek to use government power to better themselves at the expense of other groups, rather than making broad-based investments in education and infrastructure. This can involve keeping down the underdogs—slower growth in the U.S. South for much of the country's history was linked to the Southern system of white supremacy. Or it can involve seizing the surplus of ethnic groups perceived as better off—in the extreme, Nazi Germany's expropriation and genocide of the Jews, who often held professional and commercial jobs.

Of course, the solution to such divisions is not "ethnic cleansing" so that each country has only one ethnic group—in addition to being morally abhorrent, this is simply impossible in a world with 191 countries and 5,000 ethnic groups. Rather, the solution is to diminish ethnic inequalities. Once the 1964 Civil Rights Act forced the South to drop racist laws, the New South's economic growth spurt began. Easterly reports that in countries with strong rule of law, professional bureaucracies, protection of contracts, and freedom from expropriation—all rules that make it harder for one ethnic group to economically oppress another—ethnic diversity has no negative impact on growth.

If more equality leads to faster growth so everybody benefits, why do the rich typically resist redistribution? Looking at the ways that equity seeds growth helps us understand why. The importance of pressure effects tells us that the wealthy often don't think about more productive ways to invest or reorganize their businesses until they are forced to. But also, if a country becomes very unequal, it can get stuck in an "inequality trap." Any redistribution involves a tradeoff for the rich. They lose by giving up part of their wealth, but they gain a share in increased economic growth. The bigger the disparity between the rich and the rest, the more the rich have to lose, and the less likely that the equal share of boosted growth they'll get will make up for their loss. Once the gap goes beyond a certain point, the wealthy have a strong incentive to restrict democracy, and to block spending on education which might lead the poor to challenge economic injustice—making reform that much harder.

Does Economic Growth Reduce Inequality?

If inequality isn't actually good for the economy, what about the second part of the conservatives' argument—that growth itself promotes equality? According to the conservatives, those who care about equality should simply pursue growth and wait for equality to follow.

"A rising tide lifts all boats," President John F. Kennedy famously declared. But he said nothing about which boats will rise fastest when the economic tide comes in. Growth does typically reduce poverty, according to studies reviewed by economist Gary Fields, though some "boats"—especially families with strong barriers to participating in the labor force—stay "stuck in the mud." But inequality can increase at the same time that poverty falls, if the rich gain even faster than the poor do. True, sustained periods of low unemployment, like that in the late 1990s United States, do tend to raise wages at the bottom even faster than salaries at the top. But growth after the recessions of 1991 and 2001 began with years of "jobless recoveries"— growth with inequality.

For decades the prevailing view about growth and inequality within countries was that expressed by Simon Kuznets in his 1955 presidential address to the American Economic Association. Kuznets argued that as countries grew, inequality would first increase, then decrease. The reason is that people will gradually move from the low-income agricultural sector to higher-income industrial jobs—with inequality peaking when the workforce is equally divided between low- and high-income sectors. For mature industrial economies, Kuznets's proposition counsels focusing on growth, assuming that it will bring equity. In developing countries, it calls for enduring current inequality for the sake of future equity and prosperity.

But economic growth doesn't automatically fuel equality. In 1998, economists Klaus Deininger and Lyn Squire traced inequality and growth over time in 48 countries. Five followed the Kuznets pattern, four followed the reverse pattern (decreasing inequality followed by an increase), and the rest showed no systematic pattern. In the United States, for example:

- incomes became more equal during the 1930s through 1940s New Deal period (a time that included economic decline followed by growth);
- from the 1950s through the 1970s, income gaps lessened during booms and expanded during slumps;
- from the late 1970s forward, income inequality worsened fairly consistently, whether the economy was stagnating or growing.

The reasons are not hard to guess. The New Deal introduced widespread unionization, a minimum wage, social security, unemployment insurance, and welfare. Since the late 1970s, unions have declined, the inflation-adjusted value of the minimum wage has fallen, and the social safety net has been shredded. In the United States, as elsewhere, growth only promotes equality if policies and institutions to support equity are in place.

Trapped?

Let's revisit the idea of an inequality trap. The notion is that as the gap between the rich and everybody else grows wider, the wealthy become more willing to give up overall growth in return for the larger share they're getting for themselves. The "haves" back policies to control the "have-nots," instead of devoting social resources to educating the poor so they'll be more productive.

Sound familiar? It should. After two decades of widening inequality, the last few years have brought us massive tax cuts that primarily benefit the wealthiest, at the expense of investment in infrastructure and the education, child care, and income supports that would help raise less well-off kids to be productive adults. Federal and state governments have cranked up expenditures on prisons, police, and "homeland security," and Republican campaign organizations have devoted major resources to keeping blacks and the poor away from the polls. If the economic patterns of the past are any indication, we're going to pay for these policies in slower growth and stagnation unless we can find our way out of this inequality trap. ❏

Article 7.3

THE UNDESERVING RICH
Collectively produced and inherited knowledge and the (re)distribution of income and wealth.

BY GAR ALPEROVITZ AND LEW DALY
March/April 2010

Warren Buffett, one of the wealthiest men in the nation, is worth nearly $50 billion. Does he "deserve" all this money? Why? Did he work so much harder than everyone else? Did he create something so extraordinary that no one else could have created it? Ask Buffett himself and he will tell you that he thinks "society is responsible for a very significant percentage of what I've earned." But if that's true, doesn't society deserve a very significant share of what he has earned?

When asked why he is so successful, Buffett commonly replies that this is the wrong question. The more important question, he stresses, is why he has *so much to work with* compared to other people in the world, or compared to previous generations of Americans. How much money would I have "if I were born in Bangladesh," or "if I was born here in 1700," he asks.

Buffett may or may not deserve something more than another person working with what a given historical or collective context provides. As he observes, however, it is simply not possible to argue in any serious way that he deserves *all* of the benefits that are clearly attributable to living in a highly developed society.

Buffett has put his finger on one of the most explosive issues developing just beneath the surface of public awareness. Over the last several decades, economic research has done a great deal of solid work pinpointing much more precisely than in the past what share of what we call "wealth" society creates versus what share any individual can be said to have earned and thus deserved. This research raises profound moral—and ultimately political—questions.

Recent estimates suggest that U.S. economic output per capita has increased more than twenty-fold since 1800. Output per hour worked has increased an estimated fifteen-fold since 1870 alone. Yet the average modern person likely works with no greater commitment, risk, or intelligence than his or her counterpart from the past. What is the primary cause of such vast gains if individuals do not really "improve"? Clearly, it is largely that the scientific, technical, and cultural knowledge available to us, and the efficiency of our means of storing and retrieving this knowledge, have grown at a scale and pace that far outstrip any other factor in the nation's economic development.

A half century ago, in 1957, economist Robert Solow calculated that nearly 90% of productivity growth in the first half of the 20th century (from 1909 to 1949) could only be attributed to "technical change in the broadest sense." The supply of labor and capital—what workers and employers contribute—appeared almost incidental to this massive technological "residual." Subsequent research inspired by Solow and others continued to point to "advances in knowledge" as the main source of growth. Economist William Baumol calculates that "nearly 90 percent . . . of current GDP was contributed by innovation carried out since 1870." Baumol judges that his estimate, in fact, understates the cumulative influence of past advances: Even "the steam engine, the railroad, and many other inventions of an earlier era, still add to today's GDP."

Related research on the sources of invention bolsters the new view, posing a powerful challenge to conventional, heroic views of technology that characterize progress as a sequence of extraordinary contributions by "Great Men" (occasionally "Great Women") and their "Great Inventions." In contrast to this popular view, historians of technology have carefully delineated the incremental and cumulative way most technologies actually develop. In general, a specific field of knowledge builds up slowly through diverse contributions over time until—at a particular moment when enough has been established—the next so-called "breakthrough" becomes all but inevitable.

Often many people reach the same point at virtually the same time, for the simple reason that they all are working from the same developing information and research base. The next step commonly becomes obvious (or if not obvious, very likely to be taken within a few months or years). We tend to give credit to the person who gets there first—or rather, who gets the first public attention, since often the real originator is not as good at public relations as the one who jumps to the front of the line and claims credit. Thus, we remember Alexander Graham Bell as the inventor of the telephone even though, among others, Elisha Gray and Antonio Meucci got there at the same time or even before him. Newton and Leibniz hit upon the calculus at roughly the same time in the 1670s; Darwin and Alfred Russel Wallace produced essentially the same theory of evolution at roughly the same time in the late 1850s.

Less important than who gets the credit is the simple fact that most breakthroughs occur not so much thanks to one "genius," but because of the longer historical unfolding of knowledge. All of this knowledge—the overwhelming source of all modern wealth—comes to us today *through no effort of our own*. It is the generous and unearned gift of the past. In the words of Northwestern economist Joel Mokyr, it is a "free lunch."

Collective knowledge is often created by formal public efforts as well, a point progressives often stress. Many of the advances which propelled our high-tech economy in the early 1990s grew directly out of research programs and technical systems financed and often collaboratively developed by the federal government. The Internet, to take the most obvious example, began as a government defense project, the ARPANET, in the early 1960s. Up through the 1980s there was little private investment or interest in developing computer networks. Today's vast software industry also rests on a foundation of computer language and operating hardware developed in large part with public support. The Bill Gateses of the world—the heroes of the "New Economy"—might still be working with vacuum tubes and punch cards were it not for critical research and technology programs created or financed by the federal government after World War II. Other illustrations range from jet airplanes and radar to the basic life science research undergirding many pharmaceutical industry advances. Yet the truth is that the role of collectively inherited knowledge is far, far greater than just the contributions made by direct public support, important as they are.

A straightforward but rarely confronted question arises from these facts: If most of what we have today is attributable to advances we inherit in common, then why should this gift of our collective history not more generously benefit all members of society?

The top 1% of U.S. households now receives more income than the bottom 120 million Americans combined. The richest 1% of households owns nearly half of all investment assets (stocks and mutual funds, financial securities, business equity, trusts, non-home real estate). The bottom 90% of the population owns less than 15%; the bottom half—150 million Americans—owns less than 1%. If America's vast wealth is mainly a gift of our common past, what justifies such disparities?

Robert Dahl, one of America's leading political scientists—and one of the few to have confronted these facts—put it this way after reading economist Edward Denison's pioneering work on growth accounting: "It is immediately obvious that little growth in the American economy can be attributed to the actions of particular individuals." He concluded straightforwardly that, accordingly, "the control and ownership of the economy rightfully belongs to 'society.'"

Contrast Dahl's view with that of Joe the Plumber, who famously inserted himself into the 2008 presidential campaign with his repeated claim that he has "earned" everything he gets and so any attempt to tax his earnings is totally unjustified. Likewise, "we didn't rely on somebody else to build what we built," banking titan Sanford Weill tells us in a *New York Times* front-page story on the "New Gilded Age." "I think there are people," another executive tells the *Times*, "who because of their uniqueness warrant whatever the market will bear."

A direct confrontation with the role of knowledge—and especially inherited knowledge—goes to the root of a profound challenge to such arguments. One way to think about all this is by focusing on the concept of "earned" versus "unearned" income. Today this distinction can be found in conservative attacks on welfare "cheats" who refuse to work to earn their keep, as well as in calls even by some Republican senators to tax the windfall oil-company profits occasioned by the Iraq war and Hurricane Katrina.

The concept of unearned income first came into clear focus during the era of rapidly rising land values caused by grain shortages in early 19th-century England. Wealth derived *simply* from owning land whose price was escalating appeared illegitimate because no individual truly "earned" such wealth. Land values—and especially explosively high values—were largely the product of factors such as fertility, location, and population pressures. The huge profits (unearned "rents," in the technical language of economics) landowners reaped when there were food shortages were viewed as particularly egregious. David Ricardo's influential theory of "differential rent"— i.e., that land values are determined by differences in fertility and location between different plots of land—along with religious perspectives reaching back to the Book of Genesis played a central role in sharpening this critical moral distinction.

John Stuart Mill, among others, developed the distinction between "earned" and "unearned" in the middle decades of the 19th century and applied it to other forms of "external wealth," or what he called "wealth created by circumstances." Mill's approach fed into a growing sense of the importance of societal inputs which produce economic gains beyond what can be ascribed to one person working alone in nature without benefit of civilization's many contributions. Here a second element of what appears, historically, as a slowly evolving understanding also becomes clear: If contribution is important in determining rewards, then, Mill and others urged, since society at large makes major contributions to economic achievement, it too has "earned" and deserves a share of what has been created. Mill believed strongly in personal contribution and individual reward, but he held that in principle wealth "created by circumstances" should be reclaimed for social purposes. Karl Marx, of course, tapped the distinction between earned and unearned in his much broader attack on capitalism and its exploitation of workers' labor.

The American republican writer Thomas Paine was among the first to articulate a societal theory of wealth based directly on the earned\unearned distinction. Paine argued that everything "beyond what a man's own hands produce" was a gift which came to him simply by living in society, and hence "he owes on every principle of justice, of gratitude, and of civilization, a part of that accumulation back again to society from whence the whole came." A later American reformer, Henry George, focused on urban land rather than the agricultural land at the heart of Ricardo's concern. George challenged what he called "the unearned increment" which is created when population growth and other societal factors increase land values. In Britain, J. A. Hobson argued that the unearned value created by the industrial system in general was much larger than just the part which accrued to landowners, and that it should be treated in a similar (if not more radical and comprehensive) fashion. In a similar vein, Hobson's early 20th-century contemporary Leonard Trelawny Hobhouse declared that the "prosperous business man" should consider "what single step he could have taken" without the "sum of intelligence which civilization has placed at his disposal." More recently, the famed American social scientist Herbert Simon judged that if "we are very generous with ourselves, I suppose we might claim that we 'earned' as much as one fifth of [our income]."

The distinction between earned and unearned gains is central to most of these thinkers, as is the notion that societal contributions—including everything an industrial economy requires, from the creation of laws, police, and courts to the development of schools, trade restrictions, and patents—must be recognized and rewarded. The understanding that such societal contributions are both contemporary and have made a huge and cumulative contribution over all of history is also widely accepted. Much of the income they permit and confer now appears broadly analogous to the unearned rent a landlord claims. What is new and significant here is the further clarification that by far the most important element in all this is the accumulated *knowledge* which society contributes over time.

All of this, as sociologist Daniel Bell has suggested, requires a new "knowledge theory of value"—especially as we move deeper into the high-tech era through computerization, the Internet, cybernetics, and cutting-edge fields such as gene therapy and nanotechnology. One way to grasp what is at stake is the following: A person today working the same number of hours as a similar person in 1870—working just as hard but no harder—will produce perhaps 15 times as much economic output. It is clear that the contemporary person can hardly be said to have "earned" his much greater productivity.

Consider further that if we project forward the past century's rate of growth, a person working a century from now would be able to produce—and potentially receive as "income"—up to seven times today's average income. By far the greatest part of this gain will also come to this person as a free gift of the past—the gift of the new knowledge created, passed on, and inherited from our own time forward.

She and her descendents, in fact, will inevitably contribute less, relative to the huge and now expanded contribution of the past, than we do today. The obvious question, again, is simply this: to what degree is it meaningful to say that this person will have "earned" all that may come her way? These and other realities suggest that the quiet revolution in our understanding of how wealth is created has ramifications for a much more profound and far-reaching challenge to today's untenable distribution of income and wealth.

Article 7.4

CAUSE OF DEATH: INEQUALITY

BY ALEJANDRO REUSS
May/June 2001

Inequality kills.

You won't see inequality on a medical chart or a coroner's report under "cause of death." You won't see it listed among the top killers in the United States each year. All too often, however, it is social inequality that lurks behind a more immediate cause of death, be it heart disease or diabetes, accidental injury or homicide. Few of the top causes of death are "equal opportunity killers." Instead, they tend to strike poor people more than rich people, the less educated more than the highly educated, people lower on the occupational ladder more than those higher up, or people of color more than white people.

Statistics on mortality and life expectancy do not pro-vide a perfect map of social inequality. For example, the life expectancy for women in the United States is about six years longer than the life expectancy for men, despite the many ways in which women are subordinated to men. Take most indicators of socioeconomic status, however, and most causes of death, and it's a strong bet that you'll find illness and injury (or "morbidity") and mortality increasing as status decreases.

Men with less than 12 years of education are more than twice as likely to die of chronic diseases (e.g., heart disease), more than three times as likely to die as a result of injury, and nearly twice as likely to die of communicable diseases, compared to those with 13 or more years of education. Women with family incomes below $10,000 are more than three times as likely to die of heart disease and nearly three times as likely to die of diabetes, compared to those with family incomes above $25,000. African Americans are more likely than whites to die of heart disease; stroke; lung, colon, prostate, and breast cancer, as well as all cancers combined; liver disease; diabetes; AIDS; accidental injury; and homicide. In all, the lower you are in a social hierarchy, the worse your health and the shorter your life are likely to be.

The Worse off in the United States Are Not Well off by World Standards.

You often hear it said that even poor people in rich countries like the United States are rich compared to ordinary people in poor countries. While that may be true when it comes to consumer goods like televisions or telephones, which are widely available even to poor people in the United States, it's completely wrong when it comes to health.

In a 1996 study published in the *New England Journal of Medicine*, University of Michigan researchers found that African-American females living to age 15 in Harlem had a 65% chance of surviving to age 65, about the same as women in India. Meanwhile, Harlem's African-American males had only a 37% chance of surviving to age 65, about the same as men in Angola or the Democratic Republic of Congo. Among both African-American men and women, infectious diseases and diseases of the circulatory system were the prime causes of high mortality.

It takes more income to achieve a given life expectancy in a rich country like the United States than it does to achieve the same life expectancy in a less affluent country. So the higher money income of a low-income person in the United States, compared to a middle-income person in a poor country, does not necessarily translate into a longer life span. The average income per person in African-American families, for example, is more than five times the per capita income of El Salvador. The life expectancy for African-American men in the United States, however, is only about 67 years, the same as the average life expectancy for men in El Salvador.

Health Inequalities Are Not Just about Access to Health Care.

Nearly one-sixth of the U.S. population lacks health insurance, including about 44% of poor people. A poor adult with a health problem is only half as likely to see a doctor as a high-income adult. Adults living in low-income areas are more than twice as likely to be hospitalized for a health problem that could have been effectively treated with timely outpatient care, compared with adults living in high-income areas. Obviously, lack of access to health care is a major health problem.

But so are environmental and occupational hazards; communicable diseases; homicide and firearm-related injuries; and smoking, alcohol consumption, lack of exercise, and other risk factors. These dangers all tend to affect lower-income people more than higher-income, less-educated people more than more-educated, and people of color more than whites. African-American children are more than twice as likely as white children to be hospitalized for asthma, which is linked to air pollution. Poor men are nearly six times as likely as high-income men to have elevated blood-lead levels, which reflect both residential and workplace environmental hazards. African-American men are more than seven times as likely to fall victim to homicide as white men; African-American women, more than four times as likely as white women. The less education someone has, the more likely they are to smoke or to drink heavily. The lower someone's income, the less likely they are to get regular exercise.

Michael Marmot, a pioneer in the study of social inequality and health, notes that so-called diseases of affluence—disorders, like heart disease, associated with high-calorie and high-fat diets, lack of physical activity, etc.—are most prevalent among the *least affluent* people in rich societies. While recognizing the role of such "behavioral" risk factors as smoking in producing poor health, he argues, "It is not sufficient … to ask what contribution smoking makes to generating the social gradient in ill health, but we must ask, why is there a social gradient in smoking?" What appear to be individual "lifestyle" decisions often reflect a broader *social* epidemiology.

Greater Income Inequality Goes Hand in Hand with Poorer Health.

Numerous studies suggest that the more unequal the income distribution in a country, state, or city, the lower the life expectancies for people at all income levels. One study published in the *American Journal of Public Health*, for example, shows that U.S. metropolitan areas with low per capita incomes and low levels of income inequality have lower mortality rates than areas with high median incomes and high levels of income inequality. Meanwhile, for a given per capita income range, mortality rates always decline as inequality declines.

R.G. Wilkinson, perhaps the researcher most responsible for relating health outcomes to overall levels of inequality (rather than individual income levels), argues that greater income inequality causes worse health out-comes independent of its effects on poverty. Wilkinson and his associates suggest several explanations for this relationship. First, the bigger the income gap between rich and poor, the less inclined the well off are to pay taxes for public services they either do not use or use in low proportion to the taxes they pay. Lower spending on public hospitals, schools, and other basic services does not affect wealthy people's life expectancies very much, but it affects poor people's life expectancies a great deal. Second, the bigger the income gap, the lower the overall level of social cohesion. High levels of social cohesion are associated with good health outcomes for several reasons. For example, people in highly cohesive societies are more likely to be active in their communities, reducing social isolation, a known health risk factor.

Numerous researchers have criticized Wilkinson's conclusions, arguing that the real reason income inequality tends to be associated with worse health outcomes is that it is associated with higher rates of poverty. But even if they are right and income inequality causes worse health *simply by bringing about greater poverty*, that hardly makes for a defense of inequality. Poverty and inequality are like partners

MORTALITY AMONG BRITISH CIVIL SERVANTS
Based on a ten-year study beginning in 1967

Source: Michael Marmot, "Social Differentials in Mortality: The Whitehall Studies," *Adult Mortality in Developed Countries: From Description to Explanation*, 1995.

in crime. "[W]hether public policy focuses primarily on the elimination of poverty or on reduction in income disparity," argue Wilkinson critics Kevin Fiscella and Peter Franks, "neither goal is likely to be achieved in the absence of the other."

Differences in Status May be Just as Important as Income Levels.

Even after accounting for differences in income, education, and other factors, the life expectancy for African Americans is less than that for whites. U.S. researchers are beginning to explore the relationship between high blood pressure among African Americans and the racism of the surrounding society. African Americans tend to suffer from high blood pressure, a risk factor for circulatory disease, more often than whites. Moreover, studies have found that, when confronted with racism, African Americans suffer larger and longer-lasting increases in blood pressure than when faced with other stressful situations. Broader surveys relating blood pressure in African Americans to perceived instances of racial discrimination have yielded complex results, depending on social class, gender, and other factors.

Stresses cascade down social hierarchies and accumulate among the least empowered. Even researchers focusing on social inequality and health, however, have been surprised by the large effects on mortality. Over 30 years ago, Michael Marmot and his associates undertook a landmark study, known as Whitehall I, of health among British civil servants. Since the civil servants shared many characteristics regardless of job classification—an office work environment, a high degree of job security, etc.—the researchers expected to find only modest health differences among them. To their surprise, the study revealed a sharp increase in mortality with each step down the job hierarchy—even from the highest grade to the second highest. Over ten years, employees in the lowest grade were three times as likely to die as those in the highest grade. One factor was that people in lower grades showed a higher incidence of many "lifestyle" risk factors, like smoking, poor diet, and lack of exercise. Even when the researchers controlled for such factors, however, more than half the mortality gap remained.

Marmot noted that people in the lower job grades were less likely to describe themselves as having "control over their working lives" or being "satisfied with their work situation," compared to those higher up. While people in higher job grades were more likely to report "having to work at a fast pace," lower-level civil servants were more likely to report feelings of hostility, the main stress-related risk factor for heart disease. Marmot concluded that "psycho-social" factors—the psychological costs of being lower in the hierarchy—played an important role in the unexplained mortality gap. Many of us have probably said to ourselves, after a trying day on the job, "They're killing me." Turns out it's not just a figure of speech. Inequality kills—and it starts at the bottom.

Resources: Lisa Berkman, "Social Inequalities and Health: Five Key Points for Policy-Makers to Know," February 5, 2001, Kennedy School of Government, Harvard University; *Health, United States, 1998, with Socioeconomic Status and Health Chart-book*, National Center for Health Statistics <www.cdc.gov/nchs>; Ichiro Kawachi, Bruce P. Kennedy, and Richard G. Wilkinson, eds., *The Society and Population Health Reader, Volume I: Income Inequality and Health*, 1999; Michael Marmot, "Social Differences in Mortality: The Whitehall Studies," *Adult Mortality in Developed Countries: From Description to Explanation*, Alan D. Lopez, Graziella Caselli, and Tapani Valkonen, eds., 1995; Michael Marmot, "The Social Pattern of Health and Disease," *Health and Social Organization: Towards a Health Policy for the Twenty-First Centrury*, David Blane, Eric Brunner, and Richard Wilkinson, eds., 1996; Arline T. Geronimus, et al., "Excess Mortality Among Blacks and Whites in the United States," *The New England Journal of Medicine* 335 (21), November 21, 1996; Nancy Krieger, Ph.D., and Stephen Sidney, M.D., "Racial Discrimination and Blood Pressure: The CARDIA Study of Young Black and White Adults," *American Journal of Public Health* 86 (10), October 1996; *Human Development Report 2000*, UN Development Programme; *World Development Indicators 2000*, World Bank.

Article 7.5

SLICING UP AT THE LONG BARBEQUE
Who gorges, who serves, and who gets roasted.

BY JAMES M. CYPHER
January/February 2007

Economic inequality has been on the rise in the United States for 30-odd years. Not since the Gilded Age of the late 19th century—during what Mark Twain referred to as "the Great Barbeque"—has the country witnessed such a rapid shift in the distribution of economic resources.

Still, most mainstream economists do not pay too much attention to the distribution of income and wealth—that is, how the value of current production (income) and past accumulated assets (wealth) is divided up among U.S. households. Some economists focus their attention on theory for theory's sake and do not work much with empirical data of any kind. Others who *are* interested in these on-the-ground data simply assume that each individual or group gets what it deserves from a capitalist economy. In their view, if the share of income going to wage earners goes up, that must mean that wage earners are more productive and thus deserve a larger slice of the nation's total income—and vice versa if that share goes down.

Heterodox economists, however, frequently look upon the distribution of income and wealth as among the most important shorthand guides to the overall state of a society and its economy. Some are interested in economic justice; others may or may not be, but nonetheless are convinced that changes in income distribution signal underlying societal trends and perhaps important points of political tension. And the general public appears to be paying increasing attention to income and wealth inequality. Consider the strong support voters have given to recent ballot questions raising state minimum wages and the ex-tensive coverage of economic inequality that has suddenly begun to appear in mainstream news outlets like the *New York Times*, the *Los Angeles Times*, and the *Wall Street Journal*, all of which published lengthy article series on the topic in the past few years. In December 2006, news outlets around the country spotlighted the extravagant bonuses paid out by investment firm Goldman Sachs, including a $53.4 million bonus to the firm's CEO.

By now, economists and others who do pay attention to the issue are aware that income and wealth inequality in the United States rose steadily during the last three decades of the 20th century. But now that we are several years into the 21st, what do we know about income and wealth distribution today? Has the trend toward inequality continued, or are there signs of a reversal? And what can an understanding of the entire post-World War II era tell us about how to move again toward greater economic equality?

The short answers are: (1) Income distribution is even more unequal that we thought; (2) The newest data suggest the trend toward greater inequality continues, with no signs of a reversal; (3) We all do better when we all do better. During the 30 or so years after World War II the economy boomed and every stratum of society did better—pretty much at the same rate. When the era of shared growth ended, so too did much of the growth: the U.S. economy slowed down and recessions were deeper, more frequent, and harder to overcome. Growth spurts that did occur left most people out: the bottom 60% of U.S. households earned only 95 cents in 2004 for every dollar they made in 1979. A quarter century of falling incomes for the vast majority, even though average household income rose by 27% in real terms. Whew!

The Classless Society?

Throughout the 1950s, 1960s, and 1970s, sociologists preached that the United States was an essentially "classless" society in which everyone belonged to the middle class. A new "mass market" society with an essentially affluent, economically homogeneous population, they claimed, had emerged. Exaggerated as these claims were in the 1950s, there was some reason for their popular acceptance. Union membership reached its peak share of the private-sector labor force in the early 1950s; unions were able to force corporations of the day to share the benefits of strong economic growth. The union wage created a target for non-union workers as well, pulling up all but the lowest of wages as workers sought to match the union wage and employers often granted it as a tactic for keeping unions out. Under these circumstances, millions of families entered the lower middle class and saw their standard of living rise markedly. All of this made the distribution of income more equal for decades until the late 1970s. Of course there were outliers—some millions of poor, disproportionately blacks, and the rich family here and there.

Something serious must have happened in the 1970s as the trend toward greater economic equality rapidly reversed. Here are the numbers. The share of income received by the bottom 90% of the population was a modest 67% in 1970, but by 2000 this had shrunk to a mere 52%, according to a detailed study of U.S. income distribution conducted by Thomas Piketty and Emmanuel Saez, published by the prestigious National Bureau of Economic Research in 2002. Put another way, the top 10% in-creased their overall share of the nation's total income by 15 percentage points from 1970 to 2000. This is a rather astonishing jump—the *gain* of the top 10% in these years was equivalent to more than the *total income received annually* by the bottom 40% of households.

To get on the bottom rung of the top 10% of households in 2000, it would have been necessary to have an adjusted gross income of $104,000 a year. The real money, though, starts on the 99th rung of the income ladder—the top 1% received an unbelievable 21.7% of all income in 2000. To get a handhold on the very bottom of this top rung took more than $384,000.

The Piketty-Saez study (and subsequent updates), which included in its measure of annual household income some data, such as income from capital gains, that generally are not factored in, verified a rising *trend* in income inequality which had been widely noted by others, and a *degree* of inequality which was far beyond most current estimates.

The Internal Revenue Service has essentially duplicated the Piketty-Saez study. They find that in 2003, the share of total income going to the "bottom" four-fifths of house-holds (that's 80% of the population!) was only slightly above 40%. (See Figure 1.) Both of these studies show much higher levels of inequality than were previously thought to exist based on widely referenced Census Bureau studies. The Census studies still attribute 50% of total income to the top fifth for 2003, but this number appears to understate what the top fifth now receives—nearly 60%, according to the IRS.

A Brave New (Globalized) World for Workers

Why the big change from 1970 to 2000? That is too long a story to tell here in full. But briefly, we can say that beginning in the early 1970s, U.S. corporations and the wealthy individuals who largely own them had the means, the motive, and the opportunity to garner a larger share of the nation's income—and they did so.

Let's start with the motive. The 1970s saw a significant slowdown in U.S. economic growth, which made corporations and stockholders anxious to stop sharing the benefits of growth to the degree they had in the im-mediate postwar era.

Opportunity appeared in the form of an accelerating globalization of economic activity. Beginning in the 1970s, more and more U.S.-based corporations began to set up production operations overseas. The trend has only accelerated since, in part because international communication and transportation costs have fallen dramatically. Until the 1970s, it was very difficult—essentially unprof-itable—for giants like General Electric or General Motors to operate plants offshore and then import their foreign-made products into the United States. So from the 1940s to the 1970s, U.S. workers had a geographic lever, one they have now almost entirely lost. This erosion in workers' bargaining power has undermined the middle class and decimated the unions that once man-aged to assure the working class a generally comfortable economic existence. And today, of course, the tendency to send jobs offshore is affecting many highly trained professionals such as engineers. So this process of gutting the middle class has not run its course.

Given the opportunity presented by globalization, companies took a two-pronged approach to strengthening their hand vis-à-vis workers: (1) a frontal assault on unions, with decertification elections and get-tough tactics during unionization attempts, and (2) a debilitating war of nerves whereby corporations threatened to move offshore unless workers scaled back their demands or agreed to givebacks of prior gains in wage and benefit levels or working conditions.

A succession of U.S. governments that pursued conservative—or pro-corpo-rate—economic policies provided the means. Since the 1970s, both Republican and Democratic administrations have tailored their eco-nomic policies to benefit corporations and shareholders over workers. The laundry list of such policies includes

- new trade agreements, such as NAFTA, that allow companies to cement favorable deals to move offshore to host nations such as Mexico;
- tax cuts for corporations and for the wealthiest house-holds, along with hikes in the payroll taxes that represent the largest share of the tax burden on the working and middle classes;
- lax enforcement of labor laws that are supposed to protect the right to organize unions and bargain collectively.

Exploding Millionairism

Given these shifts in the political economy of the United States, it is not surprising that economic inequality in 2000 was higher than in 1970. But at this point, careful readers may well ask whether it is misleading to use data for the year 2000, as the studies reported above do, to demonstrate rising inequality. After all, wasn't 2000 the year the NASDAQ peaked, the year the dot-com bubble reached its maximum volume? So if the wealthiest households received an especially large slice of the nation's total income that year, doesn't that just reflect a bubble about to burst rather than an underlying trend?

To begin to answer this question, we need to look at the trends in income and wealth distribution *since* 2000. And it turns out that after a slight pause in 2000-2001, inequality has continued to rise. Look at household income, for example. According to the standard indicators, the U.S. economy saw a brief recession in 2000-2001 and has been in a recovery ever since. But the median household income has failed to recover. In 2000 the median household had an annual income of $49,133; by 2005, after adjusting for inflation, the figure stood at $46,242. This 6% drop in median household income occurred while the inflation-adjusted Gross Domestic Product *expanded* by 14.4%.

When the Census Bureau released these data, it noted that median household income had gone up slightly between 2004 and 2005. This point was seized upon by Bush administration officials to bolster their claim that times are good for American

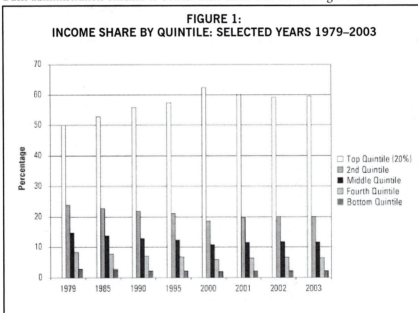

FIGURE 1:
INCOME SHARE BY QUINTILE: SELECTED YEARS 1979–2003

Source: "Further Analysis Of The Distribution Of Income And Taxes, 1979–2002," Michael Strudler and Tom Petska, Statistics of Income Division, Internal Revenue Service, and Ryan Petska, Quantitative Economics and Statistics, Ernst and Young LLP. Accompanying Excel files include data to 2003. Available at www.irs.gov/taxstats/article/0,,id=131260,00.html.

workers. A closer look at the data, however, revealed a rather astounding fact: Only 23 million households moved ahead in 2005, most headed by someone aged 65 or above. In other words, subtracting out the cost-of-living increase in Social Security benefits and increases in investment income (such as profits, dividends, interest, capital gains, and rents) to the over-65 group, workers again suffered a *decline* in income in 2005.

Another bit of evidence is the number of millionaire households—those with net worth of $1 million or more excluding the value of a primary residence and any IRAs. In 1999, just before the bubbles burst, there were 7.1 million millionaire households in the United States. In 2005, there were 8.9 million, a record number. Ordinary workers may not have recovered from the 2000–2001 rough patch yet, but evidently the wealthiest households have!

Many economists pay scant attention to income distribution patterns on the assumption that those shifts merely reflect trends in the productivity of labor or the return to risk-taking. But worker productivity *rose* in the 2000-2005 period, by 27.1% (see Figure 2). At the same time, from 2003 to 2005 average hourly pay *fell* by 1.2%. (Total compensation, including all forms of benefits, rose by 7.2% between 2000 and 2005. Most of the higher compensation spending merely reflects rapid increases in the health insurance premiums that employers have to pay just to maintain the same levels of coverage. But even if benefits are counted as part of workers' pay—a common and questionable practice—productivity growth outpaced this elastic definition of "pay" by 50% between 1972 and 2005.)

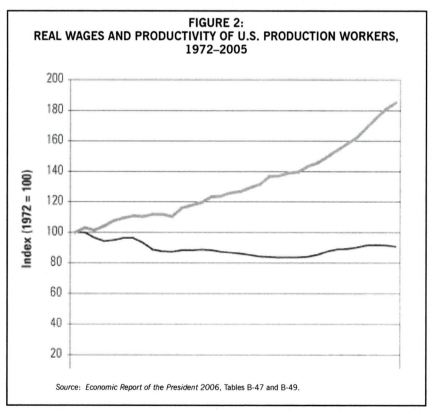

FIGURE 2:
REAL WAGES AND PRODUCTIVITY OF U.S. PRODUCTION WORKERS, 1972–2005

Index (1972 = 100)

Source: *Economic Report of the President 2006*, Tables B-47 and B-49.

And at the macro level, recent data released by the Commerce Department demonstrate that the share of the country's GDP going to wages and salaries sank to its lowest postwar level, 45.4%, in the third quarter of 2006 (see Figure 3). And this figure actually overstates how well ordinary workers are doing. The "Wage & Salary" share includes *all* income of this type, not just production workers' pay. Corporate executives' increasingly munificent salaries are included as well. Workers got roughly 65% of total wage and salary income in 2005, according to survey data from the U.S. Department of Labor; the other 35% went to salaried professionals—medical doctors and technicians, managers, and lawyers—who comprised only 15.6% of the sample.

Moreover, the "Wage & Salary" share shown in the National Income and Product Accounts includes bonuses, overtime, and other forms of payment not included in the Labor Department survey. If this income were factored in, the share going to nonprofessional, nonmanagerial workers would be even smaller. Bonuses and other forms of income to top employees can be many times base pay in important areas such as law and banking. Goldman Sachs's notorious 2006 bonuses are a case in point; the typical managing director on Wall Street garnered a bonus ranging between $1 and $3 million.

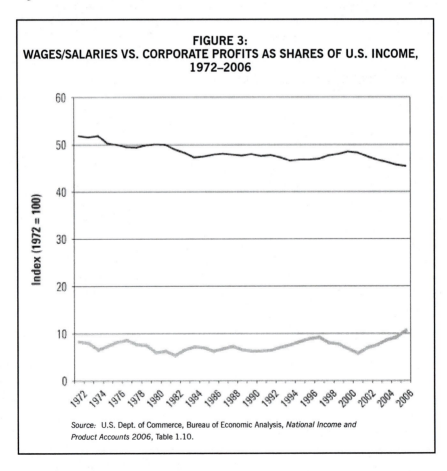

FIGURE 3:
WAGES/SALARIES VS. CORPORATE PROFITS AS SHARES OF U.S. INCOME,
1972–2006

Source: U.S. Dept. of Commerce, Bureau of Economic Analysis, *National Income and Product Accounts 2006*, Table 1.10.

So, labor's share of the nation's income is falling, as Figure 3 shows, but it is actually falling much faster than these data suggest. Profits, meanwhile, are at their highest level as a share of GDP since the booming 1960s.

These numbers should come as no surprise to anyone who reads the paper: story after story illustrates how cor-porations are continuing to squeeze workers. For instance, workers at the giant auto parts manufacturer Delphi have been told to pre-pare for a drop in wages from $27.50 an hour in 2006 to $16.50 an hour in 2007. In order to keep some of Caterpillar's manufacturing work in the United States, the union was cornered into accepting a contract in 2006 that limits new workers to a maximum salary of $27,000 a year—no matter how long they work there—com-pared to the $38,000 or more that long-time Caterpillar workers make today. More generally, for young women with a high school diploma, average entry-level pay fell to only $9.08 an hour in 2005, down by 4.9% just since 2001. For male college graduates, starter-job pay fell by 7.3% over the same period.

Aiding and Abetting

And the federal government is continuing to play its part, facilitating the transfer of an ever-larger share of the nation's income to its wealthiest households. George W. Bush once joked that his constituency was "the haves and the have-mores"—this may have been one of the few instances in which he was actually leveling with his audience. Consider aspects of the four tax cuts for individuals that Bush has imple-mented since taking office. The first two cut the top *nominal* tax rate from 39.6% to 35%. Then, in 2003, the third cut benefited solely those who hold wealth, reduc-ing taxes on dividends from 39.6% to 15% and on capital gains from 20% to 15%. (Bush's fourth tax cut—in 2006—is expected to drop taxes by 4.8% percent for the top one tenth of one percent of all households, while the median household will luxuriate with an extra nickel per day.)

So, if you make your money by the sweat of your brow and you earned $200,000 in 2003, you paid an *effective* tax rate of 21%. If you earned a bit more, say another $60,500, you paid an effective tax rate of 35% on the additional income. But if, with a flick of the wrist on your laptop, you flipped some stock you had held for six months and cleared $60,500 on the transaction, you paid the IRS an effective tax rate of only 15%. What difference does it make? Well, in 2003 the 6,126 households with incomes over $10 million saw their taxes go down by an average of $521,905 from this one tax cut alone.

These tax cuts represent only one of the many Bush administration policies that have abetted the ongoing shift of income away from most households and toward the wealthiest ones. And what do these top-tier households do with all this new-found money? For one thing, they save. This is in sharp contrast to most households. While the top fifth of households by income has a savings rate of 23%, the bot-tom 80% as a group dissave—in other words, they go into debt, spending more than they earn. Households headed by a person under 35 currently show a negative savings rate of 16% of income. Today *overall* savings—the savings of the top fifth minus the dis-savings of the bottom four-fifths—are slightly negative, for the first time since the Great Depression.

Here we find the crucial link between income and wealth accumulation. Able to save nearly a quarter of their income, the rich search out financial assets (and sometimes real assets such as houses and businesses) to pour their vast funds into. In many instances, sometimes with inside information, they are able to generate considerable future income from their invested savings. Like a snowball rolling downhill, savings for the rich can have a turbo effect—more savings generates more income, which then accumulates as wealth.

Lifestyles of the Rich

Make the rich even richer and the creative forces of market capitalism will be unleashed, resulting in more savings and consequently more capital investment, raising productivity and creating abundance for all. At any rate, that's the supply-side/neoliberal theory. However—and reminiscent of the false boom that defined the Japanese economy in the late 1980s—the big money has not gone into pro-ductive investments in the United States. Stripping out the money pumped into the residential real estate bubble, inflation-adjusted investment in machinery, equipment, technology, and structures increased only 1.4% from 1999 through 2005—an average of 0.23% per year. Essentially, productive investment has stagnated since the close of the dot-com boom.

Instead, the money has poured into high-risk hedge funds. These are vast pools of unregulated funds that are now generating 40% to 50% of the trades in the New York Stock Exchange and account for very large portions of trad-ing in many U.S. and foreign credit and debt markets.

And where is the income from these investments going? In fall 2006, media mogul David Geffen sold two paintings at record prices, a Jasper Johns ($80 million) and a Willem de Kooning ($63.5 million), to two of "today's crop of hedge-fund billionaires" whose cash is making the art market "red-hot," according to the *New York Times*.

Other forms of conspicuous consumption have their allure as well. Boeing and Lufthansa are expecting brisk business for the newly introduced 787 airplane. The commercial version of the new Boeing jet will seat 330, but the VIP version offered by Lufthansa Technik (for a mere $240 million) will have seating for 35 or fewer, leaving room for master bedrooms, a bar, and the transport of racehorses or Rolls Royces. And if you lose your auto assembly job? It should be easy to find work as a dog walker: High-end pet care services are booming, with sales more than doubling between 2000 and 2004. Opened in 2001, Just Dogs Gourmet expects to have 45 franchises in place by the end of 2006 selling hand-decorated doggie treats. And then there is Camp Bow Wow, which offers piped-in classical music for the dogs (oops, "guests") and a live Camper Cam for their owners. Started only three years ago, the company already has 140 franchises up and running.

According to David Butler, the manager of a premiere auto dealership outside of Detroit, sales of Bentleys, at $180,000 a pop, are brisk. But not many $300,000 Rolls Royces are selling. "It's not that they can't afford it," Butler told the *New York Times*, "it's because of the image it would give." Just what is the image problem in Detroit? Well, maybe it has something to do with those Delphi workers facing a

40% pay cut. Michigan's economy is one of the hardest-hit in the nation. GM, long a symbol of U.S. manufacturing prowess, is staggering, with rumors of possible bankruptcy rife. The best union in terms of delivering the goods for the U.S. working class, the United Auto Workers, is facing an implosion. Thousands of Michigan workers at Delphi, GM, and Ford will be out on the streets very soon. (The top three domestic car makers are determined to permanently lay off three-quar-ters of their U.S. assembly-line workers—nearly 200,000 hourly employees. If they do, then the number of auto-workers employed by the Big Three—Ford, Chrysler, and GM—will have shrunk by a staggering 900,000 since 1978.) So, this might not be the time to buy a Rolls. But a mere $180,000 Bentley—why not?

Had Enough of the "Haves"?

In the era Twain decried as the "great barbeque," the outrageous concentration of income and wealth eventually sparked a reaction and a vast reform movement. But it was not until the onset of the Great Depression, decades later, that massive labor/ social unrest and economic collapse forced the country's political elite to check the growing concentration of income and wealth.

Today, it does not appear that there are, as yet, any viable forces at work to put the brakes on the current runaway process of rising inequality. Nor does it appear that this era's power elite is ready to accept any new social compact. In a recent report on the "new king of Wall Street" (a co-founder of the hedge fund/ private-equity buyout corporation Blackstone Group) that seemed to typify elite perspectives on today's inequality, the *New York Times* gushed that "a crashing wave of capital is minting new billionaires each year." Naturally, the *Times* was too discreet to mention is that those same "crashing waves" have flattened the middle class. And their backwash has turned the working class every-which-way while pulling it down, down, down.

But perhaps those who decry the trend can find at least symbolic hope in the new boom in yet another luxury good. Private mausoleums, in vogue during that earlier Gilded Age, are back. For $650,000, one was recently constructed at Daytona Memorial Park in Florida—with matching $4,000 Medjool date palms for shade. Another, complete with granite patio, meditation room, and doors of hand cast bronze, went up in the same cemetery. Business is booming, apparently, with 2,000 private mausoleums sold in 2005, up from a single-year peak of 65 in the 1980s. Some cost "well into the millions," according to one the nation's largest makers of cemetery monuments. Who knows: maybe the mausoleum boom portends the ulti-mate (dead) end for the neo-Gilded Age.

Sources: Jenny Anderson, "As Lenders, Hedge Funds Draw Insider Scrutiny," *NY Times* 10/16/06; Steven Greenhouse, "Many Entry-Level Workers Feel Pinch of Rough Market," *NY Times* 9/4/06; Greenhouse and David Leonhardt, "Real Wages Fail to Match a Rise in Productivity," *NY Times* 8/28/06; Paul Krugman, "Feeling No Pain," *NY Times* 3/6/06; Krugman, "Graduates vs. Oligarchs," *NY Times* 2/27/06; David Cay Johnston, *Perfectly Legal* (Penguin Books, 2003); Johnston, "Big Gain for Rich Seen in Tax Cuts for Investments," *NY Times* 4/5/06; Johnston, "New Rise in Number of Millionaire Families," *NY Times* 3/28/06; Johnston, "'04 Income in US was Below 2000 Level," *NY Times 11/28/06*; Leonhardt, "The Economics of Henry Ford May Be Passé," *NY Times 4/5/06*; Rick Lyman, "Census Reports Slight Increase in '05 Incomes," *NY Times* 8/30/06; Micheline Maynard and Nick Bunkley, "Ford is Offering 75,000 Employees Buyout Packages," *NY Times 9/15/06*; Jeremy W. Peters, "Delphi Is Said to Offer Union a One-Time Sweetener," *NY Times 3/28/06*; Joe Sharky, "For the Super-Rich, It's Time to Upgrade the Old Jumbo Jet," *NY Times* 10/17/06; Guy Trebay, "For a Price, Final Resting Place that Tut Would Find Pleasant" *NY Times 4/17/06*.

Article 7.6

NO THANKS TO THE SUPER-RICH
We don't owe them gratitude for their "superior productivity."

BY ALEJANDRO REUSS
January/February 2012

> "Look at the industries that have dramatically improved over the past several decades, and you'll see a pattern: certain super-productive individuals have led the way. These individuals invariably fall under the 1% of income earners--often the 1% of the 1%. ...
>
> "In no other country are high achievers as free to have a vision, to act on it, to reap the rewards, and to accumulate and reinvest capital--even when they are unpopular, even when 'the 99%' disagree or are resentful or envious.
>
> "So, at a time when the 1% are the easy scapegoats, it's fitting this Thanksgiving to take a moment to thank the 1%--and to be grateful that our country rewards success. And as we approach the new year, let's resolve to keep it that way."
>
> —Alex Epstein, "Let's Give Thanks for the One Percent," FoxNews.com, November 23, 2011

Leave it to Fox News to publish an opinion piece, on the eve of Thanksgiving, titled "Let's Give Thanks for the One Percent." Author Alex Epstein, a former fellow of the Ayn Rand Institute, argues that most of "the 1%" (the Occupy Wall Street movement's designation of the richest 1% of the population) "earn their success—through superior productivity that benefits us all."

Is it true that the United States "fosters and rewards productivity like no other," as Epstein argues? Is greater inequality the price we pay for greater economic dynamism? As a first cut, let's compare Gross Domestic Product (GDP) per capita in different high-income countries. Here, the United States ranks second among large industrial countries (excluding small, oil-rich countries, city-states, etc.) behind only Norway. In 2010, Norway's GDP per capita was nearly $56,000, compared to just under $47,000 for the United States. This difference was not a one-year anomaly—Norway's GDP per capita has exceeded that of the United States for over twenty years. One doubts that Epstein would see Nordic social democracy as the kind of society—in which "high achievers [are] free to have a vision, to act on it, to reap the rewards, and to accumulate and reinvest capital"—that fosters high productivity. Yet the GDP figures suggest that it does just that.

Still, second place is not bad. The United States does outpace most of Western Europe on GDP per capita. So maybe Norway is an anomaly, and the more general picture is that the United States and its incentives to "high achievers" vastly outperform Western European "socialism" in fostering productivity. Here, we need to look at a more refined measure, GDP per hour worked, in place of GDP per capita. Average work hours per year vary dramatically among different countries. Workers in many Western European countries enjoy a shorter work week and much longer vacations than workers in the United States. Employed U.S. workers work an average of over 1700 hours per year. Their counterparts in France, Germany, the Netherlands, and Norway, in contrast, average just over 1400 hours. These differences in hours worked explain much of the variation in GDP per capita among these high-income countries. Shifting from GDP per capita to GDP per hour worked, we find that the United States (at about $59/hour) still ranks second to Norway (about $74/hour). The big difference in the rankings, however, is that the gap between the United States and several Western European countries all but disappears. Ireland, The Netherlands, Belgium, and France (yes, France!) all boast figures of over $57/hour, belying the idea that the United States "fosters ... productivity like no other" country (see Figure 1).

The idea that greater inequality fosters greater productivity is a widely held article of faith in the United States, and not only among conservatives. Even liberals may accept the idea that there is a tradeoff between equality and productivity, though they may see some loss in productivity as a price worth paying for greater equality. In fact, some countries may enjoy high labor productivity *because of,* not despite, their higher degree of economic equality (both in terms of the distribution of private incomes and the provision of public services). Near-universal access to education and health care, for example, helps people develop greater productive capabilities. Greater overall economic security (including an extensive social safety net and full-employment policies) can make it easier for people to take risks and attempt new ventures. Maybe these are some of the reasons that greater equality in many Western European countries is compatible with such high material standards of living.

While the United States does little better (or, in one case, worse) than five different Western European countries on productivity, we are clearly number one when it comes

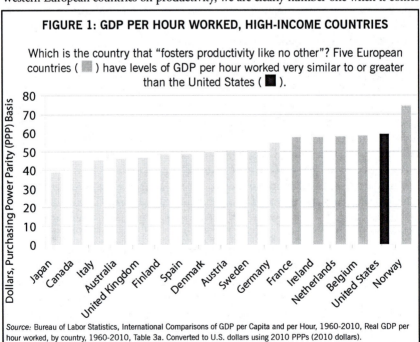

FIGURE 1: GDP PER HOUR WORKED, HIGH-INCOME COUNTRIES

Which is the country that "fosters productivity like no other"? Five European countries (▨) have levels of GDP per hour worked very similar to or greater than the United States (■).

Source: Bureau of Labor Statistics, International Comparisons of GDP per Capita and per Hour, 1960-2010, Real GDP per hour worked, by country, 1960-2010, Table 3a. Converted to U.S. dollars using 2010 PPPs (2010 dollars).

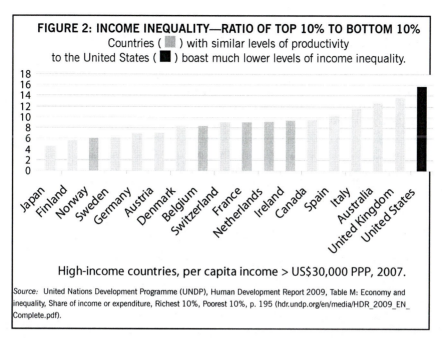

FIGURE 2: INCOME INEQUALITY—RATIO OF TOP 10% TO BOTTOM 10%
Countries (▨) with similar levels of productivity
to the United States (■) boast much lower levels of income inequality.

High-income countries, per capita income > US$30,000 PPP, 2007.

Source: United Nations Development Programme (UNDP), Human Development Report 2009, Table M: Economy and inequality, Share of income or expenditure, Richest 10%, Poorest 10%, p. 195 (hdr.undp.org/en/media/HDR_2009_EN_Complete.pdf).

to income inequality. One way to measure income inequality is to compare the share of total income going to the top 10% of the population, by income ranking, to the share going to the bottom 10%. (Using other measures does not change the basic story.) In the United States, the top 10% receives nearly 16 times as much income as the bottom 10%. In the four countries with GDP per hour very similar to the United States'—Belgium, France, Ireland, and Holland—this ratio is less than ten to one. These countries are all in the middle of the pack, in terms of income inequality, among high-income industrial economies. Norway, the country with the highest GDP per hour, has a ratio of just six to one. By this measure, it boasts the third-lowest level of income inequality among these high-income countries (see Figure 2).

Average labor productivity in the U.S. economy, measured by output per hour in the private business sector, has nearly doubled over the last thirty years. Part of the increase is explained by an increase in the education and skills of U.S. workers; part, by the fact that they are working with more and better tools. Most of the increase in income inequality in the United States is not due to an increasing gap in incomes between highly educated (and supposedly more productive) workers and less-educated workers. It is due, rather, to an increase in incomes from property (profits, rent, dividends, interest, capital gains, etc.) at the expense of incomes from labor, and to an increase in the incomes of top corporate executives (which derive from corporate control, and should be classified as part of property income).

That one person's income is higher than another's does not prove that the former is more productive than the latter. If a particular person or group's income is rising, this does not prove that they are being "rewarded" for their increasing productivity. Gains in productivity, like those in the United States in recent decades, must go to someone or other. It is the way that these gains have been split up among different groups that explains the United States' high and rising income inequality—and that has less to do with changes in the relative productivity of different people than shifts in the balance of power between owners and workers.

That does call for a response from the majority, but it's not "thank you."

Sources: Alex Epstein, "Let's Give Thanks for the One Percent," FoxNews. com, November 23, 2011; Bureau of Labor Statistics, International Comparisons of GDP per Capita and per Hour, 1960-2010, Real GDP per hour worked, by country, 1960-2010, Table 3a. Converted to U.S. dollars using 2010 PPPs (2010 dollars), (bls.gov); Bureau of Labor Statistics, Output Per Hour, Private Business Sector, Series ID number: PRS84006093 (bls.gov); United Nations Development Programme, Human Development Report 2009, Table M: Economy and inequality, Share of income or expenditure, Richest 10%, Poorest 10%, p. 195 (undp.org).

Article 7.7

NEW WELFARE POLICY, SAME SINGLE-MOTHER POVERTY

BY RANDY ALBELDA
January/February 2012

Four years into a period of deep recession and persistent economic crisis, only now has the p-word—poverty—finally surfaced. The Census Bureau's September 13 2011 announcement that the U.S. poverty rate had increased to 15.1% in 2010, up from 14.3% in 2009, put the issue of poverty onto page one, albeit briefly. In fact, poverty and how to address it have not been prominent items on the national agenda since the "welfare reform" debates of the 1980s and early 1990s.

"Welfare queens" may have disappeared from politicians' rhetoric, but poor people, disproportionately single mothers and their children, are still around. Single-mother families have been and continue to be particularly vulnerable to being poor. The September report showed the poverty rate for single mothers and their children rose as well: from 32.5% in 2009 to 34.2% in 2010.

It is remarkably hard to be the primary caregiver *and* garner enough income to support a family. This reality was built into the design of the first generation of federal anti-poverty programs in the United States. Developed beginning in the New Deal era, these programs were aimed at families with no able-bodied male breadwinner and hence no jobs or wages—single mothers, people with disabilities, and elders. Putting single mothers to work was thought to be undesirable. Or, white single mothers—there was much less reluctance in the case of black single mothers, who were largely excluded from the various anti-poverty programs until the 1960s.

The most important of the anti-poverty programs for single mothers was the cash assistance program, Aid to Dependent Children (later renamed Aid to Families with Dependent Children, or AFDC), established in 1935—also commonly referred to as "welfare." Other programs developed in the succeeding decades included Food Stamps, Medicaid, and housing assistance.

Then, in 1996, with the support of President Clinton, Congress abolished AFDC, replacing it with a block grant called TANF (Temporary Assistance to Needy Families), and passed a spate of other changes to related programs. The new anti-poverty regime implied a new social compact with the non-disabled, non-elder poor, supported by both conservatives and liberals: to require employment in exchange for—and ultimately be weaned off of—government support. In other words, the new mandate for poor adults, especially single mothers, was to get a job—any job.

And, in fact, in the ensuing years the number of poor families with wages from work increased. Moreover, welfare rolls dropped. And, in the first four years following welfare "reform," the official poverty rate for single-mother families fell too. (It has been increasing since 2000, although not quite back to its 1996 level.) But despite their higher wage income, many single-mother families are no better able to provide for their basic needs today than before the mid-1990s. Even the lower poverty rate may not reflect the real material well-being of many single moms and their children, given that their mix of resources has shifted to include more of the kinds of income counted by poverty measures and less of the uncounted kinds.

While TANF and the other legislative changes promote employment in theory, they did not reshape anti-poverty programs to genuinely support employment. Key programs are insufficiently funded, leaving many without access to child care and other vital work supports; income eligibility requirements and benefit levels designed for those with no earnings work poorly for low-wage earners; and the sheer amount of time it takes to apply for and keep benefits is at odds with holding down a job.

Ironically, there has been little or no talk of revisiting these policies despite the massive job losses of the Great Recession. With job creation at a standstill, in 2010 the unemployment rate for single mothers was 14.6% (more than one out of every seven). For this and other reasons it is time to "modernize" anti-poverty programs by assuring they do what policy makers and others want them to do—encourage employment while reducing poverty. And they must also serve as an important safety net when work is not available or possible. But changes to government policies are not enough. If employment is to be the route out of poverty, then wages and employer benefits must support workers at basic minimum levels.

Ending "Welfare" And Promoting Employment

Among the changes to U.S. anti-poverty programs in the 1990s, the most sweeping and highly politicized involved AFDC, the cash assistance program for poor parents. The 1996 legislative overhaul gave states tremendous leeway over eligibility rules in the new TANF program. For the first time there was a time limit: states are not allowed to allocate federal TANF money to any adult who has received TANF for 60 months—regardless of how long it took to accrue 60 months of aid. And the new law required recipients whose youngest child is over one year old to do some form of paid or unpaid work—most forms of education and job training don't count—after 24 months of receiving benefits.

To accommodate the push for employment, Congress expanded the Earned Income Tax Credit, which provides refundable tax credits for low-income wage earners; expanded the Child Care Development Block Grant, which gives states money to help provide child care to working parents with low incomes, including parents leaving TANF; and established the State Children's Health Insurance Program (S-CHIP), in part out of a recognition that single mothers entering the workforce were losing Medicaid coverage yet often working for employers who provided unaffordable health insurance coverage or none at all. Even housing assistance programs started promoting employment: the Department of Housing and Urban Development encouraged local housing authorities to redesign housing assistance so as to induce residents to increase their earnings.

The strategy of promoting employment was remarkably successful at getting single mothers into the labor force. In 1995, 63.5% of all single mothers were employed; by 2009, 67.8% were. This rate exceeds that of married mothers, at 66.3%. So with all that employment, why are poverty rates still so high for single-mother families? The answer lies in the nature of low-wage work and the mismatch between poverty reduction policies and employment.

Single Mothers and Low-Wage Jobs Don't Mix

There are two fundamental mismatches single mothers face in this new welfare regime. The first has to do with the awkward pairing of poor mothers and low-wage jobs. In 2009 over one-third of single mothers were in jobs that are low paying (defined as below two-thirds of the median hourly wage, which was $9.06). In addition to the low pay, these jobs typically lack benefits such as paid sick or vacation days and health insurance. Many low-wage jobs that mothers find in retail and hospitality have very irregular work hours, providing the employers with lots of flexibility but workers with almost none. These features of low-wage work wreak havoc for single moms. An irregular work schedule makes child care nearly impossible to arrange. A late school bus, a sick child, or a sick child-care provider can throw a wrench in the best-laid plans for getting to and staying at work. Without paid time off, a missed day of work is a missed day of pay. And too many missed days can easily cost you your job.

Medicaid, the government health insurance program for the poor, does not make up for the lack of employer-sponsored health insurance common in low-wage jobs. Medicaid income eligibility thresholds vary state by state, but are typically so low that many low-wage workers don't qualify. Only 63% of low-wage single mothers have any health insurance coverage at all, compared to 82% of all workers. The new Patient Protection and Affordable Care Act (also known as Obamacare) may help, depending on the cost of purchasing insurance, but for now many low-wage mothers go without health care coverage.

Finally, there is the ultimate reality that there are only 24 hours in a day. Low wages mean working many hours to earn enough to cover basic needs. Yet working more hours means less time with kids. This can be costly in several ways. Hiring babysitters can be expensive. Relying heavily on good-natured relatives who provide care but may not engage and motivate young children also has costs, as does leaving younger children in the care of older brothers and sisters, who in turn can miss out on important after-school learning. Long work hours coupled with a tight budget might mean little time to help do homework, meet with teachers, or participate in in- and out-of-school activities that enrich children's lives.

A New Mismatch

The first generation of anti-poverty programs were designed on the assumption that recipients would not be working outside the home. Unfortunately, their successor programs such as TANF and SNAP, despite their explicit aim of encouraging employment, still do not work well for working people.

What does it mean that these programs are not designed for those with employment? There are two important features. First, income thresholds for eligibility tend to be very low—that is, only those with extremely low earnings qualify. For example, only two states have income thresholds above the poverty line for TANF eligibility. To get any SNAP benefits, a single mother needs to have income below 130% of the poverty line. Working full-time at $10 an hour (that's about $1,600 a month in take-home pay) would make a single mother with one child ineligible for

Poverty Remeasured

According to the Census Bureau, 46.2 million Americans were poor in 2010. But what exactly does "poor" mean? The academic and policy debates over how to measure poverty fill volumes. Some questions relate to the establishment of the poverty threshold. On what basis should the poverty line be drawn? Is poverty relative or absolute—in other words, if the average standard of living in a society rises, should its poverty threshold rise as well? Other questions concern measuring income. What kinds of income should be counted? Before or after taxes and government benefits? Who is included in the poverty assessment? (For example, those in institutional settings such as prisons are excluded from the official U.S. poverty measure—not a minor point when you consider that nearly 2.3 million adults were incarcerated in the United States as of the end of 2009.)

Established in 1963 by multiplying an emergency food budget by three, and adjusted solely for inflation in the years since, the official U.S. poverty thresholds are notoriously low. A family of four bringing in over $22,314—*including* any TANF cash assistance, unemployment or workers' comp, Social Security or veterans' benefits, and child support—is not officially poor. In many parts of the United States, $22K would not be enough to keep one person, let alone four people, off the street and minimally clothed and fed.

An interagency federal effort to develop a more realistic poverty level has just released its new measure, known as the Supplemental Poverty Measure. The SPM makes many adjustments to the traditional calculation:

It counts the Earned Income Tax Credit and non-cash benefits such as food stamps and housing assistance as income.

It subtracts from income out-of-pocket medical costs, certain work-related expenses (e.g., child care), and taxes paid.

Its thresholds are adjusted for cost-of-living differences by region and are relative rather than absolute—basic expenses that are the building blocks of the threshold are pegged at the 33rd percentile of U.S. households.

The SPM poverty rate for 2009 was 15.7%, somewhat higher than the 14.5% official rate. More dramatic differences between the two poverty rates appeared in some subgroups, especially the elderly: 9.9% by the traditional measure versus 16.1% by the SPM, largely due to their high out-of-pocket medical expenses.

—*Amy Gluckman*

Sources: "Measure by Measure," *The Economist*, January 20, 2011; Ellen Frank, "Measures of Poverty," *Dollars & Sense*, January 2006; Center for Women's Welfare, Univ. of Wash. School of Social Work, "How Does the Self-Sufficiency Standard Compare to the New Supplemental Poverty Measure?"; U.S. Census Bureau, "How the Census Bureau Measures Poverty" and "Poverty Thresholds by Size of Family and Number of Children: 2010."

both programs in all states. Moreover, even if you are eligible, these benefits phase out sharply. With TANF (in most states), SNAP, and housing assistance, for every additional dollar you earn, you lose about 33 cents in each form of support. This means work just does not pay.

Second, applying for and maintaining benefits under these programs often takes a great deal of time. Each program has particular eligibility requirements; each requires different sets of documents to verify eligibility. While some states have tried to move to a "one-stop" system, most require separate applications for each program and, often, one or more office visits. Recertification (i.e., maintaining eligibility) can require assembling further documentation and meeting again with caseworkers. If you have ever applied for one of these programs, maybe you have experienced how time-consuming—and frustrating—the process can be.

In short, the programs were designed for applicants and recipients with plenty of time on their hands. But with employment requirements, this is not the right assumption. Missing time at work to provide more paperwork for the welfare office is just not worth it; there is considerable evidence that many eligible people do not use TANF or SNAP for that reason. Even the benefit levels assume an unlimited amount of time. Until recently, the maximum dollar amount of monthly SNAP benefits was based on a very low-cost food budget that assumed hours of home cooking.

Unlike cash assistance or food assistance, child care subsidies are obviously aimed at "working" mothers. But this program, too, often has onerous reporting requirements. Moreover, in most states the subsidy phases out very quickly especially after recipients' earnings reach the federal poverty line. This means that a worker who gets a small raise at work can suddenly face a steep increase in her child-care bill. (Of course, this is only a problem for the lucky parents who actually receive a child-care subsidy; as mentioned earlier, the lack of funding means that most eligible parents do not.)

The Earned Income Tax Credit is a notable exception. The refundable tax credit was established explicitly to help working parents with low incomes. It is relatively easy to claim (fill out a two page tax form along with the standard income tax forms), and of all the anti-poverty programs it reaches the highest up the income ladder. It even phases out differently: the credit increases as earnings rise, flattens out, and then decreases at higher levels of earnings. Most recipients get the credit in an annual lump sum and so use it very differently from other anti-poverty supports. Families often use the "windfall" to pay off a large bill or to pay for things long put off, like a visit to the dentist or a major car repair. While helpful and relatively easy to get, then, the Earned Income Tax Credit does not typically help with day-to-day expenses as the other anti-poverty programs do.

Has Employment-Promotion "Worked"?

The most striking change in the anti-poverty picture since welfare reform was enacted is that the welfare rolls have plummeted. In 1996, the last full year under the old system, there were 4.43 million families on AFDC nationwide; in 2010, amid the worst labor market in decades, the TANF caseload was only 1.86 million. In fact, when unemployment soared in 2008, only 15 states saw their TANF caseloads increase. The rest continued to experience reductions. Plus, when the TANF rolls fell sharply in the late 1990s, so did Medicaid and Food Stamps enrollments. These programs have since seen increases in usage, especially since the recession, but it's clear that when families lose cash assistance they frequently lose access to other supports as well.

Welfare reform has worked very well, then, if receiving welfare is a bad thing. Indeed, advocates of the new regime tout the rapid and steep decline in welfare use as their main indicator of its success. In and of itself, however, fewer families using anti-poverty programs does not mean less poverty, more personal responsibility, or greater self-sufficiency. During the economic expansion of the late 1990s, the official poverty rate for single mothers and their children fell from 35.8% in 1996 to 28.5% in 2000. It has risen nearly every year since, reaching 34.2% in 2010. But if a successful anti-poverty effort is measured at all by the economic well-being of the targeted families, then that slight drop in the poverty rate is swamped by the 60% decrease in the number of families using welfare over the same period. Far fewer poor families are being served. In 1996, 45.7% of all poor children received some form of income-based cash assistance; in 2009, only 18.7% did. The Great Recession pushed 800,000 additional U.S. families into poverty between 2007 and 2009, yet the TANF rolls rose by only 110,000 over this period.

Data from two federal government reports on TANF, depicted in the chart below, nicely illustrate the dilemmas of the new welfare regime. The chart shows the total average amounts of earnings and the value of major government supports ("means-tested income") for the bottom 40% of single-mother families (by total income) between 1996 and 2005. It is clear that since welfare reform, these families are relying much more on earnings. But despite the additional work effort, they find

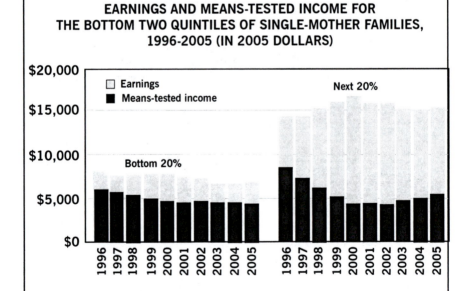

EARNINGS AND MEANS-TESTED INCOME FOR THE BOTTOM TWO QUINTILES OF SINGLE-MOTHER FAMILIES, 1996-2005 (IN 2005 DOLLARS)

Notes: Those with negative income not included. Means-tested income is the total of Supplemental Security Income, Public Assistance, certain Veteran's Benefits, Food Stamps, School Lunch, and housing benefits.

Source: U.S. Department of Health and Human Services, the Office of Assistant Secretary for Planning and Evaluation, Table 4:3 of TANF 6th Annual Report to Congress (November 2004) and Table 4:2 of TANF 8th Annual Report to Congress (June 2009), using tabulations from the U.S. Census Bureau, 1996-2005.

themselves essentially no better off. The bottom 20% saw their package of earnings and government benefits *fall*: their average earnings have not increased much while government supports have dropped off, leaving them with fewer resources on average in 2006 than in 1996. For the second quintile, earnings have increased substantially but benefits have fallen nearly as much, leaving this group only slightly better off over the period. And that is without taking into account the expenses associated with employment (e.g. child care, transportation, work clothes) and with the loss of public supports (such as increased co-payments for child care or health insurance). These women are working a lot more—in the second quintile about double—but are barely better off at all! So much for "making work pay."

More hours of work also means fewer hours with children. If the time a mother spends with her children is worth anything, then substituting earnings for benefits represents a loss of resources to her family.

What Might Be Done?

Employment, even with government supports, is unlikely to provide a substantial share of single-mother families with adequate incomes. Three factors—women's lower pay, the time and money it takes to raise children, and the primary reliance on only one adult to both earn and care for children—combine to make it nearly impossible for a sizeable number of single mothers to move to stable and sufficient levels of resources.

Addressing the time- and money-squeeze that single mothers faced in the old anti-poverty regime and still face in the new one will take thoroughgoing changes in the relations among work, family, and income.

- *Make work pay by shoring up wages and employer benefits.* To ensure that the private sector does its part, raise the minimum wage. A full-time, year-round minimum wage job pays just over the poverty income threshold for a family of two. Conservatives and the small business lobby will trot out the bogeyman of job destruction, but studies on minimum-wage increases show a zero or even positive effect on employment. In addition, mandate paid sick days for all workers and require benefit parity for part-time, temporary, and subcontracted workers. This would close a loophole that a growing number of employers use to dodge fringe benefits.

- *Reform anti-poverty programs to really support employment.* To truly support low-wage employment, anti-poverty programs should increase income eligibility limits so that a worker can receive the supports even while earning and then phase out the programs more gradually so low-wage workers keep getting them until they earn enough not to need them. Also, streamline application processes and make them more user-friendly. Many states have done this for unemployment insurance, car registration, and driver's license renewal. Why not do the same for SNAP, TANF and Medicaid?

- *Support paid and unpaid care work.* A society that expects all able-bodied adults to work—regardless of the age of their children—should also be a society that shares the costs of going to work, by offering programs to care for children and others who need care. This means universal child care and afterschool programs. It also means paid parental leave and paid time off to care for an ill relative. The federal Family and Medical Leave Act gives most workers the right to take unpaid leaves, but many can't afford to. California and New Jersey have extended their temporary disability insurance benefits to cover those facing a wide range of family needs—perhaps a helpful model.

New anti-poverty regime, but same poverty problems. Most single mothers *cannot* work their way out of poverty—definitely not without the right kinds of supplemental support. There are many possible policy steps that could be taken to help them and other low-wage workers get the most out of an inhospitable labor market. But ultimately, better designed assistance to poor and low-income families, old fashioned cash assistance, and minimal employment standards must be part of the formula. ❑

Sources: Randy Albelda and Chris Tilly, *Glass Ceilings and Bottomless Pits: Women's Work, Women's Poverty*, South End Press, 1997; U.S. Census Bureau, *Historical Tables on Poverty*; Kaiser Family Foundation, "Income Eligibility Limits for Working Adults at Application as a Percent of the Federal Poverty Level by Scope of Benefit Package," statehealthfacts.org, January 2011; U.S. Dept. of Health and Human Services, *TANF 6th and 8th Annual Report to Congress*, November 2004 and July 2009; U.S. Dept. of Health and Human Services, *Estimates of Child Care Eligibility and Receipt for Fiscal Year 2006*, April 2010; Thomas Gabe, *Trends in Welfare, Work, and the Economic Well-being of Female Headed Families with Children: 1987-2005*, Congressional Research Service Report RL30797, 2007; Randy Albelda and Heather Boushey, *Bridging the Gaps: A Picture of How Work Supports Work in Ten States*, Center for Social Policy, Univ. of Mass. Boston and Center for Economic and Policy Research, 2007; Author's calculations from the U.S. Census Bureau's Current Population Survey, various years.

Chapter 8

MARKET FAILURE, GOVERNMENT POLICY, AND CORPORATE GOVERNANCE

INTRODUCTION

M arkets sometimes fail. Mainstream economists typically focus on failures in which existing markets fall short of facilitating exchanges that would make both parties better off. When a factory pollutes the air, people downwind suffer a cost, and might be willing to pay the polluter to curb emissions, but there is no market for clean air. In cases like this, one solution is for the government to step in with regulations that ban industries from imposing pollution costs on others. The same goes when private markets do not provide sufficient amounts of public goods, such as vaccines, from which everyone benefits whether they contribute to paying for them or not. Again, government must step in. But what percentage of pollution should industries be required to eliminate? How much should be spent on public health? To decide how much government should step in, economists propose cost-benefit analysis, suggesting that the government weigh costs against benefits like a firm deciding how many cars to produce.

Orthodox economists typically see market failures as fairly limited in scope. In fact, they do not consider many negative consequences of markets to be failures at all. When workers are paid wages too low to meet their basic needs, economists do not usually call their poverty and overwork "market failures," but "incentives" to get a higher-paying job. As we saw in the last chapter, mainstream economists are less concerned about how equally the pie is distributed than the overall size of the pie, although most would agree that governments should help those most in need. Still, when economists do recognize market failures, most argue that they are best solved by markets themselves, so pollution should be reduced by allowing firms to trade for the right to pollute, and failing schools should be improved by introducing competition with vouchers and charter schools. Finally, orthodox economists worry about government failure, the possibility that government responses to market failures may cause more problems than they solve. They conclude that the "invisible hand" of the market works pretty well, and that the alternatives, especially the "visible hand" of the state, will only make matters worse.

The authors in this chapter see market failures as far more widespread and systemic. They place a high value on outcomes beyond "the size of the pie," believing that environmental sustainability, equality, and economic democracy are equally important, if not more so. In "Sharing the Wealth of the Commons" (Article 8.1), Peter Barnes challenges the way that conventional economists view issues of the environment and other goods that are shared by many people.

In "Universal Healthcare: Can We Afford Anything Less?" (Article 8.2), Gerald Friedman graphically illustrates that the cost of funding a single-payer healthcare system is entirely affordable and cost-effective. Since the benefits of such a plan outweigh the costs, why do we not have such a system?

In "Pricing the Priceless: Inside the Strange World of Cost-Benefit Analysis" (Article 8.3), Lisa Heinzerling and Frank Ackerman then point out key flaws in the use of cost-benefit analysis to guide government action. In his subsequent article; "Climate Economics in Four Easy Pieces" (8.4), Ackerman shows how this flawed concept of costs and benefits leads orthodox economists to conclude that taking action to prevent further global warming is "inefficient."

In "Car Trouble: The Automobile as an Environmental and Health Disaster" (Article 8.5), Alejandro Reuss argues that our dependence on the car has become unsustainable, and that the solution must be a new transportation system based on alternatives to the auto.

Concluding this chapter is "The Phantom Menace: Environmental Regulations are Not 'Job Killers'"(Article 8.6) by Heidi Garrett-Peltier,. The most common complaint from industry and their legions of lobbyists is that there is a rigid trade-off between all things environmental and employment. Industry chooses to link the purported cost of environmental legislation to "jobs" as opposed to "profits," since employment resonates better with the public. If you can get the public to believe in an "either/or" trade-off—a clean environment vs. employment—they will side with their most pressing need, employment. Garrett-Peltier shows this is a false dichotomy. Enforcing environmental rules and "going green" not only might not cost net jobs, but in fact might create significant new employment, especially in weaning ourselves off hydrocarbon fuels.

Discussion Questions

1) (Article 8.1) Peter Barnes says that we take for granted an enormous number of resources—including the natural environment, but also the laws and institutions that make business possible. Is his point the same as saying that there are market failures, such as pollution externalities, that prevent markets from taking into account the full value of the environment? Explain how it is the same or different. In particular, what is the connection between equality/inequality and market failures?

2) (Article 8.2) Can we afford a single-payer healthcare system in the United States? What does Friedman mean by asking, "Can we afford anything less?"

3) (Article 8.2) Is health care a "public good" or a private "commodity"? Explore this issue.

4) (Article 8.3) Make a list of types of goods that are harder to put a price on (valuate) than others. Why is it so hard to price these types of goods?

5) (Article 8.3) Lisa Heinzerling and Frank Ackerman point out a number of flaws in cost-benefit analysis. These weaknesses suggest that the cost-benefit approach will work better in some situations, worse in others. Describe when you would expect it to work better and worse, and explain.

6) (Article 8.4) Frank Ackerman provides "four easy pieces" to allow economics to better complement the science of climate change. Why are these four pieces necessary for economics as a discipline to "get it" about climate change? What don't neoclassical economists (in this case William Nordhaus) "get" about climate change?

9) (Article 8.5) Alejandro Reuss lists the many costs of using cars for transportation. Take a "devil's advocate" position, and explain why the benefits outweigh the costs. Which point of view do you find more convincing?

10) (Articles 8.5 and 5.2) Conventional economics emphasizes individual choice. But Reuss says our overdependence on cars is rooted in the evolution of an auto-based transportation system. What is a transportation system? How might it limit individual choices? Does this idea of a system help understand markets other than transportation?

11) (Article 8.6) Do environmental regulations "kill jobs?" Is this a false dichotomy? If so, how? Why is the concept "net jobs" important here?

Article 8.1

SHARING THE WEALTH OF THE COMMONS

BY PETER BARNES
November/December 2004

We're all familiar with private wealth, even if we don't have much. Economists and the media celebrate it every day. But there's another trove of wealth we barely notice: our common wealth.

Each of us is the beneficiary of a vast inheritance. This common wealth includes our air and water, habitats and ecosystems, languages and cultures, science and technologies, political and monetary systems, and quite a bit more. To say we share this inheritance doesn't mean we can call a broker and sell our shares tomorrow. It does mean we're responsible for the commons and entitled to any income it generates. Both the responsibility and the entitlement are ours by birth. They're part of the obligation each generation owes to the next, and each living human owes to other beings.

At present, however, our economic system scarcely recognizes the commons. This omission causes two major tragedies: ceaseless destruction of nature and widening inequality among humans. Nature gets destroyed because no one's unequivocally responsible for protecting it. Inequality widens because private wealth concentrates while common wealth shrinks.

The great challenges for the 21st century are, first of all, to make the commons visible; second, to give it proper reverence; and third, to translate that reverence into property rights and legal institutions that are on a par with those supporting private property. If we do this, we can avert the twin tragedies currently built into our market-driven system.

Defining the Commons

What exactly is the commons? Here is a workable definition: The commons includes all the assets we inherit together and are morally obligated to pass on, undiminished, to future generations.

This definition is a practical one. It designates a set of assets that have three specific characteristics: they're (1) inherited, (2) shared, and (3) worthy of long-term preservation. Usually it's obvious whether an asset has these characteristics or not.

At the same time, the definition is broad. It encompasses assets that are natural as well as social, intangible as well as tangible, small as well as large. It also introduces a moral factor that is absent from other economic definitions: it requires us to consider whether an asset is worthy of long-term preservation. At present, capitalism has no interest in this question. If an asset is likely to yield a competitive return to capital, it's kept alive; if not, it's destroyed or allowed to run down. Assets in the commons, by contrast, are meant to be preserved regardless of their return.

This definition sorts all economic assets into two baskets, the market and the commons. In the market basket are those assets we want to own privately and manage for profit. In the commons basket are the assets we want to hold in common and manage for long-term preservation. These baskets then are, or ought to be, the yin and yang of economic activity; each should enhance and contain the other. The role of the state should be to maintain a healthy balance between them.

The Value of the Commons

For most of human existence, the commons supplied everyone's food, water, fuel, and medicines. People hunted, fished, gathered fruits and herbs, collected firewood and building materials, and grazed their animals in common lands and waters. In other words, the commons was the source of basic sustenance. This is still true today in many parts of the world, and even in San Francisco, where I live, cash-poor people fish in the bay not for sport, but for food.

Though sustenance in the industrialized world now flows mostly through markets, the commons remains hugely valuable. It's the source of all natural resources and nature's many replenishing services. Water, air, DNA, seeds, topsoil, minerals, the protective ozone layer, the atmosphere's climate regulation, and much more, are gifts of nature to us all.

Just as crucially, the commons is our ultimate waste sink. It recycles water, oxygen, carbon, and everything else we excrete, exhale, or throw away. It's the place we store, or try to store, the residues of our industrial system.

The commons also holds humanity's vast accumulation of knowledge, art, and thought. As Isaac Newton said, "If I have seen further it is by standing on the shoulders of giants." So, too, the legal, political, and economic institutions we inherit—even the market itself—were built by the efforts of millions. Without these gifts we'd be hugely poorer than we are today.

To be sure, thinking of these natural and social inheritances primarily as economic assets is a limited way of viewing them. I deeply believe they are much more than that. But if treating portions of the commons as economic assets can help us conserve them, it's surely worth doing so.

How much might the commons be worth in monetary terms? It's relatively easy to put a dollar value on private assets. Accountants and appraisers do it every day, aided by the fact that private assets are regularly traded for money.

This isn't the case with most shared assets. How much is clean air, an intact wetlands,

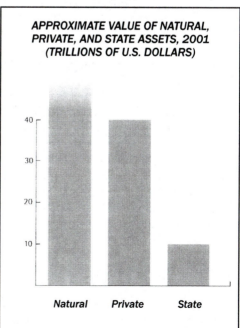

APPROXIMATE VALUE OF NATURAL, PRIVATE, AND STATE ASSETS, 2001 (TRILLIONS OF U.S. DOLLARS)

or Darwin's theory of evolution worth in dollar terms? Clearly, many shared inheritances are simply priceless. Others are potentially quantifiable, but there's no current market for them. Fortunately, economists have developed methods to quantify the value of things that aren't traded, so it's possible to estimate the value of the "priceable" part of the commons within an order of magnitude. The surprising conclusion that emerges from numerous studies is that the wealth we share is worth more than the wealth we own privately.

This fact bears repeating. Even though much of the commons can't be valued in monetary terms, the parts that can be valued are worth more than all private assets combined.

It's worth noting that these estimates understate the gap between common and private assets because a significant portion of the value attributed to private wealth is in fact an appropriation of common wealth. If this mislabeled portion was subtracted from private wealth and added to common wealth, the gap between the two would widen further.

Two examples will make this point clear. Suppose you buy a house for $200,000 and, without improving it, sell it a few years later for $300,000. You pay off the mortgage and walk away with a pile of cash. But what caused the house to rise in value? It wasn't anything you did. Rather, it was the fact that your neighborhood became more popular, likely a result of the efforts of community members, improvements in public services, and similar factors.

Or consider another fount of private wealth, the social invention and public expansion of the stock market. Suppose you start a business that goes "public" through an offering of stock. Within a few years, you're able to sell your stock for a spectacular capital gain.

Much of this gain is a social creation, the result of centuries of monetary-system evolution, laws and regulations, and whole industries devoted to accounting, sharing information, and trading stocks. What's more, there's a direct correlation between the scale and quality of the stock market as an institution and the size of the private gain. You'll fetch a higher price if you sell into a market of millions than into a market of two. Similarly, you'll gain more if transaction costs are low and trust in public information is high. Thus, stock that's traded on a regulated exchange sells for a higher multiple of earnings than unlisted stock. This socially created premium can account for 30% of the stock's value. If you're the lucky seller, you'll reap that extra cash—in no way thanks to anything you did as an individual.

Real estate gains and the stock market's social premium are just two instances of common assets contributing to private gain. Still, most rich people would like us to think it's their extraordinary talent, hard work, and risk-taking that create their well-deserved wealth. That's like saying a flower's beauty is due solely to its own efforts, owing nothing to nutrients in the soil, energy from the sun, water from the aquifer, or the activity of bees.

The Great Commons Giveaway

That we inherit a trove of common wealth is the good news. The bad news, alas, is that our inheritance is being grossly mismanaged. As a recent report by the advocacy group Friends of the Commons concludes, "Maintenance of the commons is terrible, theft is rampant, and rents often aren't collected. To put it bluntly, our common wealth—and our children's—is being squandered. We are all poorer as a result."

Examples of commons mismanagement include the handout of broadcast spectrum to media conglomerates, the giveaway of pollution rights to polluters, the extension of copyrights to entertainment companies, the patenting of seeds and genes, the privatization of water, and the relentless destruction of habitat, wildlife, and ecosystems.

This mismanagement, though currently extreme, is not new. For over 200 years, the market has been devouring the commons in two ways. With one hand, the market takes valuable stuff from the commons and privatizes it. This is called "enclosure." With the other hand, the market dumps bad stuff into the commons and says, "It's your problem." This is called "externalizing." Much that is called economic growth today is actually a form of cannibalization in which the market diminishes the commons that ultimately sustains it.

Enclosure—the taking of good stuff from the commons—at first meant privatization of land by the gentry. Today it means privatization of many common assets by corporations. Either way, it means that what once belonged to everyone now belongs to a few.

Enclosure is usually justified in the name of efficiency. And sometimes, though not always, it does result in efficiency gains. But what also results from enclosure is the impoverishment of those who lose access to the commons, and the enrichment of those who take title to it. In other words, enclosure widens the gap between those with income-producing property and those without.

Externalizing—the dumping of bad stuff into the commons—is an automatic behavior pattern of profit-maximizing corporations: if they can avoid any out-of-pocket costs, they will. If workers, taxpayers, anyone downwind, future generations, or nature have to absorb added costs, so be it.

For decades, economists have agreed we'd be better served if businesses "internalized" their externalities—that is, paid in real time the costs they now shift to the commons. The reason this doesn't happen is that there's no one to set prices and collect them. Unlike private wealth, the commons lacks property rights and institutions to represent it in the marketplace.

The seeds of such institutions, however, are starting to emerge. Consider one of the environmental protection tools the U.S. currently uses, pollution trading. So-called cap-and-trade programs put a cap on total pollution, then grant portions of the total, via permits, to each polluting firm. Companies may buy other firms' permits if they want to pollute more than their allotment allows, or sell unused permits if they manage to pollute less. Such programs are generally supported by business because they allow polluters to find the cheapest ways to reduce pollution.

Public discussion of cap-and-trade programs has focused exclusively on their trading features. What's been overlooked is how they give away common wealth to polluters.

To date, all cap-and-trade programs have begun by giving pollution rights to existing polluters for free. This treats polluters as if they own our sky and rivers. It means that future polluters will have to pay old polluters for the scarce—hence valuable—right to dump wastes into nature. Imagine that: because a corporation polluted in the past, it gets free income forever! And, because ultimately we'll all pay for limited pollution via higher prices, this amounts to an enormous transfer of wealth—trillions of dollars—to shareholders of historically polluting corporations.

In theory, though, there is no reason that the initial pollution rights should not reside with the public. Clean air and the atmosphere's capacity to absorb pollutants are "wealth" that belongs to everyone. Hence, when polluters use up these parts of the commons, they should pay the public—not the other way around.

Taking the Commons Back

How can we correct the system omission that permits, and indeed promotes, destruction of nature and ever-widening inequality among humans? The answer lies in building a new sector of the economy whose clear legal mission is to preserve shared inheritances for everyone. Just as the market is populated by profit-maximizing corporations, so this new sector would be populated by asset-preserving trusts.

Here a brief description of trusts may be helpful. The trust is a private institution that's even older than the corporation. The essence of a trust is a fiduciary relationship. A trust holds and manages property for another person or for many other people. A simple example is a trust set up by a grandparent to pay for a grandchild's education. Other trusts include pension funds, charitable foundations, and university endowments. There are also hundreds of trusts in America, like the Nature Conservancy and the Trust for Public Land, that own land or conservation easements in perpetuity.

If we were to design an institution to protect pieces of the commons, we couldn't do much better than a trust. The goal of commons management, after all, is to preserve assets and deliver benefits to broad classes of beneficiaries. That's what trusts do, and it's not rocket science.

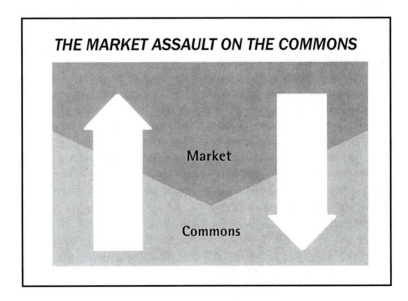

THE MARKET ASSAULT ON THE COMMONS

Market

Commons

Over centuries, several principles of trust management have evolved. These include:

- Trustees have a fiduciary responsibility to beneficiaries. If a trustee fails in this obligation, he or she can be removed and penalized.
- Trustees must preserve the original asset. It's okay to spend income, but don't invade the principal.
- Trustees must assure transparency. Information about money flows should be readily available to beneficiaries.

Trusts in the new commons sector would be endowed with rights comparable to those of corporations. Their trustees would take binding oaths of office and, like judges, serve long terms. Though protecting common assets would be their primary job, they would also distribute income from those assets to beneficiaries. These beneficiaries would include all citizens within a jurisdiction, large classes of citizens (children, the elderly), and/or agencies serving common purposes such as public transit or ecological restoration. When distributing income to individuals, the allocation formula would be one person, one share. The right to receive commons income would be a nontransferable birthright, not a property right that could be traded.

Fortuitously, a working model of such a trust already exists: the Alaska Permanent Fund. When oil drilling on the North Slope began in the 1970s, Gov. Jay Hammond, a Republican, proposed that 25% of the state's royalties be placed in a mutual fund to be invested on behalf of Alaska's citizens. Voters approved in a referendum. Since then, the Alaska Permanent Fund has grown to over $28 billion, and Alaskans have received roughly $22,000 apiece in dividends. In 2003 the per capita dividend was $1,107; a family of four received $4,428.

What Alaska did with its oil can be replicated for other gifts of nature. For example, we could create a nationwide Sky Trust to stabilize the climate for future generations. The trust would restrict emissions of heat-trapping gases and sell a declining number of emission permits to polluters. The income would be returned to U.S. residents in equal yearly dividends, thus reversing the wealth transfer built into current cap-and-trade programs. Instead of everyone paying historic polluters, polluters would pay all of us.

Just as a Sky Trust could represent our equity in the natural commons, a Public Stock Trust could embody our equity in the social commons. Such a trust would capture some of the socially created stock-market premium that currently flows only to shareholders and their investment bankers. As noted earlier, this premium is sizeable—roughly 30% of the value of publicly traded stock. A simple way to share it would be to create a giant mutual fund—call it the American Permanent Fund—that would hold, say, 10% of the shares of publicly traded companies. This mutual fund, in turn, would be owned by all Americans on a one share per person basis (perhaps linked to their Social Security accounts).

To build up the fund without precipitating a fall in share prices, companies would contribute shares at the rate of, say, 1% per year. The contributions would be the price companies pay for the benefits they derive from a commons asset, the large, trusted market for stock—a small price, indeed, for the hefty benefits. Over time, the mutual fund would assure that when the economy grows, everyone benefits. The top 5% would still own more than the bottom 90%, but at least every American would have some property income, and a slightly larger slice of our economic pie.

Sharing the Wealth

The perpetuation of inequality is built into the current design of capitalism. Because of the skewed distribution of private wealth, a small self-perpetuating minority receives a disproportionate share of America's nonlabor income.

Tom Paine had something to say about this. In his essay "Agrarian Justice," written in 1790, he argued that, because enclosure of the commons had separated so many people from their primary source of sustenance, it was necessary to create a functional equivalent of the commons in the form of a National Fund. Here is how he put it:

> There are two kinds of property. Firstly, natural property, or that which comes to us from the Creator of the universe—such as the earth, air, water. Secondly, artificial or acquired property—the invention of men. In the latter, equality is impossible; for to distribute it equally, it would be necessary that all should have contributed in the same proportion, which can never be the case .... Equality of natural property is different. Every individual in the world is born with legitimate claims on this property, or its equivalent.

Enclosure of the commons, he went on, was necessary to improve the efficiency of cultivation. But:

> The landed monopoly that began with [enclosure] has produced the greatest evil. It has dispossessed more than half the inhabitants of every nation of their natural inheritance, without providing for them, as ought to have been done, an indemnification for that loss, and has thereby created a species of poverty and wretchedness that did not exist before.

The appropriate compensation for loss of the commons, Paine said, was a national fund financed by rents paid by land owners. Out of this fund, every person reaching age 21 would get 15 pounds a year, and every person over 50 would receive an additional 10 pounds. (Think of Social Security, financed by commons rents instead of payroll taxes.)

A Progressive Offensive

Paine's vision, allowing for inflation and new forms of enclosure, could not be more timely today. Surely from our vast common inheritance—not just the land, but the atmosphere, the broadcast spectrum, our mineral resources, our threatened habitats and water supplies—enough rent can be collected to pay every American over age 21 a modest annual dividend, and every person reaching 21 a small start-up inheritance.

Such a proposal may seem utopian. In today's political climate, perhaps it is. But consider this. About 20 years ago, right-wing think tanks laid out a bold agenda. They called for lowering taxes on private wealth, privatizing much of government, and deregulating industry. Amazingly, this radical agenda has largely been achieved.

It's time for progressives to mount an equally bold offensive. The old shibboleths—let's gin up the economy, create jobs, and expand government programs—no longer excite. We need to talk about fixing the economy, not just growing it; about income for everyone, not just jobs; about nurturing ecosystems, cultures, and communities, not just our individual selves. More broadly, we need to celebrate the commons as an essential counterpoise to the market.

Unfortunately, many progressives have viewed the state as the only possible counterpoise to the market. The trouble is, the state has been captured by corporations. This capture isn't accidental or temporary; it's structural and long-term.

This doesn't mean progressives can't occasionally recapture the state. We've done so before and will do so again. It does mean that progressive control of the state is the exception, not the norm; in due course, corporate capture will resume. It follows that if we want lasting fixes to capitalism's tragic flaws, we must use our brief moments of political ascendancy to build institutions that endure.

Programs that rely on taxes, appropriations, or regulations are inherently transitory; they get weakened or repealed when political power shifts. By contrast, institutions that are self-perpetuating and have broad constituencies are likely to last. (It also helps if they mail out checks periodically.) This was the genius of Social Security, which has survived—indeed grown—through numerous Republican administrations.

If progressives are smart, we'll use our next New Deal to create common property trusts that include all Americans as beneficiaries. These trusts will then be to the 21st century what social insurance was to the 20th: sturdy pillars of shared responsibility and entitlement. Through them, the commons will be a source of sustenance for all, as it was before enclosure. Life-long income will be linked to generations-long ecological health. Isn't that a future most Americans would welcome? ❏

Article 8.2

UNIVERSAL HEALTH CARE:
CAN WE AFFORD ANYTHING LESS?

Why only a single-payer system can solve America's health-care mess.

BY GERALD FRIEDMAN
July/August 2011

America's broken health-care system suffers from what appear to be two separate problems. From the right, a chorus warns of the dangers of rising costs; we on the left focus on the growing number of people going without health care because they lack adequate insurance. This division of labor allows the right to dismiss attempts to extend coverage while crying crocodile tears for the 40 million uninsured. But the division between problem of cost and the problem of coverage is misguided. It is founded on the assumption, common among neoclassical economists, that the current market system is efficient. Instead, however, the current system is inherently inefficient; it is the very source of the rising cost pressures. In fact, the only way we can control health-care costs and avoid fiscal and economic catastrophe is to establish a single-payer system with universal coverage.

The rising cost of health care threatens the U.S. economy. For decades, the cost of health insurance has been rising at over twice the general rate of inflation; the share of American income going to pay for health care has more than doubled since 1970 from 7% to 17%. By driving up costs for employees, retirees, the needy, the young, and the old, rising health-care costs have become a major problem for governments at every level. Health costs are squeezing public spending needed for education and infrastructure. Rising costs threaten all Americans by squeezing the income available for other activities. Indeed, if current trends continued, the entire economy would be absorbed by health care by the 2050s.

Conservatives argue that providing universal coverage would bring this fiscal Armageddon on even sooner by increasing the number of people receiving care. Following this logic, their policy has been to restrict access to health care by raising insurance deductibles, copayments, and cost sharing and by reducing access to insurance. Even before the Great Recession, growing numbers of American adults were uninsured or underinsured. Between 2003 and 2007, the share of non-elderly adults without adequate health insurance rose from 35% to 42%, reaching 75 million. This number has grown substantially since then, with the recession reducing employment and with the continued decline in employer-provided health insurance. Content to believe that our current health-care system is efficient, conservatives assume that costs would have risen more had these millions not lost access, and likewise believe that extending health-insurance coverage to tens of millions using a plan like the Affordable Care Act would drive up costs even further. Attacks on employee health insurance and on Medicare and Medicaid come from this same logic—the idea that the only way to control health-care costs is to reduce the number of people with access to health care. If we do not find a way to control costs by increasing access, there will be more proposals like that of Rep. Paul Ryan (R-Wisc.) and the Republicans in the House of Representatives to slash Medicaid and abolish Medicare.

The Problem of Cost in a Private, For-Profit Health Insurance System

If health insurance were like other commodities, like shoes or bow ties, then reducing access might lower costs by reducing demands on suppliers for time and materials. But health care is different because so much of the cost of providing it is in the administration of the payment system rather than in the actual work of doctors, nurses, and other providers, and because coordination and cooperation among different providers is essential for effective and efficient health care. It is not cost pressures on providers that are driving up health-care costs; instead, costs are rising because of what economists call transaction costs, the rising cost of administering and coordinating a system that is designed to reduce access.

The health-insurance and health-care markets are different from most other markets because private companies selling insurance do not want to sell to everyone, but only to those unlikely to need care (and, therefore, most likely to drop coverage if prices rise). As much as 70% of the "losses" suffered by health-insurance providers—that is, the money they pay out in claims—goes to as few as 10% of their subscribers. This creates a powerful incentive for companies to screen subscribers, to identify those likely to submit claims, and to harass them so that they will drop their coverage and go elsewhere. The collection of insurance-related information has become a major source of waste in the American economy because it is not organized to improve patient care but to harass and to drive away needy subscribers and their health-care providers. Because driving away the sick is so profitable for health insurers, they are doing it more and more, creating the enormous bureaucratic waste that characterizes the process of billing and insurance handling. Rising by over 10% a year for the past 25 years, health insurers' administrative costs are among the fastest-growing in the U.S. health-care sector. Doctors in private practice now spend as much as 25% of their revenue on administration, nearly $70,000 per physician for billing and insurance costs.

For-profit health insurance also creates waste by discouraging people from receiving preventive care and by driving the sick into more expensive care settings. Almost a third of Americans with "adequate" health insurance go without care every year due to costs, and the proportion going without care rises to over half of those with "inadequate" insurance and over two-thirds for those without insurance. Nearly half of the uninsured have no regular source of care, and a third did not fill a prescription in the 2010 because of cost. All of this unutilized care might appear to save the system money. But it doesn't. Reducing access does not reduce health-care expenditures when it makes people sicker and pushes them into hospitals and emergency rooms, which are the most expensive settings for health care and are often the least efficient because care provided in these settings rarely has continuity or follow-up.

The great waste in our current private insurance system is an opportunity for policy because it makes it possible to economize on spending by replacing our current system with one providing universal access. I have estimated that in Massachusetts, a state with a relatively efficient health-insurance system, it would be possible to lower the cost of providing health care by nearly 16% even after providing coverage to everyone in the state currently without insurance (see Table 1). This could be done largely by reducing the cost of administering the private insurance system, with most of the savings coming within providers' offices by reducing the costs of billing and processing insurance claims. This is a conservative estimate made for a state with a relatively efficient health-insurance system. In a report prepared for the state of Vermont, William Hsiao of the Harvard School of Public Health and MIT economist Jonathan Gruber estimate that shifting to a single-payer system could lead to savings of around 25% through reduced administrative cost and improved delivery of care. (They have also noted that administrative savings would be even larger if the entire country shifted to a single-payer system because this would save the cost of billing people with private, out-of-state insurance plans.) In Massachusetts, my conservative estimates suggests that as much as $10 billion a year could be saved by shifting to a single-payer system.

Single-Payer Systems Control Costs by Providing Better Care

Adoption of a single-payer health-insurance program with universal coverage could also save money and improve care by allowing better coordination of care among different providers and by providing a continuity of care that is not possible with competing insurance plans. A comparison of health care in the United States with health care in other countries shows how large these cost savings might be. When Canada first adopted its current health-care financing system in 1968, the health-care share of the national gross domestic product in the United States (7.1%) was

TABLE 1: SOURCES OF SAVINGS AND ADDED COSTS FOR A HYPTHETICAL MASSACHUSETTS SINGLE-PAYER HEALTH SYSTEM

Change in health-care expenditures	Size of change as share of total health-care expenditures
Savings from single-payer system	
Administration costs within health-insurance system	-2.0%
Administrative costs within providers' offices	-10.1%
Reduction in provider prices through reducing market leverage for privileged providers	-5.0%
Savings:	-17.1%
Increased costs from single-payer	
Expansion in coverage to the uninsured	+1.35%
Increased utilization because of elimination of copayments, balanced by improvements in preventive care	+/- 0.0%
Total increased costs:	+1.35%
Net change in health-care expenditures:	-15.75%

Source: Calculations by the author from data in OECD Health Data 2010 (oecd.org).

nearly the same as in Canada (6.9%), and only a little higher than in other advanced economies. Since then, however, health care has become dramatically more expensive in the United States. In the United States, per capita health-care spending since 1971 has risen by over $6,900 compared with an increase of less than $3,600 in Canada and barely $3,200 elsewhere (see Table 2). Physician Steffie Woolhandler and others have shown how much of this discrepancy between the experience of the United States and Canada can be associated with the lower administrative costs of Canada's single-payer system; she has found that administrative costs are nearly twice as high in the United States as in Canada—31% of costs versus 17%.

The United States is unique among advanced economies both for its reliance on private health insurance and for rapid inflation in health-care costs. Health-care costs have risen faster in the United States than in any other advanced economy: twice as fast as in Canada, France, Germany, Sweden, or the United Kingdom. We might accept higher and rapidly rising costs had Americans experienced better health outcomes. But using life expectancy at birth as a measure of general health, we have gone from a relatively healthy country to a relatively unhealthy one. Our gain in life expectancy since 1971 (5.4 years for women) is impressive except when put beside other advanced economies (where the average increase is 7.3 years).

The relatively slow increase in life expectancy in the United States highlights the gross inefficiency of our private health-care system. Had the United States increased life expectancy at the same dollar cost as in other countries, we would have saved nearly $4,500 per person. Or, put another way, had we increased life expectancy at the same rate as other countries, our spending increase since 1971 would have bought an extra 15 years of life expectancy, 10 years more than we have. The failure of American

TABLE 2: GREATER INCREASE IN COST FOR U.S. HEALTH-CARE SYSTEM, 1971-2007

	U.S. vs. Canada		U.S. vs. 5-country average	
	Dollars	Share of GDP	Dollars	Share of GDP
Extra increase 1971-2007	$3,356	5.40%	$3,690	4.72%
Extra adjusted for smaller life expectancy gain	$4,006	5.98%	$4,480	5.73%
	As share of national health expenditures			
Extra increase 1971-2007	45%		49%	
Extra adjusted for smaller life expectancy gain	53%		59%	

Note: The first line shows how much faster health-care spending rose per person and as a share of gross domestic product in the United States compared with Canada and with the average of five countries (Canada, France, Germany, Sweden, and the United Kingdom). The second row adjusts this increase for the slower rate of growth in life expectancy in the United States than in these other countries. The third and fourth rows estimate the degree of waste in our health-care system as the proportion of total expenditures accounted for by the extra increases in health-care expenditures in the United States.

Source: Calculations by the author from data in OECD Health Data 2010 (oecd.org).

life expectancy to rise as fast as life expectancy elsewhere can be directly tied to the inequitable provision of health care through our private, for-profit health-insurance system. Increases in life expectancy since 1990 have been largely restricted to relatively affluent Americans with better health insurance. Since 1990, men in the top 50% of the income distribution have had a six-year increase in life expectancy at age 65 compared with an increase of only one year for men earning below the median.

Rising health-care costs reflect in part the greater costs of caring for an aging population with more chronic conditions. As such, the United States looks especially bad because our population is aging less quickly than that of other countries because of high rates of immigration, relatively higher fertility, and the slower increase in life expectancy in the United States. Countries also buy higher life expectancy by spending on health care; rising health expenditures have funded improvements in treatment

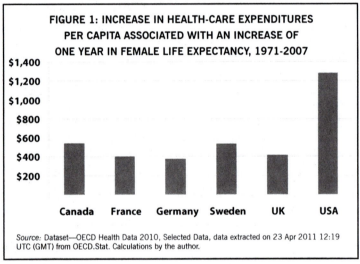

FIGURE 1: INCREASE IN HEALTH-CARE EXPENDITURES PER CAPITA ASSOCIATED WITH AN INCREASE OF ONE YEAR IN FEMALE LIFE EXPECTANCY, 1971-2007

Source: Dataset—OECD Health Data 2010, Selected Data, data extracted on 23 Apr 2011 12:19 UTC (GMT) from OECD.Stat. Calculations by the author.

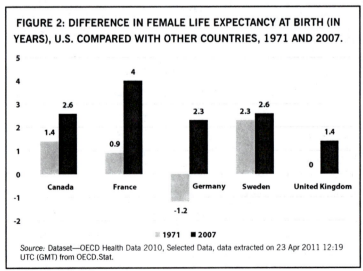

FIGURE 2: DIFFERENCE IN FEMALE LIFE EXPECTANCY AT BIRTH (IN YEARS), U.S. COMPARED WITH OTHER COUNTRIES, 1971 AND 2007.

Source: Dataset—OECD Health Data 2010, Selected Data, data extracted on 23 Apr 2011 12:19 UTC (GMT) from OECD.Stat.

that have contributed to rising life expectancy throughout the world. Female life expectancy at birth has increased by nearly nine years in Germany since 1971, by over eight years in France, by seven years in Canada and the United Kingdom, and by six years in Sweden. By contrast, the United States, where female life expectancy increased by a little over five years, has done relatively poorly despite increasing health-care expenditures that dwarf those of other countries. In other countries, increasing expenditures by about $500 per person is associated with an extra year of life expectancy. With our privatized health-insurance system, we need spending increases over twice as large to gain an extra year of life (see Figure 1, previous page).

The international comparison also provides another perspective on any supposed trade-off between containing costs and expanding coverage. In countries other than the United States, almost all of the increase in health-care spending as a share of national income is due to better quality health care as measured by improvements in life expectancy (see Figure 2, previous page). The problem of rising health-care costs is almost unique to the United States, the only advanced industrialized country without universal coverage and without any effective national health plan.

In short, the question is not whether we can afford a single-payer health-insurance system that would provide adequate health care for all Americans. The real question is: can we afford anything else? ❑

Sources: Cathy Shoen, "How Many Are Underinsured? Trends Among U.S. Adults, 2003 and 2007," Health Affairs, June 10, 2008; "Insured but Poorly Protected: How Many Are Underinsured? U. S. Adults Trends, 2003 to 2007," Commonwealth Fund, June 10, 2008 (commonwealthfund.org); David Cutler and Dan Ly, "The (Paper) Work of Medicine: Understanding International Medical Costs," Journal of Economic Perspectives, Spring 2011; Stephen M. Davidson, Still Broken: Understanding the U.S. Health Care System, Stanford Business Books, 2010; P Franks and C M Clancy, "Health insurance and mortality. Evidence from a national cohort," The Journal of the American Medical Association, August 11, 1993; Allan Garber and Jonathan Skinner, "Is American Health Care Uniquely Inefficient?" Journal of Economic Perspectives, Fall 2008; Jonathan Gruber, "The Role of Consumer Co-payments for Health Care: Lessons from the RAND Health Insurance Experiment and Beyond," Kaiser Family Foundation, October 2006 (kff.org); David Himmelstein and Steffie Woolhandler, "Administrative Waste in the U.S. Health Care System in 2003," International Journal of Health Services, 2004; "The Uninsured: A Primer: Supplemental Data Tables," Kaiser Family Foundation, December 2010; Karen Davis and Cathy Shoen, "Slowing the Growth of U.S. Health Care Expenditures: What are the Options?" Commonwealth Fund, January 2007 (commonwealthfund. org); "Accounting for the Cost of Health Care in the United States," McKinsey Global Institute, January 2007 (mckinsey.com); "Investigation of Health Care Cost Trends and Cost Drivers," Office of Massachusetts Attorney General Martha Coakley, January 29, 2010 (mass.gov); Trends in Mortality Differentials and Life Expectancy for Male Social Security-Covered Workers, by Average Relative Earnings by Hilary Waldron, Social Security Administration, October 2007; Richard G. Wilkinson, The Spirit Level, Bloomsbury Press, 2010; William Hsiao and Steven Kappel, "Act 128: Health System Reform Design. Achieving Affordable Universal Health Care in Vermont," January 21, 2011 (leg.state.vt.us); Steffie Woolhandler and Terry Campbell, "Cost of Health Care Administration in the United States and Canada," New England Journal of Medicine, 2003.

Article 8.3

PRICING THE PRICELESS
Inside the Strange World of Cost-Benefit Analysis

BY LIZ HEINZERLING AND FRANK ACKERMAN
March/April 2003

How strictly should we regulate arsenic in drinking water? Or carbon dioxide in the atmosphere? Or pesticides in our food? Or oil drilling in scenic places? The list of environmental harms and potential regulatory remedies often appears to be endless. In evaluating a proposed new initiative, how do we know if it is worth doing or not? Is there an objective way to decide how to proceed? Cost-benefit analysis promises to provide the solution—to add up the benefits of a public policy and compare them to the costs.

The costs of protecting health and the environment through pollution control devices and other approaches are, by their very nature, measured in dollars. The other side of the balance, calculating the benefits of life, health, and nature in dollars and cents, is far more problematic. Since there are no natural prices for a healthy environment, cost-benefit analysis creates artificial ones. Researchers, for example, may ask a cross-section of the affected population how much they would pay to preserve or protect something that can't be bought in a store. The average American household is supposedly willing to pay $257 to prevent the extinction of bald eagles, $208 to protect humpback whales, and $80 to protect gray wolves.

Costs and benefits of a policy, however, frequently fall at different times. When the analysis spans a number of years, future costs and benefits are *discounted,* or treated as equivalent to smaller amounts of money in today's dollars. The case for discounting begins with the observation that money received today is worth a little more than money received in the future. (For example, if the interest rate is 3%, you only need to deposit about $97 today to get $100 next year. Economists would say that, at a *3% discount rate,* $100 next year has a *present value* of $97.) For longer periods of time, or higher discount rates, the effect is magnified. The important issue for environmental policy is whether this logic also applies to outcomes far in the future, and to opportunities—like long life and good health—that are not naturally stated in dollar terms.

Why Cost-Benefit Analysis Doesn't Work

The case for cost-benefit analysis of environmental protection is, at best, wildly optimistic and, at worst, demonstrably wrong. The method simply does not offer the policy-making panacea its adherents promise. In practice, cost-benefit analysis frequently produces false and misleading results. Moreover, there is no quick fix, because these failures are intrinsic to the methodology, appearing whenever it is applied to any complex environmental problem.

It puts dollar figures on values that are not commodities, and have no price.
Artificial prices have been estimated for many benefits of environmental regulation. Preventing retardation due to childhood lead poisoning comes in at about $9,000 per lost IQ point. Saving a life is ostensibly worth $6.3 million. But what can it mean to say that one life is worth $6.3 million? You cannot buy the right to kill someone for $6.3 million, nor for any other price. If analysts calculated the value of life itself by asking people what it is worth to them (the most common method of valuation of other environmental benefits), the answer would be infinite. The standard response is that a value like $6.3 million is not actually a price on an individual's life or death. Rather, it is a way of expressing the value of small risks of death. If people are willing to pay $6.30 to avoid a one in a million increase in the risk of death, then the "value of a statistical life" is $6.3 million.

It ignores the collective choice presented to society by most public health and environmental problems.
Under the cost-benefit approach, valuation of environmental benefits is based on individuals' private decisions as consumers or workers, not on their public values as citizens. However, policies that protect the environment are often public goods, and are not available for purchase in individual portions. In a classic example of this distinction, the philosopher Mark Sagoff found that his students, in their role as citizens, opposed commercial ski development in a nearby wilderness area, but, in their role as consumers, would plan to go skiing there if the development was built. There is no contradiction between these two views: as individual consumers, the students would have no way to express their collective preference for wilderness preservation. Their individual willingness to pay for skiing would send a misleading signal about their views as citizens.

It is often impossible to arrive at a meaningful social valuation by adding up the willingness to pay expressed by individuals. What could it mean to ask how much you personally are willing to pay to clean up a major oil spill? If no one else contributes, the clean-up won't happen regardless of your decision. As the Nobel Prize-winning economist Amartya Sen has pointed out, if your willingness to pay for a large-scale public initiative is independent of what others are paying, then you probably have not understood the nature of the problem.

It systematically downgrades the importance of the future.
One of the great triumphs of environmental law is that it seeks to avert harms to people and to natural resources in the future, and not only within this generation, but in future generations as well. Indeed, one of the primary objectives of the National Environmental Policy Act, which has been called our basic charter of environmental protection, is to nudge the nation into "fulfill[ing] the responsibilities of each generation as trustee of the environment for succeeding generations."

The time periods involved in protecting the environment are often enormous—even many centuries, in such cases as climate change, radioactive waste, etc. With time spans this long, any discounting will make even global catastrophes seem trivial. At a discount rate of 5%, for example, the deaths of a billion people 500 years from now become less serious than the death of one person today. Seen in this way, discounting looks like a fancy justification for foisting our problems off onto the people who come after us.

It ignores considerations of distribution and fairness.
Cost-benefit analysis adds up all the costs of a policy, adds up all the benefits, and compares the totals. Implicit in this innocuous-sounding procedure is the assumption that it doesn't matter who gets the benefits and who pays the costs. Yet isn't there is an important difference between spending state tax revenues, say, to improve the parks in rich communities, and spending the same revenues to clean up pollution in poor communities?

The problem of equity runs even deeper. Benefits are typically measured by willingness to pay for environmental improvement, and the rich are able and willing to pay for more than the poor. Imagine a cost-benefit analysis of locating an undesirable facility, such as a landfill or incinerator. Wealthy communities are willing to pay more for the benefit of not having the facility in their backyards; thus, under the logic of cost-benefit analysis, the net benefits to society will be maximized by putting the facility in a low-income area. In reality, pollution is typically dumped on the poor without waiting for formal analysis. Still, cost-benefit analysis rationalizes and reinforces the problem, allowing environmental burdens to flow downhill along the income slopes of an unequal society.

Conclusion

There is nothing objective about the basic premises of cost-benefit analysis. Treating individuals solely as consumers, rather than as citizens with a sense of moral responsibility, represents a distinct and highly questionable worldview. Likewise, discounting reflects judgments about the nature of environmental risks and citizens' responsibilities toward future generations.

These assumptions beg fundamental questions about ethics and equity, and one cannot decide whether to embrace them without thinking through the whole range of moral issues they raise. Yet once one has thought through these issues, there is no need then to collapse the complex moral inquiry into a series of numbers. Pricing the priceless just translates our inquiry into a different language, one with a painfully impoverished vocabulary. ❑

This article is a condensed version of the report Pricing the Priceless, *published by the Georgetown Environmental Law and Policy Institute at Georgetown University Law Center. The full report is available on-line at www. ase.tufts.edu/gdae. See also Ackerman and Heinzerling's book on these and related issues,* Priceless: Human Health, the Environment, and the Limits of the Market, *The New Press, January 2004.*

Article 8.4

CLIMATE ECONOMICS IN FOUR EASY PIECES

Conventional cost-benefit models cannot inform our decisions about how to address the threat of climate change.

FRANK ACKERMAN
November/December 2008

Once upon a time, debates about climate policy were primarily about the science. An inordinate amount of attention was focused on the handful of "climate skeptics" who challenged the scientific understanding of climate change. The influence of the skeptics, however, is rapidly fading; few people were swayed by their arguments, and doubt about the major results of climate science is no longer important in shaping public policy.

As the climate *science* debate is reaching closure, the climate *economics* debate is heating up. The controversial issue now is the fear that overly ambitious climate initiatives could hurt the economy. Mainstream economists emphasizing that fear have, in effect, replaced the climate skeptics as the intellectual enablers of inaction.

For example, William Nordhaus, the U.S. economist best known for his work on climate change, pays lip service to scientists' calls for decisive action. He finds, however, that the "optimal" policy is a very small carbon tax that would reduce greenhouse gas emissions only 25% below "business-as-usual" levels by 2050—that would, in other words, allow emissions to rise well above current levels by mid-century. Richard Tol, a European economist who has written widely on climate change, favors an even smaller carbon tax of just $2 per ton of carbon dioxide. That would amount to all of $0.02 per gallon of gasoline, a microscopic "incentive" for change that consumers would never notice.

There are other voices in the climate economics debate; in particular, the British government's Stern Review offers a different perspective. Economist Nicholas Stern's analysis is much less wrong than the traditional Nordhaus-Tol approach, but even Stern has not challenged the conventional view enough.

What will it take to build a better economics of climate change, one that is consistent with the urgency expressed by the latest climate science? The issues that matter are big, non-technical principles, capable of being expressed in bumper-sticker format. Here are the four bumper stickers for a better climate economics:

- Our grandchildren's lives are important.

- We need to buy insurance for the planet.

- Climate damages are too valuable to have prices.

- Some costs are better than others.

1. Our grandchildren's lives are important.

The most widely debated challenge of climate economics is the valuation of the very long run. For ordinary loans and investments, both the costs today and the resulting future benefits typically occur within a single lifetime. In such cases, it makes sense to think in terms of the same person experiencing and comparing the costs and the benefits.

In the case of climate change, the time spans involved are well beyond those encountered in most areas of economics. The most important consequences of today's choices will be felt by generations to come, long after all of us making those choices have passed away. As a result, the costs of reducing emissions today and the benefits in the far future will not be experienced by the same people. The economics of climate change is centrally concerned with our relationship to our descendants whom we will never meet. As a bridge to that unknowable future, consider our grandchildren—the last generation most of us will ever know.

Suppose that you want your grandchildren to receive $100 (in today's dollars, corrected for inflation), 60 years from now. How much would you have to put in a bank account today, to ensure that the $100 will be there 60 years from now? The answer is $55 at 1% interest, or just over $5 at 5%.

In parallel fashion, economists routinely deal with future costs and benefits by "discounting" them, or converting them to "present values"—a process that is simply compound interest in reverse. In the standard jargon, the *present value* of $100, to be received 60 years from now, is $55 at a 1% *discount rate*, or about $5 at a 5% discount rate. As this example shows, a higher discount rate implies a smaller present value.

The central problem of climate economics, in a cost-benefit framework, is deciding how much to spend today on preventing future harms. What should we spend to prevent $100 of climate damages 60 years from now? The standard answer is, no more than the present value of that future loss: $55 at a discount rate of 1%, or $5 at 5%. The higher the discount rate, the less it is "worth" spending today on protecting our grandchildren.

The effect of a change in the discount rate becomes much more pronounced as the time period lengthens. Damages of $1 million occurring 200 years from now have a present value of only about $60 at a 5% discount rate, versus more than $130,000 at a 1% discount rate. The choice of the discount rate is all-important to our stance toward the far future: should we spend as much as $130,000, or as little as $60, to avoid one million dollars of climate damages in the early twenty-third century?

For financial transactions within a single lifetime, it makes sense to use market interest rates as the discount rate. Climate change, however, involves public policy decisions with impacts spanning centuries; there is no market in which public resources are traded from one century to the next. The choice of an intergenerational discount rate is a matter of ethics and policy, not a market-determined result.

Economists commonly identify two separate aspects of long-term discounting, each contributing to the discount rate.

One component of the discount rate is based on the assumption of an upward trend in income and wealth. If future generations will be richer than we are, they will need less help from us, and they will get less benefit from an additional dollar of income than we do. So we can discount benefits that will flow to our wealthier descendants, at a rate based on the expected growth of per capita incomes. Among economists, the income-related motive for discounting may be the least controversial part of the picture.

Setting aside changes in per capita income from one generation to the next, there may still be a reason to discount a sum many years in the future. This component of the discount rate, known as "pure time preference," is the subject of longstanding ethical, philosophical, and economic debate. On the one hand, there are reasons to think that pure time preference is greater than zero: both psychological experiments and common sense suggest that people are impatient, and prefer money now to money later. On the other hand, a pure time preference of zero expresses the equal worth of people of all generations, and the equal importance of reducing climate impacts and other burdens on them (assuming that all generations have equal incomes).

The Stern Review provides an excellent discussion of the debate, explaining Stern's assumption of pure time preference close to zero and an overall discount rate of 1.4%. This discount rate alone is sufficient to explain Stern's support for a substantial program of climate protection: at the higher discount rates used in more traditional analyses, the Stern program would look "inefficient," since the costs would outweigh the present value of the benefits.

2. We need to buy insurance for the planet.

Does climate science predict that things are certain to get worse? Or does it tell us that we are uncertain about what will happen next? Unfortunately, the answer seems to be yes to both questions. For example, the most likely level of sea level rise in this century, according to the latest Intergovernmental Panel on Climate Change reports, is no more than one meter or so—a real threat to low-lying coastal areas and islands that will face increasing storm damages, but survivable, with some adaptation efforts, for most of the world. On the other hand, there is a worst-case risk of an abrupt loss of the Greenland ice sheet, or perhaps of a large portion of the West Antarctic ice sheet. Either one could cause an eventual seven-meter rise in sea level—a catastrophic impact on coastal communities, economic activity, and infrastructure everywhere, and well beyond the range of plausible adaptation efforts in most places.

The evaluation of climate damages thus depends on whether we focus on the most likely outcomes or the credible worst-case risks; the latter, of course, are much larger.

Cost-benefit analysis conventionally rests on average or expected outcomes. But this is not the only way that people make decisions. When faced with uncertain, potentially large risks, people do not normally act on the basis of average outcomes; instead, they typically focus on protection against worst-case scenarios. When you go to the airport, do you leave just enough time for the average traffic delay (so that you would catch your plane, on average, half of the time)? Or do you allow time for some estimate of worst-case traffic jams? Once you get there, of course, you will experience additional delays due to security, which is all about worst cases: your *average* fellow passenger is not a threat to anyone's safety.

The very existence of the insurance industry is evidence of the desire to avoid or control worst-case scenarios. It is impossible for an insurance company to pay out in claims as much as its customers pay in premiums; if it did, there would be no money left to pay the costs of running the company, or the profits received by its owners. People who buy insurance are therefore guaranteed to get back less than they, on average, have paid; they (we) are paying for the security that insurance provides in case the worst should happen. This way of thinking does not apply to every decision: in casino games, people make bets based on averages and probabilities, and no one has any insurance against losing the next round. But life is not a casino, and public policy should not be a gamble.

Should climate policy be based on the most likely outcomes, or on the worst-case risks? Should we be investing in climate protection as if we expect sea level rise of one meter, or as if we are buying insurance to be sure of preventing a seven-meters rise?

In fact, the worst-case climate risks are even more unknown than the individual risks of fire and death that motivate insurance purchases. You do not know whether or not you will have a fire next year or die before the year is over, but you have very good information about the likelihood of these tragic events. So does the insurance industry, which is why they are willing to insure you. In contrast, there is no body of statistical information about the probability of Greenland-sized ice sheets collapsing at various temperatures; it's not an experiment that anyone can perform over and over again.

A recent analysis by Martin Weitzman argues that the probabilities of the worst outcomes are inescapably unknowable—and this deep uncertainty is more important than anything we do know in motivating concern about climate change. There is a technical sense in which the expected value of future climate damages can be infinite because we know so little about the probability of the worst, most damaging possibilities. The practical implication of infinite expected damages is that the most likely outcome is irrelevant; what matters is buying insurance for the planet, i.e., doing our best to understand and prevent the worst-case risks.

3. Climate damages are too valuable to have prices.

To decide whether climate protection is worthwhile, in cost-benefit terms, we would need to know the monetary value of everything important that is being protected. Even if we could price everything affected by climate change, the prices would conceal a critical form of international inequity. The emissions that cause climate change have come predominantly from rich countries, while the damages will be felt first and worst in some of the world's poorest, tropical countries (although no one will be immune from harm for long). There are, however, no meaningful prices for many of the benefits of health and environmental protection. What is the dollar value of a human life saved? How much is it worth to save an endangered species from extinction, or to preserve a unique location or ecosystem? Economists have made up price tags for such priceless values, but the results do not always pass the laugh test.

Is a human life worth $6.1 million, as estimated by the Clinton administration, based on small differences in the wages paid for more and less risky jobs? Or is it worth $3.7 million, as the (second) Bush administration concluded on the basis of questionnaires about people's willingness to pay for reducing small, hypothetical risks? Are lives of people in rich countries worth much more than those in poor countries, as some economists infamously argued in the IPCC's 1995 report? Can the value of an endangered species be determined by survey research on how much people would pay to protect it? If, as one study found, the U.S. population as a whole would pay $18 billion to protect the existence of humpback whales, would it be acceptable for someone to pay $36 billion for the right to hunt and kill the entire species?

The only sensible response to such nonsensical questions is that there are many crucially important values that do not have meaningful prices. This is not a new idea: as the eighteenth-century philosopher Immanuel Kant put it, some things have a price, or relative worth, while other things have a dignity, or inner worth. No price tag does justice to the dignity of human life or the natural world.

Since some of the most important benefits of climate protection are priceless, any monetary value for total benefits will necessarily be incomplete. The corollary is that preventive action may be justified even in the absence of a complete monetary measure of the benefits of doing so.

4. Some costs are better than others.

The language of cost-benefit analysis embodies a clear normative slant: benefits are good, costs are bad. The goal is always to have larger benefits and smaller costs. In some respects, measurement and monetary valuation are easier for costs than for benefits: implementing pollution control measures typically involves changes in such areas as manufacturing, construction, and fuel use, all of which have well-defined prices. Yet conventional economic theory distorts the interpretation of costs in ways that exaggerate the burdens of environmental protection and hide the positive features of some of the "costs."

Average Risks or Worst-Case Scenarios?

You don't have to look far to find situations in which the sensible policy is to address worst-case outcomes rather than average outcomes. The annual number of residential fires in the United States is about 0.4% of the number of housing units. This means that a fire occurs, on average, about once every 250 years in each home—not even close to once per lifetime. By far the most likely number of fires a homeowner will experience next year, or even in a lifetime, is zero. Why don't these statistics inspire you to cancel your fire insurance? Unless you are extremely wealthy, the loss of your home in a fire would be a devastating financial blow; despite the low probability, you cannot afford to take any chances on it.

What are the chances of the ultimate loss? The probability that you will die next year is under 0.1% if you are in your twenties, under 0.2% in your thirties, under 0.4% in your forties. It is not until age 61 that you have as much as a 1% chance of death within the coming year. Yet most U.S. families with dependent children buy life insurance. Without it, the risk to children of losing their parents' income would be too great—even though the parents are, on average, extraordinarily likely to survive.

For instance, empirical studies of energy use and carbon emissions repeatedly find significant opportunities for emissions reduction at zero or negative net cost—the so-called "no regrets" options.

According to a longstanding tradition in economic theory, however, cost-free energy savings are impossible. The textbook theory of competitive markets assumes that every resource is productively employed in its most valuable use—in other words, that every no-regrets option must already have been taken. As the saying goes, there are no free lunches; there cannot be any $20 bills on the sidewalk because someone would have picked them up already. Any new emissions reduction measures, then, must have positive costs. This leads to greater estimates of climate policy costs than the bottom-up studies that reveal extensive opportunities for costless savings.

In the medium term, we will need to move beyond the no-regrets options; how much will it cost to finish the job of climate protection? Again, there are rival interpretations of the costs based on rival assumptions about the economy. The same economic theory that proclaimed the absence of $20 bills on the sidewalk is responsible for the idea that all costs are bad. Since the free market lets everyone spend their money in whatever way they choose, any new cost must represent a loss: it leaves people with less to spend on whatever purchases they had previously selected to maximize their satisfaction in life. Climate damages are one source of loss, and spending on climate protection is another; both reduce the resources available for the desirable things in life.

But are the two kinds of costs really comparable? Is it really a matter of indifference whether we spend $1 billion on bigger and better levees or lose $1 billion to storm damages? In the real-world economy, money spent on building levees creates jobs and incomes. The construction workers buy groceries, clothing, and so on, indirectly creating other jobs. With more people working, tax revenues increase while unemployment compensation payments decrease.

None of this happens if the levees are not built and the storm damages are allowed to occur. The costs of prevention are good costs, with numerous indirect benefits; the costs of climate damages are bad costs, representing pure physical destruction. One worthwhile goal is to keep total costs as low as possible; another is to have as much as possible of good costs rather than bad costs. Think of it as the cholesterol theory of climate costs.

In the long run, the deep reductions in carbon emissions needed for climate stabilization will require new technologies that have not yet been invented, or at best exist only in small, expensive prototypes. How much will it cost to invent, develop, and implement the low-carbon technologies of the future?

Lacking a rigorous theory of innovation, economists modeling climate change have often assumed that new technologies simply appear, making the economy inexorably more efficient over time. A more realistic view observes that the costs of producing a new product typically decline as industry gains more experience with it, in a pattern called "learning by doing" or the "learning curve" effect. Public investment is often necessary to support the innovation process in its early, expensive stages. Wind power is now relatively cheap and competitive, in suitable locations; this is a direct result of decades of public investment in the United States and Europe, starting when wind turbines were still quite expensive. The costs of climate policy, in the long run, will include doing the same for other promising new technologies, investing public resources in jump-starting a set of slightly different industries than we might have chosen in the absence of climate change. If this is a cost, many communities would be better off with more of it.

A widely publicized, conventional economic analysis recommends inaction on climate change, claiming that the costs currently outweigh the benefits for anything more than the smallest steps toward reducing carbon emissions. Put our "four easy pieces" together, and we have the outline of an economics that complements the science of climate change and endorses active, large-scale climate protection.

How realistic is it to expect that the world will shake off its inertia and act boldly and rapidly enough to make a difference? This may be the last generation that will have a real chance at protecting the earth's climate. Projections from the latest IPCC reports, the Stern Review, and other sources suggest that it is still possible to save the planet—if we start at once. ❑

Sources: Frank Ackerman, *Can We Afford the Future? Economics for a Warming World*, Zed Books, 2008; Frank Ackerman, *Poisoned for Pennies: The Economics of Toxics and Precaution*, Island Press, 2008; Frank Ackerman and Lisa Heinzerling, *Priceless: On Knowing the Price of Everything and the Value of Nothing*, The New Press, 2004; J. Creyts, A. Derkach, S. Nyquist, K. Ostrowski and J. Stephenson, *Reducing U.S. Greenhouse Gas Emissions: How Much at What Cost?*, McKinsey & Co., 2007; P.-A. Enkvist, T. Naucler and J. Rosander, "A Cost Curve for Greenhouse Gas Reduction," *The McKinsey Quarterly*, 2007; Immanuel Kant, *Groundwork for the Metaphysics of Morals*, translated by Thomas K. Abbot, with revisions by Lara Denis, Broadview Press, 2005 [1785]; B. Lomborg, *Cool It: The Skeptical Environmentalist's Guide to Global Warming*, Alfred A. Knopf, 2007; W.D. Nordhaus, *A Question of Balance: Economic Modeling of Global Warming*, Yale University Press, 2008; F.P. Ramsey, "A mathematical theory of saving," *The Economic Journal* 138(152): 543-59, 1928; Nicholas Stern *et al.*, *The Stern Review: The Economics of Climate Change*, HM Treasury, 2006; U.S. Census Bureau, "Statistical Abstract of the United States." 127th edition. 2008; M.L. Weitzman, "On Modeling and Interpreting the Economics of Catastrophic Climate Change," December 5, 2007 version, www.economics.harvard.edu/faculty/weitzman/files/modeling.pdf.

Article 8.5

CAR TROUBLE
The automobile as an environmental and health disaster

BY ALEJANDRO REUSS
March/April 2003

(Scene: Los Angeles, the 1940s)

Eddie Valiant: A freeway? What the hell's a freeway?

Judge Doom: Eight lanes of shimmering cement running from here to Pasadena. Smooth, straight, fast. Traffic jams will be a thing of the past.... I see a place where people get off and on the freeway. On and off. Off and on. All day, all night. Soon where Toontown once stood will be a string of gas stations. Inexpensive motels. Restaurants that serve rapidly prepared food. Tire salons. Automobile dealerships. And wonderful, wonderful billboards reaching as far as the eye can see.... My god, it'll be beautiful.

Eddie Valiant: Come on. Nobody's gonna drive this lousy freeway when they can take the Red Car [trolley] for a nickel.

Judge Doom: Oh, they'll drive. They'll have to. You see, I bought the Red Car so I could dismantle it.

—*Who Framed Roger Rabbit?* (1988)

At the end of *Roger Rabbit*, a speeding train saves the day, destroying the solvent-spraying juggernaut that is set to level the fictitious Toontown for the freeway. In other words, the movie is a fairy tale about how the modern American city did *not* come into existence. In reality, Los Angeles came to represent the awful extreme of U.S. car culture. Auto companies *did* buy up the city's Red Car trolley and dismantle it. The landscape became just the cluttered wasteland of highways, fast-food joints, filling stations, and billboards dreamed by the villainous Judge Doom.

The federal government rolled out an asphalt carpet for the automobile: It built the interstate highways that fueled "white flight" to the new suburban sprawl, and carried the new "middle class" on its summer vacations. Soon, freeways criss-crossed American cities, slicing through low-income neighborhoods and consigning commuters to the twice-daily ordeal of gridlock. Roads and highways (along with the military, for which the interstates were originally intended) were politically acceptable objects of public spending even in the postwar United States. And why not? They represented an enormous subsidy to the private industries at the heart of U.S. capitalism—oil, steel, and cars.

The car effectively privatized a wide swath of the public arena. In place of the city square, it created the four-way intersection. Instead of walking or riding a trolley, the motorists sealed themselves inside their individual steel cocoons. Cars offered convenience—for grocery shopping, trips to the mall, chauffeuring the kids to school and practice, etc.—to those who got them. Their real triumph, however, was to manufacture inconvenience for those who didn't. People who could not afford cars had such unenviable choices as navigating the brave new world of speeding traffic on foot or waiting for the bus. A genuine political commitment to public transportation might have lessened the class and race divide. Most public transportation funding, however, has gone to road and highway construction geared to the motorist, and much of what remains for mass transit has been devoted to commuter trains serving the suburban middle class. Low-income city residents have largely been abandoned to an infrequent and polluting diesel bus.

As it turned out, life inside the car was not all it was cracked up to be either—especially when traffic on the freeway slowed to a crawl. In gridlock, you can practically see the steam coming out of drivers' ears. As odious as much of the time spent in cars might be, however, Americans have learned, or been convinced, to "love the car." It has become a fetish object—a symbol of freedom and individualism, power and sex appeal. The commercials always seem to show a carefree motorist speeding through the countryside or climbing a secluded mountain to gaze on the landscape below. Fortunately, not too many SUV owners actually spend their time tearing up the wilderness. Unfortunately, they spend much of it spewing exhaust into the city air.

The SUV certainly ranks among the more absurd expressions of American over-consumption (General Motors' Yukon XL Denali, to cite an extreme example, is over 18 feet long and weighs about three tons). But it is too easy to condemn this overgrown behemoth and then hop self-satisfied back into a midsize sedan. Most of what is wrong with the SUV—the resources it swallows, the dangers it poses, and the blight it creates—is wrong with the automobile system as a whole. Automobiles pollute the oceans and the air, overheat cities and the earth, devour land and time, produce waste and noise, and cause injury and illness.

Here, in more detail, is an indictment of the car as an environmental and public-health menace:

The Bill of Particulars

Oil Pollution

Transportation accounts for over two-thirds of U.S. oil consumption, according to the Department of Energy. The problem of oil pollution, therefore, lands squarely at the doorstep of a transportation system based on internal combustion. Oil tanker spills are the most visible scourge of the world's oceans. According to the National Research Council study Oil in the Sea, tankers spew 400 million tons of oil into the world's oceans each year. Technologies to prevent or contain oil spills, however, cannot solve the problem of marine oil pollution, since the main cause is not spills, but the consumption of oil. Urban consumption, including runoff from roads and used motor oil just poured down the drain, accounts for more than half of the ocean pollution, over one billion tons of oil annually. That does not count, of course, oil that does not make it to the seas, that stains roadways, contaminates the land, or spoils fresh water supplies.

Air Pollution

Automotive emissions are a major source of ozone and carbon monoxide pollution. "[I]n numerous cities across the country," according to the Environmental Protection Agency (EPA), "the personal automobile is the single greatest polluter." Ozone, a major component of urban smog, is formed by unburned fuel reacting with other compounds in the atmosphere. It causes irritation of the eyes and lungs, aggravates respiratory problems, and can damage lung tissue. Researchers at the Centers for Disease Control in Atlanta took advantage of temporary traffic reduction during the 1996 Olympic Games to observe the effects of automotive emissions on asthma attacks. Their study, published in the *Journal of the American Medical Association*, showed a 28% reduction of peak ozone levels and an 11–44% drop in the number of children requiring acute asthma care (depending on the sample). Carbon monoxide, formed by incomplete burning of fuel, impairs the oxygen-carrying ability of the blood. According to the EPA, "In urban areas, the motor vehicle contribution to carbon monoxide pollution can exceed 90 percent." A 2002 study published in the journal *Circulation* showed a link between automotive exhaust and heart attacks, and Harvard Medical School researchers called exhaust an "insidious contributor to heart disease."

Climate Change

Automotive exhaust also contains carbon dioxide, a "greenhouse gas" and the principal culprit in climate change (or "global warming"). It is produced, in the words of the EPA, by the "perfect combustion" of hydrocarbons. Internal combustion engines generate this greenhouse gas no matter how efficient or well-tuned they may be. In the United States, the country with the world's highest per capita carbon dioxide emissions, transportation accounts for over 30% of total emissions, according to a 1998 report of the United Nations Framework Convention on Climate Change. More than half that amount, reports the EPA, is due to personal transportation. As average fuel efficiency gets worse (it declined by nearly 7% between 1987 and 1997) and U.S. motorists rack up more vehicle miles (they increased by a third over the same period), the automobile contributes more and more to global warming.

Heat Islands

The temperature in a major city on a summer day can be as much as 8°F higher than that of surrounding rural areas, according to the Berkeley National Laboratory's Heat Island Group. The automobile contributes to "heat islands" mainly through increased demand for roads and parking. The asphalt and concrete used for these surfaces are among the most heat-absorbent materials in the urban environment. Paving also contributes to the loss of trees, which provide shade and dissipate heat. In the 1930s, when orchards dotted Los Angeles, summer temperatures peaked at 97°F, according to the Heat Island Group. Since then L.A. has become one of the country's worst heat islands, with summer temperatures reaching over 105°F. This does not just make the city less pleasant in the summertime. Heat islands cause increased energy use for cooling and increased ozone formation. Researchers estimate a 2% increase in Los Angeles's total power use and a 3% increase in smog for every 1°F increase in the city's daily high temperature.

Land Use

Cars occupy a huge amount of space. Paved roads occupy over 13,000 square miles of land area across the United States—nearly 750 square meters per U.S. motor vehicle—and parking occupies another 3,000 square miles, according to a report by Todd Litman of the Victoria Transport Policy Institute. In urban areas, roads and parking take up 20-30% of the total surface area; in commercial districts, 50-60%. When moving, vehicles require a "buffer zone" that varies with size and speed. Litman calculates, for example, that a pedestrian walking at 3 miles per hour (m.p.h.) requires 20 square feet of space. A cyclist riding at 10 m.p.h. needs 50 square feet. At full occupancy, a bus traveling at 30 m.p.h. requires 75 square feet per passenger. Meanwhile, a car traveling at 30 m.p.h. demands 1,500 square feet. In short, much of the road space is not required by on-road transportation as such, but by the private car. The same goes for parking space. A parked car requires twenty times the space as a parked bicycle, and eighty times the space as a person.

Materials

In the words of the EPA, "Vehicles require a lot of energy and materials to make, consume a lot of energy when used, and present unique waste disposal challenges at end-of-life." The auto industry uses nearly two thirds of the rubber, over one third of the iron, and over one fourth of the aluminum produced in the United States. Over ten million cars, moreover, are junked in the United States each year. About three fourths of the average car's weight—including the vast majority of the steel—is recycled. The rest crowds garbage dumps and contributes to toxic pollution. About 270 million tires (about 3.4 million tons) are scrapped in the United States annually. While nearly half are burned for energy, about 500 million tires now swell U.S. junk piles, where they "act as breeding grounds for rats and mosquitoes," according to the EPA, and periodically erupt into toxic tire fires. The U.S. cars scrapped each year also contain upwards of 8 tons of mercury. Meanwhile, polyvinyl chloride from scrap cars produces dioxins and other toxic pollutants. The study *End-of-Life Vehicles: A Threat to the Environment* concludes that the cars scrapped in Europe each year (75-85% as many as in the United States) produce 2 million tons of hazardous waste, about one tenth of the EU's total hazardous waste production.

Time

Car travel swallows more and more time as commutes grow longer and congestion more severe. The 2002 Urban Mobility Report from the Texas Transportation Institute calculated, on the basis of data from 75 U.S. cities, that the average motorist wasted 62 hours per year sitting in rush-hour traffic. (That's just the difference between rush-hour travel time and the normal time required to make the same trip.) In Los Angeles, the figure reached 136 hours. All told, over one third of the average rush-hour trip in the very large cities surveyed was wasted on traffic congestion. How is that an environmental or health issue? According to report Transport, Environment, and Health, issued by the World Health Organization (WHO) Regional Office for Europe, studies have connected traffic congestion with increased stress and blood pressure, as well as "aggressive behavior and increased likelihood of involvement in a crash."

Activity

Lack of exercise contributes to coronary heart disease, hypertension, some cancers, osteoporosis, poor coordination and stamina, and low self-esteem. The WHO Regional Office for Europe argues that "walking and cycling as part of daily activities should become a major pillar" of public-health strategy, and that daily travel offers the most promise to "integrate physical activities into daily schedules." Car dependence, instead, extends the sedentary lifestyle even to mobility. Half of all car trips in Europe, according to the WHO Regional Office, are under 5 km, distances most people can cover by bicycle in less than 20 minutes and on foot in well under one hour. High levels of automotive traffic, moreover, may deter people from walking or cycling—due to the unpleasantness of auto exhaust, the fear of crossing fast-moving traffic, or the dangers of riding a bicycle surrounded by cars. Some people may substitute car trips, but those without access to cars (especially children and elderly people) may simply venture outside less frequently, contributing to social isolation (another health risk factor).

Noise

Noise pollution is no mere nuisance. Researchers are beginning to document the damage that noise, even at relatively low levels, can do to human health. A 2001 study by Gary Evans of Cornell University, for example, has shown that children chronically exposed to low-level traffic noise suffer elevated blood pressure, increased changes in heart rate when stressed, and higher overall levels of stress-related hormones. In a separate study, on children exposed to low-level noise from aircraft flight patterns, Evans also documented negative effects of noise pollution on children's attention spans and learning abilities.

Collisions

Finally, the car crash ranks among the leading causes of death and injury in the United States. The statistics for 2001, compiled by the National Highway Traffic Safety Administration, were typical: over 42,000 people killed, over 360,000 people suffering incapacitating injuries, and over 3 million people injured overall. Over the last 25 years, the number of people killed per vehicle mile has declined by over 50%—undoubtedly thanks to such factors as increased availability and use of safety belts and airbags, improved vehicle design, and improved trauma care. The absolute number of deaths, however, has decreased by less than 20% (using the benchmark of 51,000 in 1980), as total vehicle miles traveled have more than doubled. Overall, the U.S. death toll from car crashes over the last quarter century is over one million people. During just the last decade, the total number of people injured in U.S. car crashes has topped 32 million.

The Path of Redemption

The environmental and public-health problems associated with the automobile have often inspired well-meaning exhortations to car-pool, drive less, or drive smaller cars, as well as dreams of "cars of the future" requiring less material or burning cleaner fuels. On the whole, however, the problems are neither individual nor technological—but social. So no individual nor technological solution will do. A comprehensive solution requires turning the "machine space" built for and dominated by the car back into human space: In the place of sprawl, compact development with work, school, stores, and recreation nearby and reachable without a car. In the place of the private car, reliable, clean, and accessible public transportation (along with small, efficient, nonpolluting vehicles for those who need them). In the place of internal combustion, the cyclist and the pedestrian—no longer marginalized and endangered, but respected as integral parts of a new, sustainable transportation system.

Cuba and China are the world's leading countries in bicycle use. Even in the rich capitalist counties, however, there are islands of sanity where public and human-powered transportation exist at least on a par with the automobile. Groningen, the Netherlands' sixth-largest city, suggests the possibilities: low speed limits reduce the dangers of urban traffic to cyclists and pedestrians; cars are not permitted on some streets, while bicycles can travel on any public way (including bike-only lanes and paths); parking for cars is restricted to garages, while secure bicycle parking facilities are plentiful (especially near train stations); cars are excluded from all squares in the city center, while careful city planning ensures that places of work and commerce are accessible to public transportation, cyclists, and pedestrians. As a result, Groningen residents now make nearly half of all in-city trips by bicycle; less than one third by car. The Dutch city of Delft, and the German cities of Freiburg and Muenster, are similar harbingers of a possible sustainable future.

The sustainable-transportation movement has shown encouraging worldwide growth in recent years. Transportation activists in the United Kingdom have carried out direct-action "street takings," closing off roads and highways and prompting spontaneous street fairs, to show what a car-free future might look like. The "Critical Mass" movement, starting in San Francisco in 1992 but quickly spreading to other cities, has brought together cyclists for rolling protest "marches" against auto hegemony. Activists have promoted worldwide car-free days, in which residents of hundreds of cities have participated. Bogotá, Colombia, a city of 7 million, held its first annual car-free day in 2000, complete with fines for any motorists caught within the city limits. Its popularity among city residents has bolstered long-term plans to exclude cars from the city, on a permanent basis, during peak morning and afternoon travel hours. In 2002, Seattle became the first U.S. city to officially host a car-free day.

With greater struggle, a more thorough-going transportation reform might be possible even within the confines of capitalism. This would require, however, a colossal economic shift—away the production of private automobiles, gasoline, and roads, and toward the reconstruction of public transportation and public space in general. It's highly unlikely, considering the ruin of former auto production centers like Detroit and Flint, that the "free market" could manage such a shift without imposing a wrenching dislocation on individuals and communities dependent on auto production. Moreover, it's virtually unimaginable, considering the trends toward privatization and commodification rampant in contemporary capitalism, that it would carry out such a transformation spontaneously. ❏

Article 8.6

THE PHANTOM MENACE
Environmental regulations are not "job-killers" after all.

BY HEIDI GARRETT-PELTIER
July/August 2011

Polluting industries, along with the legislators who are in their pockets, consistently claim that environmental regulation will be a "job killer." They counter efforts to control pollution and to protect the environment by claiming that any such measures would increase costs and destroy jobs. But these are empty threats. In fact, the bulk of the evidence shows that environmental regulations do not hinder economic growth or employment and may actually stimulate both.

One recent example of this, the Northeast Regional Greenhouse Gas Initiative (RGGI), is an emissions-allowance program that caps and reduces emissions in ten northeast and mid-Atlantic states. Under RGGI, allowances are auctioned to power companies and the majority of the revenues are used to offset increases in consumer energy bills and to invest in energy efficiency and renewable energy. A report released in February 2011 shows that RGGI has created an economic return of $3 to $4 for every $1 invested, and has created jobs throughout the region. Yet this successful program has come under attack by right-wing ideologues, including the Koch brothers-funded "Americans for Prosperity"; as a result, the state of New Hampshire recently pulled out of the program.

The allegation that environmental regulation is a job-killer is based on a mischaracterization of costs, both by firms and by economists. Firms often frame spending on environmental controls or energy-efficient machinery as a pure cost—wasted spending that reduces profitability. But such expenses should instead be seen as investments that enhance productivity and in turn promote economic development. Not only can these investments lead to lower costs for energy use and waste disposal, they may also direct innovations in the production process itself that could increase the firm's long-run profits. This is the Porter Hypothesis, named after Harvard Business School professor Michael Porter. According to studies conducted by Porter, properly and flexibly designed environmental regulation can trigger innovation that partly or completely offsets the costs of complying with the regulation.

The positive aspects of environmental regulation are overlooked not only by firms, but also by economists who model the costs of compliance without including its widespread benefits. These include reduced mortality, fewer sick days for workers and school children, reduced health-care costs, increased biodiversity, and mitigation of climate change. But most mainstream models leave these benefits out of their calculations. The Environmental Protection Agency, which recently released a study of the impacts of the Clean Air Act from 1990 to 2020, compared the effects of a "cost-only" model with those of a more complete model. In the version which only incorporated the costs of compliance, both GDP and overall economic welfare were expected to decline by 2020 due to Clean Air Act regulations. However, once the costs of compliance were coupled with the benefits, the model showed that both GDP and economic welfare would increase over time, and that by 2020 the economic benefits would outweigh the costs. Likewise, the Office of Management and Budget found that to date the benefits of the law have far exceeded the cost, with an economic return of between $4 and $8 for every $1 invested in compliance.

Environmental regulations do affect jobs. But contrary to claims by polluting industries and congressional Republicans, efforts to protect our environment can actually create jobs. In order to reduce harmful pollution from power plants, for example, an electric company would have to equip plants with scrubbers and other technologies. These technologies would need to be manufactured and installed, creating jobs for people in the manufacturing and construction industries.

The official unemployment rate in the United States is still quite high, hovering around 9%. In this economic climate, politicians are more sensitive than ever to claims that environmental regulation could be a job-killer. By framing investments as wasted costs and relying on incomplete economic models, polluting industries have consistently tried to fight environmental standards. It's time to change the terms of the debate. We need to move beyond fear-mongering about the costs and start capturing the benefits. ❑

CHAPTER 9

TAXATION

Introduction

"Only the little people pay taxes." —*Leona Helmsley*

"Taxes are the price we pay for civilization." —*Oliver Wendell Holmes, Jr.*

Taxation is a fascinating subject. It is perhaps the clearest manifestation of class struggle one can find. How a modern government funds itself in order to provide services is an elaborate study in power. The contentious tango of taxes and their inverse, subsidies, is played out daily in all three levels of government, federal, state and municipal. Who pays taxes and at what rates? What is taxed? Who bears the burden of taxation? And how are tax revenues collected? These are questions that this chapter will address.

As concern over the level of inequality in the United States spreads to such establishment figures as the chairman of the Federal Reserve, opponents of redistribution have attempted to argue that additional progressive taxation would not only be harmful to growth, but also unfair to those paying the higher taxes. Ramaa Vasudevan's article, "The 'Double-Taxation' of Corporations" (Article 9.1), refutes this claim in the context of corporate taxation.

In the next article, "Restore the Original Wealth Tax" (Article 9.2), Polly Cleveland observes that "property ownership is far more concentrated than income [and] property taxes are intrinsically far more progressive than income taxes." As there has been a serious polarization in wealth in the past few decades and the income tax appears to have been seriously "gamed" (avoided) by the wealthy, Cleveland reappraises the use of property taxes (which are difficult to avoid) as a source of governmental revenue.

"Funding a National Single-Payer System" by Gerald Friedman (Article 9.3) explores what is possible in the areas of health care and tax policy. A single-payer system has many advantages over the current dysfunctional mish-mash and Friedman proposes a redistributive funding apparatus for it.

James Tracy provides us with a case study of a corporation using its market power to blackmail its home community into granting tax breaks. "Capital Flight Across the County Line" (Article 9.4) is the story of how Twitter blackmailed San Francisco into reducing its taxes by threatening to leave town and take jobs with it.

Ellen Frank takes on supply-side economics in "Can Tax Cuts Really Increase Government Revenue?" (Article 9.5). In the Reagan era, Arthur Laffer claimed that high marginal tax rates discourage hard work, and that cutting tax rates on the rich would spur investment and economic growth. Frank reviews the empirical arguments against Laffer and the other supply-siders.

In "Elasticity and Gas Prices" (Article 9.6), Polly Cleveland walks us through that Econ 101 concept of "elasticity" as applied to gas supply and demand. Cleveland explains why, through industry market power, the suppliers would continue to have us over a barrel even with a reduction in gas taxes.

As John Miller points out in his article, "No Fooling–Corporations Evade Taxes"(Article 9.7), Forbes magazine finally acknowledged a case of a large corporation gaming the tax code, reporting that General Electric generated $10.3 billion in pretax income but ended up owing nothing to Uncle Sam. What is worse, General Electric received a tax benefit of $1.1 billion from American taxpayers as gratitude for their clever accounting.

The last essay in this chapter also explores the Helmsley-esque sense of arrogance and entitlement. "Tax Havens and the Financial Crisis" (Article 9.8) by Rachel Keeler examines the financial "offshoring" of wealth in order to avoid taxation. "The offshore world harbors $11.5 trillion in individual wealth, representing $250 billion in lost annual tax revenue. Treasury figures show tax havens sucking $100 billion a year out of U.S. coffers." Nations like Switzerland, the Cayman Islands, and Bermuda host an industry offering to give your wealth a vacation from taxes. Mitt Romney's money enjoyed some time in the Cayman Islands and returned an effective marginal tax rate to the former Bain Capital money manager of 11%. "Only the little people pay taxes."

Discussion Questions

1) (Article 9.1) While the argument against taxation is often couched in terms of the inefficiency of taxes, Vasudevan is responding to anti-tax arguments based upon the supposed unfairness of taxation. What definition of fairness do you think these opponents of taxation are employing? What definition of fairness do you think Vasudevan is employing?

2) (Article 9.1) In what way have tax policies contributed to growing inequality in the United States? Do you think there is a case for remaking tax policy to be more progressive?

3) (Article 9.2) Why does Polly Cleveland see property taxes as being "progressive?" Explain what makes a tax "progressive," "regressive," or "neutral."

4) (Article 9.2) Why would the use of property taxes be an appropriate corrective for the current trend of wealth distribution in the Unites States?

5) (Article 9.3) What elements of Gerald Friedman's funding scheme for a single-payer healthcare system would be "redistributive?"

6) (Article 9.3) What is a "Tobin Tax?" Why is this a "two birds with one stone" form of taxation?

7) (Article 9.4) How does Twitter display market power in being able to extract tax concessions from the city of San Francisco? What is it about the nature of Twitter that makes its threat of leaving "credible?" How does firm mobility reinforce neoliberal market practices?

8) (Article 9.5) What is the basis of supply-siders' claim that lowering the highest marginal tax rate will generate more tax revenue? What criticisms does Ellen Frank raise against this view?

9) (Article 9.6) Graphically illustrate Polly Cleveland's observation that the "elasticity of gas supply is much lower that (the) elasticity of demand" (draw a supply and demand function taking care to represent the relative elasticities of both). Explain why elasticity is important in determining tax policy for gasoline.

10) (Article 9.7) What are the three key corporate "loopholes" from which corporations have traditionally avoided paying their full marginal tax rate?

11) (Article 9.7) Why is Forbes suddenly noticing corporate tax evasion?

12) (Articles 9.7 and 9.8) Why do corporations complain about a corporate marginal tax rate of 35% when in fact no company actually pays that rate?

13) (Article 9.8) Seventy-five percent of the world's hedge funds are based in four Caribbean tax havens: the Cayman Islands, Bermuda, the British Virgin Islands, and the Bahamas. Why is that? Again, have the rich "won"?

Article 9.1

THE "DOUBLE-TAXATION" OF CORPORATIONS

BY RAMAA VASUDEVAN
January/February 2007

> Dear Dr. Dollar:
> My congressman, John Mica (R-Fla.), sent me a letter claiming that "the high income tax rate of 40% for U.S. corporations, unlike most competitors, does not provide relief for the double taxation of corporate income." Like the double talk? He wants to reduce the incentives for companies to move offshore by lowering corporate income taxes. But what's the best response to this claim about "double-taxation"? I don't know much about economics, but I do know enough to know that this position is a con job.
> —Sandra Holt, Casselberry, Fla.

When corporations and their friends in Washington go on about "double taxation," what they're referring to is the notion that if corporations are taxed on their income and shareholders on their dividends, then the same income is getting taxed twice, with the implication that this is unfair or unduly burdensome. You're right to view this idea as a con job. Here's why:

First, the corporation as an entity is legally distinct from its shareholders. This distinction lies at the core of the notion of limited liability and protects individual share-holders from liability for damages caused by the corporation's pursuit of profits. The claim of "double-taxation" is bogus because the two taxes apply to different taxpayers—corporations versus individual shareholders.

Second, the double taxation claim is a bit of a red her-ring since many kinds of income are in effect double taxed. For instance, along with the income tax, workers also have to pay Medicare and Social Security taxes on their earnings.

In fact, investment income is currently treated more favorably by the tax code than wage income. Investment income is taxed at an average rate of 9.6%, compared to 23.4 % for wages. One reason for this disparity is that investment income is exempt from Medicare and Social Security taxes. But a second key reason is the reduced special tax rate for investment income approved by Congress during Bush's first term. This includes cutting the top tax rate on dividends from around 35% to 15%. As David Cay Johnston of The New York Times has observed, "the wealthiest Americans now pay much higher direct taxes on money they work for than on money that works for them."

Who benefits when the tax code rewards investment rather than wage earning? The wealthy, who garner most investment income: about 43% of total investment income goes to the top 1% of taxpayers.

Repealing the dividend tax would only exacerbate that disparity. According to Federal Reserve Board data, fewer than 20% of families hold stocks outside of retirement accounts. Individual stockholdings are concentrated among the richest families, who would be the real beneficiaries of a dividend tax break. Some 42% of benefits from repealing the dividend tax would go to the richest 1% of taxpayers, and about 75% would go to the richest 10% of taxpayers.

In contrast, the vast majority of those who own any stock at all hold their stocks in retirement accounts. They neither receive dividends on these shares directly nor pay a dividend tax—but they'll find themselves paying the normal income tax as soon as they begin drawing on their retirement accounts.

Do taxes impose a disproportionately heavy burden on U.S. corporations? The oft-quoted 40% tax rate applies only to a tiny proportion of corporate income. The official tax rate for most corporate profits is 35%; the very smallest corporations (those with income under $50,000 per year) are subject to a rate of only 15%. Moreover, the official tax rates are higher than the effective tax rates that corporations actually end up paying. A variety of tax breaks allow corporations to reap tremendous tax savings, estimated at $87 billion to $170 billion in 2002-2003 alone, according to a study by Citizens for Tax Justice. The double-taxation argument would have meaning only if the actual burden of corporate taxes were excessive. But it is not. In 2002–03, U.S. corporations paid an effective tax rate of only about 23%. Forty-six large corporations, including Pfizer, Boeing, and AT&T, actually received tax rebates (negative taxes)! Far from being a crushing burden, corporate income tax in the United States has fallen from an average of nearly 5% of GDP in the fifties to 2% in the nineties and about 1.5% (projected) in 2005-2009.

Is the U.S. corporate tax burden higher that that of its competitors? Comparisons of 29 developed countries reveal that only three—Iceland, Germany, and Poland—collected less corporate income tax as a share of GDP than the United States. This represents a reversal from the 1960s, when corporate income tax as a share of GDP in the United States was nearly double that of other developed countries.

The demand for cutting dividend taxes needs to be exposed for what it is: an attempt to create yet another windfall for upper income families who earn the bulk of their income from financial investments. It would not stimulate business investment. And it would exacerbate, rather than redress, the many real inequities in the tax code. ❑

Resources: John Miller, "Double Taxation Double Speak: Why repealing the dividend tax is unfair," *Dollars & Sense*, March–April 2003; Dean Baker "The Dividend Taxbreak; Taxing Logic," Center for Economic and Policy Research, 2003; Joel Friedman, "The Decline of Corporate income tax revenues," Center on Budget and Policy Priorities, 2003; David Cay Johnston, *Perfectly Legal: The Covert Campaign to Rig our Tax System to Benefit the Super-Rich—and Cheat Everybody Else*, Portfolio, 2003.

Aricle 9.2

RESTORE THE ORIGINAL WEALTH TAX

BY POLLY CLEVELAND
Mach/April 2011

There's an alternative to the drastic cuts in public services state and local officials are proposing: restore the property tax. It's the oldest wealth tax of all, the tax that financed Chinese civilization over 2,000 years ago, the tax that until World War II financed most of government in the United States.

The property tax? Our most hated tax? The tax that New York Gov. Andrew Cuomo, a Democrat, has vowed to cap—in the face of unprecedented budget short-falls? Yes, that tax.

If you can follow me without your eyes glazing over through the briars of distribution, the brambles of tax shifting, and the thorns of tax administration, we will find the property tax to be intrinsically the most progressive tax we have. In the age of income- and corporate-tax loopholes, the property tax remains the only tax many rich people and corporations pay—even though they have already substantially crippled it by convincing ordinary folks it's a tax on the poor and middle class.

Ideally, property taxes collect a uniform percent of the market value of taxable real estate within a given jurisdiction, let's say a town or school district, or an entire state. (Govern-ment and non-profit property is exempt—a serious problem for jurisdictions dominated by universities, hospitals or government installations like Army bases.) On average, half of that real estate is homes, and half is corporate property. The assessor, an elected official, assesses—that is, estimates—that market value, based primarily on comparable sales. Then the town imposes a tax rate, say 1.5% on the assessed value—often by a vote of the residents. Very democratic.

But what makes the property tax progressive—i.e., taking a larger share from wealthier households?

Start with income and wealth. Wealth is an order of magnitude more unequal than income. All U.S. families receive some income. But a small minority holds most of the wealth. As the table shows, the top 1% of American families receive 17% of income, but hold 34% of net worth and 42% of non-home wealth. The top 20% receive about 58% of income, but hold 85% of net worth and a staggering 92.5% of non-home wealth.

At first glance, a family's non-home wealth might seem unrelated to its property tax burden. But what is non-home wealth? It's primarily stocks and bonds, that is, shares in the ownership of corporations. Real estate forms a large part of corporate assets—what is Wal-Mart, after all, but a collection of one-story buildings in huge parking lots, occupying strategic highway intersections across the nation? That makes shareholders de facto corporate property owners—and hence payers of corporate property taxes. Follow the logic here. The top 20% of property owners, the owners of over 90% of non-home wealth, also pay most of the property taxes that fall on corporations. Since about half of taxable property is corporate, it follows that the richest 20% pay close to half of all property taxes, not including taxes on their homes. That sounds very progressive to me.

What about homes? Around 60% of U.S. families own their homes. All these homeowners pay property taxes, regardless of the value of the house or the size of their mortgage. For the property tax on homes to be more progressive than an income tax, then, higher income people must own disproportionately more valuable homes. And so they do. Studies—for instance, Mason Gaffney's work on property value in Vancouver—have shown home values increasing with the 1.8 power of income.

So the property tax looks quite progressive compared to an income tax, except—wait a minute—isn't the tax "passed on" from richer to poorer people? Now obviously homeowners can't pass on the tax, because they aren't selling anything. But what about the owners of the rental units that house the poorest 40% of families? Don't they pass on property taxes to their tenants?

Perhaps counter intuitively, the answer is no. Rents go up and down with the market. When rents and property taxes rise together over long periods, it may seem as if rising taxes are driving up rents. But it's really the other way around: demand for rental housing is pushing rents up, in turn increasing property values and hence property taxes. At other times, the disconnect between rents and property taxes is more obvious. When the recession hit in 2008, rents dropped like a rock all over New York City even while property taxes continued to increase.

So here we are. For the simple underlying reason that property ownership is far more concentrated than income, property taxes are intrinsically far more progressive than income taxes. So how have most of us come to perceive them as obsolete, unfair, and a burden on the poor and middle class?

Over the last 60 years, income and sales taxes have largely replaced property taxes at the state level, leaving property taxes to local governments, school districts especially. This shift creates the primary complaint about property taxes: within the same state, rich districts can finance good schools at low property tax rates, while poor districts can only finance lousy schools at high rates. But this is not the fault of the property tax; it would be equally true of any local tax.

Since there's a broad public interest in the quality of education, it follows that schools should be financed in part at the state and even federal level. States could make school finance more fair by making rich districts share some property tax revenue with poorer ones—as New Hampshire is attempting. But most states have simply partially replaced local property taxes with state income or sales taxes.

Ironically, loopholes in the progressive income tax also may make property taxes look regressive. Many wealthy people use property to shelter income from taxes, for

CONCENTRATION OF INCOME AND WEALTH, UNITED STATES (2004)			
	Income	Net Worth	Non-Home Wealth
Top 1%	17.0%	34.3%	42.2%
Top 10%	42.9%	71.2%	80.9%
Top 20%	57.8%	84.6%	92.5%

Source: Edward Wolff, "Recent Trends in Household Wealth in the United States: Rising Debt and the Middle-Class Squeeze" Working Paper No. 502, The Levy Economics Institute of Bard College, and Department of Economics, New York University, June 2007, www.levyinstitute.org/pubs/wp_502.pdf.

example, by deducting excessive depreciation. But these people still pay property taxes. While Ronald Reagan was governor of California (1968-72), reporters found he paid heavy property taxes on his famous ranch—and zero income taxes! If an unwary researcher plots property tax payments against income as reported to the IRS, it only takes a few of these high-property tax/low-income-tax pseudo-poor in the data base to make property taxes seem a groaning burden on the poor.

In his book Revolt of the Haves (1980), Robert Kuttner described the successful 1978 campaign for Proposition 13 in California. Prop 13 rolled back and froze property taxes. Its real estate mogul promoters depicted property taxes as a burden on average homeowners. Yet large corporate property owners enjoyed the primary benefits of Prop 13. Standard Oil of California saved $25 million in annual taxes.

Prop 13 set off nationwide anti-property tax campaigns. There were copycats like Prop 2½ in Massa-chusetts. There were reductions for special classes of property, like farmland and forestland. There were tax holidays to induce businesses to move to particular states or towns. There were caps, "circuit-breakers," limits on rate increases, and other gimmicks. New York adopted a constitutional amendment limiting property taxes to 2% of real value. Assessors got into the act too, allowing assessments to fall way below market value and giving friendly breaks to large property owners. With every hole gouged into the property tax, it became more inequitable—and more vulnerable to demands for special breaks from additional groups. States replaced some local revenue with grants from state sales and income taxes, but school quality declined. California schools fell from the top to near the bottom.

Today the clamor for cutting and capping property taxes continues unabated. Only New Hampshire has resisted—so far! Tragically, leaders of the anti-property tax campaign include the union-funded group Citizens for Tax Justice—apparently befuddled by the statistics.

It's time to wake up, to recognize that even in this crisis we can still fund the services we need. The means lie right under our feet. ❑

Sources: Edward N. Wolff, "Recent Trends in Household Wealth in the United States: Rising Debt and the Middle-Class Squeeze," The Levy Economics Institute of Bard College and Department of Economics, New York University, June 2007 (levyinstitute.org); Mason Gaffney, "The Taxable Capacity of Land," 1993 (masongaffney.org); Robert Kuttner, Revolt of the Haves, Simon & Schuster (1980); Mason Gaffney, "The Property Tax is a Progressive Tax," 1971 (masongaffney.org).

Article 9.3

FUNDING A NATIONAL SINGLE-PAYER SYSTEM
"Medicare for All" would save billions, and could be redistributive.

BY GERALD FRIEDMAN
March/April 2012

"The Expanded & Improved Medicare for All Act" (HR 676) would establish a single authority responsible for paying for health care for all Americans. Providing universal coverage with a "single-payer" system would change many aspects of American health care. While it would raise some costs by providing access to care for those currently uninsured or under-insured, it would save much larger sums by eliminating insurance middlemen and radically simplifying payment to doctors and hospitals. While providing superior health care, a single-payer system would save as much as $570 billion now wasted on administrative overhead and monopoly profits. A single-payer system would also make health-care financing dramatically more progressive by replacing fixed, income-invariant health-care expenditures with progressive taxes. This series of charts and graphs shows why we need a single-payer system and how it could be funded. ❑

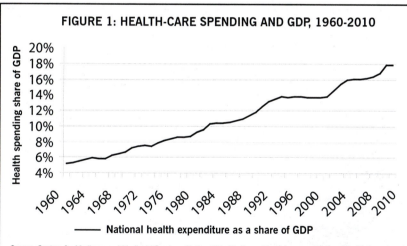

FIGURE 1: HEALTH-CARE SPENDING AND GDP, 1960-2010

Health spending share of GDP

—— National health expenditure as a share of GDP

Source: Centers for Medicare and Medicaid Services, National Health Expenditures (cms.gov/NationalHealthExpend-Data/); author's own calculations for projections of single-payer costs.

Health-care costs have risen much faster than income in the United States over the last 50 years, rising from 5% of Gross Domestic Product in 1960 to nearly 18% today. Some of the increase in costs in the United States, as with other countries, is associated with improvements in care and longevity. Costs have risen much faster in the United States, however, because of the growing administrative burden of our private health-insurance system.

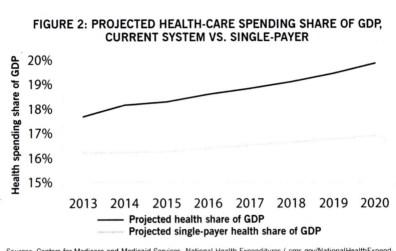

FIGURE 2: PROJECTED HEALTH-CARE SPENDING SHARE OF GDP, CURRENT SYSTEM VS. SINGLE-PAYER

Sources: Centers for Medicare and Medicaid Services, National Health Expenditures (cms.gov/NationalHealthExpend-Data/); author's own calculations for projections of single-payer costs.

With $570 billion in savings on administration and monopoly profits, a single-payer system would reduce dramatically the burden of health care costs on the United States economy. Over time, furthermore, a single-payer system would allow us to slow the growth in health-care spending.

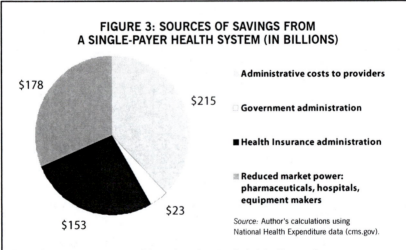

FIGURE 3: SOURCES OF SAVINGS FROM A SINGLE-PAYER HEALTH SYSTEM (IN BILLIONS)

Source: Author's calculations using National Health Expenditure data (cms.gov).

A single-payer system would produce huge administrative savings by simplifying billing operations within providers' offices and hospitals, and by redistributing the monopoly profits currently enjoyed by pharmaceutical makers and other companies.

FIGURE 4: INCREASED SPENDING ASSOCIATED WITH A SINGLE-PAYER SYSTEM (IN BILLIONS)

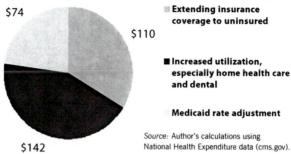

$74

$110

Extending insurance coverage to uninsured

Increased utilization, especially home health care and dental

Medicaid rate adjustment

$142

Source: Author's calculations using National Health Expenditure data (cms.gov).

The savings produced by a single-payer system would allow us to correct some of the problems within the current health-care system. In addition to extending coverage to all of those currently uninsured, we could also improve the coverage for those with inadequate insurance. Finally, we could correct the inequity in the current financing system by reimbursing providers equally for caring for the poor under Medicaid.

FIGURE 5: FUNDING FOR A SINGLE-PAYER SYSTEM, 2013 (IN BILLIONS)

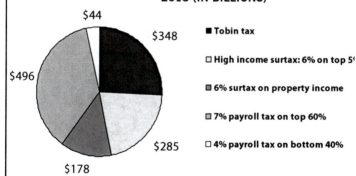

$44

$348

$496

$285

$178

Tobin tax

High income surtax: 6% on top 5⁰

6% surtax on property income

7% payroll tax on top 60%

4% payroll tax on bottom 40%

Sources: Dean Baker et al., The Potential Revenue from Financial Transactions Taxes, Political Economy Research Institute Working Paper Series (Amherst, MA.: Political Economy Research Institute, University of Massachusetts-Amherst, December 2009); author's calculations using national income data from the Bureau of Economic Analysis, bea.gov.

The single-payer system would be paid for by a variety of taxes. The Tobin tax is a tax on financial transactions that would raise revenue while discouraging the types of speculative finance that led to the current economic crisis. The remaining revenue would come from taxes targeted at those best able to pay, including those with high incomes and with incomes from property (including capital gains, dividends, interest, profits, and rents).

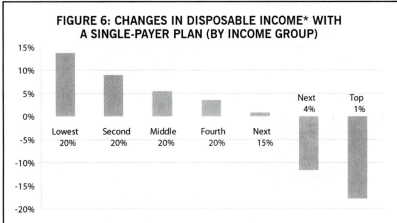

FIGURE 6: CHANGES IN DISPOSABLE INCOME* WITH A SINGLE-PAYER PLAN (BY INCOME GROUP)

*"Disposable Income" is income after taxes and health-care spending.
Source: Data on the distribution of income and its sources from the income tax as prepared by Emmanuel Saez and Thomas Piketty (elsa.berkeley.edu/~saez/).

With private health insurance, health-care expenditures are largely fixed with respect to income and, therefore, are a heavier burden on the poor and middle classes than on the wealthy. By linking health-care expenditures to income, a tax-funded single-payer system would provide savings for all Americans below the wealthiest top 5%.

Article 9.4

CAPITAL FLIGHT ACROSS THE COUNTY LINE
Twitter blackmails San Francisco and raises fears of gentrification.

BY JAMES TRACY
September/October 2011

This past April, the San Francisco Board of Supervisors granted a tax holiday to Twitter, Inc., the microblogging and social-networking company founded in the city. Twitter threatened to move south to neighboring Brisbane unless its municipal payroll taxes were forgiven. Local politicians responded not only by granting the multi-million-dollar tax break but by also approving a plan that has stoked fears of gentrification and displacement in the city's remaining working-class neighborhoods.

Twitter is fast approaching the status of Internet giant. At the time of the tax break it was valued at between $4 billion and $6 billion (although the company has yet to turn a profit and still depends on venture capital investments to operate).

Initial legislation proposed by Mayor Ed Lee would have given the Internet company a complete payroll tax break in exchange for sticking around. Modified legislation, which passed, was put forward by Supervisor Jane Kim. It granted a six-year payroll exemption only for new hires, and created an "enterprise zone" (including Twitter's new digs) on struggling Market Street and in parts of the Tenderloin and South-of-Market neighborhoods. The tax break extended to all businesses starting up, or relocating from another area, within the zone's reach.

The enterprise zone economic development strategy grants corporations tax breaks and other advantages in exchange for doing business in an economically downtrodden neighborhood. Even though it is a conservative approach, based in incentives, most enterprise zones at least require the beneficiary businesses to commit to levels of local hiring and other community benefits. One problem is that after four decades of use, they have shown little positive impact. According to the Public Policy Institute of California, employment rates within enterprise zones are no different than similar areas without them.

The Twitter legislation didn't secure any benefits in a specific, legally binding manner. Steve Woo, a community organizer with the Tenderloin Neighborhood Development Corporation, remarked, "The enterprise zone in the middle of Market Street was created by city officials without any specific commitment of addressing [the community's] needs and instead prioritized the needs of Big Business."

Even a progressive official such as Kim, who described herself as philosophically against such tax breaks, felt that she had to do business with Twitter. She pointed out in a public hearing that without the legislation, all of the revenue from Twitter's payroll tax would leave San Francisco for the suburbs and 400 jobs would disappear from the local economy. Twitter's portion of the break was estimated to sap city coffers to the tune of $22 million dollars over six years.

Advocates for the legislation pointed to the boarded-up storefronts on Market Street, and to the "seediness" of the area, claiming it was ripe for renewal. This ignored the fact that many of the storefronts had been left vacant in the past few years by speculators buying up large portions of the street and evicting small businesses.

Other community voices, such as the South of Market Community Action Network (SOMCAN), cited fears of displacement from a second dot-com economic boom. The neighborhoods bordering the "Twitter Zone" are largely working class and consist predominantly of renters. Supporters pointed out that the neighborhoods were in need of jobs and uplift and argued that because of decades of progressive zoning changes the neighborhoods were immune to gentrification.

Whether or not the legislation will bear out activists' fears remains to be seen. What is clear today is that San Francisco is in a budget crisis expected to last at least five years or more, and essential city services ranging from AIDS treatment to employment programs are fighting for survival. Angelica Cabande of SOMCAN, who led the campaign to defeat the Twitter tax break, explained, "In these hard economic times, city and state officials have been preaching that everyone needs to buckle down and make responsible decisions and make due sacrifices for the betterment of everyone; it doesn't make sense that big companies like Twitter get a tax break."

Such is the dilemma facing politicians and policy makers. Employers like Twitter are able to move their offices much more easily than factories and plants did in the past. This, combined with the current dearth of large employers, leaves cities hostage to corporate demands. It's the neoliberal economic model applied to local neighborhoods: get rid of taxes and regulation or lose the jobs.

So far, the mini-enterprise zone hasn't held its own against the sagging economy and the lack of small-business capital. As of July 2011, most of the Market Street storefronts that were vacant before the zone was created remained that way—with the exception of one small Italian restaurant that abandoned its former location a few blocks away to move into the area.

Twitter's economic blackmail has started a trend. Even before the ink had dried on this legislation, another company, Zynga.com, delivered a ransom note of its own, demanding that the city stop taxing employee stock option payments. Again the Board of Supervisors and the mayor obliged.

In early July, the *Wall Street Journal* reported that Twitter's value had been upgraded to $7 billion, raising the question of why the company needed a break in the first place. The answer may be as simple as the politics of a hostage situation: give us the money or we'll kill the jobs. ❏

Article 9.5

CAN TAX CUTS REALLY INCREASE GOVERNMENT REVENUE?

BY ELLEN FRANK
November/December 2003

> Dear Dr. Dollar:
> *A Republican friend tells me that the huge new tax cuts will actually produce more revenue than the government would have collected before the cut, because once rich beneficiaries invest the money, they will pay taxes on every transaction. He suggested that the increase could be as much as 50% more than the originally scheduled revenues. Is this possible?*
> —Judith Walker, New York, N.Y.

Back in the 1970s, conservative economist Arthur Laffer proposed that high marginal tax rates discouraged people from earning additional income. By cutting taxes, especially on those with the highest incomes, Laffer argued, governments would spur individuals to work harder and invest more, stoking economic growth. Though the government would get a smaller bite from every dollar the economy generated, there would be so many more dollars to tax that government revenues would actually rise. Ronald Reagan invoked the "Laffer curve" in the 1980s, insisting he could cut taxes, hike defense spending, and still balance the budget.

Bush's 2001 and 2003 tax packages are eerily reminiscent of the Reagan cuts. They reduce rates levied on ordinary income, with the largest rate cut going to the wealthiest taxpayers. They extend business tax write-offs and increase the child tax credit (though only for two years and only for families who earn enough to pay federal income taxes). They cut the tax on capital gains from 28% to 15%; dividend income, previously taxed at the same rate as ordinary income, now faces a top rate of 15%.

Citizens for Tax Justice estimates that two-thirds of the 2003 tax cut will accrue to the richest 10% of taxpayers. By 2006, the increased child credit will be phased out and nine out of ten taxpayers will find their taxes cut by less than $100. The top 1%, in contrast, will save an average $24,000 annually over the next four years, thanks to the 2003 cut alone.

Though inspired by the same "supply-side" vision that guided Reagan, Bush officials have not explicitly cited Laffer's arguments in defense of their tax packages. Probably, they wish to avoid ridicule. After the Reagan tax cut, the U.S. economy sank into recession and federal tax collections dropped nearly 10%. The deficit soared and economic growth was tepid through much of Reagan's presidency, despite sharp hikes in military spending. Some of the Republican faithful continue to argue that tax cuts will unleash enough growth to pay for themselves, but most are embarrassed to raise the now discredited Laffer curve.

The problem with your friend's assertion is fairly simple. If the government cuts projected taxes by $1.5 trillion over the next decade, those dollars will recirculate through the economy. The $1.5 trillion tax cut becomes $1.5 trillion in taxable income and is itself taxed, as your friend suggests. But this would be just as true if, instead of cutting taxes, the government spent $1.5 trillion on highways or national defense or schools or, for that matter, if it trimmed $1.5 trillion from the tax liability of low- and middle-income households. All tax cuts become income, are re-spent, and taxed. That reality is already factored into everyone's economic projections. But the new income, taxed at a lower rate, will generate lower overall tax collections.

To conclude that revenues will rise rather than fall following a tax cut, one must maintain that the tax cut causes the economy to grow faster than it would have otherwise—that cutting taxes on the upper crust stimulates enough additional growth to offset the lower tax rates, more growth than would be propelled by, say, building roads or reducing payroll taxes. Free-marketeers insist that this is indeed the case. Spend $1.5 trillion on highways and you get $1.5 trillion worth of highways. Give it to Wall Street and investors will develop new technologies, improve productivity, and spur the economy to new heights.

Critics of the Bush cuts contend, however, that faster growth arises from robust demand for goods and from solid, well-maintained public infrastructure. Give $1.5 to Wall Street and you get inflated stock prices and real estate bubbles. Give it to working families or state governments and you get crowded malls, ringing cash registers, and businesses busily investing to keep up with their customers.

Who is right? Die-hard supply-siders insist that the Reagan tax cuts worked as planned—the payoff just didn't arrive until the mid-1990s! But the Bush administration's own budget office is predicting sizable deficits for the next several years. Maybe, like your friend, they believe the tax cuts will pay for themselves—but they're not banking on it. ❏

Article 9.6

ELASTICITY AND GAS TAXES

Why cutting gas taxes won't lower prices, but will fatten oil companies.

BY POLLY CLEVELAND
June 2008

When Clinton and McCain proposed cutting gas taxes, I asked my environmental economics students, "So how much do you think drivers will save?" The students diligently Googled the numbers. "Well," said one, "the federal gas tax is 18.4 cents and the average state tax is 28.6 cents, so that's 47 cents a gallon drivers will save!" "But what about elasticity of demand and supply?" I asked. "Oh! Forgot about that!"

Elasticity—nemesis of Econ 101—is a vital concept even professional economists often forget. Elasticity is just the percentage change in quantity purchased or supplied, divided by the percentage change in price. An increase in price will lead consumers to buy less, and suppliers to offer more; vice versa for a price decrease; elasticity measures the size of that effect.

Elasticity of demand for gas is low, around 0.5. That means a 10% increase in gas prices will cause only a 5% decrease in gas consumption. That's because it's difficult, in the short run, for people to change their habits, for example, to buy smaller cars, to move closer to work, or to change vacation plans. But in fact some people do change; already unsold SUV's clog the dealers' showrooms and lots.

But—and here's the crucial point—elasticity of gas supply is even lower, much lower than elasticity of demand. In fact, short run elasticity of supply is near zero. Two reasons: First, it's very hard to increase supply quickly because that means expanding refining capacity. Many suppliers, especially national suppliers like Russia, Venezuela and Libya, are failing to invest in upgrading capacity. Then there's the oil production disaster in Iraq. Second, oil companies have some monopoly power, which means they are, to some degree, already holding back production in order to raise their prices. That makes it even harder for them to decrease or increase supply in response to a tax or subsidy.

A tax on a product like gasoline falls in inverse proportion to elasticity. If elasticity of demand is 0.5, and the elasticity of supply is, say, one tenth as much, or 0.05, then suppliers pay ten times as much of the tax as consumers. That is, most of the tax falls on suppliers. Another way to put it is that suppliers cannot pass on a gas tax to consumers.

Conversely, a tax cut will deliver a windfall to suppliers, without appreciably lowering prices at the pump. When some New York State counties tried lowering local gas taxes in response to consumer protests, gas prices didn't budge.

There are broader policy implications here: First, we can substantially raise gas taxes without much pushing gas prices above their market level—in the process capturing more of the windfall profits currently enjoyed by oil producers. Second, if we wish to discourage carbon emissions from cars, we need to look to other approaches besides gas taxes, for example, setting emission standards for automobiles, improving public transportation and encouraging denser development.

The United States subsidizes ethanol production by something over a dollar a gallon, supposedly to replace gasoline. On the final exam, I asked my students this question: if Congress eliminates ethanol subsidies, will suppliers or consumers suffer more, and why? Only one student got the answer completely correct: By the same logic of relative elasticity, subsidies to ethanol production accrue mostly to suppliers, not consumers. So eliminating subsidies hurts suppliers more than consumers. Elasticity is a slippery concept! ❑

Article 9.7

NO FOOLING—CORPORATIONS EVADE TAXES

Forbes Finally Notices what has Been Obvious For Years

BY JOHN MILLER
May/June 2011

WHAT THE TOP U.S. COMPANIES PAY IN TAXES

Some of the world's biggest, most profitable corporations enjoy a far lower tax rate than you do—that is, if they pay taxes at all.

The most egregious example is General Electric. Last year the conglomerate generated $10.3 billion in pretax income, but ended up owing nothing to Uncle Sam. In fact, it recorded a tax benefit of $1.1 billion.

Over the last two years, GE Capital [one of the two divisions of General Electric] has displayed an uncanny ability to lose lots of money in the U.S. (posting a $6.5 billion loss in 2009), and make lots of money overseas (a $4.3 billion gain).

It only makes sense that multinationals "put costs in high-tax countries and profits in low-tax countries," says Scott Hodge, president of the Tax Foundation. Those low-tax countries are almost anywhere but the U.S. "When you add in state taxes, the U.S. has the highest tax burden among industrialized countries," says Hodge. In contrast, China's rate is just 25%; Ireland's is 12.5%.

—Christopher Helman, "What the Top U.S. Companies Pay in Taxes," *Forbes*, April 1, 2011

When *Forbes* magazine, the keeper of the list of the 400 richest Americans, warns that corporations not paying taxes on their profits will raise your hackles, you might wonder about the article's April 1 dateline. If it turns out *not* to be an April Fool's joke, things must be *really* bad.

And indeed they are. As *Forbes* reports, General Electric, the third largest U.S. corporation, turned a profit of $10.3 billion in 2010, paid no corporate income taxes, and got a "tax benefit" of $1.1 billion on taxes owed on past profits. And from 2005 to 2009, according to its own filings, GE paid a consolidated tax rate of just 11.6% on its corporate rates, including state, local, and foreign taxes. That's a far cry from the 35% rate nominally levied on corporate profits above $10 million.

Nor was GE alone among the top ten U.S. corporations with no tax obligations. Bank of America (BofA), the seventh largest U.S. corporation, racked up $4.4 billion in profits in 2010 and also paid no corporate income taxes (or in 2009 for that matter). Like GE, BofA has hauled in a whopping "tax benefit"—$1.9 billion.

For BofA, much like for GE, losses incurred during the financial crisis erased it tax liabilities. BofA, of course, contributed mightily to the crisis. It was one of four banks that controlled 95% of commercial bank derivatives activity, mortgage-based securities that inflated the housing bubble and brought on the crisis.

And when the crisis hit, U.S. taxpayers bailed them out, not once but several times. All told BofA received $45 billion of government money from the Troubled

Asset Relief Program (TARP) as well as other government guarantees. And while BofA paid no taxes on their over $4 billion of profits, they nonetheless managed to pay out $3.3 billion in bonuses to corporate executives. All of that has made BofA a prime target for US Uncut protests (see p. 6) against corporate tax dodging that has cost the federal government revenues well beyond the $39 billion saved by the punishing spending cuts in the recent 2011 budget deal.

These two corporate behemoths and other many other major corporations paid no corporate income taxes last year, even though 2010 U.S. corporate profits had returned their level in 2005 in the midst the profits-heavy Bush expansion before the crisis hit.

An Old Story

But why is *Forbes* suddenly noticing corporate tax evasion? After all, corporations not paying taxes on their profits is an old story. Let's take a look at the track record of major corporations paying corporate income before the crisis hit and the losses that supposedly explain their not paying taxes.

The Government Accounting Office conducted a detailed study of the burden of the corporate income tax from 1998 to 2005. The results were stunning. Over half (55%) of large U.S. corporations reported no tax liability for at least one of those eight years. And in 2005 alone 25% of those corporations paid no corporate income taxes, even though corporate profits had more than doubled from 2001 to 2005.

In another careful study, the Treasury Department found that from 2000 to 2005, the share of corporate operating surplus that that U.S. corporations pay in taxes—a proxy for the average tax rate—was 16.7% thanks to various corporate loopholes, especially three key mechanisms:

- Accelerated Depreciation: allows corporations to write off machinery and equipment or other assets more quickly than they actually deteriorate.
- Stock Options: by giving their executives the option to buy the company's stock at a favorable price, corporations can take a tax deduction for the difference between what the employees pay for the stock and what it's worth.
- Debt Financing: offers a lower effective tax rate for corporate investment than equity (or stock) financing because the interest payments on debt (usually incurred by issuing bonds) get added to corporate costs and reduce reported profits.

Corporate income taxes are levied against reported corporate profits, and each of these mechanisms allows corporations to inflate their reported costs and thereby reduce their taxable profits.

And then there are overseas profits. U.S.-based corporations don't pay U.S. corporate taxes on their foreign income until it is "repatriated," or sent back to the parent corporation from abroad. That allows multinational corporations to defer payment of U.S. corporate income taxes on their overseas profits indefinitely or repatriate their profits from foreign subsidiaries when their losses from domestic operations can offset those profits and wipe out any tax liability, as GE did in 2010.

Hardly Overtaxed

Nonetheless, Scott Hodge, the president of the right-wing Tax Foundation, steadfastly maintains that U.S. corporations are overtaxed, and that that is what driving U.S. corporations to park their profits abroad (and lower their U.S. taxes). Looking at nominal corporate tax rates, Hodge would seem to have a case. Among the 19 OECD countries, only the statutory corporate tax rates in Japan surpass the (average combined federal and state) 39.3% rate on U.S. corporate profits. And the U.S. rate is well above the OECD average of 27.6%.

But these sorts of comparisons misrepresent where U.S. corporate taxes stand with respect to tax rates actually paid by corporations in other advanced countries. Why? The tax analyst's answer is that the U.S. corporate income tax has a "narrow base," or in plain English, is riddled with loopholes. As a result U.S. effective corporate tax rates—the proportion of corporate profits actually paid out in taxes—are not only far lower than the nominal rate but below the effective rates in several other countries. The Congressional Budget Office, for instance, found that U.S. effective corporate tax rates were near the OECD average for equity-financed investments, and below the OECD average for debt-financed investments. And for the years from 2000 to 2005, the Treasury Department found the average corporate tax rate among OECD countries was 21.6%, well above the U.S. 16.7% rate.

Current U.S. corporate tax rates are also extremely low by historical standards. In 1953, government revenue from the U.S. corporate income taxes were the equal of 5.6% of GDP; the figure was 4.0% of GDP in 1969, 2.2% of GDP from 2000 to 2005, and is currently running at about 2.0% of GDP.

By all these measures U.S. corporations are hardly over-taxed. And some major corporations are barely taxed, if taxed at all.

Closing corporate loopholes so that corporate income tax revenues in the United States match the 3.4% of GDP collected on average by OECD corporate income taxes would add close to $200 billion to federal government revenues—more than five times the $39 billion of devastating spending cuts just made in the federal budget in 2011. Returning the corporate income tax revenues to the 4.0% of GDP level of four decades ago would add close to $300 billion a year to government revenues.

The cost of not shutting down those corporate loopholes would be to let major corporations go untaxed, to rob the federal government of revenues that could, with enough political will, reverse devastating budget cuts, and to leave the rest of us to pay more and more of the taxes necessary to support a government that does less and less for us. ❑

Sources: "Corporate Tax Reform: Issues for Congress," by Jane G. Gravelle and Thomas L. Hungerford, CRS Report for Congress, October 31, 2007; "Treasury Conference On Business Taxation and Global Competitiveness," U.S. Department of the Treasury, Background Paper, July 23, 2007; "Six Tests for Corporate Tax Reform," by Chuck Marr and Brian Highsmith, Center on Budget and Policy Priorities, February 28, 2011; "Tax Holiday For Overseas Corporate Profits Would Increase Deficits, Fail To Boost The Economy, And Ultimately Shift More Investment And Jobs Overseas," by Chuck Marr and Brian Highsmith, Center on Budget and Policy Priorities, April 8, 2011; and, "Comparison of the Reported Tax Liabilities of Foreign and U.S.-Controlled Corporations, 1998-2005," Government Accounting Office, July 2008.

Article 9.8

TAX HAVENS AND THE FINANCIAL CRISIS

From offshore havens to financial centers, banking secrecy faces scrutiny.

BY RACHEL KEELER
May/June 2009

When an entire global financial system collapses, it is reasonable to expect some bickering over the ultimate fixing of things. Rumors of dissention and talk of stimulus-paved roads to hell made everyone squeamish going into the April summit of the G20 group of large and industrialized nations in London. French President Nicolas Sarkozy even threatened to walk out on the whole thing if he didn't get his way.

The French were perhaps right to be nervous: they were taking a somewhat socialist stand, declaring that unregulated shadow banking and offshore tax havens were at the heart of the financial crisis and had to be either controlled or eradicated. They were doing it in a city at the center of the shadow system, and at a summit chaired by British Prime Minister Gordon Brown, a man recently described by the *Financial Times* as "one of the principal cheerleaders for the competitive international deregulation of international financial markets."

But Gordon Brown had already announced his intention to lead the global crackdown on tax havens as a first step toward global financial recovery. German Chancellor Angela Merkel had long backed France in calling for regulation of hedge funds, the poster boys of shadow banking charged with fostering the crisis. And, to Sarkozy's delight, everyone kept their promises at the G20.

"Major failures in the financial sector and in financial regulation and supervision were fundamental causes of the crisis," read the summit's reassuringly clear communiqué. World leaders agreed to regulate all systemically important financial institutions, including hedge funds and those located in tax havens, under threat of sanctions for noncompliance. "The era of banking secrecy is over," they concluded, as close to united as anyone could have dreamed.

But unity that looks good on paper is always more difficult to achieve in reality. The lingering questions post-summit are the same ones Sarkozy may have pondered on his way to London: will leaders from countries made rich from offshore banking follow through to shut it down? What is at stake, and what will the globally coordinated regulation everyone agrees is necessary actually look like? Not surprisingly, there are no easy answers.

Nature of the Beast

Over the years, trillions of dollars in both corporate profits and personal wealth have migrated "offshore" in search of rock bottom tax rates and the comfort of no questions asked. Tax havens and other financial centers promoting low tax rates, light regulation, and financial secrecy include a long list of tropical nations like the Cayman Islands as well as whole mainland economies from Switzerland to Singapore.

Tax Justice Network, an international non-profit advocating tax haven reform, estimates one- third of global assets are held offshore. The offshore world harbors $11.5 trillion in individual wealth alone, representing $250 billion in lost annual tax revenue. Treasury figures show tax havens sucking $100 billion a year out of U.S. coffers. And these numbers have all been growing steadily over the past decade. A *Tax Notes* study found that between 1999 and 2002, the amount of profits U.S. companies reported in tax havens grew from $88 billion to $149 billion.

With little patience left for fat-cat tax scams, the public is finally cheering for reform. Tax havens, it seems, have become the perfect embodiment of suddenly unfashionable capitalist greed. Unemployed workers and unhappy investors grow hot with anger as they imagine exotic hideouts where businessmen go to sip poolside martinis and laugh off their national tax burden.

Reformers have tried and failed in the past to shut down these locales. But analysts say 2008, the year the global financial system finally collapsed under its own liberalized weight, made all the difference. Not only are governments now desperate for tax revenue to help fund bailouts, but a recognition of the role offshore financial centers played in the system's implosion is dawning.

Along with the G20 fanfare, economists and policymakers including Treasury Secretary Timothy Geithner have pointed to the shadow banking system as a root cause of the global crisis. They're talking about the raft of highly-leveraged, virtually unregulated investment vehicles developed over the last 20 years: hedge funds, private equity, conduits, structured investment vehicles (SIVs), collateralized debt obligations (CDOs), and other wildly arcane investment banker toys.

While most of these innovations were born of Wall Street imaginations, few found their home in New York. Seventy-five percent of the world's hedge funds are based in four Caribbean tax havens: the Cayman Islands, Bermuda, the British Virgin Islands, and the Bahamas. The two subprime mortgage-backed Bear Stearns funds that collapsed in 2007, precipitating the credit crisis, were incorporated in the Caymans. Jersey and Guernsey, offshore financial centers in the Channel Islands, specialize in private equity. Many SIVs were created offshore, far from regulatory eyes.

We now know that hedge funds made their record profits from offshore bases by taking long-term gambles with short-term loans. The risky funds were often backed by onshore banks but kept off those institutions' books as they were repackaged and sold around the world. Regulators never took much notice: one, because lobbyists told them not to; two, because the funds were so complex that George Soros barely understood them; and three, because many of the deals were happening offshore.

Beneath regulatory radar, shadow bankers were able to scrap capital cushions, conceal illiquidity, and muddle debt accountability while depending on constant refinancing to survive. When the bubble burst and investors made a run for their money, panicked fund managers found it impossible to honor their debts, or even figure out how to price them as the markets crumbled.

William Cohan writes in his book on the Bear Stearns collapse (*House of Cards: A Tale of Hubris and Wretched Excess on Wall Street*) that it took the brokerage three weeks working day and night to value illiquid securities when two of its Cayman-based hedge funds fell apart in 2007. In the end, the firm realized it was off by $1 billion from its original guesstimate, on just $1.5 billion in funds.

Mortgage-backed securities that once flourished in offshore tax havens are now the toxic assets that U.S. taxpayers are being asked to salvage through the trillion-dollar TARP and TALF programs.

Last Laughs

This convoluted network of offshore escapades is what world leaders have vowed to bring under global regulatory watch in order to restore worldwide financial stability. To their credit, the crackdown on banking secrecy has already begun in a big way.

In February 2009, secret Swiss bank accounts were blown open to permit an unprecedented Internal Revenue Service probe. Europe's UBS bank has admitted to helping wealthy Americans evade what prosecutors believe to be $300 million a year in taxes.

Switzerland, the world's biggest tax haven where at least $2 trillion in offshore money is stashed, has long refused to recognize tax evasion as a crime. Every nation has the sovereign right to set its own tax code, which is why regulators have had such a hard time challenging offshore banking in the past. The dirty secret of tax havens, as President Obama once noted, is that they're mostly legal.

Under U.S. law, tax avoidance (legal) only becomes tax evasion (illegal) in the absence of other, more credible perks. In other words, a company is free to establish foreign subsidiaries in search of financial expertise, global reach, convenience, etc., just so long as tax dodging does not appear to be the sole reason for relocation.

The IRS will tax individual American income wherever it's found, but finding it is often the key. To access account information in Switzerland, authorities had to have proof not merely of tax evasion but of fraud, which is what much white-knuckled investigation finally produced on UBS. In the wake of this success, and under threat of landing on the OECD's new list of "uncooperative" tax havens, all of Europe's secrecy jurisdictions—Liechtenstein, Andorra, Austria, Luxembourg, and Switzerland—have signed information-sharing agreements.

Following the blood trail, congressional investigators descended on the Cayman Islands in March to tour the infamous Ugland House: one building supposedly home to 12,748 U.S. companies. The trip was an attempt to verify some of the implicit accusations made by a Government Accountability Office report in January which found that 83 of the United States' top 100 companies operate subsidiaries in tax havens.

Many of those, including Citigroup (which holds 90 subsidiaries in the Cayman Islands alone), Bank of America, and AIG, have received billions in taxpayer-funded bailouts. But the report failed to establish whether the subsidiaries were set up for the sole purpose of tax evasion.

Offshore Arguments

Politicians are already patting themselves on the back for their success in tackling tax crime. Everyone is making a big deal of the new tax information-exchange standard that all but three nations (Costa Rica, Malaysia, and the Philippines—the OECD's freshly minted blacklist) have agreed to implement in the wake of the G20 meeting. What leaders aren't saying is that before it became a G20 talking point, tax information exchange was actually tax haven *fans'* favored reform measure.

The first thing most offshore officials claim when confronted with criticism is that their countries are not, indeed, tax havens. Since the OECD launched a tax policy campaign in 1996, many of the offshore centers have been working to clean up their acts. A hoard of information-exchange agreements with onshore economies were signed even before Switzerland took the plunge. Geoff Cook, head of Jersey Finance, says Jersey's agreements with the United States, Germany, Sweden, and others have long outpaced what banks in Switzerland and Singapore traditionally maintained. "Our only fear in this is that people wouldn't look into the subject deep enough to draw those distinctions," Cook said.

But analysts say the agreements lack teeth. To request information from offshore, authorities must already have some evidence of misconduct. And the information-exchange standard still only covers illegal tax evasion, not legal tax avoidance. More importantly, what is already evident is that these agreements don't change much about the way offshore financial centers function. Offshore centers that agree to open up their books still have the luxury of setting their own regulatory standards and will continue to attract business based on their shadow banking credentials.

The G20 decided that shadow banking must be subjected to the same regulation as onshore commercial activity, which will also see more diligent oversight. Financial activity everywhere will be required to maintain better capital buffers, they said, monitored by a new Financial Stability Board; and excessive risk-taking will be rebuked. But the push for harmonized regulation across all financial centers revokes a degree of local liberty. Big ideas about state sovereignty and economic growth are at stake, which is probably what made Sarkozy so nervous about taking his regulatory demands global.

"People come here for expertise and knowledge," argues head of Guernsey Finance Peter Niven, and he may have a point. Many in finance think it's wrong to put all the blame on private funds and offshore centers for a crisis of such complex origins. Havens say stripping away their financial freedoms is hypocritical and shortsighted. "It's really not about the Cayman Islands, it's about the U.S. tax gap—and we're the collateral damage," said one frustrated Cayman Island official, adding: "Everybody needs liquidity and everyone needs money. That's what we do."

Predictably, reform critics warn that responding to the global crisis with "too much" regulation will stifle economic growth, something they know world leaders are quite conscious of. "International Financial Centres such as Jersey play an important role as conduits in the flow of international capital around the world by providing liquidity in neighbouring (often onshore) financial centres, the very lubrication which markets now need," wrote Cook in a recent statement.

Overall, attempting to move beyond paltry information exchange to implementing real regulation of shadow banking across national jurisdictions promises to be extremely difficult.

Real Reform

Part of the solution starts at home. Offshore enthusiasts might be the first to point out that the Securities and Exchange Commission never had the remit to regulate *onshore* hedge funds because Congress didn't give it to them. Wall Street deregulation is often cited in Europe as the base rot in the system.

But demanding more regulation onshore won't do any good if you can't regulate in the same way offshore. A serious aspect of the tax haven problem is a kind of global regulatory arbitrage: widespread onshore deregulation over the last 20 years came alongside an affinity for doing business offshore where even less regulation was possible, which in turn encouraged tax haven-style policies in countries like Britain, the United States, Singapore, and Ireland, all fighting to draw finance back into their economies.

President Obama has long been a champion of both domestic and offshore financial reform, and a critic of the deregulation popular during the Bush years. But for global action to happen, Obama needs Europe's help (not to mention cooperation from Asia and the Middle East) and no one knows how deep Gordon Brown's commitment runs. It is only very recently that Brown transformed himself from deregulation cheerleader as chancellor of the exchequer under Tony Blair to global regulatory savior as Britain's new prime minister.

In an interview late last year, Tax Justice Network's John Christensen predicted Britain could become a barrier to reform. "Britain, I think, will become increasingly isolated, particularly in Europe where the City of London is regarded as a tax haven," he said. Even if Gordon Brown is on board, Britain's finance sector hates to see itself sink. Moreover, some say the UK's lax financial regulatory system has saved the wider economy from decay. When British manufacturing declined, the City of London became the nation's new breadwinner. It grew into the powerhouse it is today largely by luring business away from other centers with the promise of adventurous profit-making and mild public oversight.

The City now funnels much of its business through British overseas territories that make up a big faction in the world's offshore banking club. Many offshore officials have accused Britain of making a show of tax haven reform to deflect attention from its own dirty dealings onshore.

Other obstacles to reform could come from Belgium and Luxembourg, which each hold important votes at the Basel Committee on Banking Supervision (a leading international regulatory voice) and the EU. Neither country has shown much enthusiasm for Europe's reform agenda. And no one will soon forget that China nearly neutered the G20 communiqué when it refused to "endorse" an OECD tax haven blacklist that would allow Europe to chastise financial activities in Hong Kong and Macau.

Still, the regulatory tide is strong and rising; even global financial heavyweights may find it unwise or simply impossible to swim against it. For perhaps the first time since the end of World War II, the world appears open to the kind of global cooperation necessary to facilitate global integration in a socially responsible way.

But the tiny nations that have built empires around unfettered financial services will surely continue to fight for their place in the sun. Some may go the way of Darwinian selection. Declining tourism is already crippling economies across the

Caribbean. But many more are optimistic about their ability to hang on. Guernsey is pursuing Chinese markets. Jersey claims business in private equity remains strong. Bermuda still has insurance and hopes to dabble in gambling. Many offshore say they welcome the coming reforms.

"We look forward to those challenges" said Michael Dunkley, leader of the United Bermuda Party, noting that Bermuda, a tiny island with a population of just 66,000 people, is not encumbered by big bureaucracy when it comes to getting things done. Whatever new regulations come up, he said: "Bermuda would be at the cutting edge of making sure it worked."

Accusations of capitalist evil aside, one can't help but admire their spirit. ❏

Sources: Willem Buiter, "Making monetary policy in the UK has become simpler, in no small part thanks to Gordon Brown," *Financial Times*, October 26, 2008; G20 Final Communiqué, "The Global Plan for Recovery and Reform," April 2, 2009; Tax Justice Network, taxjustice.net; Martin Sullivan, Data Shows Dramatic Shift of Profits to Tax Havens, *Tax Notes*, September 13, 2004; William Cohan, *House of Cards: A Tale of Hubris and Wretched Excess on Wall Street*, March 2009; U.S. Government Accountability Office, "International Taxation: Large US corporations and federal contractors in jurisdictions listed as tax havens or financial privacy jurisdictions," December 2008; Organisation for Economic Co-operation and Development. "A Progress Report on the Jurisdictions Surveyed by the OECD Global Forum in Implementing the Internationally Agreed Tax Standard," April 2, 2009; Geoff Cook, Response to *Financial Times* Comment, mail. jerseyfinance.je; March 5, 2009; William Brittain-Catlin, "How offshore capitalism ate our economies—and itself," *The Guardian*, Feb. 5, 2009.

CHAPTER 10

TRADE AND DEVELOPMENT

Introduction

Given the economic turmoil of the last four years in the developed world, it is ironic, if unsurprising, that the developing world has been urged for several decades to adopt free markets and increased privatization as the keys to catching up with the West. These neoliberal policy prescriptions were applied across the developing world as a one-size-fits-all solution to problems as wide-ranging as poverty, malnutrition, and political conflict. While 8-10% unemployment in the United States has led to trillion-dollar increases in government spending, developing countries with double-digit unemployment were routinely assured that macroeconomic crises could only be dealt with by "tightening their belts." And while the West, having experienced a financial crisis, now called for increased financial regulation, similar calls for more regulation from developing countries were dismissed as misguided.

The contributors to this section take on different aspects of the neoliberal policy mix, raising questions that recur through this entire volume. Where do the limits of the market lie? At what point do we decide that markets cease to serve the citizens for whose well-being economists claim to advocate? And to what extent should communities, via politically representative bodies of all kinds, be able to regulate and control markets?

The first article of the neoliberal faith is the belief that openness to international trade, i.e. economic globalization, is the key to growth and development. Ramaa Vasudevan, in the primer "Comparative Advantage" (Article 10.1), starts off this chapter with a critique of the Ricardian theory of comparative advantage that is central to the neoclassical argument for free trade.

Thomas Palley offers a concise and useful metaphor for the effect of globalization and outsourcing on productive industry in the United States. "The Globalization Clock" (Article 10.2) is a metaphor for the manner in which globalization and outsourcing picks off domestic industries one at a time based on the relative exportability of the manufacturing and skill level of the jobs (inherent vs. transferable comparative advantage). Can you put your job in a box and ship it? This metaphor also illustrates how, at any given period of time, there has not been a majority consensus against outsourcing since the majority of people (consumers) benefit through lower prices from the outsourced industry; only those acutely affected through the loss of their jobs are against it. But as the clock ticks forward, more and more industries at higher and higher levels of skill become outsourced, leading the white-collar professionals to now sound the alarm over globalization. What time is it?

Ellen Frank's article, "Should Developing Countries Embrace Protectionism?" (Article 10.3), points out that contrary to the claims of globalization advocates, and the Theory of Comparative Advantage, the historical record suggests that protectionism may be a better strategy for economic development. In fact, it is hard to provide an example of successful economic growth and development from countries that "got prices right" as opposed to those that "got prices wrong"—but to their trading advantage.

Aaron Luoma and Gretchen Gordon provide us with an interesting case study in development that turns the neo-liberal "Washington Consensus" of development on its head, in "Turning Gas Into Development in Bolivia" (Article 10.4). Evo Morales in Bolivia has nationalized (not privatized) the country's oil and gas industries so as to repatriate the profits (resource rents) from the sale of these natural resources. Alejandro Reuss contributes a vital sidebar to this piece with his primer on "Resources and Rents."

In his seminal piece, "What's Wrong With Neo-Liberalism?" (Article 10.5), Robert Pollin provides a summary of the policies that constitute neoliberalism and describes their destructive impact upon the developing world. He then identifies three fundamental problems with neoliberal policy, which he calls the Marx, Keynes, and Polanyi problems. "On The Jasmine Revolution" by Fadhel Kaboub (Article 10.6) addresses the uprisings across the Middle East beginning in 2011. He explores the "fuel for the fire" in both economic and demographic terms. In the chapter's final article (Article 10.7), Arthur MacEwan takes apart the issue of American foreign aid, addressing its magnitude in total-dollar terms and as a percentage of U.S. GDP. He deflates the common misconception of an American government heaping foreign aid largesse around the globe "like a drunk sailor." MacEwan finds that though we are the largest economy in the world and we contribute the largest total amount of foreign aid by far, we contribute a far smaller percentage of our GDP in aid than most other developed countries around the globe. To add insult to injury, most of this foreign aid is "tied" to the purchase of American goods and thus is as much a subsidy to American business and agriculture as it is a benefit to the aid recipient.

Discussion Questions

1) (Article 10.1) Under what conditions might the mainstream argument about the advantages of specialization based on comparative advantage break down?

2) (Article 10.2) Thomas Palley argues that the relative benefits and costs of globalization are not evenly distributed. Some folks gain from globalization and others lose. What is "Palley's Clock"? Explain in detail the metaphor and mechanism.

3) (Article 10.2) Does Palley's assessment of globalization differ at all from your textbook? What time is it in the United States according to "Palley's Clock"?

4) (Article 10.3) What is the basic argument in favor of free trade? Ellen Frank argues that free trade can prevent poorer countries from developing, rather than helping them do so. (The same argument applies to poorer regions within the

United States.) What is her reasoning? How do you think a pro-free-trade economist would respond?

5) (Article 10.4) What is the development strategy that the Bolivian government is pursuing in its plans for the oil and gas industry? How does this strategy differ from the neoliberal development paths common in poor countries that possess valuable natural resources? Why is "rent" an important issue here?

6) (Article 10.5) According to Robert Pollin, neoliberalism as a policy regime suffers from three primary problems. Explain in your own words the Marx, Keynes, and Polanyi problems.

7) (Article 10.6) "On the Jasmine Revolution" by Fadhel Kaboub explores the forces behind the recent uprisings across the Middle East, particularly Tunisia and Egypt. What are the economic and demographic forces fueling this movement? Do you see any similar forces emerging in the United States?

8) (Article 10.6) Who is Mohamed Bouazizi?

9) (Article 10.7) How "generous" is American foreign aid? How can this type of "tied" aid actually hurt developing countries? What's up with Norway and Sweden when it comes to foreign aid? Why do they do this?

Article 10.1

COMPARATIVE ADVANTAGE

BY RAMAA VASUDEVAN
July/August 2007

> Dear Dr. Dollar:
> *When economists argue that the outsourcing of jobs might be a plus for the U.S. economy, they often mention the idea of comparative advantage. So free trade would allow the United States to specialize in higher-end service-sector businesses, creating higher-paying jobs than the ones that would be outsourced. But is it really true that free trade leads to universal benefits?*
> —David Goodman, Boston, Mass.

You're right: The purveyors of the free trade gospel do invoke the doctrine of comparative advantage to dismiss widespread concerns about the export of jobs. Attributed to 19th-century British political-economist David Ricardo, the doctrine says that a nation always stands to gain if it exports the goods it produces *relatively* more cheaply in exchange for goods that it can get *comparatively* more cheaply from abroad. Free trade would lead to each country specializing in the products it can produce at *relatively* lower costs. Such specialization allows both trading partners to gain from trade, the theory goes, even if in one of the countries production of *both* goods costs more in absolute terms.

For instance, suppose that in the United States the cost to produce one car equals the cost to produce 10 bags of cotton, while in the Philippines the cost to produce one car equals the cost to produce 100 bags of cotton. The Philippines would then have a comparative advantage in the production of cotton, producing one bag at a cost equal to the production cost of 1/100 of a car, versus 1/10 of a car in the United States; likewise, the United States would hold a comparative advantage in the production of cars. Whatever the prices of cars and cotton in the global market, the theory goes, the Philippines would be better off producing only cotton and importing all its cars from the United States, and the United States would be better off producing only cars and importing all of its cotton from the Philippines. If the international terms of trade—the relative price—is one car for 50 bags, then the United States will take in 50 bags of cotton for each car it exports, 40 more than the 10 bags it forgoes by putting its productive resources into making the car rather than growing cotton. The Philippines is also better off: it can import a car in exchange for the export of 50 bags of cotton, whereas it would have had to forgo the production of 100 bags of cotton in order to produce that car domestically. If the price of cars goes up in the global marketplace, the Philippines will lose out in relative terms—but will still be better off than if it tried to produce its own cars.

The real world, unfortunately, does not always conform to the assumptions underlying comparative-advantage theory. One assumption is that trade is balanced. But many countries are running persistent deficits, notably the United States, whose trade deficit is now at nearly 7% of its GDP. A second premise, that there is full employment within the trading nations, is also patently unrealistic. As global trade intensifies, jobs created in the export sector do not necessarily compensate for the jobs lost in the sectors wiped out by foreign competition.

The comparative advantage story faces more direct empirical challenges as well. Nearly 70% of U.S. trade is trade in similar goods, known as *intra-industry trade*: for example, exporting Fords and importing BMWs. And about one third of U.S. trade as of the late 1990s was trade between branches of a single corporation located in different countries (*intra-firm trade*). Comparative advantage cannot explain these patterns.

Comparative advantage is a static concept that identifies immediate gains from trade but is a poor guide to economic development, a process of structural change over time which is by definition dynamic. Thus the comparative advantage tale is particularly pernicious when preached to developing countries, consigning many to "specialize" in agricultural goods or be forced into a race to the bottom where cheap sweatshop labor is their sole source of competitiveness.

The irony, of course, is that none of the rich countries got that way by following the maxim that they now preach. These countries historically relied on tariff walls and other forms of protectionism to build their industrial base. And even now, they continue to protect sectors like agriculture with subsidies. The countries now touted as new models of the benefits of free trade—South Korea and the other "Asian tigers," for instance—actually flouted this economic wisdom, nurturing their technological capabilities in specific manufacturing sectors and taking advantage of their lower wage costs to *gradually* become effective competitors of the United States and Europe in manufacturing.

The fundamental point is this: contrary to the comparative-advantage claim that trade is universally beneficial, nations as a whole do not prosper from free trade. Free trade creates winners and losers, both within and between countries. In today's context it is the global corporate giants that are propelling and profiting from "free trade": not only outsourcing white-collar jobs, but creating global commodity chains linking sweatshop labor in the developing countries of Latin America and Asia (Africa being largely left out of the game aside from the export of natural resources such as oil) with ever-more insecure consumers in the developed world. Promoting "free trade" as a political cause enables this process to continue.

It is a process with real human costs in terms of both wages and work. People in developing countries across the globe continue to face these costs as trade liberalization measures are enforced; and the working class in the United States is also being forced to bear the brunt of the relentless logic of competition. ❑

Sources: Arthur MacEwan, "The Gospel of Free Trade: The New Evangelists," *Dollars & Sense*, July/August 2002; Ha-Joon Chang, *Kicking away the Ladder: The Real History of Fair Trade*, Foreign Policy in Focus, 2003; Anwar Shaikh, "Globalization and the Myths of Free Trade," in *Globalization and the Myths of Free Trade: History, Theory, and Empirical Evidence*, ed. Anwar Shaikh, Routledge 2007.

Article 10.2

THE GLOBALIZATION CLOCK

Why corporations are winning and workers are losing.

BY THOMAS PALLEY
May/June 2006

Political economy has historically been constructed around the divide between capital and labor, with firms and workers at odds over the division of the economic pie. Within this construct, labor is usually represented as a monolithic interest, yet the reality is that labor has always suffered from internal divisions—by race, by occupational status, and along many other fault lines. Neoliberal globalization has in many ways sharpened these divisions, which helps to explain why corporations have been winning and workers losing.

One of these fault lines divides workers from themselves: since workers are also consumers, they face a divide between the desire for higher wages and the desire for lower prices. Historically, this identity split has been exploited to divide union from nonunion workers, with anti-labor advocates accusing union workers of causing higher prices. Today, globalization is amplifying the divide between people's interests as workers and their interests as consumers through its promise of ever-lower prices.

Consider the debate over Wal-Mart's low-road labor policies. While Wal-Mart's low wages and skimpy benefits have recently faced scrutiny, even some liberal commentators argue that Wal-Mart is actually good for low-wage workers because they gain more as consumers from its "low, low prices" than they lose as workers from its low wages. But this static, snapshot analysis fails to capture the full impact of globalization, past and future.

Globalization affects the economy unevenly, hitting some sectors first and others later. The process can be understood in terms of the hands of a clock. At one o'clock is the apparel sector; at two o'clock the textile sector; at three the steel sector; at six the auto sector. Workers in the apparel sector are the first to have their jobs shifted to lower-wage venues; at the same time, though, all other workers get price reductions. Next, the process picks off textile sector workers at two o'clock. Meanwhile, workers from three o'clock onward get price cuts, as do the apparel workers at one o'clock. Each time the hands of the clock move, the workers taking the hit are isolated. In this fashion globalization moves around the clock, with labor perennially divided.

Manufacturing was first to experience this process, but technological innovations associated with the Internet are putting service and knowledge workers in the firing line as well. Online business models are making even retail workers vulnerable—consider Amazon.com, for example, which has opened a customer support center and two technology development centers in India. Public sector wages are also in play, at least indirectly, since falling wages mean falling tax revenues. The problem is that each time the hands on the globalization clock move forward, workers are divided: the majority is made slightly better off while the few are made much worse off.

Globalization also alters the historical divisions within capital, creating a new split between bigger internationalized firms and smaller firms that remain nationally centered. This division has been brought into sharp focus with the debate over the trade deficit and the overvalued dollar. In previous decades, manufacturing as a whole opposed running trade deficits and maintaining an overvalued dollar because of the adverse impact of increased imports. The one major business sector with a different view was retailing, which benefited from cheap imports.

However, the spread of multinational production and outsourcing has divided manufacturing in wealthy countries into two camps. In one camp are larger multinational corporations that have gone global and benefit from cheap imports; in the other are smaller businesses that remain nationally centered in terms of sales, production and input sourcing. Multinational corporations tend to support an overvalued dollar since this makes imports produced in their foreign factories cheaper. Conversely, domestic manufacturers are hurt by an overvalued dollar, which advantages import competition.

This division opens the possibility of a new alliance between labor and those manufacturers and businesses that remain nationally based—potentially a potent one, since there are approximately seven million enterprises with sales of less than $10 million in the United States, versus only 200,000 with sales greater than $10 million. However, such an alliance will always be unstable as the inherent labor-capital conflict over income distribution can always reassert itself. Indeed, this pattern is already evident in the internal politics of the National Association of Manufacturers, whose members have been significantly divided regarding the overvalued dollar. As one way to address this division, the group is promoting a domestic "competitiveness" agenda aimed at weakening regulation, reducing corporate legal liability, and lowering employee benefit costs—an agenda designed to appeal to both camps, but at the expense of workers.

Solidarity has always been key to political and economic advance by working families, and it is key to mastering the politics of globalization. Developing a coherent story about the economics of neoliberal globalization around which working families can coalesce is a key ingredient for solidarity. So too is understanding how globalization divides labor. These narratives and analyses can help counter deep cultural proclivities to individualism, as well as other historic divides such as racism. However, as if this were not difficult enough, globalization creates additional challenges. National political solutions that worked in the past are not adequate to the task of controlling international competition. That means the solidarity bar is further raised, calling for international solidarity that supports new forms of international economic regulation. ❑

Article 10.3

SHOULD DEVELOPING COUNTRIES EMBRACE PROTECTIONISM?

BY ELLEN FRANK
July 2004

> Dear Dr. Dollar:
> *Supposedly, countries should produce what they are best at. If the United States makes computers and China produces rice, then the theory of free trade says China should trade its rice for computers. But if China puts tariffs on U.S.-made computers and builds up its own computer industry, then it will become best at making them and can buy rice from Vietnam. Isn't it advantageous for poor countries to practice protectionism and become industrial powers themselves, rather than simply producing mono-crop commodities? I'm asking because local alternative currencies like Ithaca Hours benefit local businesses, though they restrict consumers to local goods that may be more expensive than goods from further away.*
> —Matt Cary, Hollywood, Fla.

The modern theory of free trade argues that countries are "endowed" with certain quantities of labor, capital, and natural resources. A country with lots of labor but little capital should specialize in the production of labor-intensive goods, like hand-woven rugs, hand-sewn garments, or hand-picked fruit. By ramping up produc-tion of these goods, a developing country can trade on world markets, earning the foreign exchange to purchase capital-intensive products like computers and cars. Free trade thus permits poor countries (or, to be more precise, their most well-off citizens) to *consume* high-tech goods that they lack the ability to *produce* and so obtain higher living standards. "Capital-rich" countries like the United States benefit from relatively cheap fruit and garments, freeing up their workforce to focus on high-tech goods. Free trade, according to this story, is a win-win game for everyone.

The flaw in this tale, which you have hit upon exactly, is that being "capital-rich" or "capital-poor" is not a natural phenomenon like having lots of oil. Capital is created—typically with plenty of government assistance and protection.

Developing countries can create industrial capacity and train their citizens to manufacture high-tech goods. But doing so takes time. Building up the capacity to manufacture computers, for example, at prices that are competitive with firms in developed countries may take several years. To buy this time, a government needs to keep foreign-made computers from flooding its market and undercutting less-established local producers. It also needs to limit inflows of foreign capital. Studies show that when foreign firms set up production facilities in developing countries, they are unlikely to share their latest techniques, so such foreign investment does not typically build local expertise or benefit local entrepreneurs.

The United States and other rich countries employed these protectionist strategies. In the 1800s, American entrepreneurs traveled to England and France to learn the latest manufacturing techniques and freely appropriated designs for cutting-edge industrial equipment. The U.S. government protected its nascent industries with high tariff walls until they could compete with European manufacturers.

After World War II, Japan effectively froze out foreign goods while building up world-class auto, computer, and electronics industries. Korea later followed Japan's strategy; in recent years, so has China. There, "infant industries" are heavily protected by tariffs, quotas, and other trade barriers. Foreign producers are welcome only if they establish high-tech facilities in which Chinese engineers and production workers can garner the most modern skills.

Development economists like Alice Amsden and Dani Rodrik are increasingly reaching the conclusion that carefully designed industrial policies, combined with protections for infant industries, are most effective in promoting internal development in poor countries. "Free-trade" policies, on the other hand, seem to lock poor countries into producing low-tech goods like garments and agricultural commodities, whose prices tend to decline on world markets due to intense competition with other poor countries.

In the contemporary global economy, however, there are three difficulties with implementing a local development strategy. First, some countries have bargained away their right to protect local firms by entering into free-trade agreements. Second, protectionism means that local consumers are denied the benefits of cheap manufactured goods from abroad, at least in the short run.

Finally, in many parts of the world the floodgates of foreign-made goods have already been opened and, with the middle and upper classes enjoying their computers and cell phones, it may be impossible to build the political consensus to close them. This last concern bears on the prospects for local alternative currencies. Since it is impos-sible to "close off" the local economy, the success of local currencies in bolstering hometown businesses depends on the willingness of local residents to deny themselves the benefits of cheaper nonlocal goods. Like national protectionist polices, local currencies restrict consumer choice.

Ultimately, the success or failure of such ventures rests on the degree of public support for local business. With local currencies, participation is voluntary and attitudes toward local producers often favorable. National protectionist polices, however, entail coerced public participation and generally fail when governments are corrupt and unable to command public support. ❏

Article 10.4

TURNING GAS INTO DEVELOPMENT IN BOLIVIA

BY AARON LUOMA AND GRETCHEN GORDON
November/December 2006

On May 1, 2006, banners reading "Nationalized: Property of the Bolivian people" were hung over filling station entrances and strung across the gates of refineries and gas and oil fields across Bolivia. From the San Alberto field in Bolivia's southern state of Tarija, President Evo Morales stood flanked by his ministers and military before a crowd of television cameras. In a carefully orchestrated public relations event, Morales made the surprise announcement that the military was at that moment securing the country's oil and gas fields.

"This is the solution to the social and economic problems of our country," Morales proclaimed. "Once we have recovered these natural resources, this will generate work; it is the end of the looting of our natural resources by multinational oil companies."

By the time Evo Morales won his unprecedented landslide electoral victory in December 2005, nationalization of Bolivia's oil and gas reserves had become a widespread popular demand. In a national referendum in 2004, 94% of Bolivians had voted to recover state ownership of oil and gas. After then-president Carlos Mesa responded to that vote with only moderate legislative proposals, protests and blockades demanding nationalization rocked the country. Morales and his Movement for Socialism (MAS) party originally supported a more limited reform of the energy sector, but as the protests mounted, MAS joined the call for nationalization. When Mesa resigned, triggering early elections, nationalization became the primary electoral issue.

On paper, the Morales government's oil and gas policy falls far short of what is traditionally meant by nationalization: government expropriation of foreign property to gain total control of an industry. Instead, his administration is taking a softer approach, opening negotiations with private investors to recover a measure of control over the industry and increase government revenues from it.

The May 1 announcement drew strong reactions from both ends of the political spectrum. Gabriel Dabdoub, president of the Santa Cruz Chamber of Commerce and Industry, told the Miami Herald, "We're very concerned about the international repercussions. This might isolate Bolivia from the world." Spanish Prime Minister Jose Luis Rodriguez Zapatero expressed his "most profound concern," warning of "consequences for bilateral relations." At the same time, many on the Bolivian left faulted the policy for not going far enough. The Bolivian Center for Information and Documentation criticized the decree for failing to "recover the oil and gas industry that was privatized in the capitalization process."

A Cochabamba cab driver named Enrique summed up the sentiment of the majority of Bolivians in the middle: "This isn't nationalization; if it were, the multinationals wouldn't be here. But if we kick them out, they'll sue us. So we have to negotiate."

Six months on, Bolivia's government has had mixed results in implementing the decree. Slow progress in negotiations to rebuild the state oil and gas company, political scandals, and logistical problems initially gave Bolivian opposition parties ample opportunity to question the government's intentions and competence. But in October the government reached agreement on new contracts with 10 oil and gas companies, including Petrobras, the Brazilian public-private energy company, and Spanish energy giant Repsol, which together control 74% of Bolivia's gas reserves. The step garnered praise from both foreign and domestic business interests. While the government continues difficult negotiations over remaining issues with foreign energy companies, Bolivians wait to see whether Morales' "nationalization through negotiation" strategy will bring about concrete improvements in their standard of living.

How Did Bolivia Get Here?

At more than 13,000 feet above sea level, the legendary colonial city of Potosi rests at the base of Cerro Rico ("Rich Hill"), once so full of silver it virtually bankrolled the Spanish empire for more than 300 years. Though the glory of Potosi faded as the silver market waned, to this day Bolivian children are taught that a bridge of silver stretching from Potosi to Madrid could have been built from Cerro Rico's bounty. For nearly five centuries, Bolivia has seen its abundant natural resources extracted by outsiders, while the people of Bolivia have remained the poorest in South America.

Today, natural gas is Bolivia's new silver. The country boasts 47.8 trillion cubic feet of certified gas reserves; in South America only Venezuela has more. And proven reserves could rise dramatically since only 15% to 40% of the oil- and gas-rich zone has been explored to date. Until a few years ago, many oil developers regarded natural gas as nothing more than a waste product of the oil extraction process. "The notion that gas might be a moneymaker would have struck most oil executives as absurd," writes Paul Roberts in The End of Oil. With oil becoming increasingly scarce, however, natural gas prices have doubled in the last six years. Gas is now seen as the bridge fuel that will help ease global demand for oil and move industry toward cleaner, non-hydrocarbon energy sources. As analysts continue to debate when oil supplies will peak, the "dash for gas" is already in full swing.

With its price rising and vast reserves to tap, natural gas has become the focus of Bolivia's politics. A keen sense of their own history drives Bolivians' demand that their gas not meet the fate of the silver, rubber, and tin before it—that the people benefit in tangible ways from the wealth beneath their feet. A leader of former state oil workers recounts the words of an Aymara woman from La Paz: "I think that if they take it all now, what will be left for my grandchildren?"

"So for this reason I have to defend it," she explains.

Giving Away the Store

On October 17, 2003, under cover of night, then-President Gonzalo Sánchez de Lozada boarded a jet for Miami after Bolivians took to the streets en masse to demand his resignation. The architect of a radical economic reform in the 1990s,

Sánchez de Lozada left behind a devastated economy and a capital in chaos. He also left over 60 people dead and over 400 wounded, casualties of his government's month-long crackdown on mounting protests.

U.S.-educated and known as "El Gringo" for his American accent, Sánchez de Lozada had worked in close collaboration with international lending institutions such as the World Bank and the International Monetary Fund to implement the economic mantra coming out of Washington: a downsized government and unfettered free markets will create a tide that will lift people out of poverty. During his first term in office (1993-1997), Sánchez de Lozada privatized all of Bolivia's most strategic state industries, including telecommunications, electricity, air and rail transportation, and the government's biggest revenue producer, oil and gas.

Sánchez de Lozada claimed his plan, dubbed "capitalization," would ensure that the public would benefit from the privatization of state-owned industries. These would be converted into public-private enterprises, with Bolivians maintaining a 51% interest in the new "capitalized" firms, while foreign investors would receive a 49% share in exchange for putting forth that same value in investment. Bolivia would still have control over the industries but would be able to double their value, spurring job creation and jumpstarting the economy. Almost half a million new jobs would be created in four years, the economy would double in size in ten years, and the dividends from the new capitalized firms would fund an ambitious pension plan for Bolivia's elderly. That was the theory, at least.

Resources and Rents

It may seem contradictory that countries can be "blessed" with valuable natural resources—gold and diamonds, petroleum and natural gas, and so on—and still remain poor. Some economists have argued that natural riches, however, can contribute to stalled economic development.

Industries like mining, oil drilling, and even forestry and fishing are called "extractive" industries. This means they are focused on "extracting" (removing) naturally existing resources. If riches can be easily found, say, by digging a hole in the ground, elites may have little reason to concern themselves with the education or skills of the people as a whole, the improvement of the country's general infrastructure, or other means of general economic development. Instead, they can grow rich and powerful by extracting and selling natural resources—especially if, like gold or oil, these are highly prized and relatively scarce.

The difference between the income that one can get from selling these kinds of goods and what it actually costs to extract them is called a "rent." (Petroleum, for example, may sell for $100 a barrel on the world market. In some parts of the world, however, it can be found relatively easily, and near the surface of the earth, and may cost only $10 a barrel to extract. The rent, then, is $90 per barrel.) In just about every place where there is a concentration of valuable and scarce resources, who will "capture" the rents from the extraction and sale of these resources is a major political issue.

Resource rents may be captured by private individuals or companies, such as those that own oil fields or gold mines. Many a fortune—from Siberia to South Africa to Texas—has come from resource rents. Even when private companies own these resources, workers in the extraction industries may organize to force the companies to "share" some of the rents with them. It may be easier for the owners to pay for labor peace, and keep the wealth flowing out of the ground, than to endure costly work stoppages. For this reason, workers in very lucrative resource-extraction industries have sometimes been comparatively well-paid (for what can be back-breaking and extremely dangerous work).

Thanks to a mix of backroom deals and grievously unrealistic economic predictions, the reality played out quite differently.

What Sánchez de Lozada's administration actually did was to divide up the assets of the state energy company YPFB (Yacimientos Petroliferos Fiscales Bolivianos) to form three public-private consortiums: two exploration and production firms and one transportation firm. Majority control of these firms—complete with over $11 billion in reserves and infrastructure—was given, free of charge, to foreign corporations such as British Petroleum and Enron in exchange for only a promise of future investment. A new oil and gas law, a condition for an IMF loan, transferred an additional $108 billion of reserves to private control and slashed oil and gas royalties on those reserves by almost two thirds, from 50% to 18%. Then, in 1999, Sánchez de Lozada's successor Hugo Banzer sold off Bolivia's refineries, pipelines, and gas storage facilities at bargain prices, completing the dismantling of YPFB.

In the end, capitalization turned out to be even more destructive than a classic privatization in which the state at least receives compensation for its assets. Under capitalization, Bolivia handed over its most strategic industries and resources, as well as, in the case of YPFB, its most profitable industry. The promised 51/49 split of public versus private control ended up the reverse, leaving Bolivians with no decision-making power over the capitalized firms. The foreign companies that took over Bolivia's oil and gas industry never invested in modernizing its domestic

---

Resource rents can also be captured by governments. In many countries, valuable natural resources like petroleum are government-owned. (In fact, more than half of all proven oil reserves worldwide are controlled by state-owned oil companies.) In some places, state oil companies engage in drilling and extraction. In some, private companies (including large multinationals) may extract and sell the oil, but have to pay "royalties" to the government for the privilege. Elsewhere, private companies may own the oilfields, but the government uses taxes to capture oil rents.

Captured resource rents can be used in many different ways. In some cases, ruling elites may use rents to enrich themselves personally or to build up armies or other forces that solidify their political power (but contribute little to overall economic development or to improving living conditions for the majority). Governments that operate in this way are sometimes known as "rentier states." ("Rentier" (pronounced *ron-tee-AY*) is a French word that means the recipient of income from (economic) rent.) Captured rents, however, may also be used to promote broader economic development (e.g., to build infrastructure or import machinery for new industries). They may be used to provide public services like schooling or education. Governments may even just transfer rents, in cash, to a broad swath of society.

Recent controversies about the control of oil and natural gas in South American countries like Venezuela and Bolivia are largely about government attempts to capture a bigger share of these rents and use them, government leaders say, to improve the lives of ordinary people. One former head of an oil-rich state put the logic of rent capture this way: "We're set up ... where it's collectively [that the people] own the resources. So we share in the wealth when the development of these resources occurs." The government was constitutionally required, this official continued, to "maximize benefits for [the people], not an individual company, not some multinational somewhere, but for [the people]." That was not, however, Venezuela's Hugo Chavez or Bolivia's Evo Morales speaking. The oil-rich state? Alaska. The former official? Sarah Palin.

—*Alejandro Reuss*

Sources: National Petroleum Council, Topic Paper #7: Global Access to Oil and Gas, Working Document of the NPC Global Oil & Gas Study, July 18, 2007; Philip Gourevitch "The State of Sarah Palin: The peculiar political landscape of the Vice-Presidential hopeful," The New Yorker, September 22, 2008.

infrastructure or technical capacity, finding it more profitable to export Bolivia's natural gas as a cheap raw material to be processed in Argentina or Brazil. While capitalization brought Bolivia a swath of new foreign investors, the promised trickle-down wealth creation never came. For Bolivians, it was like giving the mechanic the keys to your car, only to see him drive off with it.

Although average annual gas production rose by 65% between the years prior to (1990-1996) and following (1997-2004) capitalization, government gas revenues increased only 10% due to slashed royalty rates (see figure on page 25). Government revenue from oil and gas, which made up between 38% and 60% of state revenues in the years before capitalization, dropped to under 7% in 2002. Bolivia's finite natural resources were being depleted faster, and the country had little to show for it.

Mark Weisbrot, economist and co-director of the Washington-based Center for Economic and Policy Research (CEPR), views the results of the Washington Consensus experiment in Bolivia this way: "They clearly failed by any objective measure—income per person is less than it was 27 years ago." According to a CEPR report, Bolivia's per capita income has grown by less than 2% in total over the past 25 years, compared to 60% between 1960 and 1980. "In the short run it's the loss of revenue," explains Weisbrot. "Over the longer run it's the loss of control over the resources themselves, which is what you need... as a source of financing for development and as part of a development strategy."

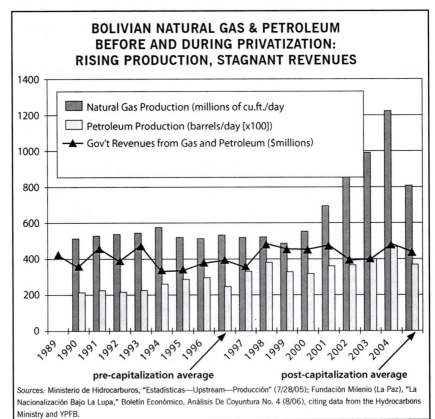

BOLIVIAN NATURAL GAS & PETROLEUM BEFORE AND DURING PRIVATIZATION: RISING PRODUCTION, STAGNANT REVENUES

Natural Gas Production (millions of cu.ft./day
Petroleum Production (barrels/day [x100])
Gov't Revenues from Gas and Petroleum ($millions)

pre-capitalization average   post-capitalization average

Sources: Ministerio de Hidrocarburos, "Estadísticas—Upstream—Producción" (7/28/05); Fundación Milenio (La Paz), "La Nacionalización Bajo La Lupa," Boletín Económico, Análisis De Coyuntura No. 4 (8/06), citing data from the Hydrocarbons Ministry and YPFB.

"The majority of government revenues in Bolivia now come from donations and loans," explains Roberto Fernandez, a professor of economics and history at San Simon University in Cochabamba. "We borrow money to pay salaries. What kind of government is this that doesn't even have the autonomy to say, 'I'm going to build a little school'? It has to look for who internationally can give us a loan."

Prohibited by law from running for a second consecutive term in 1997, Sánchez de Lozada regained the presidency in 2002. In October 2003, Bolivians' growing frustration and anger over the dismal state of the economy exploded on the streets, in what later became known as the Gas War. Thousands of primarily indigenous residents of El Alto, the sprawling municipality that surrounds the capital city of La Paz, came out to protest Sánchez de Lozada's plan to export cheap gas to the United States through Bolivia's historic rival, Chile. The protesters erected blockades, strangling La Paz. Sánchez de Lozada declared a national emergency and called out the military.

As a convoy of soldiers carrying cisterns of gas toward La Paz pushed through makeshift blockades of rocks and tires in the streets of El Alto, the city's overcrowded neighborhoods became a battlefield.

"They began to shoot at houses," remembers Nestor Salinas, a resident of El Alto, "shooting at any human being who put themselves in front of the convoy."

"Imagine children just five years old, eight-year-old girls, pregnant women, men, brothers, fathers, teenagers," he continues. "They died to defend our oil and gas."

Within days, Sánchez de Lozada fled Bolivia. As he was landing in Miami, Nestor's 29-year-old brother, David, died from a bullet wound, joining the 59 other civilians killed by government troops.

Morales' Hybrid Energy Policy

Most Bolivians viewed Evo Morales's electoral win last year as a victory for the movement to take back control of the country's natural resources and use them to tackle Bolivia's entrenched poverty. Not an outright nationalization, Morales's oil and gas decree this May set forth a complex series of steps aimed at boosting revenues from gas and regaining some control over the industry. The decree seeks to resurrect the state oil and gas company, YPFB, to assume regulatory functions, direct oil and gas development, and participate in the entire chain of production, from exploration to commercialization.

The decree requires the three public-private energy firms created by Sánchez de Lozada in the mid-1990s, along with the two private firms that bought YPFB's refineries and pipelines at the time, to sell back to the government enough shares (at market prices) to give YPFB majority ownership. To put this in context, these firms hold only 10% of Bolivia's oil and gas reserves. The rest are held exclusively by several foreign companies, including Petrobras and Repsol.

The decree placed a temporary additional tax of 32% on production in the country's two most productive fields, bringing in $32 million a month in new revenues devoted exclusively to rebuilding YPFB. It gave oil and gas companies operating in Bolivia six months to sign new exploration and development contracts.

The decree also reasserted the government's right to establish domestic and export prices. In addition to hiking tax and royalty rates, the Morales administration aims to raise the base prices on which taxes and royalties are calculated. It is currently locked in intense negotiations with Petrobras, arguing that export prices under its existing contracts are far below current market prices. In June, the administration negotiated a 48% increase in the gas price with Argentina, bringing in an additional $110 million a year in revenues—a key achievement of the May 1 decree.

Ultimately, Morales aims to transform Bolivia from an exporter of raw materials into an industrial producer of value-added goods such as electricity, synthetic diesel, fertilizers, and plastics. "The vision is that by 2010 we could see Bolivia as a main exporter of value-added products covering the entire South American market," explains Saul Escalera, a YPFB official. While some critics assert that small countries like Bolivia lack the capital and technology necessary for industrialization, Escalera disagrees. He notes that YPFB has already "received 20 project proposals with a total value of $12 billion from foreign firms that want to invest in Bolivia."

Many of those firms are not the predictable Western players. Gazprom, the Russian state energy giant with more than 25% of the world's gas reserves, has expressed interest in investing more than $2 billion in Bolivia, while inquires have also come from several Asian countries. In May, Venezuela's state oil company, PDVSA, inked a deal to build a gas separation plant to produce fertilizer both for Bolivia's domestic use and for export to Brazil. And an Indian firm, Jindal Steel, has a deal in the works to build a plant that will power the industrialization of Mutún, site of one of the largest iron ore deposits in the world. The $2.3 billion project is projected to generate more than 10,000 new jobs and $200 million a year in government revenue.

According to Hydrocarbons Minister Carlos Villegas, $2 billion of foreign investment has already been committed to expand gas production and export capacity, particularly to Argentina and Brazil. At an International Development Bank conference in Washington, D.C., this July, Villegas declared: "Bolivia has completed its cycle as an exporter of raw materials. The resources are there, but we will give them a new path."

Bolivia's Bumpy Road

The efforts of YPFB to exert control over the oil and gas industry have had mixed results. Shortly after Morales' May 1 announcement, YPFB was involved in a growing corruption scandal and admitted its inability to take over fuel distribution duties as mandated by the nationalization decree. A few weeks later the government declared the nationalization process temporarily suspended due to "a lack of economic resources," creating further unease and confirming critics' concerns that YPFB lacked the capacity, competence, and cash to carry out its new role. In late August the debacle culminated with the resignation of YPFB's president, Jorge Alvarado, who had been accused of signing a diesel contract that violated the decree. It was a major setback for a president who had asserted that YPFB would be "transparent, efficient, and socially controlled."

In August, police and prosecutors searched Repsol's Bolivia offices for the second time in six months in separate smuggling and malfeasance investigations. Repsol expressed outrage, warning that these investigations were jeopardizing the company's continued investment in Bolivia. In this case as in others, the government is pursuing a problematic strategy with foreign energy companies: wielding a strong hand to expose malfeasance and discredit them while simultaneously negotiating for their continued investment in the country.

Despite these obstacles, in late August the government became more assertive in implementing the May decree. After a four-month delay, government threats of expulsion secured the additional $32 million in monthly payments to YPFB due from Repsol, Petrobras, and France's Total, providing the state company with a critical infusion of cash.

In September political problems again flared. A resolution issued by then-hydrocarbons minister Andres Soliz Rada ordered Petrobras to hand over control of exports and domestic sales of gasoline and diesel in its two Bolivian refineries in compliance with the decree. This move backfired, however, after the Brazilian foreign minister said the measure could cause Petrobras to pull out of Bolivia, which led Vice President Garcia Linera to suspend Rada's resolution. Rada responded by tendering his resignation, another setback for the administration. Linera, feeling the political weight of the moment, was resolute in declaring that the nationalization process was "irrevocable" and that the government, while maintaining a posture of "negotiation and tolerance," would be "intransigent" in obligating companies to comply with the decree.

In October, however, the government reached agreement on new exploration and development contracts with 10 major companies operating in Bolivia—a major milestone. Under the new contracts, the foreign companies are to extract Bolivia's oil and gas and hand them over to YPFB, which compensates the companies for production costs, investment, and profit. The tax and royalty rates in the new contracts are variable depending on a company's level of production and whether or not they have recovered past investments. The government claims its take will range between 50% and 80%, although questions remain about how it will be calculated. YPFB president Juan Carlos Ortiz estimates that the new contracts will put annual revenue for 2006 at $1.3 billion; President Morales assured the public that with the increase in exports to Argentina and the new tax rates, annual oil and gas revenue will rise to $4 billion within the next four years.

"Mission accomplished," declared Morales in a press statement at the contract signing. "We are exercising as Bolivians our property rights over natural resources, without expelling anyone and without confiscating. With this measure, within 10 to 15 years, Bolivia will no longer be this little poor country, this beggar country, this country that is always looking to international assistance."

Critics, however, question whether the government got a good deal for the country, pointing out that the contracts don't commit foreign investors to substantial future investments or provide YPFB with the physical resources to participate in all phases of the industry. And tense negotiations continue over control of the five companies which used to make up the state company, prior to capitalization. Petrobras, which owns the two formerly YPFB refineries, has shown reluctance to give up any operational control of these facilities. Considering that Bolivia supplies 50% of Brazil's gas needs and that Petrobras' transactions account for 18% of Bolivia's gross domestic product, both countries have much to lose should a deal not be reached.

Opportunities and Obligations

As Bolivia struggles to work through the pitfalls of implementing Morales' decree, a clear end goal is to achieve a larger shift in power dynamics. Rather than receiving policy prescriptions from Washington or from international institutions and foreign investors, Bolivia aims to draft its own blueprint, joining a growing political shift in the region away from free-market ideology.

YPFB's Escalera describes the difference the nationalization decree has made for the state energy company. "Before, we had big plans—jobs industrialization, value added products—but didn't have the [gas]," he explains. "It was like knocking on the multinationals' door, 'Could you give me a little sugar for my tea?' If they don't want to do it, the deal is off."

"Even if they were willing to give it to me, I'd then have to go talk to Transredes [the public-private pipeline company created under capitalization] to beg for transportation," he explains, "and they would say 'forget it.'"

"Since the May 1st decree," he continues, "everything has changed. We can guarantee everything the investor wants—transportation, volume, price—now it's in my hands."

Many Bolivians hope the government's new resources and new authority will translate into concrete improvements in quality of life for the country's nine million people, including new jobs and increased state resources for education, health care, and infrastructure. But the challenges Bolivia faces in transforming its oil and gas policy cannot be overstated. Whether the nationalization decree can be fully implemented, let alone generate concrete benefits for ordinary Bolivians, depends on multiple factors: not only getting all of the pieces in place to ensure that the anticipated surge in oil and gas revenues actually materializes, but also creating strong and effective governmental and social institutions, mitigating the social and environmental impacts of energy development, and using the new revenues effectively for national development projects.

For Nestor Salinas, a member of the Association of Family Members of those Fallen in Defense of Gas, which is pushing for Sánchez de Lozada to return to Bolivia to stand trial for the killings during the Gas War, the Morales government also carries a moral debt.

"Our name says it clearly: 'Fallen in defense of gas,'" he explains. "This is the importance the country has to place on this issue. The families that lost [loved ones] didn't lose them for nothing, their loss made possible the social, economic, and political change that Bolivia is now living. The government now owes these families justice." ❑

Article 10.5

WHAT'S WRONG WITH NEOLIBERALISM?
The Marx, Keynes, and Polanyi Problems

BY ROBERT POLLIN
May/June 2004

During the years of the Clinton administration, the term "Washington Consensus" began circulating to designate the common policy positions of the U.S. administration along with the International Monetary Fund (IMF) and World Bank. These positions, implemented in the United States and abroad, included free trade, a smaller government share of the economy, and the deregulation of financial markets. This policy approach has also become widely known as *neoliberalism*, a term which draws upon the classical meaning of the word *liberalism*.

Classical liberalism is the political philosophy that embraces the virtues of free-market capitalism and the corresponding minimal role for government interventions, especially as regards measures to promote economic equality within capitalist societies. Thus, a classical liberal would favor minimal levels of government spending and taxation, and minimal levels of government regulation over the economy, including financial and labor markets. According to the classical liberal view, businesses should be free to operate as they wish, and to succeed or fail as such in a competitive marketplace. Meanwhile, consumers rather than government should be responsible for deciding which businesses produce goods and services that are of sufficient quality as well as reasonably priced. Businesses that provide overexpensive or low-quality products will then be out-competed in the marketplace regardless of the regulatory standards established by governments. Similarly, if businesses offer workers a wage below what the worker is worth, then a competitor firm will offer this worker a higher wage. The firm unwilling to offer fair wages would not survive over time in the competitive marketplace.

This same reasoning also carries over to the international level. Classical liberals favor free trade between countries rather than countries operating with tariffs or other barriers to the free flow of goods and services between countries. They argue that restrictions on the free movement of products and money between countries only protects uncompetitive firms from market competition, and thus holds back the economic development of countries that choose to erect such barriers.

Neoliberalism and the Washington Consensus are contemporary variants of this longstanding political and economic philosophy. The major difference between classical liberalism as a philosophy and contemporary neoliberalism as a set of policy measures is with implementation. Washington Consensus policy makers are committed to free-market policies when they support the interests of big business, as, for example, with lowering regulations at the workplace. But these same policy makers become far less insistent on free-market principles when invoking such principles might damage big business interests. Federal Reserve and IMF interventions to bail out wealthy asset holders during the frequent global financial crises in the 1990s are obvious violations of free-market precepts.

Broadly speaking, the effects of neoliberalism in the less developed countries over the 1990s reflected the experience of the Clinton years in the United States. A high proportion of less developed countries were successful, just in the manner of the United States under Clinton, in reducing inflation and government budget deficits, and creating a more welcoming climate for foreign trade, multinational corporations, and financial market investors. At the same time, most of Latin America, Africa, and Asia—with China being the one major exception—experienced deepening problems of poverty and inequality in the 1990s, along with slower growth and frequent financial market crises, which in turn produced still more poverty and inequality.

If free-market capitalism is a powerful mechanism for creating wealth, why does a neoliberal policy approach, whether pursued by Clinton, Bush, or the IMF, produce severe difficulties in terms of inequality and financial instability, which in turn diminish the market mechanism's ability to even promote economic growth? It will be helpful to consider this in terms of three fundamental problems that result from a free-market system, which I term "the Marx Problem," "the Keynes problem," and "the Polanyi problem." Let us take these up in turn.

The Marx Problem

Does someone in your family have a job and, if so, how much does it pay? For the majority of the world's population, how one answers these two questions determines, more than anything else, what one's standard of living will be. But how is it decided whether a person has a job and what their pay will be? Getting down to the most immediate level of decision-making, this occurs through various types of bargaining in labor markets between workers and employers. Karl Marx argued that, in a free-market economy generally, workers have less power than employers in this bargaining process because workers cannot fall back on other means of staying alive if they fail to get hired into a job. Capitalists gain higher profits through having this relatively stronger bargaining position. But Marx also stressed that workers' bargaining power diminishes further when unemployment and underemployment are high, since that means that employed workers can be more readily replaced by what Marx called "the reserve army" of the unemployed outside the office, mine, or factory gates.

Neoliberalism has brought increasing integration of the world's labor markets through reducing barriers to international trade and investment by multinationals. For workers in high-wage countries such as the United States, this effectively means that the reserve army of workers willing to accept jobs at lower pay than U.S. workers expands to include workers in less developed countries. It isn't the case that businesses will always move to less developed countries or that domestically produced goods will necessarily be supplanted by imports from low-wage countries. The point is that U.S. workers face an increased *credible* threat that they can be supplanted. If everything else were to remain the same in the U.S. labor market, this would then mean that global integration would erode the bargaining power of U.S. workers and thus tend to bring lower wages.

But even if this is true for workers in the United States and other rich countries, shouldn't it also mean that workers in poor countries have greater job opportunities and better bargaining positions? In fact, there are areas where workers in poor countries are gaining enhanced job opportunities through international trade and multinational investments. But these gains are generally quite limited. This is because a long-term transition out of agriculture in poor countries continues to expand the reserve army of unemployed and underemployed workers in these countries as well. Moreover, when neoliberal governments in poor countries reduce their support for agriculture—through cuts in both tariffs on imported food products and subsidies for domestic farmers—this makes it more difficult for poor farmers to compete with multinational agribusiness firms. This is especially so when the rich countries maintain or increase their own agricultural supports, as has been done in the United States under Bush. In addition, much of the growth in the recently developed export-oriented manufacturing sectors of poor countries has failed to significantly increase jobs even in this sector. This is because the new export-oriented production sites frequently do not represent net additions to the country's total supply of manufacturing firms. They rather replace older firms that were focused on supplying goods to domestic markets. The net result is that the number of people looking for jobs in the developing countries grows faster than the employers seeking new workers. Here again, workers' bargaining power diminishes.

This does not mean that global integration of labor markets must necessarily bring weakened bargaining power and lower wages for workers. But it does mean that unless some non-market forces in the economy, such as government regulations or effective labor unions, are able to counteract these market processes, workers will indeed continue to experience weakened bargaining strength and eroding living standards.

The Keynes Problem

In a free-market economy, investment spending by businesses is the main driving force that produces economic growth, innovation, and jobs. But as John Maynard Keynes stressed, private investment decisions are also unavoidably risky ventures. Businesses have to put up money without knowing whether they will produce any profits in the future. As such, investment spending by business is likely to fluctuate far more than, say, decisions by households as to how much they will spend per week on groceries.

But investment fluctuations will also affect overall spending in the economy, including that of households. When investment spending declines, this means that businesses will hire fewer workers. Unemployment rises as a result, and this in turn will lead to cuts in household spending. Declines in business investment spending can therefore set off a vicious cycle: the investment decline leads to employment declines, then to cuts in household spending and corresponding increases in household financial problems, which then brings still more cuts in business investment and financial difficulties for the business sector. This is how capitalist economies produce mass unemployment, financial crises, and recessions.

Keynes also described a second major source of instability associated with private investment activity. Precisely because private investments are highly risky propositions, financial markets have evolved to make this risk more manageable for any given investor. Through financial markets, investors can sell off their investments if they need or want to, converting their office buildings, factories, and stock of machinery into cash much more readily than they could if they always had to find buyers on their own. But Keynes warned that when financial markets convert long-term assets into short-term commitments for investors, this also fosters a speculative mentality in the markets. What becomes central for investors is not whether a company's products will produce profits over a long term, but rather whether the short-term financial market investors *think* a company's fortunes will be strong enough in the present and immediate future to drive the stock price up. Or, to be more precise, what really matters for a speculative investor is not what they think about a given company's prospects per se, but rather what they think *other investors are thinking*, since that will be what determines where the stock price goes in the short term.

Because of this, the financial markets are highly susceptible to rumors, fads, and all sorts of deceptive accounting practices, since all of these can help drive the stock price up in the present, regardless of what they accomplish in the longer term. Thus, if U.S. stock traders are convinced that Alan Greenspan is a *maestro*, and if there is news that he is about to intervene with some kind of policy shift, then the rumor of Greenspan's policy shift can itself drive prices up, as the more nimble speculators try to keep one step ahead of the herd of Greenspan-philes.

Still, as with the Marx problem, it does not follow that the inherent instability of private investment and speculation in financial markets are uncontrollable, leading inevitably to persistent problems of mass unemployment and recession. But these social pathologies will become increasingly common through a neoliberal policy approach committed to minimizing government interventions to stabilize investment.

The Polanyi Problem

Karl Polanyi wrote his classic book *The Great Transformation* in the context of the 1930s depression, World War II, and the developing worldwide competition with Communist governments. He was also reflecting on the 1920s, dominated, as with our current epoch, by a free-market ethos. Polanyi wrote of the 1920s that "economic liberalism made a supreme bid to restore the self-regulation of the system by eliminating all interventionist policies which interfered with the freedom of markets."

Considering all of these experiences, Polanyi argued that for market economies to function with some modicum of fairness, they must be embedded in social norms and institutions that effectively promote broadly accepted notions of the common good. Otherwise, acquisitiveness and competition—the two driving forces of market economies—achieve overwhelming dominance as cultural forces, rendering life under capitalism a Hobbesian "war of all against all." This same idea is also central for Adam Smith. Smith showed how the invisible hand of self-interest and competition will yield higher levels of individual effort that increases the wealth of nations, but that it will also produce the corruption of our moral sentiments unless the market is itself governed at a fundamental level by norms of solidarity.

In the post-World War II period, various social democratic movements within the advanced capitalist economies adapted the Polanyi perspective. They argued in favor of government interventions to achieve three basic ends: stabilizing overall demand in the economy at a level that will provide for full employment; creating a financial market environment that is stable and conducive to the effective allocation of investment funds; and distributing equitably the rewards from high employment and a stable investment process. There were two basic means of achieving equitable distribution: relatively rapid wage growth, promoted by labor laws that were supportive of unions, minimum wage standards, and similar interventions in labor markets; and welfare state policies, including progressive taxation and redistributive programs such as Social Security. The political ascendancy of these ideas was the basis for a dramatic increase in the role of government in the post-World War II capitalist economies. As one indicator of this, total government expenditures in the United States rose from 8% of GDP in 1913, to 21% in 1950, then to 38% by 1992. The International Monetary Fund and World Bank were also formed in the mid-1940s to advance such policy ideas throughout the world—that is, to implement policies virtually the opposite of those they presently favor. John Maynard Keynes himself was a leading intellectual force contributing to the initial design of the International Monetary Fund and World Bank.

From Social Democracy to Neoliberalism

But the implementation of a social democratic capitalism, guided by a commitment to full employment and the welfare state, did also face serious and persistent difficulties, and we need to recognize them as part of a consideration of the Marx, Keynes, and Polanyi problems. In particular, many sectors of business opposed efforts to sustain full employment because, following the logic of the Marx problem, full employment provides greater bargaining power for workers in labor markets, even if it also increases the economy's total production of goods and services. Greater worker bargaining power can also create inflationary pressures because businesses will try to absorb their higher wage costs by raising prices. In addition, market-inhibiting financial regulations limit the capacity of financial market players to diversify their risk and speculate.

Corporations in the United States and Western Europe were experiencing some combination of these problems associated with social democratic capitalism. In particular, they were faced with rising labor costs associated with low unemployment rates, which then led to either inflation, when corporations had the ability to pass on their higher labor costs to consumers, or to a squeeze on profits, when competitive pressures prevented corporations from raising their prices in response to the rising labor costs. These pressures were compounded by the two oil price "shocks" initiated by the Oil Producing Exporting Countries (OPEC)—an initial fourfold increase in the world price of oil in 1973, then a second four-fold price spike in 1979.

These were the conditions that by the end of the 1970s led to the decline of social democratic approaches to policymaking and the ascendancy of neoliberalism. The two leading signposts of this historic transition were the election in 1979 of Margaret Thatcher as Prime Minister of the United Kingdom and in 1980 of Ronald Reagan as the President of the United States. Indeed, it was at this point that Mrs. Thatcher made her famous pronouncement that "there is no alternative" to neoliberalism.

This brings us to the contemporary era of smaller government, fiscal stringency and deregulation, i.e., to neoliberalism under Clinton, Bush, and throughout the less-developed world. The issue is not a simple juxtaposition between either regulating or deregulating markets. Rather it is that markets have become deregulated to support the interests of business and financial markets, even as these same groups still benefit greatly from many forms of government support, including investment subsidies, tax concessions, and rescue operations when financial crises get out of hand. At the same time, the deregulation of markets that favors business and finance is correspondingly the most powerful regulatory mechanism limiting the demands of workers, in that deregulation has been congruent with the worldwide expansion of the reserve army of labor and the declining capacity of national governments to implement full-employment and macroeconomic policies. In other words, deregulation has exacerbated both the Marx and Keynes problems.

Given the ways in which neoliberalism worsens the Marx, Keynes, and Polanyi problems, we should not be surprised by the wreckage that it has wrought since the late 1970s, when it became the ascendant policy model. Over the past generation, with neoliberals in the saddle almost everywhere in the world, the results have been straightforward: worsening inequality and poverty, along with slower economic growth and far more unstable financial markets. While Margaret Thatcher famously declared that "there is no alternative" to neoliberalism, there are in fact alternatives. The experience over the past generation demonstrates how important it is to develop them in the most workable and coherent ways possible. ❑

Article 10.6

ON THE JASMINE REVOLUTION
Tunisia's political economy exemplifies a region in transition.

BY FADHEL KABOUB
March/April 2011

The success of the revolutions in Tunisia and Egypt, which put an end to two of the most oppressive police states in the Middle East, continues to spark similar popular uprisings across the region. Despite the different institutional structures, geopolitical roles, and military capabilities across the region, the experience in Tunisia, whose uprising sparked the rest, exemplifies what most countries in the region have experienced since their independence from European colonialism, and can shed some light onto their likely post-revolution paths.

In January 2011, Tunisia succeeded in toppling the 23-year Ben Ali regime via a popular grassroots revolt against injustice, corruption, and oppression. The protesters' demands in what has been dubbed the "Jasmine Revolution" were very straightforward: jobs, freedom, and dignity. Like all revolutions, the Tunisian revolution was not an overnight event but rather a long process that can be dissected into four distinct phases with important economic consequences: the neoliberal phase that started in the 1980s with the introduction of World Bank-sponsored economic policies; the plutocracy phase which began in the early 2000s with the rise of the Trabelsi-Ben Ali business empire; the uprising phase which began after the self-immolation of Mohammed Bouazizi on December 17, 2010; and finally the ongoing reconstruction phase which began after the departure of Zine El Abidine Ben Ali on January 14, 2011.

The 1980s neoliberal phase began as Tunisia's external debt soared. Its economy faced high unemployment, low currency reserves, bad harvests, decline in oil revenues, and closure of European labor market outlets for Tunisian immigrants. Like many developing countries, Tunisia was subjected to the World Bank and IMF structural adjustment program: in 1985, aggressive austerity measures led to food riots killing at least 100 people. As the crisis intensified, Ben Ali was appointed interior minister in 1986 and later prime minister in 1987. He then took over as president in a bloodless coup d'état on November 7, 1987. His immediate agenda was two-fold: crush the opposition and forge ahead with structural adjustment policies. Opposition party leaders were arrested, tortured, jailed, killed, or exiled. On the economic front, the government began privatizing state-owned enterprises, promoting free-trade zones, supporting export-oriented industries, and capitalizing on the growth of the tourism industry. Despite robust economic growth rates in the 1990s, unemployment remained stubbornly high, and socioeconomic indicators began to show signs of rising income inequality and deterioration of the economic status of the middle class.

The plutocracy phase began in the early 2000s. While the Trabelsi-Ben Ali clan was amassing billions of dollars in business deals, corruption ravaged the economy, and the Tunisian middle class slid further down the income ladder. Highly educated youth were facing humiliating life conditions and long-term unemployment with little to no hope for a better future. After more than a decade of clearing all opposition forces from the political arena and affirming Ben Ali's grip on the political and security apparatus, Leila Trabelsi, Ben Ali's second wife, expanded her First Lady duties to include securing business deals for her family. The Trabelsi-Ben Ali clan built a gigantic business empire in less than a decade. They secured quasi-monopoly deals in industries such as banking, telecommunications, media, real estate, and retail. Their aggressive and violent approach alienated even the traditional business class, which was forced to sell to or work for the Trabelsi-Ben Ali clan or face serious consequences. Banks were coerced into extending more than $1.7 billion in credit to the Trabelsi-Ben Ali clan without any repayment guarantees.

The uprising phase that followed was intense, well focused, and effective, taking only 23 days to put an end to 23 years of Ben Ali's rule. The leaderless youth movement was spontaneous, secular, fearless, and determined to put an end to an era of repression, theft, and humiliation. In a day-long general strike on January 14, the Tunisian economy was brought to a complete standstill, and men and women from all walks of life joined the protesters to unseat Ben Ali.

The reconstruction phase began as soon as Ben Ali fled the country. It is the most labor-intensive phase and it requires active participation from all facets of Tunisian society. Tunisians have faced the challenge of institutionalizing democracy head-on with popular demands to dissolve Ben Ali's RCD ruling party, free all political prisoners, rewrite the constitution, seize all the Trabelsi-Ben Ali assets, and most importantly, cleanse all socio-economic and government institutions of corrupt RCD loyalists.

While Tunisians are forging ahead with radical constitutional, judicial, and democratic reforms, they will still face a major economic challenge: unemployment among the highly educated youth. The Jasmine Revolution's achievements thus far are commendable, but the revolution will be incomplete without full employment as a means of achieving true social justice.

The challenges after Egypt's revolution are more serious than Tunisia's. The Egyptian military is very large and owns much of the country's industrial and business infrastructure; it also plays a significant role in protecting the American and Israeli interests in the region. A truly democratic civilian government in Egypt will very likely want a military that is more disengaged from the political and economic arena. Egypt is also facing a more serious economic challenge, with mass unemployment and poverty in a population that is eight times larger than that of Tunisia.

While watching events unfold in Libya, Yemen, Bahrain, and beyond, one cannot help but wonder about the extent to which a revolutionary domino effect is likely to sweep the entire region, and its significance for the political economy of the Middle East and its relationship with the United States and Europe. It is clear that there is a critical mass of empowered and fearless youth whose movements are supported by labor advocates, human rights activists, and democratic voices. The challenge, however, is to create lasting radical economic and political changes that will ensure a successful post-revolution reconstruction phase.

Western powers must also recognize that a double-standard policy cannot be an effective way of promoting peace and security in the region. The threat of an

Iranian-like anti-Western Islamic revolution is simply not plausible today, so one cannot use the anti-terrorism Bush-Cheney rhetoric to justify Western support for oppressive regimes. It is the actions taken by post-revolution movements in conjunction with the reaction of the West to these events that will determine whether the Jasmine Revolution was a turning point in world history or just a footnote in the history of the region. ❑

Article 10.7

"TIED" FOREIGN AID

BY ARTHUR MacEWAN
January/February 2012

> Dear Dr. Dollar:
> *People complaining about the ungrateful world often talk about the "huge" U.S. foreign aid budget. In fact, isn't U.S. foreign aid relatively small compared to other countries? What's worse, I understand that a lot of economic aid comes with strings attached, requiring that goods and services purchased with the aid be purchased from firms in the aid-giving country. This channels much of the money back out of the recipient country. That sounds nuts! What's going on?*
>
> —Katharine Rylaarsdam, Baltimore, MD

The U.S. government does provide a "huge" amount of development aid, far more than any of the other rich countries. In 2009, the United States provided $29.6 billion, in development aid—Japan was number two, at $16.4 billion.

But wait a minute. What appears huge may not be so huge. The graph below shows the amount of foreign development aid provided by ten high-income countries and that amount as a share of the countries' gross domestic products (GDP). Yes, the graph shows that the United States gives far more than any of these other countries. But the graph also shows the United States gives a small amount relative to its GDP. In 2009, U.S. foreign development aid was two-tenths of one percent of the country's GDP. Only Italy gave a lesser amount relative to its GDP.

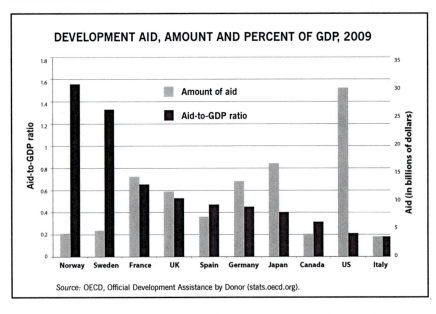

DEVELOPMENT AID, AMOUNT AND PERCENT OF GDP, 2009

Source: OECD, Official Development Assistance by Donor (stats.oecd.org).

The world's rich countries have long committed to providing 0.7% of GDP to foreign development aid. In 2009, only Norway and Sweden met this goal. The U.S. government did not come close.

Moreover, a large share of U.S. foreign aid is "tied aid"; governments that receive the aid must spend the funds by buying goods and services from U.S. firms. Generally the recipient countries could get more goods and services if they could spend the money without this restriction. So the economic development impact of the aid is less than it appears. Also, whatever the "foreign aid" does for the recipient country, it is a way of channeling money to U.S. firms.

Not only must the recipient country pay more for the goods and services, but the "multiplier impact" is much less. That is, since the money goes to U.S. companies rather than local suppliers, fewer local jobs and salary payments are created; so less is re-spent in the local economy. A 2009 report on aid to Afghanistan by the Peace Dividend Trust notes: "By using Afghan goods and services to carry out development projects in Afghanistan, the international community has the opportunity to spend a development dollar twice. How? Local procurement creates jobs, increases incomes, generates revenue and develops the Afghan marketplace —all of which support economic recovery and stability." Yet most of the aid "for Afghanistan" went to foreign "experts," foreign construction firms, and foreign suppliers of goods.

The U.S. government ties much more of its aid than do most other donor countries. A report by the Organization for Economic Cooperation and Development (OECD) estimated that in the mid-2000s, 54.5% of U.S. aid was tied. Of the 22 donor countries listed in the report (including the United States), the average share of tied aid was only 28.4%. The report notes a "widespread movement to untying [aid], with the exception of the United States."

It is important to recognize that U.S. foreign aid is an instrument of U.S. foreign policy, and is thus highly concentrated in countries where the U.S. government has what it views as "strategic interests." For example, in 2008 almost 16% of U.S. development assistance went to Afghanistan and Iraq, while the top 20 recipient countries received over 50%.

So, yes, the U.S. government provides a "huge" amount of foreign development aid—or not so much. It depends on how you look at things. ❑

Chapter 11

POLICY SPOTLIGHT: LABOR MOVEMENTS AND UNIONS

Introduction

The policy spotlight for this 19th edition of *Real World Micro* is on labor move-ments and unions, a topic routinely neglected by mainstream economics text-books. Neoclassical economics treats labor the same as any other "factor input" uti-lized in the production process. Individuals offer (supply) their labor power to the market at a market-determined wage. It is assumed that the wage recouped by the worker is equal to that worker's marginal product. Thus, we are assured a recipro-cal and mutually beneficial relationship between equal parties, the buyers and sell-ers of labor, in the sphere of production. There is no exploitation of one party by the other. "Power" disappears from the capital/labor relationship, leading to the heartwarming abstraction of mutual utility maximization by all rational economic actors involved.

This abstraction by neoclassical economics of labor and the actual process of capitalist production removes from discussion the issues of power and exploitation. In this chapter, we reintroduce these subjects with great enthusiasm. How does labor collectively respond to these issues? How does labor respond to increasing attacks on its ability to organize and collectively bargain? Are rights at work, to organize and democratically control the production process, in fact civil rights? We provide eleven articles to further the discussion.

The chapter begins with a primer, "What is Labor?" by Alejandro Reuss (Article 11.1), who explains what unions actually are, as well as the historical evolution of unions in the United States. In the next article (11.2), Reuss provides us with an analysis of the decline of unions in the United States. Then, Arthur MacEwan addresses whether unions are good or bad for the economy (Article 11.3). MacEwan provides a graph to show that as unions have declined in the United States, income inequality has skyrocketed.

In a poignant article addressing the disparate power relations between labor and capital, Josh Eidelson provides us with "Conflicting Dreams" (Article 11.4). Boeing retaliated against its union, the International Association of Machinists, in the most recent episode of a decades-long labor struggle. Punishing its Puget Sound, Washington, workers for successfully striking, the company moved assembly work to a "right to work" state, South Carolina. This labor/capital struggle takes on greater political ramifications as the National Labor Relations Board actually did the unexpected and enforced the law—barring the company from retaliating against workers for engaging in a lawful strike. John Miller follows this "right to work" issue with an "Up Against the Wall Street Journal" column where he responds to an op-ed column by "supply side" economist Arthur B. Laffer and Stephen Moore. "Wrong About Right-to-Work" (Article 11.5) explores the myths and realities about union shops, economic growth and employment.

In "Chinese Workers Stand Up" (Article 11.6), John Miller explains that Chinese workers are beginning to organize to demand higher wages and better working conditions. Contrary to the *Wall Street Journal's* proclamation that the wage increases are part of a "virtuous cycle of development," Miller suggests this is the result of the struggle of the Chinese workers themselves. Once again the issue of relative "power" comes to the forefront.

Back at home, public sector workers are being stigmatized by the right wing in the same way that "welfare moms" were in the 1990s, argues Randy Albelda in her essay, "Teachers, Secretaries and Social Workers: The New Welfare Moms?" (Article 11.7). Albelda points to one crucial difference between these public workers and single mothers: the public workers have a union and can fight back.

In "State Workers Face a Compensation Penalty" (Article 11.8), Ethan Pollack argues against the idea that public-sector workers are a privileged bunch. Data from several states show that public-sector workers are paid less than their private-sector counterparts; if we adjust for education levels, the "compensation penalty" for public-sector workers, who tend to have higher education levels, is even more pronounced.

In the final article of the chapter, "Labor Radicalism and Popular Emancipation" (Article 11.9), Steven Maher explores the political economy of the Egyptian revolution of 2011. If your only source of information about the Arab Spring was the Western mainstream media, you might have come away with the impression that middle-class university students and Twitter were the main causes of the uprisings. As Maher shows, militant labor union activism in the years leading up to the revolution played a crucial role. Egyptians were rejecting not only the brutal dictator, Hosni Mubarak, and his regime, but also the neoliberal economic order that had been enforced on the county by Western elites and international financial institutions.

Discussion Questions

1) (Article 11.1) What is a "union?" Explain the difference between a "craft" and "industrial" union. What is the relationship between "democracy" and unions?

2) (Article 11.2) Why have the number of workers represented by unions fallen in the United States over the last few decades? Which areas of the American economy are highly unionized? Which areas of the American economy are experiencing growth in union membership?

3) (Article 11.3) A case can be made that there is a positive correlation between unions, economic growth, and labor productivity. Outline such a case. Does such a case exist in Europe?

4) (Article 11.4) How did Boeing punish the International Association of Machinists? How is the threat of outsourcing and capital flight used to blackmail labor? What is "whipsawing" in labor relations?

5) (Article 11.4) Does Boeing pay a price in moving production to South Carolina? Why is the Chamber of Commerce so startled that the NLRB would actually act on this case? Is this case typical of the NLRB?

6) (Article 11.5) What are "right to work" laws? How are these laws designed to undermine the ability of a union to function? Is there really a correlation between "right to work" laws and economic growth? If so, in what direction?

7) (Articles 11.5 and 11.6) How are South Carolina and China alike in their policies towards organized labor? How do they differ? Do they both have "issues" with democracy?

8) (Article 11.6) Describe the textbook labor market explanation for rising wages. How does Miller's account of the Chinese labor market differ?

9) (Articles 11.7 and 11.8) Why the attack on public sector workers? What are the arguments being leveled against public sector workers? How is this "stigmatization" similar to that of an earlier group of poor single mothers (i.e., "welfare queens")? Why do you think conservatives dislike public-sector unions?

10) (Article 11.9) What role did organized labor play in the Egyptian revolution? What evidence does Maher provide for supposing that the revolution was driven by resistance to neoliberal capitalism?

Article 11.1

UNIONS AND THE LABOR MOVEMENT
What Are They and What Do They Do?

BY ALEJANDRO REUSS
April 2012

When we hear the word "labor" in the news, it is often being used as a synonym for organizations like unions that claim to represent and fight for the shared interests of wage-earners—people who work for someone else for pay. It can also be used to refer to the members or supporters of these organizations, or to leaders or activists in "the labor movement" or "organized labor." Note that, in most countries, union members are a minority—sometimes a small minority—of the people who work for an employer for pay. In the United States today, for example, unions represent less than one tenth of all employed workers. Therefore, when people use the term "labor" to mean only union members (or members of other labor organizations), they are referring to a much narrower group than all wage or salaried employees, or even workers in manufacturing, construction, transportation and other industries that people often think of when they hear terms like "labor" or "working class."

Labor unions (also known as "trade" unions) are defined by their membership qualifications, the issues they focus on, and the tactics they use. Union members, generally, must be wage-earners. Some unions may limit membership to workers in a particular workplace, occupation, or industry. Most unions exclude managers or supervisors. Unions usually focus much of their activity on conditions of employment—including wages, benefits, hours, working conditions, and hiring and firing. They may bargain, on behalf of workers in a particular firm or industry, for higher wages or shorter hours of work, or protest what they see as the unjust firing of a member. Unions limit competition between workers (or groups of workers). Union members, for example, may commit to accept employment only if a certain minimum hourly wage is offered. In the absence of such a commitment, an individual worker might get a job by accepting a lower wage than other workers. Unrestrained wage competition, however, forces all workers to compete for jobs by accepting lower wages, and so pushes down wages for all workers in that occupation or industry. Unions may also insist on certain conditions of work, so workers will not accept longer hours, a faster pace or work, or more dangerous conditions in order to get jobs. In other words, they take these factors "out of competition" between workers.

Historically, unions have been divided into two categories: "craft" union and "industrial" unions. Craft unions only include workers in a certain occupation. They exclude workers, even in the same workplace, who have a different occupation. In the United States today, for example, there are several unions in the airline industry: One may include only pilots; another, only machinists; still another, only flight attendants. Before the Great Depression of the 1930s, most unions in the United States were craft unions. They typically organized only highly skilled workers, ignoring the growing ranks of "unskilled" workers in growth industries like steel, auto, and trucking. Craft unions sought to organize only workers who already tended to have more bargaining power (due to their specialized skills). They did not want to risk their own position by getting mixed up in conflicts between "unskilled" workers and employers. For example, they worried that, if they accepted unskilled members, they might have to go out on strike if the unskilled workers (who formed the majority of the workforce) decided to do so.

In contrast, industrial unions aim to organize all different categories of (non-supervisory) workers in a workplace or industry. Before the Depression, for example, the main trucking union, the International Brotherhood of Teamsters, included only truck drivers—and excluded warehouse workers and other trucking-industry employees. Advocates of industrial unionism argued that the union would work better even for the drivers if it organized all these other workers as well. For example, if a group of drivers had a conflict with an employer and went on strike, they argued, union warehouse workers could refuse to handle any cargo transported by non-union drivers. This would strengthen the striking drivers' bargaining position with the employer. Moreover, advocates of industrial unions were genuinely interested in improving the conditions for all sorts of workers, not only the highly skilled who tended to be better off anyway. Finally, some union leaders realized that, as workers with specialized skills were increasingly being replaced by machines run by "unskilled" workers, the future of the unions themselves depended on a broader organizing strategy. Note that the term "industrial" union, in this context, does not mean that it organizes "industrial workers" (workers in manufacturing or in "blue collar" occupations). It means that the union organizes, or seeks to organize, all the workers in an industry, not just those in a particular "craft."

Before the Depression, workers often had to go on strike to get employers to bargain with their union. A strike is a joint action by a group of workers in which the workers "walk out" at the same time, refusing to return to work until the employer meets certain demands. A successful strike will prevent the struck company from operating normally, depriving it of sales and profits. During a "strike for recognition," workers demand that the employer "recognize" union representatives' authority to deal with the employer on the workers' behalf. (They may also make additional demands—about wages, hours, or working conditions, against the firing of union members or leaders, and so on.) Strikes for recognition often turned into violent clashes—between striking workers and "strikebreakers" (workers, known pejoratively as "scabs," hired to replace strikers), between strikers and company-hired thugs, or between strikers and police or state militia troops.

Since the 1930s, U.S. federal law has established another way for workers to organize unions. The National Labor Relations Act of 1935 established a system of union elections, to be overseen by a National Labor Relations Board (NLRB). When the majority of workers in an NLRB-defined "bargaining unit" have signed union membership cards, the NLRB orders a secret-ballot election. If a majority of the votes are for the union, the employer is required by law to recognize the union and to bargain with its representatives (over a contract, or "collective-bargaining agreement," covering all the workers in the bargaining unit). Union members are required to pay dues to the union, which pays for union operations including the salaries of paid officials and organizers. Workers covered by a union contact can decline to join the union, but may be required to pay a union fee (depending on the law in the state where they live), on the grounds that they benefit from union bargaining and protections, and should not be able to "free ride" while others pay.

During the 1930s, policymakers were alarmed by the growing conflict between workers and employers. They were afraid that strikes could sweep across the country and paralyze industry, and even that such a movement could threaten the entire capitalist economic system based on private ownership of industry. The National Labor Relations Act and other changes in labor law were a way to cushion the clash between workers and employers. After the Depression and World War II, the new system of labor relations may have made it easier for unions to gain employer recognition (at least in some areas and industries). However, workers and unions also faced many important constraints. Most collective-bargaining agreements contained "no-strike" clauses barring the union from striking for the contract's duration. Under this system, instead of striking to protest employer actions—including contract violations—workers bring complaints to their union representatives, who then file a "grievance" with the employer. (If not resolved, a grievance can eventually go before an arbitrator agreed upon by the employer and union.) Strikes for recognition became rare after the establishment of union-election system, but strikes were still frequent when union contracts expired and the two sides could not come to terms on a new agreement. U.S. labor law, however, barred unions from physically blocking entrance to the workplace in order to keep out strikebreakers. In some other countries, labor laws bar employers from hiring replacements during a strike. In the United States, however, this practice is legal, and makes it more difficult for workers to win strikes.

The overall structure of U.S. labor law has largely limited unions to two basic functions—negotiating contracts, which usually last for several years, and enforcing them through grievance procedures. Collective bargaining has come to define U.S. unions so completely that that other workers' organizations—those that do not engage in collective bargaining—are usually not considered unions at all. In recent years, for example, organizations known as "workers' centers" have emerged in many cities. These organizations usually focus on workers without union representation, especially in industries with large numbers of immigrant workers. Workers' centers may advise workers about their legal rights at work and how to fight for them (for example, how to contact state or federal agencies enforcing labor laws). They may even organize protests against employers who violate workers' rights (by paying less than the minimum wage, requiring workers to work "off the clock" without pay, breaking workplace safety or health regulations, etc.). These can include demonstrations outside a place of business, calls for consumer boycotts of a business, and other pressure tactics. Efforts like these may improve the pay or conditions for workers at offending businesses. Since workers' centers do not engage in collective bargaining with employers, however, they are not normally considered unions.

While some unions may "organize" only a single workplace, most local unions are affiliated with national organizations, often focused on a particular occupation or industry. (In the United States, these are typically called "international unions" or just "internationals." Workers in other countries, however, rarely form more than a small percentage of the membership of these organizations. For simplicity, we will call them "national unions" or "national organizations.") National unions can offer assistance to their "locals," strengthening the latter's bargaining power with employers. For example, if members of a local vote to go on strike against a particular employer, the national organization may offer financial assistance to the strikers (who are going without pay during the strike). This can help strikers "hold out" longer, making them more likely to win a long strike—and so might actually make employers more likely to settle quickly and avoid a prolonged shutdown.

In many countries, different national unions are affiliated into a union federation. In the United States, for example, the American Federation of Labor-Congress of Industrial Organizations (AFL-CIO) is the main union federation. Most of the country's largest national unions are members. The AFL-CIO itself was the product of the 1955 merger of two separate federations, the AFL and CIO. More recently, in 2005, several large national unions split from the AFL-CIO to form a new federation, known as Change to Win (CtW). Many national unions or labor federations, in the United States and other countries, try to influence public policy more broadly—especially on issues affecting the conditions of work (for

---

Reform or Revolution?

In addition to labor-based "reform" movements, there is a long history of labor-based "revolutionary" movements in capitalist countries. The word "revolutionary," in this context, refers to the aim of a fundamental transformation of the economic system—that is, the replacement of capitalism with some other system. (It does not imply anything about the means used to bring about this change, like whether to work through existing political institutions or not, whether to use violence or not, and so on.) Leaders and members of these movements argued that it was not possible to fix certain problems—like inequalities of wealth and power, "boom-and-bust" economic cycles, or "exploitation" of workers by employers—within a capitalist economic system. Instead, they believed, it was necessary to change the system itself.

Such movements and political parties have often used terms like "social democratic" or "socialist" to describe themselves, so it is not always easy to tell from a party name whether its politics are "reformist" or "revolutionary." At the beginning of the First World War, "social democratic" parties across Europe split between reformist and revolutionary wings. In many cases, the revolutionary side adopted the name "communist." This word has since been used by many different parties and movements across the world. Some have ruled or advocated dictatorial systems like those of the Soviet Union and its Eastern European "satellites." Others have visions of a future "communist" society—often emphasizing democratic decision-making from the workplace on up through all levels of the society—that are in many ways the opposite of these dictatorial systems.

To complicate things further, many self-styled "revolutionary" movements still call themselves "socialist" (and may reject the term "communist" because of its association with a system they reject). Meanwhile, in some countries, there are influential "communist" parties that have, in practice, long since adopted reformist politics, and do not really aim at the replacement of the capitalist system. Good luck sorting them out!

both union and non-union workers). Unions may campaign directly on issues like the minimum wage, occupational safety and health regulations, or workers' rights to organize unions. They may also support candidates for public office who they perceive as "pro-labor."

In many capitalist countries, there are major political parties whose names and political platforms link them to the labor movement. The British Labour Party (or, simply, "Labour"), for example, is one of the United Kingdom's two largest political parties, and recently ended more than a decade as the majority party in parliament and the party of the prime minister. Some former British colonies have similar parties. The Australian Labor Party is the governing party in that country. Canada, too, has a major party in the labor tradition, though it does not have the word "labor" (or "labour") in its name. The New Democratic Party is currently the second-largest party in the Canadian parliament. In many European countries, similar parties are more likely to be called "social democratic" or "socialist." In Germany, for example, the Social Democratic Party is one of the two largest parties, and was the party of the chancellor (Germany's name for its prime minister) as recently as 2005. In France, the Socialist Party is also one of the top two parties. The party last held the office of prime minister in 2002. Parties with similar traditions also exist in many lower-income countries. In Brazil, for example, the Workers' Party (founded only in 1980) has held the office of president since 2002. The South American countries of Bolivia and Venezuela are both governed by parties that self-identify as "socialist." In Chile, the Socialist Party held the presidency from 2000 to 2010. In many countries, "labor," "social democratic," or "socialist" parties have formal ties to labor unions or union federations.

Major political parties with the words "labor," "workers," "socialist," or "social democratic" in their names are almost always "center-left" parties. They tend to favor government interventions in economic life such as regulation of labor conditions (like wages, hours, occupational safety and health, and hiring and firing), "social welfare" programs (like unemployment, disability, and retirement benefits), public provision of some basic goods and services (like education and health care), full-employment policies, regulation of important industries, and perhaps government ownership in some industries (especially utilities, transportation, communications, etc.). They also emphasize protections for workers' rights to join unions, bargain collectively, and go on strike. They do not propose, however, to get rid of the "capitalist" economic system—defined by private ownership of the "means of production" (like land, machinery, factories, and mines), wage labor (some people working of others for pay), and production for exchange (sale of goods in markets)—in favor of a different system. ❑

Article 11.2

WHAT'S BEHIND UNION DECLINE IN THE UNITED STATES?
The role of the "employers' offensive" has been key.

BY ALEJANDRO REUSS
May/June 2011

The total number of union members in the United States peaked in the late 1970s and early 1980s, at over 20 million. As of 2010, it remained near 15 million. The story of union decline in the United States, however, does not begin in the 1980s, nor is it as modest as these figures would suggest.

Union density (or the "unionization rate"), the number of workers who are members of unions as a percentage of all employed workers, has been declining in the United States for over half a century. The share of U.S. workers in unions peaked in 1954, at just over 25%. For nonagricultural workers, the high-water mark—at more than one third of employed workers—came even earlier, in 1945. It would reach nearly the same percentage again in the early 1950s, before beginning a long and virtually uninterrupted decline.

By 2010, the U.S. unionization rate was less than 12%. It would be even lower were it not for the growth of public-sector unions since the 1960s. For private-sector workers, the unionization rate is now less than 7%.

There are multiple reasons for union decline, including shrinking employment in highly unionized industries, falling unionization rates within these traditional bastions of unionism, and failures to unionize in new, growing sectors.

Employers' determination to rid themselves of unions has certainly played a major role in declining unionization rates. Where employers could not break unions by frontal assault, they were determined to find ways around them. Unionized companies established parallel non-union operations, a practice sometimes known as "double breasting," gradually shifting production and employment away from their unionized facilities. Some employers began contracting out work formerly done by union employees to non-union subcontractors (the original meaning of "outsourcing"). Some established new operations far from their traditional production centers, especially in less unionized and lower-wage areas. Many companies based in the Northeast and Upper Midwest, for example, set up new production sites in the South and West, and eventually in other countries. (For a great historical account on one company, see Jefferson Cowie's *Capital Moves: RCA's 70-Year Quest for Cheap Labor.*) Finally, new employers entering highly unionized sectors usually remained non-union. The auto industry is a good example. So-called "transplants" (factories owned by non-U.S. headquartered companies) have accounted for an increasing share of the industry's shrinking labor force, and have remained largely non-union.

Historically, union growth has come primarily in short spurts when unions expand into new industries. Since the 1940s, however, U.S. unions have failed to organize in growing industries to compensate for the declines in employment and unionization rates in traditional union strongholds. The public sector represents the one major exception. Since the early 1970s, union density for public-sector workers

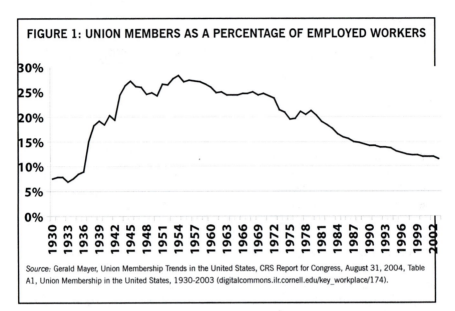

FIGURE 1: UNION MEMBERS AS A PERCENTAGE OF EMPLOYED WORKERS

Source: Gerald Mayer, Union Membership Trends in the United States, CRS Report for Congress, August 31, 2004, Table A1, Union Membership in the United States, 1930-2003 (digitalcommons.ilr.cornell.edu/key_workplace/174).

has increased from about 20% to over 35%. This has not been nearly enough, however, to counteract the decline among private-sector workers. To maintain the overall unionization rates of the 1950s or 1960s, unions would have had to enlist millions more workers in the private sector, especially in services.

Since the 1970s, employers have fought unions and unionization drives with increasing aggressiveness, as part of what labor historian Michael Goldfield calls the "employer offensive." Many employers facing unionization drives fire vocal union supporters, both eliminating pro-union campaigners and spreading fear among the other workers. Researchers at the Center for Economic and Policy Research (CEPR) have found that, between 2001 and 2005, pro-union workers were illegally fired in around one-fourth of all union election campaigns. Meanwhile, during many campaigns, employers threaten to shut down the facility (at least in part) if the union wins. Labor researcher Kate Bronfenbrenner reports, in a study from the mid 1990s, that employers threatened plant closings in more than half of all unionization campaigns, and that such threats cut the union victory rate (compared to those in which no such threat was made) by about 30%.

The employer offensive has unfolded, especially since the 1980s, against a bacdrop of government hostility towards unions. The federal government has often turned a blind eye to illegal tactics (or "unfair labor practices") routinely used by employers to fight unionization drives. Employer retaliation against workers (by firing or otherwise) for union membership, union activity, or support for unionization is illegal. So is an employer threatening to close a specific plant in response to a unionization drive. However, since the 1980s, union supporters argue, the government agencies tasked with enforcing labor law have increasingly ignored such practices, imposed only "slap on the wrist" punishments, or delayed judgment, somtimes for years, long after the unionization drive is over and done with.

Many labor historians point to the Reagan administration's mass firing of striking air-traffic controllers (members of the Professional Air Traffic Controllers

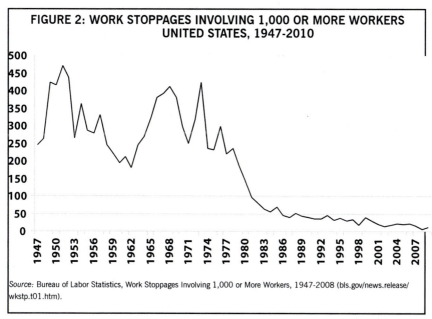

FIGURE 2: WORK STOPPAGES INVOLVING 1,000 OR MORE WORKERS
UNITED STATES, 1947-2010

Source: Bureau of Labor Statistics, Work Stoppages Involving 1,000 or More Workers, 1947-2008 (bls.gov/news.release/wkstp.t01.htm).

Organization, or PATCO) in 1981 as a signal that the government approved of private employers' own union-busting activities. Before the PATCO strike, it was relatively rare for employers to fire striking workers and hire "permanent replacements." (Sometimes, employers would bring in replacements during a strike, but striking workers would get their jobs back after a settlement was reached.) After PATCO, private employers increasingly responded to strikes by firing the strikers and bringing in permanent replacements—a practice that is illegal in many countries, but not in the United States. The number of large strikes, already in sharp decline during the preceding few years (possibly due to the employer offensive, rising unemployment, and other factors), has since declined to microscopic proportions.

At this point, unions in the United States—including less than a tenth of private-sector workers—are almost back down to the level they were on the eve of the Great Depression. The 1930s turned out to be the greatest period of union growth in U.S. history, with substantial additional growth in the 1940s and 1950s largely an aftershock of that earlier explosion. There is no guarantee, however, that history will repeat itself, and that the weakness of organized labor today will give way to a new burst of energy. In the midst of a deep recession, and now the beginnings of a halting recovery, there have been few signs of a labor revival. Ironically, only the recent attacks on public-sector workers and unions have provoked a mass-movement fightback. Labor supporters, however, should understand this, soberly, as coming from a very defensive position. ❑

Sources: Michael Goldfield, "Labor in American Politics—Its Current Weakness," *The Journal of Politics*, Vol. 48, No. 1. (Feb., 1986), pp. 2-29; Kate Bronfenbrenner, "Final Report: The Effects of Plant Closing or Threat of Plant Closing on the Right of Workers to Organize," *International Publications*, Paper 1, 1996 (digitalcommons.ilr.cornell.edu/intl/1); Gerald Friedman, *Reigniting the Labor Movement: Restoring Means to Ends in a Democratic Labor Movement* (New York:

Routledge, 2008); Gerald Mayer, "Union Membership Trends in the United States," CRS Report for Congress, August 31, 2004, Table A1, Union Membership in the United States, 1930-2003 (digitalcommons.ilr.cornell.edu/key_workplace/174); Bureau of Labor Statistics, "Work Stoppages Involving 1,000 or More Workers," 1947-2008 (www.bls.gov/news.release/wkstp.t01.htm); John Schmitt and Ben Zipperer, "Dropping the Ax: Illegal Firings During Union Election Campaigns," Center for Economic and Policy Research, January 2007 (www.cepr.net/documents/publications/unions_2007_01.pdf).

Article 11.3

UNIONS AND ECONOMIC PERFORMANCE

BY ARTHUR MacEWAN
November/December 2011

Dear Dr. Dollar:

I know unions have shrunk in the United States, but by how much? And how best to respond to my right-wing friends who claim that unions are bad for the economy?
—Rich Sanford, Hardwick, Mass.

Take a look at the graph below. The two lines on the graph show for the period 1917 through 2007 (1) labor union membership as a percentage of the total U.S. work force and (2) the percentage of all income obtained by the highest 1% of income recipients. So the lines show, roughly, the strength of unions and the distribution of income for the past century. (John Miller and I developed this graph for our book *Economic Collapse, Economic Change.*)

The picture is pretty clear. In periods when unions have been strong, income distribution has been less unequal. In periods when unions have been weak, income distribution has been more unequal. In the post-World War II era, union members were about 25% of the labor force; today the figure is about 10%. In those postwar years, the highest-income 1% got 10% to 12% of all income; today they get about 25%.

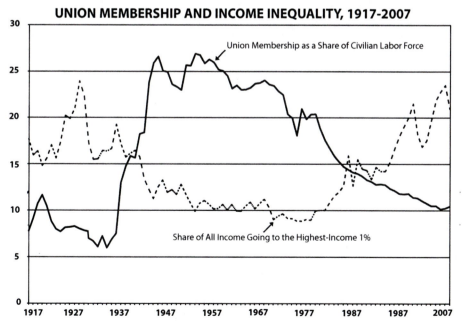

UNION MEMBERSHIP AND INCOME INEQUALITY, 1917-2007

Source: Arthur MacEwan and John A. Miller, *Economic Collapse, Economic Change: Getting to the Root of the Crisis* (M.E. Sharpe, 2011).

The causation between union strength and income distribution is not simple. Nonetheless, there are some fairly direct connections. For example, when unions are strong, they can push for higher wages and thus we see a more equal distribution of income. Also, strong unions can have an impact on the political process, bringing about policies that are more favorable to workers.

But causation can work in the other direction as well. Great income inequality puts more power in the hands of the rich, and they can use that power to get policies put in place that weaken unions—for example, getting people who are hostile to unions appointed to the National Labor Relations Board.

And then there are other factors that affect both union strength and income distribution—for example, the changing structure of the global economy, which places U.S. workers in competition with poorly paid workers elsewhere. Yet the structure of the global economy is itself affected by the distribution of political power. For example, the "free trade" agreements that the United States has established with other countries generally ignore workers' rights (to say nothing of the environment) and go to great lengths to protect the rights of corporations. So, again, causation works in complex ways, and there are certainly other factors that need to be taken account of to explain the relationship shown in the graph.

However one explains the relationship, it is hard to imagine that we can return to a more equal distribution of income while unions remain weak. This means, at the very least, that the interests of unions and of people at the bottom of the income distribution are bound up with one another. Building stronger unions is an important part of fighting poverty—and the hunger and homelessness that are the clear manifestations of poverty.

One important thing to notice in the graph: In the post-World War II years, economic growth was the best we have seen. Certainly no one can claim that it is impossible for strong unions and a more equal distribution of income to co-exist with fairly rapid economic growth. Indeed, we might even argue that strong unions and a more equal distribution of income create favorable conditions for economic growth!

Stronger unions, it turns out, could be good preventive medicine for much of what ails our economy. ❑

Article 11.4

CONFLICTING DREAMS
The Strikes That Made Boeing a Flashpoint

BY JOSH EIDELSON
September/October 2011

Boeing makes the future. That's the recurring message of Boeing's "Future of Flight" tour, which brings visitors from around the world through its Everett factory in Washington State. The tour begins with a sign announcing that Boeing will "shape the future," and then carries you through employee elevators encouraging riders to "embrace the future."

As of September 2011, Boeing was in a high-profile legal battle with national implications. It's the latest round in a decades-long labor struggle. At stake: Do workers at Boeing get to shape their own future, and Boeing's? Or do they just have to embrace—or rather, submit to—the corporation's plan?

The National Labor Relations Board case against Boeing drew national headlines in the summer of 2011, and it will again as the case winds through the board's process and Republicans seize more opportunities to bash President Obama for appointing board members who may actually enforce labor law against employers. Though several media outlets have run with Republican claims that the case is an effort to punish South Carolinians for their state's right-to-work law, it's actually about Boeing's alleged effort to punish its Puget Sound workers for striking by moving work to South Carolina. The NLRB's General Counsel issued the complaint (roughly comparable to an indictment) after Boeing executives publicly and repeatedly declared that they would be producing a new line of Dreamliner aircraft in South Carolina because Puget Sound workers kept going on strike—four times since 1989. The National Labor Relations Act protects the right of workers to strike without actual or threatened retaliation.

I went to Puget Sound to hear directly from workers there why they've chosen time and again to strike.

The International Association of Machinists represents 29,000 workers at Boeing's Puget Sound plants in Renton, Seattle, and Everett. A dozen of them told me how strikes have allowed them to achieve and sustain their standard of living.

Safety and Sane Scheduling

Workers went on strike in 1989 to win protections for safety and restrictions on overtime. John Jorgenson, who just retired from Boeing after 45 years, is one of six employees in his building who were diagnosed with kidney cancer, which he blames in part on the chemicals they worked with before the 1989 strike. The strike won new protective gear and the elimination of dozens of chemicals judged unsafe.

Jorgenson says excessive overtime is one reason that so many Boeing workers from the pre-1989 period are now divorced, himself included. He remembers working eleven hours a day without a day off for 16 weeks. He would worry about falling asleep at work or while driving home. Brian Pelland, who started work at Boeing in 1988, says he hardly saw his kids in his first year on the job. "You're always looking at the future," Pelland says, "and you think you're always going to have time." But eventually the mandatory overtime left him feeling "deadbeat" and "numb." Since the 1989 strike he's been able to make enough money at Boeing to support his kids, while spending enough time outside of work to be in their lives. Without the strike, he says, "I wouldn't know them. They wouldn't know me."

When I asked Jorgenson what his life would be like without that strike, he said "I'd probably still have to work," despite the back injuries that put him out on medical leave for the final six months prior to his retirement at age 65. Before he could describe what that would be like, his wife cut him off. "I don't think so, John. I think with all those chemicals and the stuff you were exposed to... you wouldn't be here."

Defending Their Dream

Though workers have won additional improvements over the past two decades, the dozen employees I spoke to all described the strikes since 1989 primarily as defensive actions aimed at simply maintaining what had been won before. That includes robust pensions and an affordable family health-care plan for workers and retirees.

(Reached by phone, Boeing labor relations spokesperson Tim Healy said that both sides share responsibility for the frequency of strikes.)

The Boeing medical coverage pays for prescription medicine for 15-year employee Jason Redrup's stepson, who's had a liver transplant. Without Boeing benefits, Redrup said, "It would bankrupt me." Then he paused, contemplating what would happen next. "He'd be dead."

Bob Merritt, a 32-year employee, described rushing his daughter to the emergency room after she collapsed on the volleyball court. As he drove, he watched her fingers ball up as she lay in a fetal position in the back seat. "Talk about scared," he says. "We got her in [the ER] and I flashed my health card—damn right I got that insurance." He questioned whether his daughter, who fully recovered, would have gotten adequate treatment if she hadn't had adequate insurance. "There goes your whole life."

The strikes have also given workers confidence that their contract can be enforced. Pelland believes that without the credibility the union has established through striking, Boeing would have found an excuse to fire him. Twenty years ago, working under pressure on a wing line, Pelland slipped on leaking oil and badly sprained his thumb. His doctor sent him back to work with instructions not to grasp with his right hand for two weeks. With a mix of anger and embarrassment, he described his manager announcing at a morning crew meeting, "Oh Brian, he's got some pussy restriction—he can't do his job." "That changed me for life," said Pelland. Without strikes, he said, "they'd throw me away," and the union would lack the clout to stop them.

Dave Swann, who was hired in 1989, says the contract language and clout won through the strikes created opportunities for him to advance at Boeing despite management racism. Growing up, Swann was one of three or four African-American students bussed into a majority white school district in West Seattle. For years before the recent strikes won a new promotions system, managers looked at him "like I was a ghost."

A Changed Membership

The strikes were transformative experiences. For Jorgenson, the scariest was in 1977, when he was recently married to his first wife and making house payments. He says he went into the strike unsure "whether I'm going to have a job or not." He remembers managers swerving their cars towards picketing strikers on their way into work, and then taking photos of picketers from inside the plant.

Jorgenson joined a group calling itself the "Everett Raiders" that worked to discourage replacement workers and keep the spirits of the other strikers up. He compared going through a strike together to going through a war. "You're not really going to desert each other, and you're a lot more willing to endure the pain of going through all of it. And it is painful." The percentage of the workforce on strike went up during the course of the strike rather than down. By the end, he felt "pretty powerful," and when he went back to work, co-workers told him he had helped give them the strength to stay out on strike.

Wilson "Fergie" Ferguson, a military veteran who plays Santa at union Christmas parties, says going on strike for the first time in 1977 "scared the shit out of me." But "anger trumps fear every time. I'm scared until you piss me off."

Pelland says if he had crossed the picket line, "a part of me would have died, and I wouldn't be who I am." Having been guided through the 1989 strike by the veterans, by the time of the 2008 strike Pelland was seeking out newer employees on the picket line. "Can I talk to you about how the company bluffs?" he would ask them. "We hold a straight flush and the company's always bluffing."

Several workers mentioned they were struck by the degree of support from the community. Twenty-five-year employee Diana Loggins was moved in 1989 when her mailman, seeing the strike stickers on her car, would say, "Hang in there, you're on strike for us." Jorgenson says Boeing provides most of the middle-class jobs in Puget Sound. Boeing workers make significant contributions to the local tax base and the demand for local businesses. The other major private employer in the area is Microsoft, whose educational requirements leave its jobs out of reach for many.

A History of Retaliation

None of the dozen workers I met with doubted that Boeing was retaliating for Puget Sound strikes by locating production of its new Dreamliner line in South Carolina. For these workers, threats to shift production are more of the same. What's new is that this time, Boeing is actually making good on its threat to build commercial airplanes outside of Puget Sound.

Several workers said they've heard managers threaten to shut down or transfer production during past contract fights. Pelland says prior to "every strike" he's heard managers threaten to move lines of airplanes out of state. He says friends of his in management told him they were specifically instructed to warn workers that "they could take their business somewhere else." Merritt says co-workers informed him that managers told them, "We're pretty sick of this—you keep striking, we'll move your jobs."

During the 2002 contract fight, Jorgenson was pulled into a meeting where managers tried to convince him and other shop stewards to support the company's offer. Jorgenson says a manager told them that if the workers voted to strike, a Sonic Cruiser line planned for Everett would be built somewhere else instead. Jorgenson and other stewards did their best anyway to round up the two-thirds support the union requires to authorize a strike. But with the airline industry still recovering from 9/11, they fell just short. That meant management's final offer was accepted, including weakened subcontracting protections and language that prevented the union from filing charges over past threats. Fifteen-year employee Paul Veltkamp thinks that after managers "managed to scare just enough people" to vote against striking in 2002, they convinced themselves they were "vote-counting wizards" who could get workers to agree to more concessions in subsequent contracts. But after Boeing lost the 2005 and 2008 strikes, says Veltkamp, now the company is "trying something else, a different kind of threat."

Some workers said their co-workers have been intimidated by managers telling reporters that Boeing denied Puget Sound the second line of airliners because of strikes. Veltkamp, a shop steward, says he was approached by employees holding up newspapers and telling him that in the 2012 contract negotiations "we're just going to have to give them what they want." However, he says, "We don't stay scared for long."

Boeing spokesperson Healy said the lesson Puget Sound employees should take from the choice of South Carolina is that "we need to be competitive," and added that Boeing would "talk to our unionized employees here" about paying a greater share of health care costs in their next contract.

Different Dreams

Machinists Union members at Boeing are defending a dream too few American workers have in place or see in reach: Work hard, and don't live paycheck to paycheck. Get sick, and don't worry whether you can afford a doctor's visit. Put in enough decades, and expect a comfortable retirement. They didn't just win that dream through the beneficence of their bosses or the worthiness of their work (though the particulars of the industry make strikers less vulnerable to permanent replacement). It was birthed and maintained through strikes. Four times over the past 22 years, they held together and outlasted the company.

Dave Swann proudly relates that his great-grandfather was a porter, "one of the highest-paid jobs an African-American could have back in those days ... Everybody came to their house to eat, because he was in the union and they made good money." His grandfather was a longshoreman and his father, like him, was a Machinists member at Boeing. "I feel threatened," he says, because if his sons can't land their dream jobs of moviemaker and sportscaster, he wants union jobs at Boeing to be there for their whole lives. "It's a hurting feeling, because you want to see your kids do better than you."

Boeing has its own dreams. Take its tour and you'll hear about a future of faster, smoother production. When all the pieces are in place, my tour guide said, parts will arrive from several sources and become a Dreamliner in three days. "Most of the people who will ride on this plane," a pre-tour video brags, "haven't been born yet."

Bob Merritt describes the attitude he gets now from the company: "We want our airplanes to be plug and play, we want our workers to be plug and play." Pelland says Boeing is trying to become "a Lego building company" more focused on assembling parts than creating them. "They're sending a message to their customers and their shareholders that they're done with us," said Redrup. He says Boeing is trying "to break our stranglehold on their production system" just as General Motors did to the UAW half a century ago. "They've got to deal with the workers, and they don't like that. If they can't housebreak us, they gotta find a way to get away from us."

Now Boeing is at the center of a national controversy over how robust the right to strike should be. The workers I spoke to were divided over whether the company had arrogantly stumbled into legal danger or intentionally set out to see what they could get away with. It's good to see that, under the Obama-era labor board, publicly declaring you are denying production of a line of airplanes to a group of workers because they keep going on strike at least earns you a labor board complaint (Obama has been at pains to keep his distance from the case).

Reached by phone, Boeing government operations spokesperson Tim Neale maintained that management has "been honest about the fact that strikes have harmed the company and that we as a company very much are looking for production stability," but insisted Boeing hasn't broken the law. Its Republican defenders claim that the complaint signifies a shift toward Soviet-style central planning or Chicago-style machinations. But it's the prospect of an acquittal—or a management-friendly settlement—that would signal a further departure from the stated purpose and promise of the National Labor Relations Act, which set forth as its intent the promotion of collective bargaining and enshrined a right to collective action without threat of retaliation.

And if Boeing does pay a heavy price for telling its employees that their collective action cost them an expansion of their plant, it won't take a high-priced anti-union consultant to interpret the lesson for other companies: Don't be so obvious. All too often, employers get away with anti-union retaliation when they don't go bragging about it in the newspaper.

So whatever the result, the Boeing case is less a story about the potency of current labor law than about the power of the strike on the one hand and the threat of retaliation on the other. It's the story of workers who have refused to believe that they should cede a hard-won package of middle-class wages and workplace protections in the face of a major company's multi-year effort to persuade or intimidate them into backing down. Now, after decades during which Puget Sound has been the only place Boeing assembles commercial aircraft, workers are right to recognize that the power to move work elsewhere has become a powerful weapon in management's arsenal.

Boeing workers expect to have to strike every few years until they retire. One can imagine new attacks from Boeing spurring them to leverage their solidarity in other ways as well, be it international coordination, secondary picketing, or directing their political mobilization (which has successfully helped the company win tax breaks) towards demanding that the U.S. government, a major Boeing customer, insist on better behavior. As Boeing and the Machinists both look to the future, their struggle across decades shows both the enduring power of collective action and the still-unmet challenge that capital mobility poses for the labor movement.

Successive generations of Boeing workers have figured out that it's better to shape the future than to passively accept it. Meanwhile, Boeing and its peers are working to foist their own dreams on the rest of us—sometimes loudly, often not. My "Future of Flight" tour guide boasted about the ways the Dreamliner represents a new achievement in illusion. Scientific innovations in materials and lighting mean that passengers won't feel the altitude, the humidity, or the time difference as Boeing's airplane takes them somewhere new. "By the time you get there," he said, "we can trick your body to make you think you've already been there a long time." It was easy to forget he was referring to an airplane. ❏

Article 11.5

WRONG ABOUT RIGHT-TO-WORK

Laffer throws another curve-ball.

BY JOHN MILLER
July/August 2011

> BOEING AND THE UNION BERLIN WALL
>
> Two policies have consistently stood out as the most important in pre-
> dicting where jobs will be created and incomes will rise. First, states
> with no income tax generally outperform high income tax states.
> Second, states that have right-to-work laws grow faster than states with
> forced unionism.
>
> As of today there are 22 right-to-work states and 28 union-shop
> states. Over the past decade (2000-09) the right-to-work states grew faster
> in nearly every respect than their union-shop counterparts: 54.6% versus
> 41.1% in gross state product, 53.3% versus 40.6% in personal income,
> 11.9% versus 6.1% in population, and 4.1% versus -0.6% in payrolls.
>
> The Boeing incident makes it clear that right-to-work states have a
> competitive advantage over forced-union states. So the question arises:
> Why doesn't every state adopt right-to-work laws?
>
> —Arthur B. Laffer and Stephen Moore, *Wall Street Journal*
> op-ed, May 13, 2011

What do you get when you mix a *Wall Street Journal* editorial writer with a supply-side economist?

That's right: more of the same.

This time, however, it's right-to-work laws, not taxes, that come in for the full
Laffer treatment (although without the illustration on the back of a cocktail napkin).

In May 2011, the National Labor Relations Board (NLRB) issued an injunction
to stop defense giant Boeing from moving a jet production line from its unionized
factories in Washington state to right-to-work South Carolina. The International
Association of Machinists & Aerospace Workers union had filed a complaint that
the planned move was in retaliation against strikes the union conducted over the
last decade, and thus illegal.

The NLRB decision amounts to "a regulatory wall with one express purpose:
to prevent the direct competition of right-to-work states with union-shop states,"
insist Arthur Laffer, the supply-side economist, and Stephen Moore, former head
of the far-right economics think tank Club for Growth and now on the *Wall Street
Journal*'s editorial board. Right-to-work laws enforced in 22 states, mostly in the
southern and western United States, prohibit businesses and unions from agreeing to contracts that stipulate that an employer will hire only workers who join
the union or pay union dues. In right-to-work states, unions confront a free-rider
problem: they have to organize workers who can benefit from collective bargaining
without joining (or staying in) the union or paying dues.

The disadvantages that right-to-work states impose on unions give those states a competitive advantage that will enrich them, according to Laffer and Moore. And their report, "Rich States, Poor States," has the numbers to prove it, or so they claim. Right-to-work states grow faster, add more income, create more jobs, and attract more people than states hamstrung by pro-union labor laws.

But it turns out that the claim that right-to-work laws lead states to prosper is no more credible than Laffer's earlier claim that cutting income taxes would spur such an explosion of economic growth that government revenues would actually rise despite the lower tax rates. Much like what Laffer had to say about tax cuts and economic growth, Laffer and Moore make the case for right-to-work laws as the key to economic prosperity through sleight of hand and half-truths.

Let's take a look at exactly where their story goes wrong.

Something Up Their Sleeve

To begin with, Laffer's and Moore's report needs to be read carefully. Their claim is that the economies of states with right-to-work laws grow faster, not that their citizens are better off.

And they are not. For instance, while it is true that both output and income have grown faster in right-to-work states than in other states over the last decade, the growth is from a much lower starting point. In fact, output and income in those states still lag well behind the levels in non-right-to-work states. Personal income per capita averaged $37,134 (in 2010) and real GDP per capita averaged $39,365 (in 2009) in right-to-work states, but $41,312 and $42,513 respectively in the other 28 states.

The positive job creation numbers that Laffer and Moore report for right-to-work states over the last decade haven't resulted in superior job prospects for those out of work. With their faster growing populations, right-to-work states had unemployment rates averaging 8.0% in April of this year, just below the 8.2% average in non-right-to-work states.

And in practice, right-to-work laws are very much "right-to-work-for-less" laws, as union critics call them. In a recent Economic Policy Institute briefing paper, economists Elise Gould and Heidi Shierholz looked closely at the differences in compensation between right-to-work and non-right-to-work states. Controlling for the demographic and job characteristics of workers as well as state-level economic conditions and cost-of-living differences across states, they found that in 2009:

- Wages were 3.2% lower in right-to-work states vs. non-right-to-work states—about $1,500 less annually for a full-time, year-round worker.

- The rate of employer-sponsored health insurance was 2.6 percentage points lower in right-to-work states compared with non-right-to-work states.

- The rate of employer-sponsored pensions was 4.8 percentage points lower in right-to-work states. On top of that, in 2008 the rate of workplace deaths was 57% higher in right-to-work states than non-right-to-work states, while the 2009,poverty rate in right-to-work states averaged 15.0%, considerably above the 12.8% average for non-right-to-work states.

But here is the real kicker: once their effect is isolated from the effects of other factors, right-to-work laws seem to have little or no impact even on economic growth itself. For instance, a 2009 study conducted by economist Lonnie Stevans concludes that:

While ... right-to-work states are likely to have more self-employment and less bankruptcies on average relative to non-right-to-work states, there is certainly no more business capital. ... Moreover, from a state's economic standpoint, being right-to-work yields little or no gain in employment and real economic growth. Wages and personal income are both lower in right-to-work states, yet proprietors' income is higher.

Those lower wages and lower personal incomes are especially detrimental in today's fragile economic recovery, still plagued by a lack of consumer spending.

A Bad Move

The evidence above militates against the notion that right-to-work laws are the key to economic prosperity for state economies, and in favor of the notion that anti-union laws, much like deregulation and tax cuts targeted at the rich, are another mechanism for securing more and more for the well-to-do at the expense of most everyone else.

That is especially clear when it comes to Boeing's planned move from Washington state to South Carolina. Ironically, union-heavy Washington tops right-to-work South Carolina in Laffer's and Moore's Economic Outlook Rankings for 2010 and in their Economic Performance Rankings for 1998- 2008. Personal income, output, and employment all grew considerably faster in Washington state than in South Carolina from 1998 to 2008. And personal income per capita and GDP per capita in Washington state ($43,564 and $45,881 respectively) far exceed their levels in South Carolina ($33,163 and $30,845).

Beyond that, unemployment and poverty rates in Washington state are both well below those in South Carolina. By all those measures, Washington's economy is far and away the more vibrant of the two.

Working conditions are a lot better in Washington state too, something not lost on Boeing. Wage workers in Washington state on average make $11,020 a year more than their counterparts in South Carolina. Production workers in Washington state earn $5,560 a year more. South Carolina workers are 69% more likely to die on the job than workers in Washington. And not surprisingly, just 6.2% of wage and salary workers in right-to-work South Carolina were union members in 2010, versus more than 20% in Washington.

So then why does Boeing want to leave the Evergreen State for the Palmetto State? To benefit from a more vibrant economy? Or to take advantage of workers whose ability to organize is hindered by right-to-work laws, whose bargaining power has been eroded by high unemployment and poverty, who have few alternatives than to endure working in far more dangerous conditions while getting paid less than workers in Washington? The numbers speak for themselves.

No wonder the NLRB filed an injunction against Boeing's planned move. Labor board members saw it for what it is: not a mere relocation, but an exercise of raw power intended to bust a union. ❏

Sources: Arthur B. Laffer and Stephen Moore, "Rich States, Poor States: ALEC-Laffer State Economic Competitiveness Index, 3rd edition," Wall Street Journal, April 7, 2010; Lonnie K. Stevans, "The Effect of Endogenous Right-to-Work Laws on Business and Economic Conditions in the United States: A Multivariate Approach," Review of Law & Economics, Vol. 5, Issue 1, 2009; Elise Gould and Heidi Shierholz, "The Compensation Penalty of 'Right-to-Work' Laws," Economic Policy Institute Briefing Paper #299, February 17, 2011 (epi.org); Gordon Lafar, "'Right-to-Work': Wrong in New Hampshire," Economic Policy Briefing Paper #302, April 5, 2011 (epi.org); Carl Horowitz, "NLRB Sues Boeing; Seeks End to Commercial Jet Production in South Carolina," National Legal and Policy Center, May 4, 2011 (nlpc.org).

Article 11.6

CHINESE WORKERS STAND UP

What is the real cause of increasing wages in China?

BY JOHN MILLER
September/October 2010

> "THE RISE OF CHINESE LABOR:
> WAGE HIKES ARE PART OF A VIRTUOUS CYCLE OF DEVELOPMENT"
>
> The recent strikes at Honda factories in southern China represent another data point in an emerging trend: Cheap labor won't be the source of the Chinese economy's competitive advantage much longer.
>
> The auto maker has caved and given workers a 24% pay increase to restart one assembly line. Foxconn, the electronics producer that has experienced a string of worker suicides, has also announced big raises. This is all part of the virtuous cycle of development: Productivity increases, which drive wages higher, forcing businesses to adjust, leading to more productivity growth.
> —*Wall Street Journal* op-ed, June 9, 2010

Wages in China are in fact rising. But that hardly constitutes a "virtuous cycle of development" that is the inevitable result of market-led economic growth, as the *Wall Street Journal* editors contend.

Rather, higher wages in China are the hard-fought gains of militant workers who have used tightening labor markets as a lever to pry wage gains out of employers whose coffers have long been brimming with cash.

Labor unrest taking advantage of tightening labor markets is the story in China today—not abstract economic forces lifting wages, the tale the *Journal's* editors want to pass off as a paean to free-market economics.

A Changing Labor Outlook

In recent years rapid economic growth has indeed tightened the Chinese labor market, drying up the seemingly bottomless pool of jobseekers from the countryside. As of May 2010, job vacancies in China outnumbered the number of job applicants, according to the Chinese Labor Market Information Center.

And wages are rising for many. Pay for China's 150 million or so internal-migrant workers increased 16% in 2009 despite the global financial crisis, according to Cai Fang, head of the Institute of Population and Labor Economics at the Chinese Academy of Social Sciences.

Higher wages aren't about to break the corporate piggybank. In recent years the biggest increase in China's extraordinarily high national savings (which includes household and business savings) has come from retained earnings—the undistributed profits of Chinese corporations. Retained earnings did so much to boost the country's savings because low wages kept corporate profits high. For more than a decade, labor's share of national income has been on the decline in China as the corporate share has increased dramatically. On top of that, the strong productivity growth that the *Journal* editors laud has offset wage increases, keeping labor costs per unit of output in check. At the beginning of 2010 Chinese unit labor costs were no higher than in 2004.

Wage increases notwithstanding, working conditions in China remain oppressive, as even the *Journal* editors seem to recognize. In May 2010 a thirteenth worker attempted to commit suicide at a Foxconn factory in southern China. The world's largest maker of computer components, Foxconn supplies Apple, Dell, and Hewlett-Packard, among others. While working conditions at this Taiwanese-owned company are far from the worst in China, the hours are long, the assembly line moves too fast, and managers enforce military-style discipline.

Foxconn's string of suicides is just the tip of the iceberg. Early in 2008, the *New York Times* reported that worker abuse is still commonplace in many of the Chinese factories that supply Western companies. The *Times* quoted labor activists who reported unfair labor practices—child labor, enforced 16-hour days, and sub-minimum wages, among others—in factories supplying several U.S. firms including Wal-Mart, Disney, and Dell. The activists also reported that factories routinely withhold health benefits, employ dangerous machinery, and expose workers to lead, mercury, and other hazardous chemicals. According to government statistics, an average of 187 Chinese workers die each day in industrial accidents; the equivalent U.S. figure is three.

The Real Virtuous Cycle

Rapid economic growth and rising productivity undoubtedly laid the groundwork for higher wages. But it is labor militancy that has exploited workers' improved bargaining position. The number of labor disputes in China doubled from 2006 to 2009. Workers have won wage increases in excess of 20% at several large export factories, including Foshan Fengfu Autoparts, the company that supplies exhaust pipes to Japanese automaker Honda, and Hon Hai Precision Industry Co., the Taiwan-based electronics manufacturer that supplies iPads and iPhones for Apple and a range of gadgets for Hewlett-Packard and Nintendo.

Predictably, the editors misrepresent how social improvement comes about with economic development. Not just in China but in the developed economies as well, improvements in working conditions have come about not due to market-led forces alone, but when economic growth was combined with social action and worker militancy.

The history of sweatshops in the United States makes that clear. The shirtwaist strike of 1909, the tragedy of the Triangle Shirtwaist fire two years later, and the hardships of the Great Depression inspired garment workers to unionize and led to the imposition of government regulations on the garment industry and other industries, beginning with the New York Factory Acts and extending to the Fair Labor

Standards Act of 1938. The power of those reforms along with the postwar boom nearly eradicated sweatshops in the United States.

Since then, sweatshops have returned with a vengeance to the U.S. garment industry. Why? Declining economic opportunity is part of the answer. But severe cutbacks in the number of inspectors and a drop-off in union density paved the way as well. The U.S. experience confirms the take-away message from rising Chinese wages: Economic development by itself will not eliminate inhuman working conditions. Improve-ments in working conditions are neither inevitable nor irreversible.

Not only is labor organizing crucial for improving working conditions, but those organizing efforts need to be international if workers are to succeed in reaping durable gains from economic development.

China's case makes that clear. Rising wages in China have prompted footwear and apparel firms to shift their manufacturing elsewhere—to Indonesia, Bangladesh, and Vietnam, for example. Jim Sciabarrasi, head of sourcing and procurement at U.S.-based sneaker company New Balance, was clear about the reason for the firm's move. "Indonesia has a ready supply of workers and their wages are not going up as fast as in China," he told the *Boston Globe*.

Chinese workers attempting to organize and improve their situation always face the threat that their employer will simply pack up and depart for even lower-cost countries. This kind of threat, which helps employers resist demands for better wages and working conditions not just in China but elsewhere in global South and in the developed economies as well, has been increasingly effective as globalization has weakened limits on the mobility of corporations. It throws into sharp relief the common interests of workers in all countries in improving conditions at the bottom, in robust full-employment programs that raise their incomes and enhance their bargaining power.

In that way, the rise of China's workers and the bold labor unrest there should benefit manufacturing workers across the globe, a virtuous cycle the *Wall Street Journal* editors would not only be loathe to recognize but have gone out of their way to obscure. ❑

Sources: David Barboza, "In Chinese Factories, Lost Fingers and Low Pay," *New York Times*, Jan. 5, 2008; William Foreman, "13th worker attempts suicide at Foxconn tech factory in southern China, report says," *Los Angeles Times*, May 27, 2010; Jenn Abelson, "Local sneaker firms are making it in Indonesia," *Boston Globe*, May 29, 2010; Norihiko Shirouzo, "Chinese Workers Challenge Beijing's Authority," *WSJ*, June 13, 2010; Elizabeth Holmes, "U.S. Apparel Retailers Turn Their Gaze beyond China," *WSJ*, June 15, 2010; "NW: Wage disputes in China put world on notice," NIKKEI, June 14, 2010; Aileen Wang and Simon Rabinovitch, "Why labor unrest is good for China and the world," Reuters, June 2, 2010; World Bank, China Quarterly Update, June 2010; James Areddy, "Accidents Plague China's Workplaces," *WSJ*, July 28, 2010.

Article 11.7

ARE TEACHERS, SECRETARIES, AND SOCIAL WORKERS THE NEW WELFARE MOMS?

BY RANDY ALBELDA
May/June 2011

Conservatives have had their sights on public-sector workers for a while and for good reason. Public-sector workers represent two favorite targets: organized labor and government. I am a public-sector employee and union member, so I can't help but take these attacks and struggles personally. I am also a veteran of the welfare "reform" battles of the 1990s, and the debates over public-sector workers are strikingly similar.

Like welfare moms, public-sector workers have been painted as greedy [fill-in-the-blank barnyard animals], feeding from the public trough and targeted as the primary source of what's wrong with government today.

Like 1990s welfare-reform debates, this one is dominated by more fiction than fact. For example, previous and recent research consistently shows public-sector workers actually earn less than private-sector workers with comparable skills and experience. While many, but not all, public-sector workers who work long enough for the public sector have a defined-benefit pension, the unfunded portions of those pensions are often due to bad state policy, not union negotiations.

In some states, like my own, Massachusetts, current workers are paying most of their pension costs through their own contributions into interest-bearing pension funds. Because state and local governments with defined pensions do not contribute to social security, there are currently cost savings. The upshot is that the cost of pensions may not be as high as some are arguing.

It is true that health-insurance costs for current retirees are expensive and worrisome. But this is because of the rising costs in private health insurance. Making workers pay more for their health-care benefits will erode the compensation base of public-sector workers, but it won't get at the real problem of escalating health-care costs.

During the welfare debates, one of the arguments used to justify punitive legislative changes was spun around the fact that welfare moms who did get low-wage employment could also get child-care assistance—while other moms could not. Sound familiar? Public-sector workers do have employer-sponsored benefits many private-sector workers no longer get. But benefits haven't improved in the public sector over the last 20 years; indeed most public-sector workers are paying more for the same benefits.

Over the same period, many private-sector workers have been stripped of their employer-provided benefits even as profits have soared. Instead of asking why corporate America is stripping middle-class workers of decent health-care coverage and retirement plans, the demand is to strip public-sector workers of theirs.

The new Cadillac-driving welfare queens are the handful of errant politicians who game the pension system and a few highly paid administrators getting handsome pensions. Sure they exist, but are hardly representative. The typical public-sector worker is a woman, most often working as a teacher, secretary or social worker. Women comprise 60% of all state and local workers (compared to their 47% representation in the private work force). And those three occupations make up 40% of the state and local work force.

Shaking down public-sector unions may make some feel better about solving government fiscal problems, but the end result will be more lousy jobs for educated and skilled workers. It will also not stem the red ink that is causing states to disinvest in much-needed human and physical infrastructure with budget cuts. But eroding wages and benefits combined with public-sector bashing will send a very loud market signal to the best and brightest currently thinking about becoming teachers, librarians, or social workers to do something else.

Wisconsin Governor Scott Walter is leading the attack on public-sector workers today. In the 1990s it was another Wisconsin governor, Tommy Thompson, who was a leader in demanding and implementing punitive changes to his state's welfare system. His plan became a model for the rest of the states and federal welfare legislation in 1996. Then there were horror stories and welfare bashing, but not much in the way of discussing the real issue of decent paying jobs that poor and low-income mothers on and off welfare needed to support their families. The main result of welfare reform was the growth in working-poor moms.

There is one important difference. Public-sector workers, unlike welfare moms, have unions and a cadre of supporters behind them. ❑

Article 11.8

STATE WORKERS FACE A COMPENSATION PENALTY

BY ETHAN POLLACK
March/April 2011

The campaign against state and local workers is often justified with claims that they are privileged relative to their private-sector peers or have somehow been cushioned from the effects of the recent recession and slow recovery. Data from Wisconsin as well as Indiana, New Jersey, and Ohio prove that these claims are clearly false.

In Wisconsin, which has become a focal point in this debate, public servants already take a pretty hefty pay cut just for the opportunity to serve their communities, according to findings by Rutgers economist Jeffrey Keefe. The figure below shows that when comparing the total compensation (which includes non-wage benefits such as health care and pensions) of workers with similar education, public-sector workers consistently make less than their private-sector peers. Workers with a bachelor's degree or more—who make up nearly 60% of the state and local workforce in Wisconsin—are compensated between $20,000 a year less (if they just have a bachelor's degree) to over $82,000 less (if they have a professional degree).

True apples-to-apples comparisons require controlling for worker characteristics such as education in order to best measure a worker's potential earnings in a different sector or industry. Controlling for a larger range of earnings predictors—including not just education but also age, experience, gender, race, etc., Wisconsin public-sector workers face an annual compensation penalty of 11%. Adjusting for the slightly fewer hours worked per week on average, these workers still face a compensation penalty of 5% for choosing to work in the public sector.

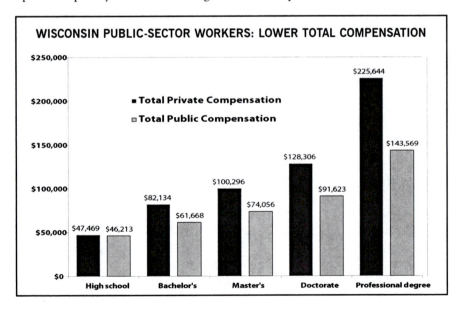

WISCONSIN PUBLIC-SECTOR WORKERS: LOWER TOTAL COMPENSATION

PUBLIC AND PRIVATE-SECTOR WORKERS COMPARED					
		Job experience		% w/ 4-yr degree	
	Public-sector Penalty	Public	Private	Public	Private
Indiana	7.5%	24.1 years	21.6	49%	24%
New Jersey	4.1%	24	22	57%	40%
Ohio	6%	23.2	21.7	49%	26%
Wisconsin	11%	22.5	21.3	59%	30%

The story is similar in Indiana, New Jersey, and Ohio. Public-sector workers in all of these states also face an annual compensation penalty—of 7.5%, 4.1%, and 6%, respectively. As in Wisconsin, a higher percentage of public-sector workers than private-sector workers in these states have a four-year college degree, as well as more job experience on average (see table).

The deficit that these states face is caused by the economic downturn and, in Wisconsin, a recent tax-cut package. It has nothing to do with the compensation of the people that educate our children, keep the streets safe and clean, keep dangerous chemicals out of our water, and keep insurance companies from taking advantage of us. These public servants are already paid less than those in the private sector, and nationally, this gap has actually been increasing over the past few decades, according to a report by University of Wisconsin-Milwaukee economists Keith Bender and John Heywood.

Instead of opportunistically using these hard times to target workers who—because of their public service—already take a substantial pay cut, state politicians should focus on creating jobs and boosting the incomes of all workers. ❑

A version of this article originally appeared as a "Snapshot" at the Economic Policy Institute website (epi.org).

Sources: Keith Bender and John Heywood, "Out of Balance: Comparing Public and Private Sector Compensation over 20 Years," National Institute on Retirement Security, Washington, D.C., April 2010, (sige.org); Jeffrey H. Keefe, "Are Wisconsin Public Employees Overcompensated?," Economic Policy Institute, Washington, D.C., February 10, 2011 (epi.org); Economic Policy Institute, Reports on public-sector worker undercompensation in Ohio, Indiana, and New Jersey, Washington, D.C., February 18, 2011 (epi.org).

Article 11.9

LABOR RADICALISM AND POPULAR EMANCIPATION
The Egyptian uprising continues.

BY STEPHEN MAHER
November/December 2011

In mid-August 2011, the eminent Marxist philosopher Slavoj Žižek wrote, "Unfortunately, the Egyptian summer of 2011 will be remembered as marking the end of revolution, a time when its emancipatory potential was suffocated." Indeed, the forcible clearing of protestors from Tahrir Square, the outlawing of labor strikes, and the imprisonment of thousands by the military that was taking place as Žižek wrote did not bode well for the revolution. In the months since his words were published, things have not gotten much better: the military has reinstated Mubarak's Emergency Law, the International Monetary Fund has issued grim predictions for Egypt's economic performance as interest rates soar, and Moody's has again downgraded Egypt's bond rating and that of several of its major banks. Meanwhile, the Islamists, marginalized in the earlier days of the revolutionary uprising, have returned, well organized and poised to play a significant part in the constitution-writing process that will commence following the upcoming elections.

Yet since the overthrow of Mubarak, industrial actions against low wages and poor working conditions have persisted, and a multitude of new, independent labor unions have been formed. In the fall of 2011, a new wave of labor strikes exploded across the country on a scale "not seen since the earliest weeks of the revolution," as the *Washington Post* put it. But in view of the monumental challenges they face, what can these ongoing labor and leftist popular political movements still hope to accomplish? Is the revolution doomed, as Žižek suggests, or is a brighter future, and a truly radical social transformation, away from the domination of Egyptian society by capital, still within reach for Egypt?

Rise to Rebellion

The years leading up to the overthrow of Hosni Mubarak saw the development of a democratic social movement unprecedented in the history of the modern Middle East. This movement developed partly in resistance to the neoliberal policies imposed after a 1991 debt restructuring by the Egyptian state in collaboration with the International Monetary Fund (IMF) and the World Bank. The "reforms" consisted of the familiar neoliberal package: liberalized capital flows, deregulation and privatization of industries, and the gutting of the national health care and education systems along with the retreat of the state from other areas of social provision. As Marxist theorist David Harvey has argued, "the evidence strongly suggests that the neoliberal turn is in some way and in some degree associated with the restoration or reconstruction of the power of economic elites." Egypt's neoliberal transformation was no exception, with the breakdown of the powerful nationalist solidarity that held sway during the presidency of Gamal Abdel Nasser, followed by the ascendance of a powerful bourgeoisie linked to global capitalism. Despite increased production and strong GDP growth—between 4% and 7% per year—much of the new wealth was concentrated into the hands of Egypt's ruling class, while workers were left with barely enough to eat and social services for the poor were degraded or eliminated outright.

These programs were accelerated after 2004 with the inauguration of the "reform cabinet" of Ahmad Nazif. But alongside this push grew fierce resistance: between 2004 and 2010, there were more than 3,000 labor actions in Egypt, as workers exercised leverage from within the labor process against the ruling class and an authoritarian, unresponsive state apparatus. A sudden spike in inflation (which doubled in 2009), partly spurred by the liquidity that flooded the market as a result of the U.S. Federal Reserve's $2 trillion Quantitative Easing program, exacerbated the social crisis as the pitifully low wages paid out to Egyptian workers proved inadequate to meet basic needs. Egyptian society—beginning with the workers in the factories—was increasingly pushed toward revolutionary social transformation. The spread of high technology linked together workers in the industrial towns and an urban youth movement chafing under the authoritarian state apparatus, expanding conceptions of the revolutionary potential for the future. An 18-day popular uprising, which eventually saw millions gather in Cairo's central Tahrir Square, led on February 11 to the resignation of Hosni Mubarak, the suspension of the constitution, the repeal of the dreaded Emergency Law (which effectively circumvented all constitutional protections) and the transfer of power to the Egyptian army under the auspices of the Supreme Council of the Armed Forces (SCAF).

Reaction and Normalization

Despite Mubarak's resignation, large-scale protests and labor actions continued across Egypt. Such ongoing actions have made clear that the uprising is fundamentally social: it seeks to challenge not just the leadership of one individual, but rather an entire social-institutional order. Concern that the movement could turn explicitly anti-capitalist and lead to a more radical transformation of Egyptian society led the IMF to cloak its proposed post-revolution loan programs—negotiated in secret with Mubarak-appointed finance minister Samir Radwan—behind claims of "social justice" and an "orderly transition" to democratic rule. Meanwhile, after supporting Mubarak until his final days in office, the United States hurriedly expressed its support for the revolutionary movement, which it claimed had achieved its goals and urged the activists to return home and get back to work.

But soon after Mubarak's resignation, 5,000 employees from the Tawhid wa-Nur department store chain descended on Cairo, winning a 12-hour workday and a significant pay increase. Then, on March 3, planned protests against newly appointed Prime Minister Ahmad Shafiq, widely viewed to be a member of Mubarak's old guard, caused him to resign, replaced by Essam Sharaf. Ongoing industrial actions also forced the army to permit the organization of independent labor unions. But by the end of March, ongoing mass demonstrations across the country led the Egyptian cabinet to order a law criminalizing all strikes and protests, which were made punishable by huge fines or imprisonment.

Still, the revolutionaries were not deterred. On April 1, "Save the Revolution Day," tens of thousands again filled Tahrir in defiance of the new measures. Massive protests continued on May 27 in opposition to the repression of SCAF, in particular the practice of subjecting civilians to military trials. The ongoing demonstrations forced SCAF to hastily announce on June 30 that it would reject all loans from the IMF and World Bank, which had been negotiated by Finance Minister Radwan just three weeks previously. This powerful mass movement was able to retain its momentum throughout July, before the military forcibly cleared Tahrir in early August. After arresting thousands of demonstrators, by September SCAF had reinstated the despised Emergency Law, one of the primary targets of the revolution.

Slowly but surely, the U.S.-backed Egyptian military and the ruling elite to which it is intimately connected seemed to consolidate their grip on power, ensuring that Egypt would remain closely linked to global capitalism and stay within the U.S. imperial system. Harsh repression, aimed at stifling a democratic social transformation and solidifying the hegemony of the army and the bourgeoisie, proceeded even as the show trial of Mubarak and a few of his closest associates got underway. Designed to demobilize the population and create the impression that justice has been achieved and "the system is working," the trial of Mubarak is perhaps the most effective measure the SCAF has taken so far toward the goal of preserving the existing social order.

Dark Clouds

Thorough the maintenance of a debt cycle, international capital keeps Egypt on a short leash. The establishment of a self-reinforcing cycle of debt means that as Egypt needs constant access to new credit in order to service its long-term obligations, the government will have to do whatever is necessary to keep new loans coming in. The result is a net *outflow* of capital from Egypt to international lenders. Between 2000 and 2009, net transfers on Egypt's long-term debt (the difference between received loans and debt payments) reached $3.4 billion. In the same period, Egypt's debt *grew* by 15%, despite the fact that it repaid a total of $24.6 billion in loans. This self-reinforcing cycle of dependency, which redistributes billions from Egypt's poor to Western financiers, gives these institutions tremendous leverage over Egypt's government. This, despite the fact that much of this debt is what is referred to as "odious" debt, contracted by an unelected dictatorship with the encouragement of the IMF, World Bank, and others. Mubarak's inner circle and the capitalist class were enriched to the tune of billions of dollars, while millions of Egyptians were kept in desperate poverty.

Keeping the economy open to foreign investment by eliminating trade barriers and capital controls is another way Egyptian dependence on foreign capital is maintained, establishing what is often referred to as a "virtual parliament." If the Egyptian government does not serve the interests of capital, Western investors can literally defund the country by rapidly withdrawing capital, thereby driving up interest rates and destroying the Egyptian currency. Not surprisingly, the maintenance of liberalized capital flows is a key demand made on the new Egyptian government, likewise tied to the continued extension of aid and credit, as the Egyptian business class warns the ongoing revolutionary movement of the dangers of capital flight. Ominously, Moody's

Investor Service downgraded its rating for five major Egyptian banks, a move certain to provoke a reaction in international markets. Further liberalization and privatization, on the other hand, would almost certainly improve such ratings.

The downgrades bode ill for Egypt's ability to borrow on international markets. With Egypt in danger of bankruptcy, Egyptian finance minister Hazem el Beblawi has suggested that Egypt would again consider returning to the IMF for a loan, regardless of the popular outrage sparked by the deal made by his predecessor. Beblawi has already concluded a deal for $400 million from the World Bank to finance various public works projects, and Saudi Arabia and the United Arab Emirates have sought to preserve the rule of Egypt's capitalist class by lending Egypt $5 billion in budget support, and to finance new infrastructure projects. By soaking up unemployment through the implementation of Keynesian programs and making financing available for capitalistic activities, these loans seek to stabilize an Egyptian capitalism whose future—in the face of a massive new labor uprising—seems uncertain at best.

An IMF report on the Egyptian economy issued in late September further clarified the dark clouds on Egypt's horizon, projecting just 1.5% growth in 2011, mildly recovering to 2.5% in 2012. Gaping budget deficits, as the state seeks to buy off dissent and agitation for a more radical transformation by increasing the wages of public sector workers, are meeting with soaring interest rates that led the Cairo Central Bank to halt the sale of two- and three-year bonds on September 19. On September 22, Egypt gained $1.3 billion through the sale of six-month and one-year bonds, but at an average interest rate of 13.9%. Even at this astronomical interest rate, government borrowing risked crowding out private investment, according to the IMF report, which suggested that Egypt might have to return to the IMF after all in order to meet its budgetary shortfall.

A New Explosion

During Mubarak's rule, the only labor organization permitted to operate was the regime-dominated General Federation of Trade Unions, which supported the neoliberal agenda and worked to keep labor in line with state and ruling-class objectives. Before the uprising, labor organizers risked arrest, imprisonment, and torture to organize workers underground, but since the resignation of Mubarak labor organization has exploded: 130 new unions have been formed in the past seven months. In recent weeks, laborers from a broad swath of Egyptian society have taken advantage of the gains of the revolution, with a tidal wave of strikes engulfing the country on an unprecedented scale. While Mubarak never hesitated to obstruct labor action by deploying brute force, today's empowered strikers confront the state and the bourgeoisie with demands to reverse many of the neoliberal measures and redistribute the vast wealth that was concentrated in the hands of the upper classes in the neoliberal era.

Doctors staging sit-ins at hospitals are demanding better pay and insisting on a trebling of health spending in order to reverse the neoliberal gutting of what was once a strong public-health system. Striking teachers demanding the restructuring of the educational system to include classes on democracy and human rights, pay increases, and the firing of the education minister have forced the total or partial shutdown of 85% of Egyptian schools. Transit workers, demanding better pay, have brought the Cairo metro system to a screeching halt. Dockworkers at the port of Ain Al Sokhna are also refusing to work, disrupting trade with the Far East. This growing class consciousness, and willingness to confront the authorities, is taking hold of ever-wider segments of Egyptian society, and now, according to a *Washington Post* report, "appears to be spreading to private factories and farms, fueled by the breaking of a barrier of fear that served to curb union activity here for decades." As Abdel Aziz El Bialy, deputy director of the Independent Teachers' Union, put it: "This is a social revolution to complete the political revolution."

The Road Ahead

Given the organizational head start of the Islamists, the upcoming parliamentary elections are likely to bring victories to such conservative social forces, which will give them a tremendous hand in the constitution-writing process that will follow. The Islamists, who were an integral component of social stability during the Mubarak regime, are likely to accept the privilege of the army and the ruling class in exchange for increased ideological dominance. But as this tremendous labor uprising makes clear, the Egyptian people do not want the restoration of economic growth based on the gross exploitation of poorly paid workers by the owners of capital. Egypt has already been through that, with much of the vast wealth produced by workers in the neoliberal period simply concentrated in the hands of the bourgeoisie. Indeed, the IMF and World Bank issued one glowing assessment after another on Egypt's economic performance during the period of its neoliberal transformation (including one issued just days before the beginning of the uprising), which saw social inequalities grow to unprecedented heights amid severe state repression of labor and other dissent.

The purpose of the revolution was not to preserve market stability and assuage global capitalism; on the contrary, capitalist exploitation of labor in factory towns like Mahalla was the target of the uprising in the first place. A true, democratic social transformation is possible for Egypt, but this means discarding the advice and interests of capitalists, local and international, and their affiliates and agents. It means the democratic management of production and social life, the construction of a society in which despair and unemployment are impossible and true human flourishing is the foremost social goal, not the senseless accumulation of capital. In other words, the revolution must seek a true social transformation: one that puts an end to the exploitation of the workers and the violent deprivation of the poor and brings about genuine democratic management of social and political life. Such a radical social transformation will not be looked upon kindly by global capitalism and those at its head. But, again in the words of Slavoj Žižek, "liberation hurts." ❑

Sources: Slavoj Žižek. "Shoplifters of the World Unite," *London Review of Books*, August 19, 2011; Slavoj Žižek and Eric Dean Rasmussen, "Liberation Hurts: An Interview with Slavoj Žižek," *Electronic Book Review*, July 1, 2004; Anthony Faiola, "Egypt's Labor Movement Blooms in Arab Spring," *Washington Post*, September 25, 2009; David Harvey, *A Brief History of Neoliberalism*, Oxford University Press, 2005; Ismail Arslan, World Bank Independent Evaluation Group, *Egypt, Positive Results From Knowledge Sharing and Modest Lending: An IEG Country Assistance Evaluation, 1999-2007*, World Bank

Publications, 2009; Adam Morrow and Khaled Moussa al-Omrani "Economists Blame 'Neo-liberalism' for Region's Woes," *Inter Press Service*, January 18, 2010; Walter Armbrust, "A Revolution Against Neoliberalism?" Al-Jazeera English, February 24, 2011; "The Struggle For Worker Rights in Egypt," The Solidarity Center, February, 2010 (www.solidaritycenter.org/files/pubs_egypt_wr.pdf); "IMF agrees to $3bn Egypt loan for post-Mubarak transition," Bloomberg, June 5, 2011; Anand Gopal, "Egypt's Cauldron of Revolt," *Foreign Policy*, February 16, 2011; Steve Hendrix and William Wan, "Egyptian prime minister Ahmed Shafiq resigns ahead of protests," *Washington Post*, March 3, 2011; Yassin Gaber, "Egypt workers lay down demands at new trade union conference," *Al-Ahram*, March 3, 2011; Klaus Enders, "Egypt: Reforms Trigger Economic Growth," IMF Middle East and Central Asia Department, February 13, 2008; Abigail Hauslohner, "Has the Revolution Left Egypt's Workers Behind?" Time Magazine, June 23, 2011; "Tens of Thousands attend 'Save the Revolution' Day," Al-Ahram, April 1, 2011; "Tens of thousands of Tahrir protesters demans swift justice in 'Second Friday of Anger'," *The Daily News Egypt*, May 27, 2011; Edmund Blair, "Egypt says will not need IMF, World Bank funds," Reuters, June 25, 2011; Malika Bilal, "Egypt: An incomplete revolution," *Al-Jazeera English*, August 19, 2011; Shahira Amin, "Activists fight revival of emergency law," *CNN*, September 19, 2011; "IMF: Egypt economy to grow just 1.5 per cent in 2011," *Al Ahram*, September 21, 2011; Alaa Shahine, "Arabs May Buy Egypt Debt to Cut Highest Yield Since 2008," *Bloomberg Businessweek*, September 23, 2011; Tim Falconer, "Moody's Downgrades Egypt's Ratings," *Wall Street Journal*, March 16, 2011; "Standard & Poor's Downgrades Egypt Debt Rating," CBS/AP, February 1, 2011; Tarek El-Tablawy, "Moody's downgrades five Egyptian banks," *The Daily News Egypt*, February 3, 2011; Sharif Abdel Kouddous, "Hot Teachers," *Foreign Policy*, September 21, 2011; Michael Robbins and Mark Tessler, "What Egyptians mean by democracy," *Foreign Policy*, September 20, 2011; International Monetary Fund, "Arab Republic of Egypt—2010 Article IV Consultation Mission, Concluding Statement," Cairo, February 16, 2010.

CONTRIBUTORS

Frank Ackerman an economist with the Stockholm Environment Institute, and a founder of *Dollars & Sense*. His latest book is *Can We Afford the Future? Economics for a Warming World* (Zed Books, 2009).

Randy Albelda, a *Dollars & Sense* Associate, teaches economics at the University of Massachusetts-Boston.

Gar Alperovitz is a professor of political economy at the University of Maryland and co-author, with Lew Daly, of *Unjust Deserts: How the Rich Are Taking Our Common Inheritance and Why We Should Take It Back* (New Press, 2009).

Dean Baker is co-director of the Center for Economic and Policy Research.

Peter Barnes, co-founder of Working Assets, is a senior fellow at the Tomales Bay Institute.

Heather Boushey is a senior economist at the Center for American Progress.

Marc Breslow is co-chair of the Massachusetts Climate Action Network and a former *Dollars & Sense* collective member.

Jim Campen is a founder of *Dollars & Sense*, is a professor emeritus of economics at University of Massachusetts-Boston and former executive director of Americans for Fairness in Lending.

Polly Cleveland is executive director of the Association for Georgist Studies and adjunct professor of economics at Columbia University's School of International and Public Affairs.

James M. Cypher is professor-investigador, Programa de Doctorado en Estudios del Desarrollo, Universidad Autonoma de Zacatecas, Mexico and a *Dollars & Sense* Associate.

Lew Daly is a senior fellow at Demos and co-author, with Gar Alperovitz, of *Unjust Deserts: How the Rich Are Taking Our Common Inheritance and Why We Should Take It Back* (New Press, 2009).

Alan Durning founded Sightline Institute (formerly Northwest Environment Watch) and is a former senior researcher at the Worldwatch Institute.

Josh Eidelson is a freelance journalist and a contributor at *The American Prospect* and *In These Times*. After receiving his MA in Political Science, he worked as a union organizer for five years.

Anne Fischel teaches media and community studies at Evergreen State College in Olympia, Wash.

Ellen Frank teaches economics at the University of Massachusetts-Boston and is a *Dollars & Sense* Associate.

Gerald Friedman is a professor of economics at the University of Massachusetts-Amherst.

Heidi Garrett-Peltier is a research fellow at the Political Economy Research Institute at the University of Massachusetts, Amherst.

Amy Gluckman is a former co-editor of *Dollars & Sense*.

Gretchen Gordon is a research associate with the Cochabamba-based Democracy Center. She is a contributor to the Democracy Center's anthology *Dignity and Defiance: Stories from Bolivia's Challenge to Globalization*.

Lisa Heinzerling is a professor of law at Georgetown University Law School, specializing in environmental law.

Edward Herman is an economist and co-author of *The Global Media: The New Missionaries of Corporate Capitalism* (Continuum, 1997).

Marianne Hill is an economist who has published articles in the *Journal of Human Development*, *Feminist Economics*, and other economics journals. She also writes for the American Forum and the Mississippi Forum.

Fadhel Kaboub is an assistant professor of economics at Denison University.

Mara Kardas-Nelson is a freelance writer currently based in Capetown, South Africa. She has written on health, the environment, and human rights for the *Globe & Mail* and the *Mail & Guardian*.

Rachel Keeler holds an MSc in Global Politics from the London School of Economics and is a freelance international business journalist.

Marie Kennedy is professor emerita of Community Planning at the University of Massachusetts-Boston and visiting professor in Urban Planning at UCLA. She is a member of the board of directors of Grassroots International.

Rob Larson is assistant professor of economics at Ivy Tech Community College in Bloomington, Indiana.

Jonathan Latham, PhD, is co-founder and executive director of the Bioscience Resource Project, which is the publisher of Independent Science News (independentsciencenews.org).

Aaron Luoma is a research associate with the Cochabamba-based Democracy Center. He is a contributor to the Democracy Center's anthology *Dignity and Defiance: Stories from Bolivia's Challenge to Globalization.*

Arthur MacEwan, a *Dollars & Sense* Associate, is professor emeritus of economics at the University of Massachusetts-Boston.

Steven Maher is an MA candidate in U.S. Foreign Policy and the Middle East at the School of International Service in Washington, DC. He is currently writing his thesis on the Palestinian Authority's relationship with the United States and Israel.

John Miller, a *Dollars & Sense* collective member, teaches economics at Wheaton College.

William G. Moseley is a professor of geography at Macalester College.

Lin Nelson teaches environmental and community studies at the Evergreen State College in Olympia, Wash.

Thomas Palley is an economist who has held positions at the AFL-CIO, Open Society Institute, and the U.S./China Economic and Security Review Commission.

Raj Patel is a journalist and activist, and author of *Stuffed and Starved: The Hidden Battle for the World Food System* (2007) and *The Value of Nothing: How to Reshape Market Society and Redefine Democracy* (2010).

Ethan Pollack is a Senior Policy Analyst at the Economic Policy Institute.

Robert Pollin is professor of economics and co-director of the Political Economy Research Institute at the University of Massachusetts, Amherst.

Paddy Quick is a professor of economics at St. Francis College.

Smriti Rao (co-editor of this volume) is a member of the *Dollars & Sense* collective and teaches economics at Assumption College in Worcester, Mass.

Alejandro Reuss (co-editor of this volume) is an economist and historian and a former co-editor of *Dollars & Sense*.

Helen Scharber is a staff economist for the Center for Popular Economics in Amherst, Massachusetts.

Bryan Snyder (co-editor of this volume) is a senior lecturer in economics at Bentley University.

Chris Sturr (co-editor of this volume) is co-editor of *Dollars & Sense*.

Chris Tilly is a *Dollars & Sense* Associate and director of UCLA's Institute for Research on Labor and Employment and professor in the Urban Planning Department.

James Tracy is a San Francisco-based economic justice organizer and writer. He is co-author of *Hillbilly Nationalists, Urban Race Rebels, and Black Power* (Melville House Publishing).

Ramaa Vasudevan teaches economics at Colorado State University and is a *Dollars & Sense* Associate.

Jeannette Wicks-Lim is an economist and research fellow at the Political Economy Research Institute at the University of Massachusetts-Amherst.

Thad Williamson, a *Dollars & Sense* Associate, is assistant professor of leadership studies at the University of Richmond. He is the author of four books, including *Sprawl, Justice, and Citizenship: The Civic Costs of the American Way of Life* (Oxford, 2010).

Richard Wolff is professor of economics at the University of Massachusetts, Amherst. He is co-author of *Knowledge and Class: A Critique of Political Economy, Economics: Marxian vs. Neoclassical*, and *Bringing It All Back Home: Class, Gender, and Power in the Modern Household*.

CPSIA information can be obtained at www.ICGtesting.com
Printed in the USA
BVOW082343310712

296670BV00002B/12/P

9 781878 585929